ACE OF SPIES

The True Story of

SIDNEY REILLY

D0851385

ACE OF SPIES

The True Story of
SIDNEY REILLY

TEMPUS

TO MY PARENTS

First published 2002
This edition first published 2004

Tempus Publishing Limited
The Mill, Brimscombe Port,
Stroud, Gloucestershire, GL5 2QG
www.tempus-publishing.com

British Library Cataloguing in Publication Data.
A catalogue record for this book is available from the British Library.

ISBN 0 7524 2959 0

Typesetting and origination by Tempus Publishing Limited
Printed in Great Britain by Midway Colour Print, Wiltshire

CONTENTS

About the Author

Andrew Cook worked for many years as a foreign affairs and defence specialist, and was aide to George Robertson (former Secretary of State for Defence, now Lord Robertson of Port Ellen and Secretary General of NATO) and John Spellar (former Minister of State for the Armed Forces). The contacts he made enabled the author to navigate and gain access to classified intel-ligence services archives. During his ten years researching this book, he was only the fifth historian to be given special permission, under the 1992 'Waldegrave Initiative' by the Cabinet Office, to examine closed MI6 documents that will never be released, documents not seen by any previous biographer of Reilly. Since working directly as a foreign affairs and defence specialist, Andrew Cook has worked as a professional historian in colleges and universities. He is a regular contributor on espionage history to *The Guardian*, *The Times* and *BBC History Magazine* and has appeared on national radio and television. His next book, *M: MI5's First Spymaster*, will be published by Tempus. The author's Sidney Reilly website is www.sidneyreilly.com. He lives in Bedfordshire.

ACKNOWLEDGEMENTS

I owe a debt of gratitude to all those involved in the development of this book. It took many years to research and a large number of people were involved in the project from inception to completion.

My particular thanks go to the principal researchers who assisted me: Jordan Auslander (USA); Dmitry Belanovsky (Russia); Vladislav Kiriya (Ukraine); Dr Sylvia Moehle (Germany); and Stephen Parker and Graham Salt (UK). I would also like to thank Michel Ameuw (France), Dr Michael Attias (UK), Marc Bernstein (USA), Norman Crowder (Canada), Alex Denisenko (Poland), Lynda Fagan (UK), Dr Tatiana Filimonova (Russia), Sigita Gasparaviciene (Lithuania), Maria Herman (Brazil), Geoffrey Hewlett (UK), Reinhard Hofer (Austria), Sinan Kuneralp (Turkey), Sean Malloy (USA), Mary Morrigan (Eire), Irina Mulina (Russia), Danna Paz Prins (Israel), Mikhail Sachek (Belarus), Ishizu Tomoyuki (Japan) and Mark Windover (USA) for additional assistance with research.

In the pursuit of source material, I am much indebted to ministers and former ministers for whom I have previously worked, for their advice concerning access to UK records. As a result of an approach to the Cabinet Office, the government agreed to provide me with a briefing based on the records of Sidney Reilly's service with the Secret Intelligence Service (SIS), for the purpose of this book. This has helped enormously, as indeed has the opportunity to compare UK records with those of the Federal Security Service (FSB) in Russia and the US Bureau of Investigation (the forerunner of the FBI) in Washington DC.

The help and co-operation of the families of those who played a role in Reilly's story has been greatly appreciated, as has the assistance of Francis & Francis (private investigators), who helped in tracing them. Special gratitude is owed to Diane Briscoe, George Burton, Carmel Callaghan-Sinnott, Teodor Gladkov, Boris Gudz, Edward Harding-Newman, Charles Lewis, Gustav Nobel, Trevor Melville, Anne Thomas, Viscount Thurso and Brigid Utley.

I have been most grateful to those who have previously written on this and related subjects for speaking or corresponding with me – Gill Bennett, Gordon Brook-Shepherd, Alan Judd, the late Michael Kettle, Margot King, Robin Bruce Lockhart, Professor Ian Nish, Gail Owen, Professor Richard Spence, Carol Spero and Oleg Tsarev.

A special thank you to Lisa Adamson, Laura Ager, Caroline Beach, Daksha Chauhan, Alison Cook, Julia Edwards, Elaine Enstone, Janet Jacobs, Bob Sheth, Selina Short and Chris Williamson for their hard work at various stages of this project. Also to Eurotech Ltd for their sterling work in translating the masses of source material from Russian, German and French into English.

There are equally a number of individuals I would like to thank for their help, but cannot name for reasons of protocol. However, they are already aware of my gratitude and have been thanked in person. Last, but certainly not least, my thanks go to my editor Joanna Lincoln and to my publisher Jonathan Reeve for his support, enthusiasm and advice throughout.

Introduction to the Second Edition

When the first edition of this book was published in October 2002, it received a great deal of media coverage, not only in Britain but around the world. Since then, the first edition has been reprinted in this country and translated into several foreign editions. When the idea of writing a revised and updated second edition was suggested by my publisher Jonathan Reeve, I saw it as an ideal opportunity to follow up several further lines of enquiry that were still outstanding at the time of submitting the manuscript for the first edition. As a result, a wealth of new evidence has been uncovered that sheds new light on significant episodes in Reilly's life.

For example, photo-forensic work by Ken Linge, which was still being undertaken at the time the first edition was being printed, is now concluded and has made a major contribution to establishing Reilly's parentage and family lineage. Another mystery concerning his involvement in a crime that forced him to flee from France to England in 1895 is also solved thanks to new research in France by Michel Ameuw. Other new discoveries include German files on Reilly's shady commercial dealings in the Ottoman Empire before the First World War, letters he wrote in 1917 which clear up the mystery of his whereabouts in the autumn of that year, and the discovery of a repository of papers belonging to Major J.D. Scale, the intelligence officer who recruited Reilly to the Secret Intelligence Service (better known today as MI6) in 1918.

In Moscow, new finds include the personal testimonies of Reilly's mistresses Olga Starzhevskaya and Elizaveta Otten, written during their captivity in Butyrka Prison. These previously unpublished accounts not only provide a glimpse of their personal relationships with Reilly but give a unique insight into the secret life he was living in Russia during the spring and summer of 1918. Perhaps the most astonishing new account, however, is that of Boris Gudz, a former OGPU officer who took part in the 1925 'Trust' operation that resulted in Reilly's arrest and execution. Gudz, who celebrated his 100th birthday shortly before I met him in Moscow in August 2003, was able to provide first-hand recollections that were invaluable in piecing together the last few weeks of Reilly's life.

Taken together, these and other new sources, many of which are published in this book for the first time, make a unique contribution to this definitive work of reference on the life of the Ace of Spies, Sidney Reilly.

The idea of writing a spy novel had apparently been in Ian Fleming's mind for a decade before he finally decided to commit the book to paper. Little did he know the phenomenon he was about to create when he sat down behind his typewriter on the morning of 15 January 1952 to start the first chapter of *Casino Royale*. Working at 'Goldeneye', his Jamaican holiday home, he completed the 62,000-word manuscript in a little over two months.[1] On the shelf in his study was the book that had gifted him the name of his hero, *Field Guide to Birds of the West Indies*, by the ornithologist James Bond.[2] Not long after its publication in April 1953, Fleming told a contemporary at the *Sunday Times*, where he worked as foreign manager, that he had created James Bond as the result of reading about the exploits of the British secret agent Sidney Reilly in the archives of the British Intelligence Services during the Second World War.[3]

PREFACE

As personal assistant to the Director of Naval Intelligence during the Second World War, Cmdr Ian Fleming was a desk-bound intelligence officer who liaised closely with other agencies involved in the clandestine world of espionage. He learnt a great deal about the operational history of his own department, including its role in the greatest intelligence coup of the First World War – the cracking of the German diplomatic code 0070, which gave Fleming the inspiration for Bond's own code number 007.[4] This background knowledge enabled him to draw on a rich seam of characters, experiences and situations that would prove invaluable in creating the fictional world of James Bond.

One of Fleming's wartime contacts, for example, was Charles Fraser-Smith, a seemingly obscure official at the Ministry of Supply. In reality, Fraser-Smith provided the intelligence services with a range of fascinating and ingenious gadgets such as compasses hidden inside golf balls and shoelaces that concealed saw blades.[5] He was the inspiration for Fleming's Major Boothroyd, better known as 'Q' in the Bond novels and films.

Having a fascination for gadgets, deception and intrigue, Fleming was particularly attracted to the 'black propaganda' work undertaken by the Political Warfare Executive, headed by former diplomat and journalist Robert Bruce Lockhart, with whom he also struck up an acquaintance.[6] In 1918 Lockhart had worked with Sidney Reilly in Russia, where they became embroiled in a plot to overthrow Lenin's fledgling government. Within five years of his disappearance in Soviet Russia in 1925, the press had turned Reilly into a household name, dubbing him a 'Master Spy' and crediting him with a string of fantastic espionage exploits.

Fleming had therefore long been aware of Reilly's mythical reputation and no doubt listened in awe to the recollections of a man who had not only known Reilly personally but was actually with him during the turmoil and aftermath of the Russian Revolution. Lockhart had himself played a key role in creating the Reilly myth in 1931 by helping Reilly's wife Pepita publish a book purporting to recount her husband's adventures.[7] As a journalist at the time, Lockhart also had a hand in the deal that led to the serialisation of Reilly's 'Master Spy' adventures in the *London Evening Standard*.

Although Reilly was a spark or catalyst for Fleming's 'Master Spy' concept, Bond's personality was a fictional cocktail, culled from a range of characters, including Fleming's own.[8] There are certainly threads of Reilly's hard-edged personality to be found in the Bond who inhabits the pages of Fleming's books. The literary Bond was visibly a much darker, more calculating and altogether more sinister character than his big screen counterpart, who has tended to dilute Fleming's original concept over the years.

Like Fleming's fictional creation, Reilly was multi-lingual with a fascination with the Far East, fond of fine living and a compulsive gambler. He also exercised a Bond-like fascination for women, his many love affairs standing comparison with the amorous adventures of 007. Unlike James Bond, though, Sidney Reilly was by no stretch of the imagination a conventionally handsome man. His appeal lay more in the elusive qualities of charm and charisma. He was, however, equally capable of being cold and menacing. In many ways, the closest modern fictional character to resemble Reilly is Al Pacino's Michael Corleone in

The Godfather, a man of controlled coldness and deadpan calculation. Like Corleone, the equally calculating Reilly had a powerful hold over women – or, at least, a particular kind of woman – which he never failed to exploit.

But who was Sidney Reilly and what were the forces that drove him? To lovers, friends and enemies alike, Reilly remained a mystery. In spite of the many books that have been written about him, often themselves making contrary claims, major questions still remain unanswered about his true identity, place of birth and the precise facts surrounding his disappearance and death. During his life Reilly laid an almost impenetrable fog of mystery and deception around his origins as he adopted and shed one identity after another. Those who entered this ruthlessly compartmentalised life knew only what Reilly himself had told them.

Over a century of falsehood and fantasy, both deliberate and intentional, has obscured the real Sidney Reilly. Reilly's tendency to be something of a Walter Mitty character, telling tall tales of great espionage feats, has only added to the legend and muddied the water still further. To piece together an accurate picture of his extraordinary life it has been necessary to shed all preconceptions and to return to square one, starting from scratch in gathering together as many primary sources as possible.

The ability to draw on many classified, restricted and hitherto unpublished sources in Britain, Canada, Germany, Japan, Poland, Ukraine and the United States has helped this task immeasurably. The descendants of a number of those who played key roles in Reilly's story have also been tracked down and interviewed. Their help in particular has provided many of the missing pieces in the jigsaw of his life, and revealed for the first time how he was propelled at the age of only twenty-five into the life of an international adventurer.

ONE

A SUDDEN DEATH

Of Newhaven there is little to say, except that in rough weather the traveller from France is very glad to reach it, and on a fine day the traveller from England is happy to leave it behind.[1]

These rather unflattering words were written by the travel writer E.V. Lucas in 1904. However, it is often in unremarkable places such as this that some of the most remarkable things happen. Indeed, some six years before Lucas wrote these words, Newhaven's London & Paris Hotel was the unwitting host to an event that was to have far reaching repercussions, not only for a twenty-four-year-old heiress, but also for a man who was to become the epitome of the twentieth-century spy.

Incorporated into the design of Newhaven Harbour Station, the imposing three-storey stucco building was luxuriously furnished with thirty bedrooms and was everything the discerning Victorian traveller could possibly want or expect. It was here, at the quayside platform on the afternoon of Friday 11 March 1898, that a sixty-three-year-old invalid was helped down from the train into his wheelchair. Accompanied by his nurse, Anna Gibson, the Reverend Hugh Thomas[2] proceeded to the reception desk to announce his arrival. He and the nurse had booked two rooms up to and including Monday 14 March, when his twenty-four-year-old wife, Margaret, was due to arrive from London. The three would then take the 11.30 a.m. boat train to Paris en route to a holiday in Egypt.

Despite the trappings of her social status, Margaret may well have felt that a part of her life was somehow empty. It was almost certainly her need for attention and affection that ultimately led her to respond to the overtures of Sigmund Rosenblum, of the Ozone Preparations Company.[3]

Hugh Thomas and Sigmund Rosenblum first met in 1897. Thomas, a sufferer from Bright's Disease, a chronic inflammation of the kidneys, was one of many who succumbed to the siren voice of the patent medicines popular at the time, peddled by companies such as Ozone Preparations Company as offering miracle cures. These companies' claims were greater than those of conventional medicine, who only prescribed bed rest, a low protein diet, massive doses of Jalap, and blood letting – the attraction of patent medicines to sufferers such as Thomas was obvious.

Hugh Thomas and Sigmund Rosenblum met regularly throughout 1897 at the Manor House, Kingsbury, and at 6 Upper Westbourne Terrace, London. Indeed, it was at the Manor House, in the summer of 1897, that Thomas introduced Rosenblum to Margaret.[4] It has been claimed that the Thomases first met Sigmund Rosenblum in Russia, during a tour of Europe they undertook in 1897.[5] It has been claimed, too, that Margaret's relationship with Rosenblum developed as he accompanied them from hotel to hotel on a melodramatic journey back to England.[6] The facts, however, tell a very different story. Although a passport was not as necessary as it is today for foreign travel, to enter Russia, Hugh and Margaret Thomas would most certainly have required one. British passport records show, however, that the Thomases never at any time applied for, or were ever granted, passports for Russia.[7] Furthermore, Thomas household records make no reference to any foreign trips or holidays undertaken in 1897, although in December of that year, plans were made for a holiday in Egypt the following March.

Whose idea this Egyptian holiday was we do not know. Whether these plans were made with a straightforward holiday in mind or something a good deal more sinister is very much dependent upon one's interpretation of the evidence.[8] What we do know, however, is that the planning, arrangements and bookings were made by Margaret, as Thomas Cook records show. Shortly before their departure, Margaret arranged an appointment for her husband and herself to visit a local solicitor. On Friday 4 March they made their way to 13 St Mary's Square, Paddington, a short distance from their home. Before a clerk, Hugh Thomas appointed the Thomas family solicitor, Henry Lloyd Carter, and Margaret as his Executors. The Will itself declared the following:

> I direct that my funeral and testamentary expenses and debts be paid. I give devise and bequeath to my said wife for her own absolute use and benefit all my real estate and the residue of my personal estate and all the property over which I have any power of disposition and whereas in the event of issue being born to me of my said wife Margaret such issue will under the Will of my late uncle, Hugh Thomas of Trevor Anglesey aforesaid become entitled to certain real estate and personal estate. Now I hereby declare that the gift devise and bequest to my said wife here in before contained shall include all real and personal estate which I may have power to dispose of as heir at law or next of kin of any such issue as aforesaid and I give devise and bequeath the same to my wife accordingly for her own absolute use and benefit.[9]

Margaret also made a Will, assigning Henry Lloyd Carter as Executor. On the morning of Friday 11 March, exactly one week after making the Will, Hugh Thomas and his nurse, Anna Gibson, left Upper Westbourne Terrace bound for Victoria Station. Arriving at Newhaven Harbour Station during the late afternoon, their trunks were put into storage and the hand luggage taken to their adjoining rooms. Little did Hugh Thomas know, as he retired to bed early, that he had less than twelve hours left to live.

Saturday 12 March was a cold and wet day and the Reverend Thomas and his nurse were confined to the hotel. He retired to bed shortly before 11.00 p.m. It was early the following morning that John Simmons knocked on the door of the Reverend Thomas's room; being an invalid, he had ordered breakfast to be served in his room. Getting no reply to his knocking, Simmons used his key to open the door. Inside the room was dark and seemingly all was normal.

Having seen a good number of slumbering guests in the three years he had worked at the hotel, Simmons' instinct quickly told him that something was not as it should be. He therefore rushed from the room to alert the hotel manager, Alfred Lewis.[10] It took a further half-hour before Lewis telephoned the Newhaven police to report that the Reverend Hugh Thomas had been found dead in bed. This was probably because his first reaction was to summon the Reverend's nurse and a doctor, who by chance was also staying at the hotel, having arrived late the previous evening. Dr T.W. Andrew examined the body of Hugh Thomas and spent some time talking with Anna Gibson, the nurse, before advising Lewis that the death was the result of heart failure.

Hugh Thomas's body was taken to a Chapel of Rest, and it may well have surprised the undertaker that, on her arrival the next day, Margaret voiced her intention to have her husband taken back to his place of birth in Anglesey for burial, rather than to London. What might have surprised him even more was the speed at which Mrs Thomas wanted the arrangements made. Eight to ten days was not an unusual period of time from death to burial in 1898, yet Margaret wanted a funeral on Wednesday 16 March, which gave the undertaker a mere day and a half to carry out the necessary rituals, make a coffin and convey the body to its final resting place in Llansadwrn Church Yard.[11]

Not surprisingly, Hugh Thomas's death caught the attention of the local press, much to the concern of Alfred Lewis, the hotel manager, who no doubt resented the unwelcome attention such a story brought to his hotel. It is interesting to note that one journalist referred in his account to the fact that 'a young medical man having been able to certify the cause of death, it was not deemed necessary to hold an inquest'.[12]

Six weeks later, probate of the Will of Hugh Thomas was granted to Margaret, who became the inheritor of £8,094 12s (something in the region of half a million today). If Henry Lloyd Carter, Hugh Thomas's solicitor and co-executor of the Will, had any doubts arising from the fact that the Reverend had expired within nine days of writing the Will, or indeed the fact that he was buried within three days of his sudden death, he did not say so publicly, and possibly did not say so privately either. Had he done so, and the authorities had conducted an investigation, what would they have discovered?

The police would, initially, have wanted to be sure about the cause of death. According to Dr Andrew, the cause of death was 'Influenza Morbus Cordis Syncope', which essentially means 'influenza; a fainting of the heart'.[13] It is as non-specific a diagnosis as is possible to record and most certainly one that would not be acceptable today. It could encompass virtually any heart condition, and taken literally and logically means quite simply that death occurred because the heart stopped beating!

The police would therefore have wanted to establish a more precise cause of death. They would have wanted to interview the Reverend Thomas's own doctor about his general state of health, and most certainly Dr Andrew. It would have been at this point that what began as a routine enquiry would have turned into something more serious, for they would quickly have discovered that no such person as Dr T.W. Andrew MRCS actually existed.[14] The Royal College of Surgeons, with whom Andrew claimed membership, would have confirmed that no one of that name was a member of the college. The General Medical Council would have consulted its register, which listed all doctors authorised to practice medicine in Great Britain. No T.W. Andrew MRCS would have been found there either. The police may well have contacted Dr Thomas Andrew LRCS, the only T. Andrew on the

Hugh Thomas during his tenure as Vicar of Old Newton, Suffolk (c.1860).

register.[15] They would have found that this sixty-one-year-old doctor from Doune in Perthshire had not crossed the border into England during the entire thirty-six years that he had been practising medicine. Besides which, it would have been very obvious that this elderly Scotsman could not possibly have been the 'young medical man' referred to by the *Sussex Express* or the man recalled by Louisa Lewis, the daughter of the hotel manager.[16]

In light of this disturbing development, the police would have proceeded to interview Margaret Thomas, Anna Gibson, other members of the below-stairs household, and friends and acquaintances of the Thomases. They would also have taken steps to have the body of Hugh Thomas exhumed to confirm the cause of death.

From what is known of Margaret's personality, she would probably have held up well under the pressure of questioning. It is likely, however, that others interviewed would have mentioned a Mr Rosenblum and the fact that he was a regular visitor to the Thomas household, both at Upper Westbourne Terrace and at the Manor, Kingsbury. Would the police have harboured any suspicions about the purpose of his visits and his relationship with Margaret Thomas? Would the fact that Sigmund Rosenblum was a consultant chemist, and a Fellow of the Institute of Chemistry and the Chemical Society, with easy access to drugs, further fuel their suspicions? Would the police have made a connection between the 'young medical man' and the young chemist? The police may well have stumbled on the fact that the twenty-five-year-old Rosenblum had been in the country for a little over two years and was 'known' to Scotland Yard's Special Branch.

Of course, no such investigation ever took place, much to Sigmund Rosenblum's very great fortune. However, looking at all the available evidence, what can we conclude was the likely chain of events over the weekend of Hugh Thomas's death?

Assuming that Thomas's death was not a convenient and timely coincidence, we must consider the issues of motive, method, and opportunity. For Sigmund Rosenblum, Hugh Thomas was an inconvenient obstacle who stood between him and the achievement of two major ambitions. With Thomas's death, Margaret would not only become a widow but a very rich widow, and by marrying Margaret, Rosenblum would achieve at least one ambition and effectively gain control of her new fortune. Rosenblum's second ambition, the achievement of a new identity, would also benefit from this marriage.

A further motivational clue in terms of the timing of Thomas's death is possibly concealed within his Will. Fourteen innocuous words raise a scenario never before suggested – 'in the event of issue being born to me of my said wife Margaret'. Was this merely wishful thinking on the part of a sixty-three-year-old man with Bright's Disease, or were his words motivated by the fact that Margaret was already pregnant? According to London lawyers Kingsford, Stacey, Blackwell, who studied the contents of the Will, this passage is very significant as, 'it is not a standard clause or a clause that would have been included in error, as it refers to his issue receiving a share of the estate of his uncle which is quite specific'.[17] If Margaret was pregnant, it is more likely to be by Rosenblum than Hugh Thomas. If nature had been allowed to take its course, the child may well have betrayed its paternity. After all, as Gordon Brook-Shepherd pointed out in his book *Iron Maze*, Reilly himself was someone whose Jewish heritage was, 'written in capital letters on his face'. Had the child's parentage been equally obvious, Margaret would surely have been divorced and cut off without a penny, hardly a scenario that she or Rosenblum would have welcomed. If Margaret had found herself pregnant in late 1897, the forthcoming holiday might well have presented the perfect cover for Thomas's death. Indeed, Margaret, who had arranged the holiday, was conveniently absent from the London & Paris Hotel over that critical weekend, having left London four days after her husband.

Furthermore, it is unlikely that Rosenblum could have plotted the demise of Hugh Thomas without the assistance and connivance of Margaret. Margaret was by this time very much under Rosenblum's spell and very much in love with him, as evidenced by anecdotal accounts from, among others, British diplomat HM Vice-Consul Darrell Wilson (see Chapter Five). Assuming that Thomas had been suffering from Bright's Disease for some eight years, Rosenblum may well have decided to use the symptoms of the disease as a convenient cover for slow and progressive arsenic poisoning, the results of which would appear very similar to those of Bright's Disease. Both progressive arsenic poisoning and Bright's Disease would have resulted in a swelling of the limbs, especially the legs, caused by fluid retention; a loss of appetite; and blood in the urine.

The poison could have been administered progressively through the patent medicine he was supplying to Hugh Thomas. Equally, Margaret could also have administered it on Rosenblum's instructions through food and drink. Neither possibility, however, would account for or enable the fatal dose to be administered at the London & Paris Hotel on the night of Saturday 12 March. If we assume that Rosenblum was at the hotel in the guise of Dr T. W. Andrew,[18] he

---

on August 17th.

SUDDEN DEATH.—On Sunday morning a gentleman named Mr. Hugh Thomas, of Manor House, Kingsbury, was found dead in bed at the London and Paris Hotel. The deceased, who is stated to have been an invalid, arrived at the hotel on Friday with a nurse and was waiting for his wife to arrive.

News of Thomas's sudden death was very quickly picked up by the local press.

would not have wanted to risk being seen by or in the vicinity of Hugh Thomas, or risk direct involvement in administering the fatal dose. With Rosenblum keeping a low profile and Margaret sixty miles away in London, we must take a closer look at Anna Gibson who, after all, was best placed in terms of opportunity, being Thomas's nurse and occupying the neighbouring room.

According to Thomas family records, Miss Anna Gibson was a twenty-eight-year-old born in Clerkenwell, London, who joined the household in March 1897. This would mean that her date of birth would have been somewhere between March 1868 and April 1869. An exhaustive search of birth records for an Anna Gibson during that period reveal only one person of that name, who was born in Blofield in Norfolk. As this Anna Gibson was not born in London, let alone Clerkenwell, we must either assume an error or omission in the records or that, for whatever reason, Anna misled the family about her name, age or place of birth. The nearest national census to Anna's year of birth was 1871. By methodically searching the Clerkenwell census returns for two-year-old girls by the name of Anna, we find only one such candidate – Anna Luke, daughter of William and Elizabeth Luke. Anna Luke's birth certificate shows that she was born on 5 January 1869, and more revealingly that her mother's maiden name was Gibson.[19]

Can we therefore assume that the Anna Gibson employed by the Thomas household and Anna Luke are one and the same? If so, what motive or reason could Anna have had for adopting her mother's maiden name? The answer may lie in the circumstances surrounding Anna's departure from her previous position in Japan, where she had held a post working for a wealthy family. Shortly before Anna's return to England, a *crime passionnel* hit the headlines in the Japanese press. In Yokohama, on 22 October 1896, Walter Carew died of arsenic poisoning, and his wife was arrested amid a storm of publicity. As it later emerged in court, Mrs Carew had been having an affair with a young bank clerk. Although found guilty and sentenced to death, Mrs Carew's sentence was commuted and she was sent back to England to serve out her sentence at

Aylesbury Prison. At her trial she maintained her innocence and continued to do so on her release from prison in 1910. Until the day she died at the age of ninety in June 1958, she was to maintain that one 'Anne Luke' had been involved in her husband's death.

To tell the full story of the Carew case, with its many twists and turns, would require a book in its own right. In the context of Hugh Thomas, however, the central question is whether or not there is any tangible evidence to connect 'Anna Gibson' with the Carew case. If Anna Gibson spent two years in Japan, and returned to England in late 1896 or early 1897, she must have initially left in late 1894 or early 1895. An exhaustive search of British passport records indicated that no passports were issued to anyone under the name Gibson during late 1894 and early 1895. However, a second search undertaken for the name Luke revealed that on 13 December 1894 a passport was indeed issued to 'A. Luke'.[20] While there is no conclusive proof that Anna Gibson was Anna Luke, or that she was involved in Carew's death, the circumstantial evidence does point very strongly to this conclusion.

Had Rosenblum somehow discovered Anna's secret and involved her, willingly or unwillingly, in the plot? Towards the end of her life, Margaret spoke of a 'great wrong' she had committed earlier in her life, which preyed on her conscience. Was this perhaps a reference to her involvement in the death of her first husband?[21]

Rosenblum, however, was a man without a conscience. The planning and execution of the Thomas murder had all the hallmarks of the skilful cunning, deceit and daring that characterised his later career. If ever there was such a thing as a perfect murder, this is surely a prime candidate. On 22 August 1898 he married Margaret Thomas at Holborn Registery Office. The marriage brought not only the wealth he desired but provided the pretext for the fulfilment of his second major ambition, to discard Sigmund Rosenblum and assume the identity that was to bring him such notoriety: that of Sidney Reilly. This new and plausible identity was, as we shall see later, the key to achieving his desire to return to the land of his birth.

Two

THE MAN FROM NOWHERE

Sigmund Rosenblum's identity and origins have confounded writers, researchers, governments and their intelligence agencies for well over a century. It has almost become an accepted fact that his real name was Sigmund Rosenblum, partly because of the sheer number of times that this 'fact' has been repeated and printed over the passage of time. Many authors have written about Reilly's origins and his supposed family background. According to Robin Bruce Lockhart, Reilly was born, 'not far from Odessa'.[1] Edward Van Der Rhoer similarly has his birth, 'in Odessa, a Black Sea port',[2] as do John Costello and Oleg Tsarev.[3] Michael Kettle, however, claims his place of birth to be Russian Poland,[4] an assertion supported by Christopher Andrew[5] and Richard Deacon.[6]

Reilly himself told numerous stories about his supposed origins. He was, at different times, the son of: an Irish sea captain; an Irish clergyman; or a Russian aristocrat. His first wife Margaret was under the impression that he was the son of a wealthy landowner and came from Poland or Russia.[7] In his book, *British Agent*, Robert Bruce Lockhart, an envoy sent to Russia by Lloyd George in 1918, stated that Reilly's parents came from Odessa, although he made no pronouncements upon Reilly's own place of birth.[8] Among the places in Ireland Reilly claimed to have been born were Clonmel in Tipperary and Dublin.[9] While accompanying Brig.-Gen. Edward Spears on a business trip to Prague in 1921, however, Reilly was alleged to have lunched at the British Legation where he recounted stories of his childhood in Odessa. When asked by a Legation official why it was that his passport gave his place of birth as Tipperary, Reilly apparently replied, 'There was a war and I came over to fight for England. I had to have a British passport and therefore a British birthplace, and, you see, from Odessa, it's a long way to Tipperary!'[10] He told Pepita Bobadilla, whom he married in 1923, that being born in Ireland was a cover, and that he had actually been born and educated in St Petersburg, of an Irish merchant seaman and a Russian mother.[11]

Not only was Reilly's place of birth a mystery, but so too was his age. In 1931 Pepita Bobadilla stated in the first edition of her biographical account of Reilly that he was born in 1872.[12] When she published a longer version in book form, his year of birth became 1874.[13] Robert Bruce Lockhart stated that when they first met, Reilly was in his forty-sixth year, indicating 1873 as his year of birth.[14]

Marriage certificates, immigration documents and passports prior to 1917 equally point to 1873 as being his year of birth.[15] From the date of his recruitment into the Royal Flying Corps (RFC) in late 1917, however, Reilly gives 1874 as his year of birth on all official documents.[16] It has been suggested that the main motivation for these conflicting stories was a desire to protect his family, as he was engaged in espionage on behalf of a foreign power, and was thus anxious for their safety should this ever become known.[17] The more we discover about Reilly's real motivations and behaviour in the ensuing years, however, the more we are led to an alternative theory, namely that he had little or no interest in his family or their fate after he left them, and that instead he was more concerned with masking his Jewishness.[18]

If Reilly had actually written an autobiography,[19] or authorised a biography, the story told would almost certainly have closely resembled that which appears in Robin Bruce Lockhart's *Ace of*

Spies. This is hardly surprising, given the fact that a significant part of this book is based upon the anecdotal stories Reilly told his friends, colleagues and acquaintances, particularly Capt. George Hill.

In essence, *Ace of Spies* is Reilly as he would like to have been seen by posterity. According to this story, he was born into a minor aristocratic landowning Russian family, in or near Odessa, and christened Georgi. His father was apparently a minor aristocrat and a colonel with connections to the court of the Tsar himself. Georgi and his older sister led a privileged life, being educated by tutors. To retain an air of mystery around this story, Reilly was always careful never to divulge the family's name. At the age of sixteen, Georgi embarked on a three-year course in chemistry at the university in Vienna, where he made the acquaintance of Dr Rosenblum, his mother's doctor. Here Georgi was a great success, excelling in his studies and living a somewhat debauched life to the full. He also became involved in a socialist political group which led to his arrest by the Imperial Russian Secret Police, the Ochrana. His family used their connections to secure his release, by which time his mother, who had been unwell for some time, had died. It was on the day of his release from prison that his uncle revealed to the assembled family that Georgi was in fact a bastard, the offspring of an adulterous relationship between his mother and Dr Rosenblum, the Jewish doctor from Vienna, who had treated her.

Unable to come to terms with the shame of being a bastard, he disowned his family, adopted the name Rosenblum, faked his death in Odessa Harbour and stowed away on a boat bound for South America. For three years he went from job to job, before being recruited as a cook by three British army officers who were to lead an expedition to explore the Amazonian jungle. All went well until natives attacked the party. In typical melodramatic style, Rosenblum grabbed an officer's pistol and with expert marksmanship fought off the natives single handed. As it turned out, one of the three officers, Maj. Fothergill, was a member of the British Secret Service and rewarded him with a cheque for

£1,500, a passage to Britain, a British passport and a job with the Secret Service. As compelling a story as this is, it totally fails to stand up when subjected to scrutiny.

Over and above the fact that the British Secret Service did not exist in the 1890s, birth records kept by the State Archives of Odessa Region contain no mention of a boy by the name of Georgi whose father was a colonel, for either 1872, 1873 or 1874.[20] No Dr Rosenblum is listed in the Vienna City Censuses during the 1890s,[21] and neither the University of Vienna nor the Vienna Technical University have any record of a student from Odessa, born in the relevant time period, studying chemistry.[22] Furthermore, newspaper and archive records in both Britain and Brazil fail to mention any Amazonian expeditions during the time period in question, neither are any references to be found to British army officers or to a Maj. Fothergill.[23] Such findings are hardly surprising, for Reilly's family were neither Russians nor aristocrats.

Abram Rosenblum was born in the Grodno gubernia around 1820.[24] He and his wife, Sarah, were the first of their family to leave Poland to settle in the Kherson gubernia, in which Odessa is located, in the early 1850s. His elder brother, Jankiel (Jacob),[25] married Hana (Henrietta) Bramson[26] in Lomza in the Bialystok province in 1840. Their sons Zeev (Vladimir) and Gersh (Grigory) were born in the province in 1843 and 1845 respectively.[27] Grigory married Perla (Paulina), a reputedly attractive girl some seven years younger than himself, who hailed from a well-to-do family in Kherson. By all accounts their marriage was 'strained'. According to later family trees, they had three children, Mariam (Maria), Shlomo (Salomon – the future Sidney Reilly) and Elka (Elena).[28] Family speculation, however, raises the possibility that Grigory might not have been Salomon's father. According to one account, Paulina had an adulterous liaison with a close relative of Grigory's who was more of her own age. Another alludes to Paulina leaving her husband and returning to the south. Whether Paulina and Grigory were reconciled at a later date is uncertain. These rumours perhaps suggest that although the story Reilly told

George Hill about his origins is essentially fiction, it would be wrong to dismiss every aspect of it as a fabrication. The rumour of Paulina's infidelity certainly seems to strike a chord with the part of the story in which Georgi finds out that he is the product of an adulterous affair between his mother and Dr Rosenblum. If this speculation has any substance and Grigory was not, in fact, Salomon's father, then who was?

Grigory's brother Vladimir has been put forward as a possible candidate, largely, it would seem, on the basis that he was reputedly a doctor. A serious dispute apparently arose between the two brothers during this approximate period, which ultimately led to them breaking off contact with one another, and thus giving credence to this theory. Vladimir was, of course, older than Grigory, which does not fit in with the plausible view that the father was of a similar age to Paulina. If, as we have already seen, there was no Dr Rosenblum in Vienna, was there possibly one in the vicinity of Odessa who might be another candidate for Salomon's natural father?

Odessa was an important naval and military district at this time and the services had their own doctors, many of whom lived in the Odessa region when they were not on active duty. Although no Dr Rosenblums are in evidence in the early/mid-1870s, Russian military archives reveal a Dr M. Rosenblum of 24 Marazliyevskaa Street, Odessa, who qualified in 1879. His military service file reveals him to be none other than Mikhail Abramovich Rosenblum, the son of Abram Rosenblum, and therefore Grigory's cousin. Born in Kherson, some ninety miles east of Odessa in 1853, he was one year younger than Paulina.[29] Mikhail must therefore be considered a serious candidate for the identity of the 'close family relative' who might possibly have fathered Salomon.

A recent discovery, while not providing conclusive proof, does make a very persuasive case in favour of this theory. Among a collection of family photographs unearthed in Odessa during May 2001 was one in particular, which was considered at first sight to be of Reilly himself during his teens. It was, however, later established that the picture was of one Boris Rosenblum, the son of Mikhail Rosenblum.[30] When this photograph is compared with one of Reilly at approximately the same age,[31] the likeness is profound. If Mikhail Rosenblum was Reilly's father, then the likeness is uncanny in the extreme, bearing in mind that they had only one parent in common, not two. In the belief that hypotheses raised by investigation and research should be subject to independent analysis, the phototgraphs were presented to the forensic imaging expert Ken Linge BA, MSc, FBIPP. Linge, one of the UK's leading experts on facial mapping and a veteran Old Bailey forensic witness, explained that on the basis that the human face and its features are effectively a unique genetic fingerprint, it is now scientifically possible to examine genetic similarities and determine the odds of two people being related. The results of computer analysis using morphological, anthropometric and biometric techniques found numerous and significant similarities between the two faces, which led Linge to conclude that, 'in my opinion the persons depicted on these images are almost certainly genetically linked'. In terms of whether they shared a common parent, Linge described the likelihood as, 'a strong possibility' (Linge's computer analysis appears in full on the author's website, www.sidneyreilly.com).

The hunt for documentary evidence of Reilly's birth has, thus far, remained elusive,[32] although new evidence revealed later in this chapter strongly suggests Kherson, the home town of Mikhail and Paulina Rosenblum, to be his place of birth. Although this would mean he was not born in Odessa itself, it is still the most likely place for him to have grown up. Reilly's ability as a linguist may have been inherited from the multi-lingual Mikhail Rosenblum, or could equally have resulted from being brought up in such a cosmopolitan city as Odessa. By the mid-1880s the Russian-speaking population of Odessa constituted some 49.3% and Ukrainian speakers 9.4%. The remaining 41.3% of the population spoke an amazing forty-nine different languages.[33] Germans settled in Odessa in their tens of thousands, forming the colonies of Bol'shoi Libental, Malyi Libental and Liustdorf. There were also English, French, Italians and Greeks, along with almost every ethnic group represented within the Russian Empire. In short, Odessa was the perfect environment for someone like Reilly who had a natural inclination for languages.

Reilly's education, like many other aspects of his early life, has been shrouded in mystery. His OGPU file declares that he attended the 3rd Odessa Gymnasium (grammar school) and proceeded from there to study for two years in the physico-mathematics department of the Novorossiysky University in Odessa.[34] Unfortunately, no records of the 3rd Odessa Gymnasium exist today. Comprehensive Novorossiysky University records have survived, but contain no record of Reilly entering, leaving or graduating. It is significant, as well as coincidental, that the academic career attributed to him in the OGPU file bears more than a passing resemblance to that of Mikhail Rosenblum.[35]

On first meeting his future wife Margaret Thomas, Reilly told her that he had been studying chemistry at a Russian university but had left due to his involvement in a student political group,[36] which of course also features in the 'Georgi' story he told George Hill two decades later. According to the story he told Margaret, he completed his studies in Germany, although no trace can be found of him in the archives of any German university. However, the Ochrana kept card index records of Russian students studying abroad who were considered to have dissident sympathies or contacts.[37] One index card of particular note is that on a chemistry student from Odessa, Leon Rosenbaum, also known as Rosenblatt. These names are significant as the file kept on Reilly by the French Deuxième Bureau lists Leon Rosebaum and Leon Rosenblatt among the aliases he used. If he did spend any time in Germany following his departure from Russia, it would be at this point that he adopted the Germanic name Sigmund in place of Salomon.

Whatever the reason for his departure from Russia, we know that he left in haste. In addition to the 'Georgi' story in which his departure results from the shame of being exposed as a bastard, we also have the possibility that he was involved in a radical student political group. Various other theories have equally been advanced. Michael Kettle, for example, claims he 'fell violently in love with his first cousin', which was greeted with horror by the two families who 'firmly forbade the match'.[38] This apparently led him to sever all connections with his family and go abroad.[39] Although not mentioned by name, it is clear from references elsewhere in Kettle's book that he is referring to Felitsia,[40] the daughter of Reilly's uncle Vladimir. Gordon Brook-Shepherd is probably right to reason in *Iron Maze* that lacking any moral scruples, 'he would have been more likely to have eloped with the forbidden cousin, rather than tamely abandoning her'.[41] In fact, the cousins never lost touch, as we shall see later. Of the two stories, the more plausible is the one given to Margaret Thomas. This view is reinforced by the fact that in 1892 there was student unrest in Odessa. This resulted in a number of the students involved in groups suspected of fomenting trouble being sought by the Ochrana.[42]

If Reilly's outward journey from Russia began from Odessa – and it is only an if – there is no record of a passport being issued to him, under his own name or under any of his known aliases.[43] He could, of course, have left legitimately by another route, although his behaviour in the years to follow makes this seem unlikely. To leave the country illegally was very risky, and would only be resorted to by someone with little alternative. It was a criminal offence and could, for someone of Reilly's age, be perceived as evading compulsory military service. Should he ever wish to return or pass through Russian Empire territory in the future, he would first have to establish a new identity, or risk possible arrest and punishment. Like many other exiles before him, Reilly headed for France. According to his Deuxième Bureau file,[44] he used the aliases Rosenblatt and Rosenbaum while residing in Paris during 1894–95.[45] Paris was not only a centre for Russian exiles of radical persuasion, but also the largest Ochrana operational centre outside Russia itself. In Paris, Rosenblum no doubt made the acquaintance of a good many Russian political exiles.

However, any affinity or attraction on his part to the anti-Tsarist émigrés was more than likely a reaction against the anti-Semitism of the Tsar's autocratic regime than any positive identification with an alternative political creed. It would be a great mistake to believe that he had any strong ideological views or loyalties in the accepted sense, either during this period or at any other time in his life. His prime motivation lay not with ideology, but with money and the pleasures it could bring. Indeed, the illegitimate pursuit of money would seem to be the reason for his disappearance from France after little more than a year.

It was generally assumed by solicitor Arthur Abrahams,[46] who later became acquainted with Rosenblum in England, that his sudden arrival in London in December 1895 was the direct result of him having dishonestly come into a sizeable sum of money in France and having to leave there post haste. Indeed, four decades later Yan Voitek (alias Alexander Matseboruk), a Russian émigré residing in Paris, contacted Britain's Secret Intelligence Service volunteering to supply information on Reilly's criminal past in exchange for passage to England. While SIS rejected Voitek's overtures, he later related his story to Nikolai Alekseev, a Paris-based journalist. According this account, Reilly and an accomplice were responsible for attacking two anarchists on board a train, relieving them of a substantial sum of money in the process. Until now, this story has remained uncorroborated. However, a detailed investigation by French researcher Michel Ameuw, concluded in spring 2003, unearthed documentary evidence confirming Voitek's story. From this, contemporary French press reports of the robbery were tracked down. According to the 27 December 1895 edition of *Union Républicaine de Saône et Loire*:

A dramatic event occurred on a train between Paris and Fontainebleau... on opening the door of one of the coaches, the railway staff discovered an unfortunate passenger lying unconscious in the middle of a pool of blood. His throat had been cut and his body bore the marks of numerous knife wounds. Terrified at the sight, the station staff hastened to inform the special investigator who started preliminary enquiries and sent the wounded man to the hospital in Fontainebleau.

The report went on to relate how, on the afternoon following the attack, 26 December, the man had briefly regained consciousness and been questioned by the public prosecutor's department. Apart from revealing that he was a thirty-seven-year-old Italian citizen by the name of Constant Della Cassa, he was unable or unwilling to give them anything more than an elementary account of what had happened to him. According to Della Cassa he had been attacked at Saint-Maur by two men. He refused to say how much cash had been stolen or whether he was alone in the compartment at the time of the attack. The public prosecutor's office were certainly of the view that it had been a sizeable sum due to the fact that 362 francs had been left behind by the attackers. A ticket found in his jacket pocket indicated that he had boarded the train at Maisons-Alfort. Although Della Cassa gave no description of his attackers, the two men had been seen alighting the train at the station after Saint-Maur.

The following day, 28 December, Le Centre reported that Della Casa, of 3 rue de Normandie, Paris, had died from his wounds in Fontainebleau Hospital. The report also stated that he had been identified by police as an anarchist. Although an enquiry was immediately set up by the French authorities, it failed to shed any further light on the robbery or lead to any arrests in connection with the crime. By the time Le Centre announced Della Cassa's death, at least one of the culprits was already on his way to England. London was an obvious destination, where émigrés from Europe were welcomed as refugees, in keeping with Britain's tradition of providing sanctuary for victims of political persecution.

Rosenblum's most likely route from Paris would have been the boat train service from the Gare du Nord to London, via Dieppe and Newhaven. According to the 1895 timetable, the ferry *Tamise* departed from Dieppe at 1.15p.m., bound for Newhaven. The London & Paris Hotel would therefore have been among his first

sights of England. It would be another decade before any meaningful controls were placed on entry to the UK by foreign nationals,
and he would therefore have passed unhindered through the quayside customs point and proceeded by rail to London.

Being well supplied with money and being a creature of habit,
Rosenblum would more than likely have spent a short period
in a comfortable hotel before finding a more permanent
residence. We know from local government records that he
moved into Albert Mansions, a newly completed prestigious
apartment block in Rosetta Street, Lambeth, in early 1896.[47]
He was also able to acquire business premises, albeit just two
rooms, at 9 Bury Court, in the City of London, from where he
established 'Rosenblum & Company'.[48] Ostensibly a consultant
chemist, Rosenblum was, to all intents and purposes, a patent
medicine salesman who went to extraordinary lengths to acquire

85

Date of Admission.	FELLOWS.
A. 2/4/83 F. 28/5/86	Reed, Lester, "Hyrsthof," South Park Hill Road, South Croydon.
A. 30/3/83 F. 16/12/90	Reeks, Trenham Howard, Assoc.R.S.M., 106, Queen Victoria Street, London, E.C.
F. 4/7/88	* Reid, Walter Francis, Fieldside, Addlestone.
F. 21/12/77	¶ Reynolds, Professor James Emerson, Hon. M.D., Hon. D.Sc. (Dub.), L.R.C.P., L.R.C.S. (Edin.), F.R.S., Trinity College, Dublin ; and Burleigh House, Burlington Road, Dublin.
F. 22/3/87	Reynolds, Richard, 13, Briggate, Leeds.
F. 19/2/78	Reynolds, William James, M.A. (Cantab.), 10, Tor Gardens, Campden Hill, W.
A. 27/10/91 F. 3/6/94	Richards, Percy Andrew Ellis, Charing Cross Hospital, W.C., and Town Hall, St. Martin-in-the-Fields.
F. 25/8/97	Richardson, Frederic William, 2, Farcliffe Place, Bradford.
F. 2/12/87	Richmond, Henry Droop, Rodbourne, Claremont Road, St. Margaret's, Twickenham.
A. 30/7/95 F. 4/1/99	Ridding, Howard Charles, Assoc.R.S.M., 8, Grove Place, Shelton, Stoke-on-Trent.
F. 23/3/87	* Rideal, Samuel, D.Sc. (Lond.), 28, Victoria Street, Westminster, S.W.
F. 21/12/87	Ridsdale, Charles Henry, Hutton Grange, Guisbrough, Yorkshire.
F. 12/12/94	Rigby, William Thomas, Public Health Laboratory, Unity Buildings, Temple Street, Birmingham.
F. 1/2/78	Riley, Edward, 14A, Finsbury Square, E.C.
F. 16/3/78	Roberts, Thomas Vaughan, B.Sc. (Lond.), 31, Fern Road, Canonbury, London, N.
F. 21/8/97	Robertson, Robert, D.Sc., M.A. (St. Andrew's), Royal Gunpowder Factory, Waltham Abbey, Essex.
F. 2/2/78	Robinson, George Carr, Chemical Laboratory, Bond Street, Hull.
F. 3/7/93	Robson, James, Glasgow and West of Scotland Technical College, 204, George Street, Glasgow, N.B.
F. 4/3/97	Rosenblum, Sigmund Georgievitch, 6, Upper Westbourne Terrace, Hyde Park, London, W.
A. 23/7/94 F. 26/1/98	Ross, Arthur, 1, Glengall Road, Old Kent Road, London, S.E.
F. 26/1/97	Ross, Raymond St. George, 5, Lavender Road, Worcester.
F. 19/8/97	Rossiter, Edmund Charles, A.C.G.I., Bloncidge House, Langley, Birmingham.

Sigmund Rosenblum's entry in the Institute of Chemistry's Register of Fellows, where he elevated his Paddington address to 'Hyde Park'.

a cloak of professional respectability for himself. Within six months he had succeeded in being admitted to the Chemical Society as a Fellow,[49] although it would take a further nine months to gain a fellowship of the more prestigious Institute of Chemistry.[50]

In order to have gained a fellowship, he would not only have to have demonstrated degree level knowledge of chemistry,[51] but would also have needed the support and sponsorship of other Fellows. Circumstantial evidence indicates that Reilly set about gaining this. We know, for example, that his neighbour at Albert Mansions, William Fox,[52] had been a Fellow of the Institute of Chemistry since 1889, and that another Fellow, Boverton Redwood, was a member of the Russian Technical Society, of which Rosenblum was also a member. A further Russian connection with the Institute of Chemistry, albeit an indirect one, was another institute member, Lucy Boole, the sister of the novelist Ethel Voynich (*née* Boole).

According to Robin Bruce Lockhart, Ethel met Sigmund Rosenblum in London in 1895 and became his mistress.[53] He further asserts that they went to Italy together with the last £300 he had. During this sojourn Rosenblum apparently 'bared his soul to his mistress', and revealed to her the story of his mysterious past. After their brief affair had ended, she published in 1897 a critically acclaimed novel, *The Gadfly*, the central character of which, Arthur Burton, was, according to Rosenblum, largely based on his own early life.[54]

In reality, this is but one more example of Rosenblum's ability to turn reality on its head. The truth about this remarkable book, and how its equally remarkable author came to write it, can be found in Appendix 1.

Ethel Voynich was a significant figure not only on the late Victorian literary scene but also in Russian émigré circles. It is surprising that her political role has received only minimal attention from those writing about Sidney Reilly, for it is through her connections that important clues concerning Reilly and his activities in England are to be found. It was at her mother's house at 16 Ladbroke

Grove, Notting Hill, that Ethel first met Sergei Kravchinsky, a lynchpin in London's Russian émigré community. Kravchinsky, or Stepniak as he now called himself, had fled from St Petersburg in 1878, where, in broad daylight, he had stabbed to death Gen. Mezentsev, the head of the Ochrana. Ethel offered to support Stepniak in his revolutionary work, and immediately began helping him in organising the 'Society of Friends of Russian Freedom'. She soon became a member of the society's council and worked on the editorial of their monthly publication, *Free Russia*. Through Stepniak she became acquainted with other revolutionaries such as Eleanor Marx, Friedrich Engels, Georgi Plekhanov, and the man she would eventually marry, Wilfred Voynich.

In 1895 Stepniak died in a rail accident and Wilfred Voynich, among others, began to play a more central role in the society's covert activities. Ostensibly a London bookshop owner, Voynich became instrumental in smuggling the society's texts and propaganda into Russia through a network of couriers under the cover of his book business. The Ochrana had good reason to believe that his business dealings were also a front for the raising and laundering of revolutionary funds. There seems little doubt that the British authorities as well knew a great deal about Voynich and his activities. Clearly someone close to Wilfred was supplying inside information, but who? What grounds are there for suspecting that it might have been Rosenblum? He certainly had a great deal in common with Wilfred, being a fellow chemist with a keen interest in medieval art and antiquarian books. This would almost certainly have helped him to win Wilfred's acceptance and confidence. Wilfred was also born in the same district of Kovno in Lithuania as Rosenblum's cousin Lev Bramson.[55] Being of a similar age and sharing radical political views, Wilfred and Bramson no doubt moved in the same circles and knew each other long before Wilfred and Sigmund Rosenblum came to reside in London.

The fact that they were indeed friends and associates is confirmed by an Ochrana report concerning members of the

society of Friends of Russian Freedom which states that
Rosenblum was, 'a close friend of Voynich's and especially his wife's.
He accompanies her everywhere, even on her trips to the continent'.[56] Whether this statement should be interpreted as implying
or confirming any romantic attachment between Sigmund and
Ethel is a highly debatable point. It is clear from Ethel's own
statements about this period that she was an active courier for the
'Free Russia' cause and travelled abroad frequently. Wilfred may
well have felt that Ethel needed a protective companion to accompany her, knowing full well that the Ochrana would no doubt be
keeping an eye on her movements. Who better than his trusted
friend Sigmund? Besides which, anecdotal family sources indicate
that Ethel's sexual preferences may well have precluded a romantic
attachment to Rosenblum, or indeed any other man, come to that.[57]

According to the same Ochrana report, other active émigré
members of the Society of Friends of Russian Freedom included:

Aladyin, A.F. (43 Sulgrave Road, Hammersmith): moved to London
from Paris, first attended all gatherings of Russian and Polish revolutionaries, but now, in view of suspicion of espionage, has broken all
such ties and meets only with Goldenberg.

Goldenberg, Leon (15 Augustus Road, Hammersmith): since his arrival
from New York in 1895 he has been the manager of the office of the
'Society of Friends for Russian Freedom'. He maintains relations with
almost all Russian and Polish revolutionaries.

Volkhovsky, Felix (47 Tunley Road, Tooting): an active revolutionary,
often gives lectures on his exile to Siberia. Took over from Kravchinsky
after his death.

Chaikovsky, Nikolai (1 College Terrace, Harrow): a famous emigrant,
the Poles believe him to be an agent of the Russian government. He
has recently been seen meeting the Greek Mitzakis, who frequently
travels to St Petersburg.

Rothstein, Fedor (65 Sidney Street, Mile End): made a speech at the last socialist congress in London under the name of Duchowietzky. A very active revolutionary, moves in Russian and Polish revolutionary circles. Took an active part in the last revolutionary rally on Trafalgar Square, standing next to other speakers by the pedestal of Nelson's Column.

Voynich, Wilfred, alias Kelchevsky (Great Russell Mansions, Great Russell Street, Office Soho Square): took an active part in the revolutionary movement, but now is more inclined to literary work, also on revolutionary issues. Holds an annual international revolutionary library. His wife is British, a novelist.

Wilfred Voynich's remarkable and consistent success in acquiring rare medieval manuscripts prompted a number of theories regarding the sudden appearance of these previously unknown items. According to one theory, he was acquiring supplies of unused medieval paper from Europe and using his knowledge as a chemist to replicate medieval inks and paints, thus enabling him to create 'new' medieval manuscripts to order. One of Voynich's early employees, Millicent Sowerby, confirms that he sold blank fifteenth-century paper to select customers for a shilling a sheet.[58] While this confirms that he at least had access to the paper, what evidence is there to suggest that either he or Rosenblum had the capability to recreate medieval paints and inks? The best source for anyone wanting to research the composition of such properties was the British Museum Library, whose extensive collection contained numerous volumes on medieval art and manuscripts.

Perusal of the museum's records reveals that on 17 December 1898 the principal librarian received a letter of application from one Sigmund Rosenblum seeking a reader's ticket to enable him to use the Reading Room. According to his letter of application he was a 'chemist and physicist' wishing to study medieval art; a character reference provided by Leslie Sandford of the legal firm Willett and Sandford intriguingly states that Rosenblum was 'engaged in scientific research of great importance to the community'.[59] A reader's ticket was issued and Rosenblum began his research on 2 January 1899. Of course, he could have had other or indeed additional motives for his research, which are explored later in this chapter.

If Rosenblum was informing on Voynich, to whom was he supplying the information? Prior to the creation of the Secret Service Bureau in 1909 (the forerunner of MI5 and MI6), émigré matters were the preserve of the Metropolitan Police Special Branch. 'The Branch' had been created in 1887 as a successor to the Special Irish Branch. Unlike the SIB, however, the new Special Branch had a much wider 'anti-subversion' remit than purely countering Irish Republican terrorism. Under its first chief, Scotsman John Littlechild, the Branch consisted of no more than thirty officers. Littlechild resigned in April 1893, to establish his own private detective agency, and was succeeded by William Melville, under whose leadership the Branch grew in size and reputation, establishing itself as a power in the world of secret agencies.[60]

Born a Roman Catholic in Sneem, County Kerry, on 25 April 1850, William Melville joined the Metropolitan Police on 16 September 1872, and was a member of the SIB from its inception in 1883.[61] He was, without doubt, one of the most intriguing and distinguished men ever to lead the Special Branch, holding the post for ten years before mysteriously resigning at the peak of his police career in 1903. Prior to his appointment he had been in Section B, in charge of 'counter-refugee operations', a responsibility that gave him an intimate knowledge of political exiles, émigré groups and 'undesirables' of all varieties. He was described by colleagues as a 'big broad-shouldered man with tremendous strength and unlimited courage'.[62] From contemporary police reports and newspaper coverage, Melville comes across as an effective and single-minded officer who was the antithesis of almost everything the Scotland Yard detective chief inspector was portrayed to be by the popular media of the time.

Sigmund Rosenblum gave the name of solicitor L.J. Sandford to vouch for his application to be allowed to research into medieval art at the British Museum.

The secret of Melville's success was undoubtedly his intelligence network. He was a meticulous man whose records suggest that he carefully checked out the backgrounds of his key informants. It is thanks to his intimate knowledge of those who were part of his network that we come closest to finally establishing solid documentary evidence concerning Reilly's place and date of birth. Prior to his election as a Fellow of the Chemical Society, on 18 June 1896, Rosenblum had been required to submit official Russian documentation to establish his date and place of birth. While still in the possession of the society, pending the committee's decision on membership, the document was perused by one of Melville's officers, who, satisfied by the document's authenticity, recorded in his report that Rosenblum was born on '11 March 1873 in Kherson, Russia'.[63] At this time Russia was still using the Julian calendar, which was thirteen days behind the Gregorian calendar in use elsewhere. The date on the Russian document would therefore equate to 24 March in terms of the Gregorian calendar.

Agents and informers were the most significant intelligence sources Special Branch had in terms of the Russian and Polish

William Melville, the redoubtable Head of Scotland Yard's
Special Branch, who created 'Sidney Reilly'.

émigré communities, and were recruited in a variety of ways.
Some were approached by detectives either on recommendation
or through the course of everyday enquiries. A minority offered
their services to officers. Whether they were approached or had
volunteered, the motive was usually the same – money. Each
officer had his own private circle of informers, whom he paid out
of his own pocket and then claimed from his expenses. Sigmund
Rosenblum, although well endowed with money when he arrived
in England, had a propensity to spend his ill-gotten gains almost
as quickly as he had come by them. Money was, as so often in his
life, his prime motivator and the reason he became a Special
Branch informer.

To Melville, this émigré intelligence network was money well
spent. As the chief commissioner of the Metropolitan Police made
clear in a memorandum to the under secretary of the Home
Department, this area of intelligence gathering was one that was
very difficult for officers to participate in directly due to the
language and cultural barriers of the community they were
seeking to infiltrate.[64] Rosenblum was particularly useful in that he
had a network of his own contacts that transcended the narrow

STREET DIRECTORY, 1896.   **BUR-**

h, dress maker
bel, dressma
aker
rna rd....
ott rd.....
DE.
eorge
tments
William
na road....
hompson
hos. architect
erdale road
o: 30)....
fectioner
grocer&oilman
rne road....
tt road....
ryman
Edgware rd.
t. to Bell st.
8.
DE.
RAILWAYSTAT
refrshmnt.rms

EDWARDS' ALMSHOUSES
SOUTH SIDE.
2 Corso Marco, hairdresser
4 Brown Thomas, grocer

Burton crescent,
29 *Marchmont street* (W.C.)
MAP K7.
1 Page Stephen, dairyman
3 Siddons Miss Mary, boarding ho
5 Erbsmehl Mrs. Louisa, dressmkr
6 Southgate Thomas, gun manfr
7 McCrae Kenneth
8 Ward James Furness
10 Deane William, boarding house
11 Jewell Mrs
13 Daines Miss
14 Piaggio Augustus
15 Butler Mrs
16 Newbery Mrs
18 Simmons Jas. Jsph. L.D.S.dentist
20 Jaeger Mrs; Elise, apartments
21 Gregg Mrs; Mary, apartments
22 Isaacs Mrs. Martha, apartments
24 Menn Arnold
25 Eagles Mrs
26 Mitchinson Chas.Calthrop,surgn
...*here are Hastings street &*
Mabledon place......

3 Price E. H. & Co. mat manufrs
3 Vellinghausen W. S. & Co. iron
agents
3 *Benfleet Brick & Tile Works Limtd*
4 Seale John Bernard, merchant
9 Adolph Wm. & Co. merchants
9 Watson Joseph Albt. comsn.agt
9 De Salis Chas.&Co. who. tea dlrs
9 Rosenblum&Co.consltg.chemsts

Bury st. *Bloomsbry.* (W.C.)
2 *New Oxford street.*
MAP K 8.
EAST SIDE.
1 Harold Miss
Morrell Miss
Rossel Mrs
Fleck A. E
Boyazoglu Nicholas
Davis George
Zusman Charles
Collins Ernest
Howard Percy
2 Hare Denby
Hedley John, jun
Hayward Mrs
Carter Maximilian William
3 Smith Charles
Bingham Mrs

Russell chambers.

5 Butler Harry
5 Hopwood John Tur
5 Rashleigh J. C. S
6 Roberts Mrs
6 Ambiant Mark
6 Cookson Joseph
7 Greenhill Geo.& Co.
7 Saxby William, apa
8 Jones, Yarrell & Co.
8 Poulter Reginld.Clif
8 Scott Montague
9 Scarlett John Rober
... *here is Ryder*
10.& 11 *Pearce's hotel,*
12 *Couriers' Society.*
Ed. Ernest
13 Quartly Mrs. Wm. R
14 George, Mrs. Marion
15 Hall Joseph, apartm
15 Drysdale Gen. Sir W
15 Evans Arthur
16 Timmins William, a
17 Menday William, a
17 Cowles Lieut.-Com
Sheffield [U.S. nav
19 Kitson Frederick, a
19 Alexander Geo C
19 Burke Sir Theobald
19 Holland Francis C

Rosenblum & Company was to all intents and purposes a patent medicine racket set up in 1896.

world of émigré politics. By courting journalists, professional contacts and those he encountered in the gambling clubs and other less than salubrious establishments he frequented, he had a unique pool of sources. He kept his ear to the ground and reported back to Melville on anything that struck him as being of interest.

Apart from selling information, Rosenblum was also developing his legitimate business interests. In 1897 he moved Rosenblum & Co. from Bury Court to Imperial Chambers at 3 Cursitor Street, Holborn, where he also took up residence. Unlike South Lambeth Road, Cursitor Street was at the hub of London life, adjacent to the law courts, Fleet Street and the City. Rosenblum, who later in life would be dubbed 'The Man Who Knew Everything',[65] was in his element at Cursitor Street, where several well-connected Fleet Street journalists also lived.[66] It is not hard to imagine the gregarious and avuncular Rosenblum keeping the drinks flowing for his journalist friends in the Imperial Club on the ground floor of 3 Cursitor Street, listening avidly to their gossip and inside stories.

At the same time as he moved his business to Cursitor Street, he also changed its name to the 'Ozone Preparations Company'. Unlike most consultant chemists, Rosenblum's business activity lay more in the field of patent medicine peddling than in the more professional field of consultancy work. The patent medicine racket was almost totally dependent upon advertising miracle cures to the gullible. The Institute of Chemistry had, since 1893, taken a strong line against its members advertising – a contentious issue among its membership, a number of whom dissented from this ruling.[67] Not wishing to court expulsion from such a prestigious body and thus losing his FIC suffix, Rosenblum concocted a scheme which would enable him to continue advertising unhindered, while at the same time retaining his membership of the institute. By changing the name of the business from his own to that of a corporate trading identity, he concealed his connection with the business. He also covered the tracks of Rosenblum & Co. by moving the business to new premises. Although the accommodation at Cursitor Street was somewhat restricting, space was not a major consideration as he was not actually manufacturing the products himself, but buying from drug manufacturers and selling on the repackaged potions to customers.

While the patent medicine business was booming, both in Britain and in the United States, it was certainly not making the kind of money necessary for Rosenblum to finance the lifestyle to which he had become accustomed. The fact that he moved from the well-appointed and spacious apartment in Albert Mansions to a smaller one in Cursitor Street, from where he also ran his business, suggests that by 1897 the money he had initially brought with him from France was running low, and he was looking to make economies. It was in the summer of that year that he first met Margaret Thomas. As we have already seen, she was a temptation he could not resist in more ways than one, but was she all she seemed to be?

To all intents and purposes, anyone meeting Margaret Thomas for the first time in the late 1890s would, no doubt, have taken her at face value, as an educated and cultured Englishwoman of the

Victorian upper classes. The reality, however, was anything but. Margaret Callaghan was born in the southern Irish fishing village of Courtown Harbour, County Wexford, on 1 January 1874,[68] the eldest daughter of Edward and Anne Callaghan.[69] She and her brothers and sisters grew up in a small cottage very close to that of her cousins Patrick, James and Elizabeth. She left Courtown Harbour in 1889 to join her elder brother, James,[70] who had headed for England in search of better prospects, and was now living in Didsbury, Manchester. She found a position in the household of Edward Birley, in nearby Altrincham, and three years later moved to London to work for Birley's cousin, the Reverend Hugh Thomas. This much is on the official record. It is once she arrives in London, however, that the manipulation and fabrication of her life begins in earnest, instigated primarily by herself.

When she married Hugh Thomas in 1895, for example, she wrote in the marriage register that her father's name was Edward Callaghan, a seaman.[71] Whilst not being an outright lie, it was certainly a profound exaggeration. Edward Callaghan was a small-time fisherman who, like generations of his family before him, had worked the fishing grounds off the coast of Wexford, with his brothers John and David. Less than three years later her story had been refined and further embellished. When she married Sigmund Rosenblum in August 1898, she stated on the marriage register that her father was deceased, and that his name was Edward Reilly Callaghan, a captain in the navy.[72] Apart from the fact that Edward Callaghan was still very much alive in 1898, his fictional promotion from naval rating to an officer and captain was certainly more in keeping with her social pretensions.

According to the marriage register, the two witnesses at the ceremony were Charles Cross and Joseph Bell. Bell at this time was a clerk at the Admiralty, while Charles Cross was a local government official. Whether they were acquaintances of the bride or groom is not immediately apparent. However, it is noteworthy that both eventually married daughters of Henry Freeman Pannett, a one-time associate of William Melville.[73]

It has been claimed that Sigmund Rosenblum adopted the name Reilly from his father-in-law's middle name.[74] If this was indeed the case, why had Margaret not declared this middle name on her 1895 marriage certificate? If Reilly was her father's middle name, then it would have been given to him at baptism. His baptismal records show, however, that this was not the case.[75] Why then did Margaret introduce the name Reilly into the official record when she married Sigmund Rosenblum?

The answer lies in the fact that Rosenblum wanted a new, legitimate identity, not merely the assumption of a *nom de plume* as he had used on many occasions in the past. If he was to return to Russia in the future, his new identity would need to be a watertight one that would be able to stand up to official scrutiny. This would best be achieved by acquiring a British passport. Obtaining a passport through official channels would have been no simple matter for Rosenblum. The easiest way, theoretically, would have been to apply for naturalisation on the grounds that he had married a British subject. Having been resident in England for less than three years at this point, he could not have applied for citizenship on residential grounds. If, having gained naturalisation, he then applied for a British passport, under the regulations it would have been issued with 'Naturalised British Subject' emblazoned on it.[76]

This would have been useless to Rosenblum as it would indicate quite clearly to anyone examining it that he had previously been a citizen of another country and was not British by birth. Furthermore, by adopting this approach, the passport would have been issued under the name Rosenblum, which again would have defeated the whole object of seeking a new identity. Rosenblum therefore needed a British passport in a new name, indicating the holder to have been born in Britain. Obtaining such a passport was motivated purely by the need to provide a new identity in Russia or in Russian-held territory. Although returning to Russia had been on his mind for some while, he certainly had every intention of retaining his British connections

1868 , Marriage solemnized at *the Register Office* in the *District* of *Holborn* in the County of *London*							
No.	When Married.	Name and Surname.	Age.	Condition.	Rank or Profession.	Residence at the time of Marriage.	Father's Name and Surname.	Rank or Profession of Father.
186	Twenty second August 1898	Sigmund Georgiewich Rosenblum	25 years	Bachelor	Consulting Chemist	3 Bartilett Street Chancery Lane Holborn	Grigory Jackovliewich Rosenblum	Landed Proprietor
		Margaret Thomas	24 years	Widow		6 Upper Melbourne Terrace Paddington	Edward Reilly Callahan deceased	Captain in the Navy

Married in the *Register Office* according to the Rites and Ceremonies of the by *Licence Before* us,

This Marriage was solemnized between us, { *Sigmund Georgiewich Rosenblum* *Margaret Thomas* } in the Presence of us, { *Charles James Cross* *Joseph Harold Bell* } *J. J. Sibley, Registrar* *Arthur J. Read, Superintendent Registrar*

Sigmund Rosenblum married Margaret Thomas five months after her husband's sudden death.

and wished, in due course, to adopt the Reilly identity legitimately under English law by Deed Poll. This was why Margaret included the name Reilly on their marriage record. Should the question ever be raised in the future as to why they wished to adopt the name Reilly, they could fall back on the claim that it was her father's name and produce the marriage certificate. It was not unusual for Jews either to anglicise their surnames or to change them completely. The story that it came from his father-in-law was therefore a justification or validation for using the name Reilly, not the origin of it.

In terms of manufacturing a new identity, who better to assist than William Melville? Prior to Sigmund and Margaret's marriage, Melville had found a suitable Irish identity for Rosenblum to use – Sidney Reilly. A comprehensive search through Irish records of birth from their inception in 1864 (when the civil registration of births, deaths and marriages began in Ireland) found only one Sidney Reilly in the whole of Ireland.[77] Interestingly, the child died soon after birth. More intriguingly, research conducted during the spring of 2003 into the family tree of William Melville revealed that his first wife Catherine's maiden name was Reilly. According to family records, her father came from the same Mayo village as Michael Reilly, the father of the deceased infant Sidney.[78] The provision of a new identity was not something Melville would have provided for any common-or-garden informer who was simply supplying émigré 'tittle-tattle'.

In late August 1898, according to Margaret, Sigmund went to Spain for an unspecified period, well supplied with money.[79] Spain was a major terrorist centre during the 1890s and had witnessed a number of notable outrages. The previous August the Spanish Prime Minister, Canovas del Castillo, had been assassinated in Santa Agueda by the anarchist Angiolillo and in July 1896 twelve people had been killed in a bomb explosion in Barcelona. The Spanish government had made specific proposals to the British government for closer police co-operation to combat anarchism and had also referred a number of requests for action or further investigation to Melville through the appropriate diplomatic channels.[80]

While Sigmund was away in Spain, Margaret 'liquidated' the Manor House in Kingsbury.[81] Initially acquired as an out-of-town retreat for Hugh Thomas, the house was now surplus to their requirements. On his return from Spain, Sigmund settled into a life of leisure at 6 Upper Westbourne Terrace, Paddington, typically giving the address a more prestigious tone by re-styling it 6 Upper Westbourne Terrace, Hyde Park, London.[82] Ever the gambler, he also took to horse racing (apparently with disastrous consequences) and set about enlarging his collection of objets d'art, at Margaret's expense.[83] Robin Bruce Lockhart has stated that within a few months of their marriage, Margaret sold 6 Upper Westbourne Terrace, putting the proceeds into a joint bank account and together they moved to St Ermin's Chambers in Caxton Street, Westminster.[84] The house was the property of the church commissioners, from whom Hugh Thomas had leased it since 1891, and Margaret could not possibly have sold it. Church records show that the Rosenblums moved out of the property in June 1899 and that a new lease was given to the incoming tenant, Ormonde Crosse.[85]

Rather than heading for the bright lights of Westminster, documentary evidence strongly suggests an alternative scenario. According to Foreign Office passport records, a passport was issued in the name of S.G. Reilly on 2 June 1899, shortly before their departure from Upper Westbourne Terrace.[86] Margaret also alluded to the issuing of a passport in a meeting she had in Brussels with the British vice-consul on 29 May 1931 when she was attempting to renew her current passport.[87] According to the minute of the meeting, she stated that a passport had been issued in the name of 'Sidney Reilly and wife' in 1901. Study of the original document clearly suggests that the officials considering the matter questioned this claim. The date 1901 has been underlined and a question mark placed by it. This scepticism is born out by an examination of Foreign Office passport records that indicate the only passport issued to an S.G. Reilly between 1898 and 1903 was on 2 June 1899 (No. 38371). Although the 1899 register does not refer to Margaret, she may have travelled with him on the same document. Prior to the British Nationality and Status of Aliens Act 1914, passports were single sheets of paper, without photographs, and were issued for single journeys. It was common practice for a wife travelling with her husband to have her name entered on a passport issued under her husband's name.

The consensus of other Reilly writers is that they left England for the Far East between 1900 and 1902. Michael Kettle places their departure 'about 1900',[88] whereas Robin Bruce Lockhart has Reilly playing a role in Holland in the Boer War, spying on Dutch aid bound for South Africa. When the Boer War ended in 1902, Lockhart states, Reilly was sent to Persia to report on the possibilities of oil exploration in the area, and was eventually sent to Port Arthur in Manchuria around 1903. He also writes that Margaret stayed in England[89] while Reilly was away on these missions, taking to drink in his absence. Jay Robert Nash makes similar claims to Lockhart in terms of missions in Holland and Persia, although he asserts that Reilly was at this time in the employ of NID, the Naval Intelligence Department.[90]

While Margaret's own recollections refer to proceeding to China in 1901,[91] this does not necessarily imply they went directly from England to China. Although she does not give a specific date for the liquidation of the Manor House in Kingsbury, we know that this occurred after August 1898. Her account also claims that following the liquidation Reilly wished to return to Russia due to 'homesickness', and that in 1901 they changed their name to Reilly[92] and proceeded to China. It therefore follows that they left England in June 1899 for Russia, and thence to China.

The timing of their departure from these shores was opportune to say the least, as they left at the very same time as a top-level Russian investigation was in progress in London. On 17 April, Petr Rachkovsky, chief of the Paris Ochrana, had written to William Melville at Scotland Yard seeking information concerning individuals residing in London who were 'without any doubt' involved in a massive rouble-counterfeiting ring operating in London. He concluded by:

> …warmly recommending my friend Mr Gredinger, Deputy State Prosecutor in St Petersburg, who is leaving for London tomorrow, with the aim of taking charge of this case. It would be much appreciated if you could help Mr Gredinger out with whatever he might need and do everything in your power to make his job easier. My friend, will refund you… all of the costs which you have incurred in collecting information.[93]

This was no amateur racket. The counterfeiters had a contact inside the currency-printing firm of Bradbury and Wilkinson, and the contact obtained a plate that was copied by an engraver. The counterfeiters then carried out the printing themselves using their own ink and paper. Rosenblum's name was not initially connected with the investigation. It emerged when attention turned to how the forged money was being shipped out of the country.

According to Ochrana records, Rosenblum had an interest in the Polysulphin Company, in Keynsham, Somerset.[94] The factory produced a host of chemical products including soap, which it exported abroad. This was an ideal vehicle for smuggling money and indeed other commodities. Although the file itself is now incomplete, and therefore inconclusive, Polysulphin must be considered a prime suspect in terms of the counterfeiters' distribution network.

In order to perpetrate such a scheme, an expert knowledge of printing inks would have been required. As a chemist with some experience in this line, Rosenblum may therefore have played a wider role outside that of mere distribution. Once Rosenblum's role was uncovered, Melville would have had good grounds to fear that his connection with Scotland Yard might prove a severe embarrassment if discovered by Gredinger and the Ochrana. The safest thing all round would clearly be for Rosenblum's planned departure to be brought forward post haste with Melville's assistance. With his new passport and new identity, Rosenblum and his wife were thus able to leave the country, and head for probably the last place the Ochrana would think of looking for them – Russia. It would not be the first, or indeed the last time that he would disappear just as the net was tightening around him.[95]

The coat of arms on Rosenblum's letter-head incorporated the double-headed Russian eagle and shamelessly appropriated the Thomas family motto 'no faith in the world'.

Three
GAMBIT

Leaving London behind, Margaret and Sidney Reilly proceeded to Russia in June 1899 where they remained until the autumn of the following year. During the summer of 1900, Reilly travelled around the oil-rich Caucasus, visiting the ports of Petrovsk and Baku while Margaret remained in St Petersburg. It is noteworthy that during these months, War Office records note that: 'Mr Stevens (at the British Consulate in Baku) has an agent who travels between Petrovsk, Baku and along the T.C. Railway and reports to Stevens by word of mouth'.[1]

Whatever the nature of the information being supplied, it would appear that it was of sufficient interest to warrant payment being made to the informant. The scenario certainly fits Reilly's 'modus operandi', although there is no positive proof that the informant was actually Reilly.

In September 1900, the Reillys made their way to Constantinople and took a ship to Port Said in Egypt. Here the SS *Rome* departed for Colombo, where they again changed ships for the final stage of their journey to Shanghai via Penang, Singapore and Hong Kong. After several months in Shanghai, they proceeded to Manchuria, arriving in Port Arthur during the early months of 1901.[2]

Life in Port Arthur was not only primitive by comparison to the one they had led in England and Russia, it was also at the very epicentre of a simmering regional conflict of interest between Russia and Japan, which before too long would break out into open hostility. Located at the tip of the Liaotung peninsula, the port held great strategic significance, due to its commanding position on the Gulf of Chihli, which gave access to the Chinese capital of Peking. In 1898 the Chinese had, by way of a lease, conceded the peninsula to the Russians, with the greatest of reluctance and much to the chagrin of the Japanese. The Russians had renamed the Port of Lushun Port Arthur and made it the base for their Pacific fleet. The harbour was, without doubt, the perfect defensive location, shielded by 'the tiger's tail', a natural deep-lying peninsula. This natural fortification was further reinforced by what was reputedly the strongest fortress in China.

To the Japanese, Port Arthur was a token of Russia's desire for naval supremacy in the region, an aspiration that they, as an emerging naval power themselves, could not countenance. On the economic front, the two powers were equally at loggerheads in that they were both competing for the same unexploited natural resources in Manchuria and Korea. In the same way that Japan saw Russia's annexation of the Liaotung peninsula as an ominous sign in the military and naval sphere, the continued expansion of Russia's railway empire into Manchuria raised economic danger signals for the Japanese. While trying to contain Russian expansion by diplomacy, the Japanese were at the same time preparing for the contingency of war.

Reilly entered this cauldron of intrigue determined to make the most of the business opportunities that beckoned. At first sight, his reported activities in Port Arthur seem to have little or no logical connection. Records, for example, indicate his involvement in lumber trading, real-estate speculation and shipping. Closer inspection, however, reveals that all these ventures were effectively linked by the mutual involvement of one Moisei Akimovich Ginsburg.

Ginsburg, born on 5 December 1851 in Radzivilov in the Ukraine, had long-standing associations with the Rosenblum family. His early life was quite typical of any Jew in the Russian Empire. Born into poverty, he started work at the age of eleven by writing out labels at the local customs house. At fifteen he went to the seaport of Odessa from where he proceeded to Germany, England and America. Having saved $90 working in San Francisco, he bought a third-class ticket for a ship heading for China. On the way the ship docked at the Japanese port of Yokohama, where Ginsburg took an immediate liking to Japan and decided to stay there. By 1877 he had set up his own trading company in Yokohama supplying ships sailing in Japanese waters. He soon gained a reputation as 'the only Russian in Japan who knew perfectly the local conditions'.[3] The Russian Pacific fleet, then based at the port of Vladivostok, was only in its early stages of development and its facilities struggled to supply the fleet with even the barest of essentials. Ginsburg therefore stepped in and within a few short years had become indispensable to the Russian navy.

Duke Kirill Vladimirovich, who raised the Russian tricolour over Port Arthur in 1898, recalled Ginsburg as a 'benefactor on whom the entire Pacific navy depended... everything – from a pin to an anchor, and from rivets to a smoke stack – we got everything from Ginsburg'.[4] It was here, at the new base of the Russian Pacific fleet, that M. Ginsburg & Co. set up its new head office on Port Arthur's main thoroughfare. The import-export company now had branches in Nagasaki, Yokohama, Chemulpo, Odessa and Singapore, and an annual turnover of over 1 million roubles.

With his flair for languages and business, Reilly was seen as a distinct asset when he joined the staff of Ginsburg & Co., where he worked initially under G.M. Gandelman, Ginsburg's office manager.[5] In addition to 'direct' trading, the company also acted as agents for other enterprises such as the East-Asiatic Company, a steamship line with branches in Odessa, St Petersburg and

Copenhagen. Reilly was charged by Ginsburg to deal directly with all the line's business and in this connection Reilly attended a major trade conference on behalf of the company in February 1902.[6] Reilly's responsibilities as representative for both companies thus explains why East-Asiatic's business address in Port Arthur is the same as that of Ginsburg & Co.[7] Also trading from the same address was 'Grunberg & Reilly', which along with the American firm Clarkson & Company was the main importer of American lumber.[8] Reilly's business partner in the lumber business, V. Grunburg, was, according to East-Asiatic records, also a representative of the naval steamship company and the Chinese East railway.[9]

The approaching war with Japan was no secret for Moisei Ginsburg, who had a web of agents in Japan and China picking up news and speculation from some of the most informed sources. After the war, Ginsburg was to claim that he had warned the Russian navy of Japanese intentions, but had been overlooked or ignored.[10] It is equally possible that this claim may have been made to deflect criticism that he had been profiteering during the war. He further countered later criticism by claiming, with some justification, that his foresight had enabled the Russian garrison to hold out for two or three months longer than they would otherwise have been able to do.

Thoroughly convinced that war with Japan was inevitable, Ginsburg and Reilly had been purchasing enormous amounts of food, raw materials, medication and coal. On 10 July 1903, for example, the Russian War Ministry in St Petersburg wrote to the Russian-Asiatic shipping company in Port Arthur, asking them to make enquiries about provisions sent to Grunberg and Reilly, intended for delivery to the 4th East-Siberian Rifle Regiment. Needless to say, the regiment was adamant that the shipment had never arrived. What happened to this and indeed other missing shipments remains a mystery. There were also reports that Reilly was speculating in ground-lots during this period, another indication that he was well aware of what was looming.[11] In addition to the ample provisions that were ordered and purchased from Ginsburg & Co. by the Russian Naval Ministry, the company amassed a stockpile at its own expense. For example, 150,000 roubles worth of medication and dressings were purchased some months before the first shot was even fired.

While the growing gulf between Russia and Japan was creating understandable tension in the Far East, and within the Port Arthur community in particular, closer to home Reilly's marriage to Margaret was also under strain. What for him had always been a marriage of convenience was, for her, something very different. It is highly unlikely that she would ever have taken the risks she did five years earlier if the objective had been anything less than marriage to a man she truly loved. While Margaret no doubt found her socially restricted life dull, Reilly himself found the colonial atmosphere of Port Arthur very much to his liking. With Chinese servants to cater for his every whim at home, and the drinking and gaming clubs to while away the evenings, he lived to the full the persona of the English gentleman, albeit one with an 'Irish father and Russian mother'. A recreation even more to his liking was afforded by the social circumstances of colonial life. Among the 4,000-strong European community was a large band of wives who, like Margaret, were often bored and neglected. Such opportunities to philander were ones that a man of his character found hard to resist. Like a good many serial philanderers of that era, his success with women seems to have relied on a judicial use of gentlemanly charm, and his undoubted ability to make a woman feel that she was the centre of his universe without resorting to obvious or overt flattery. This approach, combined with a steady stream of gifts and affectionate letters almost always seemed to do the trick. One relationship in particular, with a lady by the name of Anna, may well have resulted in Margaret's premature departure from Port Arthur.

With his knowledge of the impending Japanese attack, now possibly only months away, he insisted that a town under siege was no place for Margaret and had her pack her things and return to

England. In the autumn of 1903 she left Port Arthur for Yokohama, then journeyed to Europe across the Pacific, via San Francisco and New York.[12] Now free to continue his dalliance with Anna unhindered, their affair began to attract attention. Whether this was another relationship of short-term convenience, or the beginning of a much longer term liaison depends very much on how one interprets Reilly's connections with the Japanese and his own hasty departure from Port Arthur the following year.

His undoubted knowledge of Japanese intentions would later lead to questions being raised about his role in Port Arthur and the allegation that he was in fact a spy in the pay of the Japanese. Authors Winfried Ludecke and Richard Deacon state clearly their view that Reilly was a Japanese spy,[13] while Robin Bruce Lockhart portrays Reilly as being distinctly anti-Japanese in his account of events.[14] Professor Ian Nish, of the London School of Economics, and author of *Causes of the Russo-Japanese War*, is therefore right to refer to Reilly's role as 'one of the unsolved riddles about the Russo-Japanese War'.[15]

The first known and recorded suggestion that Reilly had been a Japanese spy is contained within a US Bureau of Investigation report written by Agent L. Perkins on 3 April 1917.[16] Written while Reilly was living in New York during the First World War, the report refers to information volunteered to the Bureau by one Winfield Proskey, an engineer with the Flint Arms Company, who stated that Capt. Guy Gaunt,[17] the British Naval attaché in New York, had told him that Sidney Reilly had once spied for Japan. Gaunt was certainly in Manchuria at the time the Russo-Japanese War broke out, where he was serving on HMS *Vengeance* in the summer of 1904.[18] It is, therefore, not unlikely that Gaunt either encountered Reilly while in Manchuria or had heard stories of his alleged spying there.

Although Richard Deacon's stated belief that Reilly's Japanese intelligence contact was Col. Akashi Motojiro is not supported by Akashi's own records,[19] a letter written by Reilly to an unknown correspondent simply referred to as 'ECF', on 3 December 1902, does clearly suggest that he did have an interest and knowledge of intelligence matters at this time:

> The Manchu's are finished. It is only a matter of time before China becomes the playground of the great powers. Their intelligence service, such as it is, for all practical purposes simply does not exist. But I should warn you that in this vacuum which is left a new and much more dangerous Secret Service will eventually spring up. Today it is like a sperm in the womb. Tomorrow? Perhaps a fully fledged child.[20]

Although not stated openly in the letter, the 'sperm in the womb' can only mean the Japanese Secret Service, who had a growing network of agents in Manchuria at this time to help them gauge Russian intentions. Britain was also keeping a watching brief on developments in the area through its Military and Naval Intelligence Departments with a view to her future policy. Her first preference would have been an agreement with the Russians to preserve the status quo in the region. Unable to achieve this objective, Britain concluded a treaty with Japan in January 1902, by which she hoped to achieve the next best thing. At the time of the treaty, the Japanese had six capital ships, Russia six, France six and Britain four. Under the treaty, Britain or Japan would come to the other's aid in the event of one of them being at war with more than one of the other great powers. Should Japan be unable to get the Russians to come to some agreement concerning their ongoing expansionism, the treaty would at least now make it possible for Japan to contemplate war with Russia as a last resort, in the full knowledge that the French would be kept in check by the British.

Understandably, Britain took a greater degree of interest after the treaty and particularly as tensions between the Russians and the Japanese were seen to be heightening. War Office Military Intelligence records confirm that in 1903, 'the first four officers were sent to Japan as language students'.[21] The thrust of Britain's intelligence gathering was therefore through the armed forces, although this is not to discount information picked up by diplomatic posts and newspaper correspondents. Russian espionage files, for example, refer to a *Daily Telegraph* correspondent in Manchuria, a retired lieutenant colonel, Joseph Newman, who appears to have been well connected within the European business community.[22] He would, more than likely, have relayed back anything of interest he had heard and could well have come across Reilly during his stint in Manchuria. Whoever Reilly was supplying information to, it was certainly not the Russians. While not expecting to lose any future conflict with Japan, they were certainly sensitive to Japanese efforts to obtain information about Port Arthur and were keen to keep a watchful eye on those suspected of being foreign spies, particularly among the European residents of Port Arthur. Comprehensive records still exist in Moscow, providing a wealth of detail about the numerous agents they themselves were running in Port Arthur and in the region generally.[23] Reilly's name is nowhere to be seen.

When the inevitable conflict between Russia and Japan broke out into open hostility on 8 February 1904, it was as a result of a surprise Japanese attack against the Russian Pacific fleet at Port Arthur. With no declaration of war prior to the attack, it bore many of the hallmarks that would characterise the assault on the American Pacific fleet at Pearl Harbor some thirty-six years later. Although the attack on Pearl Harbor was carried out in daylight by air and the attack on Port Arthur was at night by torpedo boats, the theory behind both acts of war was the same. The Japanese had calculated that the only possible way they could defeat a larger and theoretically stronger power was by attacking without warning and in so doing striking a blow from which the enemy would have great difficulty recovering.

As a result of superior intelligence, Japan's Admiral Togo was not only aware of the positions of all Russian ships but was equally aware of the layout of Russian minefields and search-light locations. This enabled the Japanese to move through the minefields unhindered and to emerge from the darkness unseen by Port Arthur's search lights, which on the night of the attack were mysteriously disabled. Although Togo's attack succeeded in crippling the Russian Pacific fleet, it was not until 1 January 1905 that the Japanese actually captured the port. Neither side had foreseen the lengthy siege of Port Arthur and the Japanese in particular were not prepared for a winter campaign. Although ultimately victorious, 58,000 Japanese lives were lost in comparison to the 31,000 Russians who perished defending the town.

Credit for Togo's initial attack on Port Arthur, which was one of the most brilliantly conceived and co-ordinated assaults ever undertaken, was very much the result of the advance intelligence operation which enabled him to access Russian defence plans. How he managed to obtain these has been shrouded in mystery for nearly a century. When the US army, led by Gen. MacArthur, arrived in Japan in August 1945, it set about examining Japanese intelligence records. A large consignment of material was taken away by MacArthur's intelligence chief, Gen. Willoughby, and sent to Washington for detailed analysis. Students of the Russo-Japanese War hoped that here at last would be revealed the answer to the mystery. Sadly, no hint as to the identity of the agent who procured the plans for Togo was ever found in the records, copies of which now reside in America's National Archives in Washington DC. As a result, it was widely assumed that the solution to the riddle had been lost or destroyed.

In Moscow's Military Historical Archives 6,000 miles away, however, a dusty file of intelligence reports finally exposes the Russians' number-one suspect. The file, not seen by unauthorised eyes before the downfall of Soviet communism, contains a report from April 1904 addressed to 'His Excellency the Commandant of Port Arthur' and marked 'Secret'.[24] In it, the conclusions of an in-depth investigation into the theft of harbour defence plans are revealed, and the culprit named as one Ho-Liang-Shung, a Chinese engineer who worked under the Head Marine Architect, Svirsky. Ho-Liang-Shung had a detailed knowledge of the harbour, its fortifications and mine field. He also had access to the harbour defence plans. According to the report, he had prior knowledge of the Japanese attack as early as 26 January 1904. On 23 February and again on 8 March, large sums of money were deposited into his bank account. On 10 April he attempted to leave without an exit permit and was detained by the port gendarme. In spite of this, he managed to escape confinement and was never seen again.

While convinced of Ho's guilt, the Russians were clearly of the view that he had not acted alone and was very much a minor player in a wider web. The identity of his 'go-between', the person to whom he had given the plans and who had paid the money into his bank account, was never established. Intriguingly, some twenty-seven years later, when Margaret Reilly wrote a manuscript about her husband's life, she referred in passing to a port engineer acquaintance he had known in Port Arthur – 'Ho-Ling-Chung'.[25] While the spellings are at variance, the chances of there being two engineers with such similar names, moving in similar circles, must be viewed as somewhat remote. Bearing in mind the intimate relationship between Ginsburg & Company and the Pacific fleet, it is highly probable that Reilly would have come into regular contact with port and naval officials at all levels. In fact, many of the naval contacts he utilised in later years were initially made during his time in Port Arthur.

Reilly and Ho are further linked by their mutual disappearance, for shortly after Ho's escape, Reilly too departed. In 1917 Moisei Ginsburg recalled that Reilly had 'suddenly vanished', leading the local Russians to conclude that he was a spy.[26] Winfried Ludecke and Richard Deacon have both maintained that Reilly concluded the Russians had their suspicions about him after discovering someone associated with East-Asiatic was in the employ of Russian intelligence.[27] This theory again finds corroboration in Moscow archives, which reveal that one of Russia's most valuable espionage finds was a British citizen by the name of Horace Collins who indeed happened to work for the East-Asiatic Company. Collins was born on 12 March 1870 in Hever, Kent.[28]

His father was a well-to-do farmer, and Horace grew up working with horses, eventually taking up an apprenticeship as a jockey at the nearby Lingfield stables. On completion of his apprenticeship in 1893 he went to the Far East, where he eventually secured a job at the stables of the Japanese Emperor. It was during this period that he learnt to speak Japanese and a Chinese language. Although moderately successful as a jockey, it was not long before he took to business, making the most of his oriental languages and travelling widely on behalf of various trading houses in China, Korea, Japan and eastern Russia.

There is no indication in Russian records as to how Collins was recruited as a spy, although money may well have been a factor. It would seem from the commentary in his file that he was not exactly prospering in business when he was first recruited. From the Russian point of view, he was most useful by virtue of his language abilities and his knowledge of Japan and her people. Accordingly, the Russians were paying him $300 per month plus expenses.[29]

Whether Reilly's discovery of the Russian agent was made by chance or through a third party is unknown. However, bearing in mind the suggestion that he was involved in an affair with a woman by the name of Anna, one candidate stands out in particular – Anna Grigoryevna Collins, Horace Collins' Russian-born wife.[30] She not only knew of his work for the Russians, but was also known to be having an affair with an associate of her husband.

Having made a swift exit from Port Arthur, Winfried Ludecke suggests that Reilly headed for Japan in the company of 'a lady with whom he had been flirting'.[31] Whether Anna and the lady companion are one and the same is conjecture. If Reilly did go to Japan, he could not have stayed there very long, for in June 1904 we find him in Paris.[32] During the brief time he spent in the city he renewed his acquaintance with William Melville, whom he had last seen in 1899, shortly before his hurried departure from London. Reilly's meeting with Melville is most significant, for within a matter of weeks Melville was to enlist his help in what would later become known as the D'Arcy Affair.

Authors writing about Reilly's role in the D'Arcy Affair have often relied on Reilly's own tale of what happened. Other sources lead to a rather different train of events. The background to the affair is succinctly set out in a letter of reminiscence dated 30 April 1919 from E.G. Pretyman MP to Sir Charles Greenway, the chairman of The Anglo-Iranian Oil Company,[33] in which Pretyman recounts his own involvement some fifteen years earlier, as Civil Lord of the Admiralty, in securing the Persian oil concession for Britain, which led indirectly to the founding of the Anglo-Iranian Oil Company:

In 1904 it became obvious to the Board of the Admiralty that petroleum would largely supersede coal as the source of fuel supply to the Navy. It was also clear to us that this would place the British Navy at a great disadvantage, because, whereas we possessed, within the British Isles, the best supply of the best steam coal in the world, a very small fraction of the known oilfields of the world lay within the British Dominions, and even those were situated in very distant and remote regions. Lord Selborne therefore decided to appoint a small Standing Committee to deal with this question and to take any steps they found possible to bring additional sources of petroleum supply under British control. I was appointed Chairman of this Committee and was assisted by Sir Boverton Redwood and the late Sir Henry Gordon Miller, then Mr Gordon Miller, Director of Navy Contracts. In the course of our investigations we learned through Sir Boverton Redwood that the late Mr D'Arcy had secured a valuable concession from the Persian government of the oil rights in southern Persia, and that he was negotiating for a similar concession from the Turkish Government for oil rights in Mesopotamia. We also ascertained that Mr D'Arcy was desirous of disposing of his rights under the Persian Concession to some financial Syndicate with the necessary capital and experience to undertake development operations. We further ascertained that D'Arcy was, at that moment, in the Riviera negotiating for the transfer of his concession to the French Rothschilds. I therefore wrote to Mr D'Arcy explaining to him the Admiralty's interest in petroleum development and asking him, before parting with the concession to any foreign interests, to give the Admiralty an opportunity of endeavouring to arrange for its acquisition by a British Syndicate.

I further asked him to come and see me on the subject. Mr D'Arcy accepted my invitation and returned from the Riviera to discuss the position with me. As a result of our conversation, the Committee approached the Burmah Oil Company with whom arrangements had already been made for emergency supplies of Naval Oil fuel, and, after investigating the prospects of the Persian Oil Field, they agreed to undertake its development and to form a Syndicate.

D'Arcy had already spent over £150,000 in the search for oil over and above what he had spent in obtaining the concession in the first place. It was clear that he could not continue in this way. He soon found, however, that he was very much in a 'chicken and egg' position, as potential backers, including the British government, would have nothing to do with the project until oil was found. Then, in December 1903, there seemed to be hope in that Lord Rothschild, who had heard of D'Arcy's venture, had expressed the view that it was of 'great importance'. D'Arcy's intermediary, Sir Arthur Ellis, met with Lord Rothschild and on 30 December wrote to D'Arcy to inform him that Rothschild would be writing to his cousin Baron Alphonse de Rothschild in Paris. It was indicated to the Rothschilds by Sir Arthur Ellis that £2 million would have to be spent in Persia. A personal meeting was therefore arranged between D'Arcy, who was accompanied by John Fletcher Moulton, and Baron de Rothschild in Cannes. According to the records of the Anglo-Iranian Oil Company, this meeting took place towards the end of February 1904.[34]

Pretyman's letter also raises a number of other questions: why, for example, had the British government had such a quick and fundamental change of heart in now wanting to assist D'Arcy? Back in November of the previous year they had shown a distinct lack of enthusiasm for assisting him. Now, three short months later, they had not only a dramatic change of mind but were positively pursuing him to the negotiating table.

It may well be that in December 1903 the government view was that in the absence of any other potential D'Arcy backers they could afford to wait for a sign of the concession's potential before committing any money. The situation changed dramatically the following month, however, when it seemed not only that D'Arcy had now found potential funding, but that potential funding was sourced abroad and might purchase the concession outright.

In *Ace of Spies*, Robin Bruce Lockhart repeats one of Reilly's oft-recited tales of how, at the British Admiralty's behest, he tracked down D'Arcy and covertly approached him in the south of France. According to Reilly, he boarded de Rothschild's yacht disguised as a priest and persuaded D'Arcy to break off negotiations and return to London to meet with Pretyman and the Admiralty.[35] This story is clearly fantasy on Reilly's part, for in February 1904 he was thousands of miles away in Port Arthur. However, this should not discredit the theory that the Admiralty was engaged in efforts to entice D'Arcy from the clutches of the Rothschilds.

As D'Arcy and the Rothschilds were making the first tentative moves towards exploratory talks, William Melville mysteriously resigned as head of Special Branch on 1 December 1903. No known reason was given for his sudden departure. His Metropolitan Police Service File would have contained the answer to this puzzle, but unlike those of other Special Branch heads, it is no longer to be found. Had he made too many anarchist enemies, and decided to disappear from view, or had he accepted a lucrative position outside the force? All the signs are that this was a speedy and unplanned departure. Patrick Quinn was appointed to succeed him, and as an indication of the haste involved, was promoted to superintendent without sitting the usual examination, which he would have done well in advance if his promotion had been planned and anticipated.

Where then did Melville go? It seems unlikely that his departure was motivated by a desire to avoid the attentions of anarchists or any other undesirable element, as his name and address continue to appear in the London Post Office Directory from the time of his resignation in 1903 to the time of his death in 1918.[36] There is no indication either, from any source, that he set up in business in Britain or abroad. It was not until after his death on 1 February 1918,[37] that a clue to this mystery presented itself in the 'Funerals' column of *The Times* on Wednesday 6 February 1918. Under the heading 'Mr William Melville', the report referred to his funeral the previous day at St Mary's Cemetery in Kensal Green, and went on to state that he was 'formerly a superintendent of Special Police at Scotland Yard, and recently of the Military Intelligence Department of the War Office'. Among those listed as attending the funeral was one Lt Curtis Bennett RN, who author Nicholas Hiley[38] believed was a naval intelligence officer. This led Hiley to speculate that Melville had been recruited by NID, the Naval Intelligence Division, in 1903 and that he later joined MI5 during the First World War, as stated by *The Times* report.[39] Research by this author has confirmed that Henry Curtis Bennett was indeed an intelligence officer, but was an MI5 officer with no connection to the Naval Intelligence Division.[40]

It was not, however, until November 1997, when MI5 released material on Melville to the Public Record Office, that Hiley's theories were finally corroborated, if only in part.[41] It revealed that 'W. Melville, MVO, MBE, was employed with effect from 1 December 1903' by the War Office.[42] It further indicated that he initially worked in the second auxiliary of the Military Intelligence Investigation Branch, which was later incorporated into MI5 when the new service was created in 1909. Those working in this branch are described as 'shadowing staff', whose responsibility it was to 'watch and report' on designated persons.

We know from contemporary records that the Admiralty and the War Office worked closely together on a number of intelligence matters, and shared the cost of such operations.[43] Had the Admiralty decided in December 1903 that a close eye should be kept on developments between D'Arcy and a possible French source of funding? It is highly unlikely that Pretyman would have written such a letter to D'Arcy completely out of the blue, particularly bearing in mind that there does not appear to have been any contact between them since the rejection of D'Arcy's approach to the Admiralty the previous November. It is therefore probable that some reconnaissance work took place prior to Pretyman's approach. The impression given by Pretyman in his letter to Sir Charles Greenway is significant, in that it states, 'we further ascertained that Mr D'Arcy was, at that moment, in the Riviera negotiating for the transfer of his concession to the French Rothschilds'. This very much suggests that such information had come to them literally at a moment's notice, necessitating prompt action.

D'Arcy was staying at the Grand Hotel while the Rothschild negotiations were taking place, and there would seem little point in the kind of approach featured in Reilly's story. Where better to approach D'Arcy than at his own hotel, and who better to do so than a fellow guest?

Le Littoral very helpfully lists comings and goings during the period that Alphonse de Rothschild and William Knox D'Arcy were in Cannes. Of the many British visitors passing through, one particular couple stand out – Mr and Mrs William Melville, who stayed at the Grand Hotel throughout D'Arcy's stay there.[44]

Melville was no stranger to France,[45] and was a fluent French speaker.[46] Whatever transpired during the Melville's 'holiday' in Cannes, D'Arcy was soon in receipt of Pretyman's letter and on his way back to London to meet with the Admiralty's Oil Committee, who approached Burmah Oil to undertake the formation of a British syndicate.

This process was not, however, quite as speedy and seamless as Pretyman implied fifteen years after the event. In fact, negotiations between D'Arcy and the Burmah Group did not begin for another six months. In the intervening period D'Arcy was experiencing more difficulties with Lloyds Bank, who were pressing him to put forward the concession itself as security against his overdraft, something D'Arcy fiercely resisted. As a result, D'Arcy once again turned to Alphonse de Rothschild, although this time he did not negotiate directly, but sent John Fletcher Moulton to Cannes as his representative.[47] Melville, by virtue of the fact that he was now a known quantity so far as Fletcher Moulton was concerned, perhaps felt that his presence could compromise the situation, and appears at this point to have enlisted Reilly's assistance.

Back in February, the threat that the oil concession might slip into foreign hands had been successfully averted. Now, three short months later, the possibility was again in contention, and it was deemed essential from the Admiralty's point of view that the renewed talks be stopped dead in their tracks. Unable to again play the same hand that had worked so well before, namely to appeal to D'Arcy's patriotism, other means of stalling the negotiations had now to be found.

One of the surest ways of scuttling the discussions would have been to sow seeds of doubt in de Rothschild's mind concerning the chances of oil being found in the location D'Arcy was drilling. By the time the talks commenced in June, Fletcher Moulton was already complaining that de Rothschild's terms were now somewhat less favourable than when they had last met.[48] His despondence was even more evident when, on 24 June, he cryptically referred to an 'unhelpful outside interest' whose influence had led to de Rothschild questioning the location of drilling.[49] Although the 'unhelpful outside interest' is never actually identified by Fletcher Moulton, it seems clear that there is a distinct connection between this involvement and de Rothschild's acquisition of a report that seems to have been the source of his misgivings.

Meanwhile, some 30km down the coast, where 'Mr and Mrs Reilly' were guests at the Continental Hotel in St Raphael, Reilly wrote a letter dated 30 June, in which he referred to 'a most useful report' that had helped him 'turn the tide'.[50] The tide had indeed turned for Fletcher Moulton, who apparently found that there was little he could do to dispel de Rothschild's misgivings or to reassure him. Their discussions finally broke down during the first week of July 1904.[51] On cabling Knox D'Arcy in London with the regrettable news, Fletcher Moulton was surprised to find that his friend was not at all downcast by the news. On the contrary, out of the blue, the Admiralty-sponsored talks with Burmah Oil were suddenly back on the agenda with a renewed sense of urgency.[52] An agreement was finally signed on 20 May 1905 and, almost three years later, oil was struck at Masjid-i-Suleiman. In April 1909 the Anglo-Persian Oil Company was founded, today known as BP Amoco. Apart from making D'Arcy and his syndicate rich beyond their wildest expectations, the find also guaranteed the Royal Navy a substantial and dependable source of oil.

The Reillys appear to have stayed on the Côte d'Azur for the remainder of the summer. Apart from the mystery report referred to by both Reilly and Fletcher Moulton, a secondary puzzle in this episode concerns the identity of 'Mrs Reilly'. If, as will later become evident, there is a strong case for believing that Reilly bigamously remarried after the Russo-Japanese War, we can confidently discount the possibility that the 'Mrs Reilly' at the Continental was in fact Margaret, as she herself declared that the first occasion on which she saw her husband after their parting in Port Arthur was Christmas 1904.[53]

Following his departure from the Continental Hotel, Reilly returned to Brussels.[54] In the new year he moved on to St Petersburg, where he arrived alone on 28 January 1905, checking into room 93 at the Hotel Europe on Nevsky Prospect.[55] If he had remarried, where was the new Mrs Reilly, and why did he go to such extraordinary lengths to successfully keep the marriage a secret?

Four
THE BROKER

If Reilly did marry bigamously after the Russo-Japanese War, the question arises as to how he managed to conceal his second wife's existence for so long. The most likely explanation is that she was found secreted away in 'backwater' locations where he had contacts and connections who would ensure she was well taken care of. Odessa and Port Arthur are two such possibilities.[1] After Russia's defeat in the war of 1904/05, the Liaotung peninsula became a Japanese possession, eventually becoming part of the Japanese puppet state of Manchukuo. Whatever the reality of Reilly's connections with the Japanese during the war, it is evident that he had, and continued to have, very close business connections with a number of businesses in Japan and her occupied territories. As someone known to the Japanese authorities, Reilly would have had no trouble in accommodating his new spouse in Port Arthur, which after the war was rebuilt and restored by the Japanese. His representative and principal agent in Japan was William Gill, in Narunouchi, Tokyo.[2] Again, Gill would have been well placed to act as conduit and to ensure that Reilly's wife was well provided for.

Likewise, Alexandre Weinstein became a trusted lieutenant of Reilly's before the Russo-Japanese War, and remained such for over a quarter of a century. If Reilly did take a second wife, then Weinstein above all would not only have been aware of her, but would more than likely have played a pivotal role in liaising between 'husband and wife'. When a decade later Reilly joined the Royal Flying Corps, he named his next of kin as his wife, 'Mrs A. Reilly', who in the event of his death could be contacted at 120 Broadway, New York City, a business address being run on his behalf at the time by Alexandre Weinstein.[3] Further evidence concerning a possible second marriage is examined in later chapters.

In contrast to the comings and goings of wives, ex-wives and mistresses, one female relationship that survived the test of time was that with his first cousin Felitsia. Born in the Grodno gubernia of Russian Poland, she later moved to Vienna during the closing years of the 1890s. The city's large Jewish population lived principally in the old quarter, and it was here that Reilly visited Felitsia[4] whenever he could. She was the only member of his immediate family that he kept in touch with after leaving Odessa in 1893, and her existence was kept a closely guarded secret from all who knew him. It was through these visits to Vienna that he made the brief acquaintance of an influential businessman whose precise role in Reilly's story has since become a source of some controversy.

Josef Mendrochowitz, an Austrian Jew, was born in 1863 and came to St Petersburg in 1904.[5] In partnership with Count Thaddaeus Lubiensky he founded a firm of brokers, Mendrochowitz and Lubiensky, who successfully secured the right to represent Blohm & Voss shortly thereafter. Under the representation contract, Blohm & Voss undertook to pay Mendrochowitz and Lubiensky a commission of 5% on each successful business deal.[6] In *Ace of Spies*, Robin Bruce Lockhart argues that 'Mendrochovitch and Lubensky' were awarded the rights of representation in relation to Blohm & Voss in 1911, as a result of Reilly's chicanery with the Russian Admiralty. Blohm & Voss archives and Mendrochowitz and Lubiensky's own business records demonstrate quite clearly that this was not the case. At the time the contract was awarded, Reilly was not even in Russia. According to the St Petersburg Police Department, Reilly first arrived in the city en route from Brussels on 28 January 1905,[7] where he seems to have stayed for a comparatively short period of time before moving on to Vienna. By the summer of 1905 he was back in St Petersburg, this time with the intention of staying on a more or less permanent basis.

Thanks to a chance meeting with George Walford, a British born lawyer, whom he accompanied to St Petersburg's Warsaw Railway Station on 10 September 1905, an account of his activities at this time have found their way into Ochrana records. Walford was under Ochrana surveillance, and Reilly was watched and followed from 11–29 September as a result of his being seen with him. Why Walford was under surveillance is unclear, although it was routine practice for the Ochrana to keep a watchful eye on foreign citizens, a task they took even more seriously in the wake of the Russo-Japanese War. The surveillance on Reilly yielded nothing of value for the Ochrana, although it is most helpful to us in confirming that on arrival in St Petersburg, Reilly made contact with Mendrochowitz and Lubiensky, and actually lived in their apartment building at 2 Kazanskaya. According to the surveillance report, Reilly also visited the offices of the China Eastern Railway and introduced himself as a telephone supplier. Whether or not he succeeded in making a sale is unknown. Bearing in mind that Ochrana 'tailers' often gave their targets nicknames in written reports, Reilly was appropriately referred to as 'The Broker'.[8]

If Reilly had nothing to do with Mendrochowitz and Lubiensky securing the right to represent Blohm & Voss, did he have any connection or dealings at all with the firm? Details of the firm's dealings are contained in six volumes of files containing over 1,000 pages of correspondence and records now held by the Hamburg State Archive. In addition to the two partners, there appear to have been four other employees, including deputy manager Jachimowitz, who ran the office in the absence of the partners and was particularly well connected with influential Russian politicians. Reilly's name is not among those employed by the firm, but is mentioned in letters and invoices concerning his work on behalf of Blohm & Voss, as a freelance broker during the winter of 1908 and the spring of 1909. During this time he was working with Mendrochowitz and Lubiensky, assisting them in marketing a new Blohm & Voss boiler system. Company records show that agents or brokers like Reilly were often used to 'influence' people in favour of the company.

Exchanges of correspondence and telegrams between Mendrochowitz and Lubiensky and Blohm & Voss in Hamburg during this period give some impression of the working relationship between the firm and the freelance Reilly. His name first surfaces in a telegram dated 14 December 1908[9] in which Blohm & Voss are told that 'Reilly asks for advance payment of 1,000 roubles urgently. Please notify us whether we should pay'. It is apparent from Blohm & Voss records in Hamburg that Reilly was not only waging his campaign for a higher fee through Mendrochowitz but was also making personal representations to Blohm & Voss. On 13 April, while staying at the Hotel Bristol in Berlin, he sent them a handwritten letter:

Dear Mr Frahm,

I am here in Berlin on my way to Paris, where I will stay only tomorrow.

At the initiative of Mr Mendrochowitz (who is in Vienna right now) I dare to ask you whether it would be convenient for you if I came by on my way back and visited you in Hamburg. Mr Mendrochowitz was of the opinion that the unsolved matter between us would be dealt with best by a meeting. I will be at the Grand Hotel Paris tomorrow until 1 p.m. and would be grateful for a telegram.

Yours faithfully,

Sidney G. Reilly[10]

The following day, while he was in Paris, a telegram duly arrived from Blohm & Voss: 'Nothing against a visit this week, next week not possible'.[11] Whatever the outcome of this meeting, it seems clear that despite the impression he sought to create, namely that his approach was being made at Mendrochowitz's instigation, Mendrochowitz had no idea he was doing anything of the kind. In ignorance of the meeting, Mendrochowitz wrote to Blohm & Voss on 23 April[12] expressing some frustration at Reilly's demands for a higher commission:

> In this matter we inform you that with utmost respect that Mr Reilly does not want to accept the application made to him on the part of Mr Frahm. He asserts that the amount offered him is not even enough to satisfy his background men and otherwise considers the sum not nearly commensurate with his services. It will not be easy for us to reach agreement with this stubborn man. We request by all means a response from you, after which the matter will be further dealt with.

Reilly's stock with Blohm & Voss was clearly somewhat higher than it was with Mendrochowitz, for on 26 April they sent a telegram agreeing to raise Reilly's portion from 6,700 roubles to 10,000 roubles.[13]

On 27 April Blohm & Voss sent Mendrochowitz and Lubiensky a cheque for 27,500 roubles made payable to the firm's bankers, Crédit Lyonnais, St Petersburg, and a statement[14] setting out how the money should be dispersed:

For yourself:	15,000 roubles
For Mr Reilly:	10,000 roubles
For payments already made to Mr Reilly:	300 roubles
For Dr Polly:	1,000 roubles
For payments already made to Dr Polly:	1,000 roubles
For your typist:	200 roubles

The fact that Reilly had clearly been asking for more than 10,000 roubles is apparent from Mendrochowitz' reply on 27 April:

We confirm receipt of your dispatch in which you increase the portion in question by 3,300 roubles. We have not yet, however, informed the person in question because he continues to insist on the preposterous standpoint: 'all or nothing at all'. Relenting immediately on your part would certainly at this point in time not serve its purpose and to the contrary strengthen the view of the person in question that he should succeed. It appears to be the case that he has a difficult standpoint, which is his own fault. In view of your very noble concessions, we hope to reach a result in the course of the next few days, about which we will inform you.[15]

When Mendrochowitz issued Blohm & Voss with a receipt[16] he informed them:

We confirm with thanks the receipt of your valued letter from 27 of this month with the enclosed cheque for 27,500 roubles (twenty-seven thousand five hundred roubles). With exception to the money

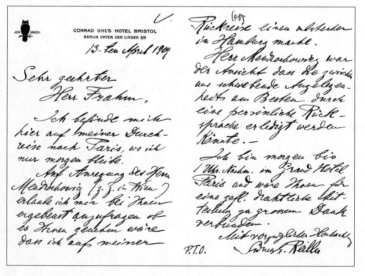

While staying at the luxury Hotel Bristol in Berlin in April 1909, Reilly wrote to Blohm and Voss, in an attempt again to undermine Josef Mendrochowitz.

intended for Mr Reilly we have used the amount according to your deployment. We are not yet finished with Mr Reilly and withhold the money at his disposal until he declares his agreement to the amount. He believes he is able to act in our interests in the course of the next few days by his friends getting the German boiler system accepted. We therefore want to wait a few days until the meeting in question takes place, and we hope then agreement is achieved. We thank you in the name of all involved for transmitting the amounts in question.

Mendrochowitz was clearly unwilling to give in to Reilly and his demands and was waiting to see if his behind-the-scenes work actually got the results in terms of the boiler order. Unfortunately, the file contains no more correspondence between Reilly and the firm of Mendrochowitz & Lubiensky on this or any other matter. This absence may, in itself, tell a story, namely that having already had a taste of Reilly's business methods, the firm had no further associations with him from that time on. This episode also contrasts sharply with Robin Bruce Lockhart's argument that Mendrochowitz offered Reilly a fifty-fifty partnership in the firm, and that Reilly was effectively running the firm in all but name by 1911.[17] Lockhart further states that Reilly ousted Lubiensky as Mendrochowitz' partner and replaced him with a banker named 'Chubersky',[18] yet not a single reference to a Chubersky or Shubersky is to be found anywhere in the company's records or indeed those of Blohm & Voss. On the contrary, they show Lubiensky playing a key role for many years to come.

Mendrochowitz' chagrin is understandable because, if Reilly's demands were met, his earnings from the transaction would be comparable with Mendrochowitz' own. What, then, was Reilly actually doing for Blohm & Voss to warrant such rewards? Rapid industrialisation coupled with a massive naval rearmament programme created a heaven-sent opportunity, not only for Russian firms but also for those in Britain, France and Germany. Competition for contracts was little short of cut-throat and almost any means, fair or foul, were sanctioned to gain an advantage over a competitor.

Kurt Orbanowsky, a Blohm & Voss engineer who spent considerable time in St Petersburg negotiating with Russian officials about shipbuilding contracts, wrote several hundred pages of reports back to the company in Hamburg, which provide a most revealing insight into the role Reilly played.[19] It would seem that Reilly's main function was to oil the wheels of business, working primarily behind the scenes, something at which he had always excelled. As a master of intrigue and corruption in its many forms, Reilly was clearly someone whose services would be invaluable in the cut-throat market place that existed in pre-war St Petersburg.

Orbanowsky's reports are peppered with references to Reilly, who clearly has a pipeline into the Ministry of Marine. On 28 April 1909,[20] for example, Orbanowsky reported that 'Reilly thinks he will know the day after tomorrow whether the Programme discussions will be postponed'. In another report a year later, it is again clear that Blohm & Voss were receiving inside information from Reilly via Orbanowsky:

> …the gentlemen have not yet decided which type of ship they should choose. I will have the opportunity to talk about this with Reilly… it would be desirable if they chose to order a smaller number of ships of higher quality because we have the greatest experience in the building and profitability of this type of ship.[21]

The modus operandi for one such as Reilly would appear to be something along the lines of identifying potential opposition and spreading misinformation about them and their product. Through a web of political, court and ministerial contacts, listening posts could be established that would pick up news of new contracts, specifications, deadlines, budgets and costings. Of course, this network would need to be supplied with suitable rewards, be they monetary gifts or other favours and services. Such 'representational' work would also involve paying journalists and editors to write favourable articles about Blohm & Voss and negative ones about competitors. Reilly had particularly cosy relationships with the *Novoe Vremia* (New Times) and *Vechernee Vremia*.[22] Perusal of these, and indeed other, newspapers during this period will bear testimony to the success of such tactics. Under Reilly would be a lower tier of 'rear-rank' or 'background' men, who would be employed by him on a retainer basis to do the low-level footwork.

In addition to clarifying Reilly's relationship with Mendrochowitz and Lubiensky and his role in representing Blohm & Voss, the correspondence files also indicate that while Reilly was based in St Petersburg, his business took him all over Europe, where he stayed in style at the best hotels in cities like Odessa, Kiev, Paris, Berlin, Vienna and London.[23] His visits to Paris appear quite frequent and were no doubt motivated by two new obsessions in his life – aviation and Eve Lavallière, the wife of the director of the Parisian Théâtre des Variétés.[24] The Wright brothers may have been the first into the air in 1903, but it was not until 1909, when French engineers invented the rotary engine,[25] that the aviation age dawned. Blériot's cross-channel flight in the same year kindled the imagination of thousands and before too long an aviation boom was underway. The Farman brothers, Henri and Maurice, quickly established the Farman Aviation works near Paris and set about displaying their aeroplanes at air shows throughout Europe. Despite the pioneering steps taken by the French, they were still, at this stage, very much reliant on German magnetos, which had to be imported.

Robin Bruce Lockhart relates a tale about Reilly's supposed involvement in obtaining a newly developed German magneto at the Frankfurt International Air Show.[26] According to his account, a German plane lost control on the fifth day of the air show and nosed-dived to the ground, killing the pilot. The plane was alleged to have a new type of magneto that was far ahead of other designs. An SIS agent by the name of Jones, posing as one of the exhibiting pilots, enlisted Reilly's help in diverting attention while he removed the magneto from the wreck of the plane, substituting it for another. According to Lockhart:

Later, Jones made rapid but detailed drawings of the German magneto and, when the engine had been removed to its rightful place in the hangar of the German pilot, Jones and Reilly managed to switch the magnetos once again, restoring the original.[27]

As with so many of these *Ace of Spies* tales of derring do, the facts tell a very different story. SIS at this point was barely ten months old and could count its agents on the fingers of one hand. None of its agents fit Lockhart's description of 'an engineer commander in the Royal Navy who had been working for 'C' for some time'. The official exhibition catalogues and guides of the air show equally fail to mention anyone by the name of Jones. The Frankfurt Institute for Urban History contains well over 1,000 pages of material on the Air Show, including newspaper accounts and some 300 original photographs. From these records it is clear that there were no accidents at all during the show involving any aircraft, be they of German or any other nationality.[28] This is not to say that Reilly was not at the Air Show or that he had no interest in German magnetos. On the contrary, as a bona fide agent of Bosch, the leading manufacturers of German magnetos, he was enthusiastically promoting their virtues to Farmans and enjoying a good commission into the bargain.

Apart from his growing interest in aviation, patent medicine was a racket never too far from his heart. In 1908 and 1909 he made regular visits to London in order to re-establish the Ozone Preparations Company he had wound down on his departure from England ten years previously. It was during a visit in the autumn of 1908 that he finally took steps to legally change his name from Rosenblum to Reilly. Sandford & Company, the solicitors who made the application on his behalf, had been associated with Reilly since 1896. Although the wording of his petition,[29] submitted to the High Court on 23 October 1908, is dressed in the appropriate legal verbiage it is none the less significant:

For all to whom these presents may come, I Sidney George Reilly at present residing at the Hotel Cecil in the County of London – Gentlemen send Greeting. By Deed Poll under my hand and seal and under my then name of Sigmund George Rosenblum dated in or about the month of June 1899 I absolutely renounce and abandon the use of my then birth or initial name of Rosenblum and in lieu there of assumed and adopted the initial name of Sidney and the surname of Reilly and have ever since that date assumed, adopted and been known by the name of Sidney George Reilly.

And whereas the said Deed Poll was never enrolled and has since been lost or destroyed. And whereas I am desirous of confirming the said Deed Poll and of perpetuating and evidencing my change of names by executing these presents and causing them to be enrolled in His Majesty's Supreme Court.

Now I the said Sidney George Reilly do therefore abandon the use of my said birth or initial name of Sigmund and my surname Rosenblum and in lieu thereof assume and adopt the initial name of Sidney and the surname of Reilly. And for the purpose of evidencing such change of names I hereby declare that I shall at all times hereafter in all records deeds documents and other writings and in all actions and proceedings as well as in all dealings and transactions matters and things whatsoever and upon all occasions use and subscribe the said names of Sidney George Reilly as my names in lieu of the said names of Sigmund George Rosenblum. And I therefore expressly authorise and require all persons whatsoever at all times to designate describe and address me by such adopted names of Sidney George Reilly. In witness whereof I have here unto subscribed my adopted and substituted names of Sidney George Reilly this twenty-third day of October one thousand nine hundred and eight.

It confirms the fact that a much earlier move to change his name by Deed Poll had, 'never been enrolled and has since been lost or destroyed'. This is almost certainly a reference to the Deed Poll application that was being drawn up on behalf of Sigmund and Margaret in the summer of 1899, which was more than likely

480

of Sigmund and my surname of Rosenblum and in lieu thereof assume and adopt the initial name of Sidney and the surname of Reilly And for the purpose of evidencing such change of names I hereby declare that I shall at all times hereafter in all records deeds documents and other writings and in all actions suits and proceedings as well as in all dealings and transactions matters and things whatsoever and upon all occasions use and subscribe the said names of Sidney George Reilly as my names in lieu of the said names of Sigmund George Rosenblum. And I therefore expressly authorise and require all persons whomsoever at all times to designate and describe and address me by such adopted names of Sidney George Reilly.

The Deed Poll application to the High Court in October 1908 finally made Rosenblum's adoption of the name Reilly legal.

Statute made for that purpose —

Reilly to — Deed Poll of — 1461

To all to whom these Presents may come I Sidney George Reilly ... residing at the ... Stand in the County of ... Gentleman Send Greeting.

Whereas by a Deed Poll under my hand and under my ... name of Sigmund George Rosenblum dated ... or about the month of June One thousand eight hundred and ninety nine I absolutely renounced and abandoned the use of my then Birth or ... name of Sigmund ... ... of Rosenblum and in lieu thereof assumed and adopted the initial name of Sidney and the surname of Reilly and have ever since those acts assumed and adopted and been known by the names of Sidney George Reilly.

And whereas the said Deed Poll was now mislaid and has since been lost or destroyed. —

abandoned in the wake of their swift departure from England. It is most likely that he now resolved to make the change of name official in light of his plans to resume business in England. Robin Bruce Lockhart also refers to his return to the patent medicine business in *Ace of Spies*.[30] According to his version, Reilly entered into a partnership with a young American chemist by the name of Long and launched the company Rosenblum & Long from 3 Cursitor Street. Although he gives no precise dates for this venture, the implication is that the company was in existence for a four-year period somewhere between 1905 and 1911. Lockhart relates that despite a great deal of hard work on Reilly's part, the company failed to prosper, due in part to Reilly being 'something of an innocent in business'. The business finally collapsed when Long absconded with £600 and Reilly was forced to wind the company up with the assistance of a solicitor by the name of 'Mr Abrahams'. The fact that no trace of Rosenblum & Long has ever been found is due to the fact that the business adopted the name he had first used in 1897, the Ozone Preparations Company.

A search of City of London records confirms that the Ozone Preparations Company traded for some three years between 1908 and 1910, occupying not 3 Cursitor Street, but the first floor of 97 Fleet Street on a sub-lease from the owner, S.R. Cartwright.[31] Reilly certainly had a partner in the venture, William Calder.[32] It is most unlikely, however, that he absconded with company funds, as he was involved in other Reilly business ventures in the 1920s. The business was indeed wound up in 1911 by Michael Abrahams Sons & Co., other associates of long standing.

The Fleet Street address was within walking distance of the Hotel Cecil in the Strand, where Reilly occupied a suite whenever he was in London. In Edwardian times the Cecil was England's largest and most luxurious hotel to which the rich flocked and where foreign heads of state were received. The Savoy next door was very much the poor relation by comparison. Opened in 1896, the Cecil had 1,000 rooms and boasted interiors of multi-coloured marble, and corridors with hand-wrought tapestries.[33] The adjacent Cecil Chambers housed a number of businesses, which at the time included the British Tobacco Company at No. 86 and a number of its European and Empire subsidiaries. Two decades later Stephen Alley, George Hill, Ernest Boyce and William Field Robinson (all of whom we shall meet later in our story) were to work for the company. In 1908, however, one Basil Fothergill worked at the company's Cecil Chambers office and was a known acquaintance of Reilly. Fothergill's father, Charles, was a retired British Army major and may well have been known to Reilly through his son.[34] To what extent, if any, Fothergill senior served as an inspiration for the Maj. Fothergill in Reilly's Amazon story is very much open to debate.

It was also at the Cecil that one Louisa Lewis disappeared without trace, on the evening of 25 October 1908. Louisa had worked at the hotel for four years, having moved to London from Sussex. She was last seen early that evening in her coat and hat speaking to a gentleman at the foot of the hotel's main staircase.[35] It was assumed that they left the hotel together. The gentleman was described as being between thirty and forty years of age, medium height with dark hair. Whilst this description could easily apply to a good many men who were in London on 25 October 1908, one particular thirty-five-year-old, who was 5ft 10ins with dark hair, might have had good cause to remember Miss Lewis. In fact, more to the point, she might well have had good cause to remember him – ten years previously Louisa Lewis lived and worked at the hotel managed by her father, Alfred – the London & Paris at Newhaven. On the morning of 13 March 1898 she had encountered Dr T.W. Andrew, who had examined the dead body of the Reverend Hugh Thomas, and declared his death to be by natural causes. Such a death was not an everyday occurrence at the London & Paris, and it would no doubt have remained etched forever in her mind. Is it too much to speculate that ten years later, by pure chance, she happened to meet Dr Andrew again at the Hotel Cecil? Reilly's face was not one that could be forgotten in a hurry. Had such a crossing of paths occurred, what might Reilly's reaction have been? Although Hugh Thomas's death was never suspected of being anything other than natural if untimely, could he afford to take the chance of allowing someone who could match his face with the identity of Dr Andrew seeing him again?

We know from his Deed Poll petition that Reilly was residing at the Hotel Cecil on 23 October 1908, two days before Louisa's disappearance. Such evidence is purely circumstantial, but compelling all the same. Equally of interest is a story related by Donald McCormick[36] in his book, *Murder by Perfection*, which concerns the activities of Arthur Maundy Gregory, the honours tout,[37] and his possible involvement in the death of Edith Rosse. McCormick relates how Gregory established his own private detective agency and was apparently observing the comings and goings in the West End's major hotels. On one such observation, he was initially suspicious of a 'free-spending foreigner who was masquerading as an Englishman'.[38] This suspicious character turned out to be none other than the 'flamboyant womaniser' Reilly.

McCormick, who had no knowledge of the fact that the Hotel Cecil was Reilly's home from home, mentions that Gregory was exploring the possibility of leasing a small theatre in John Street, off the Strand. Although there is no street off the Strand by the name of John Street today, John Adam Street is the nearest fit, running parallel with the Strand from Villiers Street, next to Charing Cross Station, to Adam Street. According to London County Council records,[39] in 1940, streets by the names of John Street and Duke Street were administratively joined, and properties renumbered, to create John Adam Street.

Contemporary records also indicate there was indeed a small theatre in John Adam Street during this period,[40] which turns out to have been briefly let to one A.J.P Maundy Gregory. Anyone walking down John Adam Street today cannot help but be aware of the imposing former Shell Mex House, which overshadows the street. Shell Mex House was built in 1930 following the controversial demolition of one of the Strand's great landmarks – The Hotel Cecil. This places Maundy Gregory in the near vicinity of Reilly at this time. Maundy Gregory's nocturnal detective activities are corroborated by Superintendent Arthur Askew of Scotland Yard, who investigated the mysterious death of Mrs Rosse and the 'honours for sale' charge against Maundy Gregory.[41] Whether there was any connection at all between Reilly and Louisa Lewis's disappearance, and whether Reilly met Maundy Gregory at this stage can only remain speculation. However, the fact that all three were in the same place at virtually the same time can no longer be in any doubt.

If, on his return to St Petersburg in late October or early November 1908, Reilly felt any sense of relief, this was to be short lived, for the reappearance of another face from the past was about to set in motion a chain of events that would end in tragedy.

FIVE

THE COLONEL'S DAUGHTER

Six years had elapsed since Margaret Reilly left Port Arthur at the behest of her husband. Although her departure was nominally on grounds of impending war, to Reilly she had already served her purpose and he had effectively discarded her. She had seen little of him in the intervening years, and when she did see him or receive letters from him, he was always insistent that he was on his 'beam ends', with little or no money to spare her. While Reilly's finances before the First World War certainly had their ups and downs, we can take it as read that he wished to have as little to do with her as possible. He married her for her money and unashamedly used her to adopt a new identity to conceal his Russo-Jewish origins.

Unsurprisingly, his account of their parting put a somewhat different gloss on matters. According to Reilly, she had turned to drink and become a liability to him during their time in Port Arthur. Robin Bruce Lockhart has also stated that on Reilly's return from the Far East, he found that she had left him and disappeared.[1] This view of Margaret has been unquestioningly accepted by almost all those who have ever written about Reilly over the years. Of course, we have only his word for this assumption, which is hardly the best of recommendations.

Margaret's reappearance in St Petersburg in 1909 was almost certainly triggered by the fact that what little money she had left was now running low. Unwelcome in the best of circumstances, Margaret would no doubt have received an even frostier reception from Reilly being in such a penurious state. Knowing Reilly as we do, it might well be asked why he had not already sought to dispose of her permanently. After all, he is reputed to have threatened to kill her on at least one occasion, although there is no evidence for this assertion. Having shown no such mercy to others who had crossed his path in the past, this is a question that begs an answer, albeit a speculative one. Margaret, we know, was not naïve in the ways of the world. Even before she met Reilly she had managed to advance her interests well enough. She was certainly not beyond gilding the truth, and was, without doubt, a quick-witted and resourceful woman. It is likely that if Reilly had actually wanted to kill her he could have done so quite easily. On the basis that he made no such efforts, we can only assume that Margaret had some kind of preventive hold over him. Being a party to the guilt and responsibility for the death of Hugh Thomas, she must also have been aware of other matters that Reilly would no doubt wish to keep secret. If she effectively held an insurance policy against any untoward accidents that might befall her, it might well have been in the form of a written statement or testimony against Reilly that was held in safe keeping as security. Should she meet a sudden or unnatural end, whoever had custody of the document would be under instruction to make it public or, more likely, direct it to the appropriate authorities.

Margaret's own brief account[2] of Reilly's life is completely silent on personal and marital matters generally. In fact, one could be forgiven for gaining the impression that they were anything but a devoted, albeit distant, couple. Some twenty years later, while working in Brussels as a governess in the household of Robert Messenger and his wife, she confided to Mrs Messenger that she had loved Reilly 'with complete abandon, but that his many betrayals and affairs with other women had turned her love into hatred'.[3] Although particularly hurt by his affair with Eve Lavallière, the wife of the director of the Parisian Théâtre de Variétés, she was never disparaging in any way about her husband, at least not in the hearing of Mrs Messenger.[4] It would not appear, however, that it was this particular betrayal that caused Margaret the greatest distress, but a much greater sin in her eyes – that of bigamy.

This traumatic discovery while in St Petersburg apparently led Margaret to make an attempt on her own life. According to Mrs Messenger, Margaret had taken a pistol that Reilly kept in his desk drawer and shot herself in the eye. By some miracle she survived, but spent six weeks in a coma. As a result of losing her right eyeball she was given a glass eye.[5] How Margaret managed to shoot herself in the eye without causing serious brain damage, let alone killing herself, is at first hard to fathom. It has been known, however, for those attempting suicide in this way to place the gun against the temple, behind the eye socket, rather than further back to the ear. A shot in the region of the ear would impact into the brain, whereas a shot to the forward region of the temple would enter the cavity behind the eye socket and depending upon the angle, exit through the eye or nose. Even this lucky escape would have meant tissue, skin and bone damage to the temple, eye and nose. British diplomat Darrell Wilson, who met Margaret in May 1931, when she was seeking to renew her passport, gives confirmation of this.[6] According to Wilson, 'Mrs Reilly is of a nervous disposition and bears the trace of an attempt to commit suicide by shooting herself through the right temple, when she found her husband had committed bigamy'.[7]

When, after six weeks, she came out of the coma, Reilly was nowhere to be found. The issue of bigamy does, of course, raise the question of with whom it was committed, for it was to be another two years before he met Nadezhda Zalessky and a further four years before they married. This account therefore gives further credence to the possibility that Reilly had indeed married a hitherto unknown bride at some point after the Russo-Japanese war, as discussed at the end of Chapter Three.

No word of Margaret's attempted suicide appears in *Ace of Spies*, which contends that Reilly bribed her to leave St Petersburg.[8]

Through Boris Suvorin, part of the Suvorin family, proprietors of the *Novoe Vremia* newspaper, Reilly then supposedly planted a story in *Novoe Vremia* that a Red Cross ambulance had swerved off a mountain road in Bulgaria and fallen into a ravine killing several nurses, 'including a Mrs Reilly who until recently was a resident in St Petersburg'.[9] One can only assume that Lockhart himself was somewhat unsure about this tale, as in his follow-up book on Reilly[10] he refers to him 'placing a false news item in the Russian press about a railway accident in which several people had been killed, including Mrs Reilly'.[11] A comprehensive search of *Novoe Vremia* during this period failed to unearth any item about the death of a Mrs Reilly, in either an ambulance or a train accident.

Although the ambulance story is somewhat out of place, in that no situation requiring the presence of Red Cross volunteers existed in Bulgaria in 1909, *Novoe Vremia* coverage of the first and second Balkan wars, fought between October 1912 and August 1913, yielded a surprise result. On 8 November 1912 *Novoe Vremia*[12] reported that an English medical team of thirty-eight persons had arrived in Sophia, Bulgaria. According to the Red Cross, the female volunteers included a Mrs M. Reilly.[13]

As a ten-year-old, Leon Messenger was enthralled by the fact that his governess, whom he knew as Daisy, was the wife of the legendary spy Sidney Reilly. His recollections provide a rare window into Margaret's personality and outlook on the world, which was no doubt shaped by her earlier life. Although Irish by birth, it is clear that Margaret not only regarded herself as English, but as belonging to the upper class. Messenger remembers her as 'well educated and well read... in every respect a cultured Englishwoman who spoke in upper-class accents and was to everybody who met her... the perfect embodiment of a cultured lady'.[14] His reminis-cences on her outlook are equally fascinating: on their long walks in the woods and parks, 'she would talk about the glories of England... the greatness of the British Empire and the white man's burden'.[15]

Although Margaret and Sidney were clearly leading separate lives, and always would, there was never any possibility in her mind that she would grant him a divorce. Whether this was dictated by her Catholic faith or by a hardheaded recognition that while she was legally Mrs Reilly she would always have a financial call on him, is open to question. By 1910 she was thirty-six years old, down on her luck and physically disfigured. In these circumstances it is hardly surprising that she would not voluntarily sever her hold over him. Whether Margaret was ever aware of Nadezhda Zalessky is unknown. Certainly Nadezhda had no knowledge of her. Margaret was long gone from St Petersburg by the time Reilly met Nadezhda, to whom he presented himself as a bachelor.

Born Nadezhda Massino in Poltava, Ukraine, on 26 March 1885,[16] the daughter of Lt-Col. Petr Massino and his wife Varvara Kondratyevna Brodskaya, she was the second of four children.[17] Both parents were Jewish by origin, but had converted to Orthodox Christianity. Like Reilly, Nadezhda later drew a veil over her family origins by claiming they were Swiss by descent. In 1907 she married Petr Ivanovich Zalessky, a naval lieutenant who had taken part in the defence of Port Arthur during the siege of 1904.[18] It was in Port Arthur that Zalessky first met Admiral Grigorovich, to whom he was appointed aide-de-camp when the admiral became Minister for Marine. This was a particularly important time for the Ministry of Marine, which was responsible for rebuilding the Russian fleet which had suffered such a catastrophic defeat at the hands of Japan. Their home at 2 Admiralty Quay, St Petersburg,[19] was often the venue for parties and receptions, which were attended by high-ranking military and naval officials as well as senior politicians and members of the Russian Court.

In 1912 the Duma approved funds for the next phase of the rebuilding of the Russian naval fleet. Shipyards from all over Russia would shortly be competing for these orders that had the potential to keep their yards in work and their coffers full for many years to come. It was at one such reception that Reilly met Nadezhda. As a renowned beauty, she would have caught his eye immediately. At 5ft 3ins, of slight build, with dark hair and complexion, she had a captivating personality and spoke fluent

French and English.[20] Compared with his other mistresses at this time, such as Myrtil Paul, Ganna Walska and Paulette Pax, Nadezhda's attractions were clearly unique. He was drawn not only by her outstanding beauty, but perhaps more so by the connections and influence that might be had through her. Not only was her husband the right-hand man to Admiral Grigorovich, who would decide the tendering arrangements for navy contracts, but ultimately he would also carry great weight in deciding to whom the contracts would be awarded. By the time they met, her father had been promoted to colonel, and her younger brother, Georgi, had graduated from the Elisavetgradsky Cavalry School, and enlisted in the 3rd Hussar Regiment.[21] Reilly was introduced to her family, who also lived in St Petersburg, and the evidence suggests that the family themselves provided him with a great deal of inspiration in terms of the cover identities he would use in the future.

It is worth thinking back, at this point, to the story Reilly often related to George Hill and others, concerning his origins. We have already noted Lockhart's account of how his name at birth was apparently Georgi, the son of 'a colonel in the Russian army with connections at the Court of the Tsar'. We are also told that Georgi had a passion for swordsmanship and 'took up pistol shooting to reveal marksmanship quite remarkable in one so young'. It is quite evident, however, that this is a description not of the young Reilly, but of Nadezhda's brother, Georgi Petrovich Massino, whose military service file reveals him to be the mirror image of Reilly's 'Georgi' character. Reilly's fascination with the Massino family went somewhat further a decade later, when he adopted the name Konstantin Markovich Massino when he was working undercover in Russia after the Revolution. He also claimed on a different occasion that his mother's maiden name was Massino.[22]

While Reilly's Georgi character might be a perfect fit for Nadezhda's brother, how close a match is her father for Reilly's colonel, who had 'connections at the Court of the Tsar'? If Col. Massino did have such connections, this would have been yet a further attraction for Reilly in terms of forming a relationship with Nadezhda.

According to Col. Massino's military service file,[23] he had an exemplary career from the time he joined the army as a private on 28 May 1853. Promotions followed swiftly to under-officer (1855), ensign (1859), lieutenant (1862), captain (1868), major (1872), lieutenant-colonel (1877) and finally to colonel (1901). However, his career came to sudden halt when, on 2 May 1905, he was relieved of his command in the Siberian Military District and placed under arrest. The military authorities in St Petersburg confirmed his dismissal on 17 June 1905. After a long investigation, he was charged with corruption, profiteering and abuse of power. Finally, on 24 August 1906, he appeared before the Siberian Military District Court in Irkutsk.[24] The court was told that Massino had used a military hospital train to transport duty free commercial goods, including food and alcohol, from Yekaterinoslav to Irkutsk. On arrival in Irkutsk, the goods were unloaded by a merchant by the name of Mrozovsky, who then sold the goods on at a significant profit. The verdict of the court was that while insufficient evidence had been presented by the prosecution to demonstrate that Massino had received money from Mrozovsky, he was clearly guilty of an abuse of power. He was therefore sentenced to serve sixteen months imprisonment in a civilian jail, and given a dishonourable discharge from the army. As a consequence of his discharge he also lost his rank, medals and, more importantly, his pension.

He filed an appeal against the verdict, and an appeal hearing was scheduled to be heard in St Petersburg on 12 October 1906. Each and every point on which he appealed was rejected and the original verdict and sentence were upheld. This, under normal circumstances, would have been the end of the matter. However, three months later on 14 January 1907, Tsar Nicholas II himself intervened in the case and issued a decree commuting Massino's sentence to discharge and loss of rank only. Such an intervention was most unusual to say the very least. What happened eight months later was even more so. On 19 August 1907 the Tsar issued a further decree, reinstating Massino's former rank, along with his pension, medals and additional privileges. Who or what could possibly have accounted for this near miraculous turn of events? Who could have interceded on Massino's behalf, at the highest level, to secure his release? Whilst high-level decisions could, at a price, be influenced, securing the release of prisoners like Massino was not any everyday occurrence.

However, Massino's rehabilitation was engineered, it must have been done at Court level. Those with access to the Tsar's immediate circle would have included ministers, high-ranking military officials and Rasputin. The Tsar's former ministers and their fabled misdemeanours were a particular target for the Provisional Government which came to power after the Tsar's abdication in March 1917. One of its first acts was to set up, in March of that year, 'The Extraordinary Commission of Enquiry for the Investigation of Illegal Acts by Ministers and Other Responsible Persons'. One of the principal areas for investigation was Rasputin and the influence he had on ministers and the Royal family. The enquiry also had access to the Ochrana reports which catalogued the comings and goings at Rasputin's apartment and a general digest of those he met. Although the commission's investigations were still in progress at the time of the Bolshevik takeover in October, the new government disbanded the commission and its conclusions were never published.[25] However, the enquiry's transcripts survived and provide a rare insight into the activities of those in high places. It would seem that statements from some twenty-two people associated with Rasputin were taken, which provides a vivid picture of the influence he wielded at the Royal Court.

Alexei Filippov, a banker and publisher, provided interesting testimony as to how some of those within Rasputin's close circle exploited the influence he had with the Tsar and Tsarina by accepting 'gifts' from those whose interests were forwarded by Rasputin. Whether this was with or without Rasputin's knowledge is not clear. In 1906 and 1907, Rasputin's connections with the Court were not so well known as they became in later years, but it is interesting to note that the person who first introduced Rasputin to those of influence in St Petersburg was

Bishop Feofan, who was born in Poltava. He himself had very close royal connections, particularly to the Tsarina, and is another possible link between the Massinos and the Royal Court.

Filippov himself had very close associations with Rasputin and became the semi-literate peasant's publisher. Some six years after Col. Massino's re-instatement, there is also evidence that Rasputin's aide Sophia Volynskaya had links with Varvara Massino, who like herself was a converted Jew from Poltava. Filippov told the 1917 enquiry that Rasputin shifted from charitable acts of help to the exploitation of clients with the help of Volynskaya. Her husband, an agronomist, had been tried and imprisoned, but had been pardoned on representations from Rasputin. Rasputin, however, justified these acts as part of his teaching. The Tsarina had written down his words in her notebook, 'Never fear to release prisoners, to restore sinners to a life of righteousness... Prisoners... become through their sufferings in the eyes of God – nobler then we'.[26]

Another Rasputin acolyte, Pyotr Badmaev, may also have had a connection with Reilly, according to Richard Deacon.[27] Badmaev, known as the 'cunning Chinaman', was a doctor in Tibetan medicine, or so he claimed. In reality he was, like Reilly, a cross between a patent medicine salesman and a businessman-cum-broker. A Buryat of Asiatic descent, Badmaev was born in Siberia in 1857. His brother had established a Tibetan pharmacy in St Petersburg, and Pyotr followed him to the capital and soon established himself practising Tibetan medicine. His patients were predominantly in the upper echelons of St Petersburg society and, thanks to Rasputin, his influence permeated to the very top. He established a trading company, Badmaev & Ko, which was involved in land speculation and also sought to market a range of commodities including his Tibetan herbal remedies. These claimed to treat such complaints as pulmonary disease, neurasthenia, venereal disease and impotence. It is significant that while most patent medicine companies in England at this time promoted home-grown remedies or those imported from America, the Ozone Preparations Company was unique in having amongst its stock 'Tibetan Remedies'.[28]

The banker and publisher Alexei Filippov, as well as having associations with Rasputin, also knew Vladimir Krymov, the accountant of the Suvorin family, the proprietors of the *Novoe Vremia* newspaper. Krymov, who had power of attorney from Alexei Suvorin due to Suvorin's ill health, was closely involved in the affairs of the family, from which perspective he provides an interesting insight into Reilly's life during the period 1910–1914. Krymov relates how Reilly visited the newspaper's editorial office nearly every day and was treated by the staff there as 'one of their own'.[29] Reilly's ability to network and keep his ear to the ground was obviously well recognised by editor Mikhail Suvorin and utilised accordingly.

Mikhail's younger brother Boris shared Reilly's interest in aviation. According to Robin Bruce Lockhart they formed a flying club called The Wings Aviation Club,[30] which sponsored the St Petersburg–Moscow Air Race.[31] The reality, however, was somewhat different. Although Reilly was a member of a flying club, the All-Russian Aviation Club,[32] Krylia (Wings) was, in fact, a commercial company set up principally by Boris Suvorin, at Reilly's instigation. In other words, it was Reilly's idea but Suvorin's money was used to launch it. The Krylia Joint-Stock Company opened for business at Apartment 42, 12 Bolshaya Morskaya on 21 April 1910, amid a flurry of interest from the press, aviators and central government.[33] The Ministry for the Interior in particular seems to have taken a close interest in the company, requesting that the Ochrana make routine enquiries into the five directors of the company – Frenchman Ludovic Arno, Mikhail Efimov, Boris Suvorin, Konstantin Veygelin and 'Englishman' Sidney Reilly.[34] All five were given a clean bill of health by the Ochrana, which would seem to indicate that up to this point they had nothing on Reilly and furthermore did not identify or associate him with one Sigmund Rosenblum who was still on their 'wanted list'. Such official interest might also reflect the fact that the Russian government was now taking a particular interest in the development of aviation for military purposes. In

Advertisement in *Vozdukhoplavatel* announcing the opening of the Krylia Aerodrome in September 1910 another Reilly project financed by other people's money.

fact, Tsar Nicholas had, only a few months before, announced the creation of the Imperial Russian Air Service under the command of Grand Duke Alexandr Mikhailovich.

Suvorin invited the famous Russian aviator Nikolai Evgrafovich Popov to open the office, and arranged for the event to be exclusively covered by *Novoe Vremia*. The company was the first to commercially market aircraft in Russia. Reilly's interest in aviation had apparently been kindled by Wilbur Wright's demonstration of the 'Wright Flyer' at the Hunaudières Racecourse at Le Mans in August 1908. The Wrights had, by this time, concluded that there was more to be gained from displaying their machines in public than from continued secrecy. It is clear from the European press at the time that there was certainly widespread scepticism concerning the merits of the Wright aircraft owing to their publicity-shy reputation. This attitude changed dramatically when Wilbur Wright arrived in France three months before the Le Mans demonstration and began touting the merits of the 1905 'Flyer', a machine capable of flying up to twenty-five miles at a time when

Henry Farman was endeavouring to achieve one kilometre in his Voisin.

Reilly was among the large crowd that gathered at Hunaudières on 8 August to watch Wilbur Wright take to the air. All scepticism vanished as he rose to a height of thirty feet and made three circuits of the racecourse before making a perfect landing within fifty metres of where he had taken off. Louis Bleriot, who was also in the crowd, told the *New York Herald* that, 'for us in France and everywhere, a new era in mechanical flight has begun... my view can best be conveyed in the words – it is marvellous!'

The new era reached Germany the following year, when Orville Wright visited Berlin to give a similar flying demonstration. Reilly arranged to meet him afterwards and discovered the Wrights planned to withdraw from active participartion in flying demonstrations in order to concentrate on the commercial exploitation of their machines. When, the following year, they launched the Wright Brothers Company, Reilly shrewdly negotiated an agreement to be their sole representative within the Russian Empire and to market their aircraft there. Before too long Reilly had also signed a similar deal with the Farman Company.

The objective of Krylia was, according to Suvorin, to 'assist the development of aeronautics and aviation in Russia'. This, however, did not extend to organising the St Petersburg–Moscow air race, which was in fact a competition rather than a race, meaning that competitors were judged on performance in certain areas and not just on their times.

It was actually organised by the Imperial Aero-Club of St Petersburg and the Moscow Aeronautical Society. There is no record of Krylia or Reilly in particular providing any of the sponsorship. The event cost 107,500 roubles, which was met by a donation of 100,000 roubles from the Russian government, the remainder being made up of smaller sums donated by the Imperial Aero Club, the Moscow Aeronautical Society, Moscow City Council, the Riga Section of the Imperial Aero Club, the Imperial Russian Automobile Society, and the Russian Hunting Club. The

Nobel Oil Company and the Vacuum Oil Company donated their products to the event.[35] Lockhart is correct in stating that the competition was won by Vasilyev, although it is unlikely that Reilly was there to meet him in Moscow. After landing in Moscow, Vasilyev publicly lambasted the organisers of the event for incompetence. The Imperial Aero Club retaliated by boycotting his victor's banquet, which as a consequence had to be cancelled![36]

Reilly can, however, justifiably claim the credit for founding St Petersburg's first airport.[37] According to Vladimir Krymov, this too was an example of Reilly knowing something no one else knew. He had found out that, under an eighteenth-century right of use going back to the time of Peter the Great, the Commandant of St Petersburg had the right to use a large piece of land on the outskirts of the city, known as Komendantskoe Pole (the Commandant's Field). In practice, however, this right had never been taken up. Reilly also discovered that the long-term tenant of the land was an elderly Englishwoman who was paying a small annual rent and sub-letting plots to allotment keepers. Reilly traced her and arranged to pay her a visit. In Krymov's words, 'Reilly charmed her with his manners and beautiful English and obtained from her the right to let the whole field as an aerodrome'.[38]

To provide capital for the aerodrome venture, Alexei Suvorin was persuaded to become a backer. Work to convert the land to an aerodrome with hangers and workshops was completed in time for Krylia to host the first St Petersburg Flying Week, held between 25 April and 2 May 1910.[39] Aviators from France, Belgium, Switzerland and Holland, as well as Russia, took part and prizes were awarded for height reached and length of time spent in the air. The Russians enthusiastically supported their own man, Popov, who came second and flew the highest.[40] The main purpose of the event was, however, a commercial opportunity for the display and sale of aircraft, from which Krylia did particularly well. In May 1911 a second flying week was held, during which Reilly himself participated as one of the aviators. While the aerodrome was a great success, Krymov was at pains to point out that, as a result of Reilly's aerodrome business dealings, and having power of attorney from Alexei Suvorin, he had to honour several promissory notes issued by Suvorin. This resulted in Suvorin losing over 100,000 roubles, while Reilly avoided liability and collected a salary as a Krylia director.[41]

While fully engaged in exploiting the providence brought about by the onset of the aviation age, Reilly lost no opportunity to cash in on the escalating naval arms race that was now gaining pace among the great powers. Procuring Russian maritime contracts on behalf of Blohm and Voss was not, however, the limit of Reilly's brokering ambitions. Constantinople, the capital city of the sprawling Ottoman Empire on Russia's southern border, was not only well known to Reilly but was a ready market for German armaments. Indeed, a decade later when working undercover in Russian, Reilly would adopt, among other identities, that of Turkish merchant 'Mr Constantine'.

Although regarded by Germany as being in terminal decline, an alliance with the faltering Ottoman Empire was seen as key to Berlin's plan for imperial expansion eastwards. Sultan Abdul Hamid was equally looking for a new and powerful European ally to act as a bulwark against Russia, the Turks' traditional foe, following his falling out with Great Britain over the control of Egypt. In the decade before the outbreak of the First World War, the Turks therefore looked principally to their new-found German ally to help them develop a twentieth-century army and navy. However, competition for orders was fierce and Blohm & Voss were having little success in obtaining major naval contracts. Since May 1904 they had been represented in Constantinople by one Walther Berghaus.[42] From July 1905, when the first announcement of the rebuilding of the Turkish navy was made, until March 1909, not a single deal was successfuly negotiated for Blohm & Voss by Berghaus.

On 7 December 1909 Berghaus wrote to Blohm & Voss questioning the status of a Herr Reilly, who had recently arrived in Constantinople and was representing himself as acting on behalf of Blohm & Voss.[43] Reilly had good contacts in the Ottoman capital where both Ginsburg & Company and the East-Asiatic

Company, for example, were well established and had good connections with Ottoman government officials. What transpired during the next three months is very much open to conjecture, as little of the correspondence between the company and Berghaus has survived. However, we do know that on 9 February 1910 Blohm & Voss wrote to Berghaus, formally dismissing him as their Ottoman representative. It would seem that they had come to the conclusion that he had passed on compromising information to a rival company.[44] The prime source of the allegations against him would appear to be 'Herr R'. With Berghaus now deposed, Reilly set about negotiating with the Ottoman authorities and on 14 February the Turkish navy agreed to send a delegation to Germany to finalise a deal to purchase one battleship and a floating dock from Blohm & Voss.[45] Reilly took the commission for the deal, leaving Berghaus out in the cold. Little further trace of Reilly's activites in Constantinople appear in either German or Ottoman records, suggesting that his endeavours there on behalf of Blohm & Voss were shortlived. This view is further confirmed by the fact that on 6 September 1911, Blohm & Voss reappointed Berghaus as their Ottoman representative.[46]

According to Vladimir Krymov, Reilly's finances before the First World War were 'dire',[47] a situation that was not remedied until the outbreak of war when the arms trade came to his rescue. Throughout his life Reilly seemed to spend money as quickly as he obtained it. One consequence of this was a short spell of having to share a flat during the autumn of 1911. His flatmate was apparently one Eduard Fedorovich Gofman. Not long after the flat-share arrangement began, Gofman was found dead, a bullet in his head and a pistol in his hand.[48] Police enquiries revealed that a large sum of money was missing from his employers the East-Asiatic Company, which Gofman had apparently embezzled. According to the police, a suicide note had been found stating that Gofman had lost the money gambling. Gofman was not a known gambler and the police could find no evidence that he had ever frequented any of the usual gambling haunts in St Petersburg.

Reilly too stated that he had no knowledge of his flatmate being a gambler. The police were never able to solve the riddle and the money was never recovered. If Reilly had a hand in the embezzlement, Gofman's death or the disappearance of the money, he had, once again, managed to avoid the consequences.

If Reilly's finances were, in Vladimir Krymov's words, 'dire', then it was down, as ever, to his expensive tastes and lifestyle. If his income was in any doubt, he would not be travelling throughout Europe and staying at such hotels as the Cecil in London, the Grand Hotel in Paris and the Hotel Bristol in Berlin and Vienna. Neither would he have been a regular at St Petersburg's exclusive Vienna Restaurant in Ulitsa Gogolya and the Café de Paris at 16 Bolshaya Morskaya, next door to the East-Asiatic Company. The Café de Paris[49] was better known by the name of its owner, Kiuba. It was a chic restaurant with French cuisine and high prices and was frequented by the high aristocracy. The artist Milashevsky recalls that 'all the waiters were formerly soldiers of the Guard and so they never take his Highness for his nobleness'. It was the first restaurant to have an electric sign – each letter in the word was made of electric lamps – 'may your name shine forever' was an in-joke among Kiuba's customers at the time.

In addition to the Café de Paris, Reilly also frequented the St Petersburg English Club at 16 Dvortsovaia Naberezhnaia, where the aristocratic élite gambled at cards. Card gambling became particularly widespread during the first decade of the twentieth century, and flourished most of all in the so-called 'new-style clubs' or businessmen's clubs. The English Club was the oldest in St Petersburg, and although founded by the English community in 1770, it was, by the late nineteenth century, a thoroughly Russian institution. Reilly, although an enthusiastic card player, was rarely a successful one. The club was, however, yet another opportunity to associate with the influential élite of St Petersburg.

Another costly expense that Reilly may well have faced was that of medical treatment. As we shall see later in our story, the likelihood was that he suffered throughout his life from a mild form of epilepsy, known as *petit mal*. This milder form has associations with migraine, something we know Reilly regularly experienced. We also know, for example, that between 2 March and 6 March 1911, Reilly stayed at the Weiner Cottage Sanitarium in Vienna,[50] although no details of the treatment he received have survived.

Despite the fact that he represented himself as an Irishman with a Russian mother, Reilly did not openly associate himself with the self-styled 'English colony' in St Petersburg. By the turn of the twentieth century there were some 4,000 British citizens in St Petersburg, most of them living on the Vasilyevsky Ostroff or in the mill districts. Many families had lived in Russia for several generations, and avoided having to become Russian citizens by sending pregnant wives back to England to give birth. It was from among this community that the 'New English Club'[51] was founded in 1905. Unlike the English Club, it was essentially an English membership institution where members drank Scotch whisky and English beer, played football, cricket, golf and billiards and held dinners to mark British national holidays. Among its 400 members was the club president, Ernest Durrent, and his nephew Alfred Hill, who joined British intelligence in the war.[52] Alfred's cousin, George Hill, would also become an intelligence officer and an associate of Reilly's in the aftermath of the October Revolution of 1917. Another member of the club, Cecil Mackie, who was a secretary at the British Embassy in St Petersburg, later recalled that, 'at one time we had some doubt as to his right to British nationality, but the matter was never thrashed out'.[53]

It would take a world war to provide Reilly with the opportunity of making more money than he could actually spend. In the meantime, the ubiquitous wheeler-dealer soldiered on with mixed results in the scramble for naval contracts. A letter written by Reilly on 25 April 1912 to Kurt Orbanowsky gives some very pertinent clues to his relationship with the various players involved in the naval warship programme. The purpose of the letter was, ostensibly, to explain why Blohm & Voss had not been successful with a particular tender:

Dear Mr Orbanowsky,

Yesterday evening I looked into the dock dossier and gather from this that the rejection of our project and the acceptance of the Russian or English offer resulted mainly from technical reasons.

I am at a loss to judge to what extent the General Director K, on the basis of purely technical decisions, can contend the *fait accompli*. The only contentious point I could discover was that the weight was incorrectly given, for in the N^{54} project the weight is 15310 and not 15910 – thus, the difference between the two projects is not nearly so great. There is no doubt that a second swindle occurred with the price, and that RSO have been informed about the price of the N project, but this cannot be proved. The final price of RSO project is 4,800,000 roubles (earlier it was 4,960,000). The final price from N is 4,930,500 roubles (compared to 5,175,000 roubles earlier). The final N price is 4,709,000 has for some reason gone totally without mention.

The Count[55] informed me yesterday that the General Director K takes great comfort in the hope (I believe as a result of his discussions yesterday with Georg) that the decisions can be changed to his favour. My most recent information is that it is more or less a waste of energy.

The engineer from the technical committee who will supervise construction of the dock steamed to England yesterday at the expense of RSO. I heard yesterday from my friend Grigorovich, who is in the south with Georg, that progress made by RSO in their shipyard construction is very admirable. Georg is convinced that everything RSO has ordered will be ready by the date and has sent an enthusiastic telegram to SM. In contrast, Georg found that the situation at N is extremely miserable. Furthermore, I hear that P is as good as delivered and that B himself will leave soon as a precaution. I also hear that Professor B's days in the inter-departmental commission are numbered because there is opposition to his belonging to the Nicolai direction at the same time.

The general opinion among them is that the gr.Kr[56] project will be built after the Admiralty plans. I was strongly advised that you and Bisch should contact Georg often to keep him continuously informed about Putt and their suggestions. Georg is very interested in this and it is very important that his interest is maintained and that in the future

SIDNEY G. REILLY

Telepn. 430-98.
Telegramm
„SIDNEY—ST. PETERSBURG"
(Code A.B.C. V. Ed.)

22, Novo-Isaakiewskia
St. Petersburg, 23/5 April 1912

Sehr geehrter Herr Orbanowsky ,

      Gestern Abend habe ich in das Dockdossier Einsicht
genommen und ersehe daraus, dass die Ablehnung unseres Projects &
die Ahnahme des russischen . beziehungsweise englischen) hauptsäch
lich aus rein technischen Gruenden erfolgt ist .

    Im Beschluss der Technischen Commission, die die Projecte be -
urteilte , werden unter anderen – folgende Gruende angefuehrt .

    Soweit es die verwickelte technische Sprache erlaubt , will ic
Ihnen hier die Gruende angeben :

   ✳ Vom Gesichtspunkte der allgemeinen Construction ist das Dock
der R.S.O. dem Nikolajewschen vorzuziehen; beim Ersteren sind die
Waende gans und nicht zerschnitten. wie beim Zweiten, was die Längs
festigkeit des Dockes garantirt; weiterhin sind die Schotten in der
Pontons der R.S.O. zweckmaessiger verteilt und lassen die Eintei –
lung in eine groessere Zahl von Abschnitten zu ; die Groesse der
mentacentrischen Hoehe im kritischen Moment der Hebung des Schiffes
ist groesser, als beim N. Project; die Wohn-& Dienstraeume befinden
sich im Aufbau auf dem Oberdeck und nicht unter dem Oberdeck, wie
beim N. Project .

    Vom mechanischen Standpunkte ist folgendes bemerkt :
  I). Anwendung von Diesel ist unpraktisch, da, obgleich diese

On 25 April 1912 Reilly hypocritically complained to Obanowsky of insider dealing.

he is informed about us directly by you or Bisch and not from P or B.
I am furthermore told (but I must have your word that this remains
between you and I) that Jach is very unwelcome at Georg's and that in
our own interests we should not send him there. You know how dear
this common friend is to me but I consider it my duty to tell you this.
It is doubtful whether it is planned to build the gr.Kr in Germany, and
indeed there are national and political reasons for this. In regard to the
kl.Kr,[57] it is probable that no one except B and V would be considered.

It can be assumed that the programme will be settled in the Duma
at the start of May; there is no doubt that money will be received.
Serious work should get going immediately after Easter and the contracts
will be allocated by the end of July. During the holidays I will have various
opportunities to see my friends and will work with them on the aspects
that interest you. For now and wishing you the most pleasant of holidays,
Your very loyal
Sidney G. Reilly[58]

In reality, the letter is a subtle example of Reilly's 'divide and rule' approach to life. He not only casts aspersions on the judgement of Count Lubiensky and his ability to get a more favourable verdict on the proposal, he also tries, in a very underhanded way, to drive a wedge between Orbanowsky and his 'dear friend', Lubiensky's senior colleague Jachimowitz. Ironically, Reilly is the first to complain in this letter about the 'insider-information' swindles being perpetrated on Blohm & Voss, but his own hands were far from clean when it came to obtaining the particulars of rival tenders. In September of that year, Sir Charles Ottley, of the British shipbuilders Armstrongs, visited St Petersburg with a view to tendering for contracts.[59] Although Armstrongs had initially shown some reluctance to participate, they seem to have been persuaded to do so by Alexei Rastedt, who was ultimately appointed their Russian representative. Alexei Rastedt was no newcomer to the shipping business, and had, several years previously, been one of Reilly's 'background men'. When eventually Armstrongs did decide to enter a last-minute tender, this caused much friction between themselves and their Tyne-side neighbours, Vickers, which was gleefully picked up by the St Petersburg press. When the contracts were eventually awarded, there was a very strong suspicion that Armstrong's bid had been reported to one of their rivals.

Vickers' ruthless and unscrupulous representative Basil Zaharoff was the biggest player in the arms trade at this time, and it is hardly surprising that his name has been subsequently linked with the equally unsavoury Reilly. Zaharoff was featured as a prominent character in Troy Kennedy-Martin's television adaptation of *Ace of Spies*,[60] despite the wholesale lack of evidence linking the two. Richard Deacon, who also proffered the theory that Reilly was an Ochrana agent, believed that 'one of the tasks which the Russian Secret Service set for Sidney Reilly was to build up a dossier on the notorious international arms salesman, Basil Zaharoff'.[61] Ochrana records at the Hoover Institute in California and in the State Archive of the Russian Federation in

Moscow contain no corroboration for this belief, nor for any kind of association between Reilly and Zaharoff.

Not unsurprisingly, Reilly was viewed with suspicion by many of those he came into contact with in St Petersburg. Some thought he was an English spy, others said he was spying for the Germans. In November 1911 the Suvorins had been concerned enough to make enquiries about Reilly and his activities. Boris Suvorin initially asked his associate Ivan Manasevich-Manuilov, a *Novoe Vremia* journalist, to check with Stephan Beletsky, the head of the St Petersburg Police Department. Beletsky referred the enquiry to Gen. Nicolai Mankewitz, head of counter-intelligence. As a result Reilly was briefly kept under close surveillance and had his mail intercepted. As with the previous year's check initiated by the Interior Ministry, nothing that would give any cause for concern was found and Mankewitz called off the surveillance and closed the file.[62]

Among the regular correspondents Reilly kept in touch with was his cousin Felitsia, now living in Warsaw. Their close relationship is evident from a verse from the 29th stanza of the Rubaiyat of Omar Khayyam he sent her:

> Into this universe, and why not knowing,
> Nor whence, like water, willy-nilly flowing,
> And out of it, as wind along the waste,
> I know not whither, willy-nilly blowing

Ironically, Manasevich-Manuilov was himself an Ochrana agent and had supplied information on Boris Suvorin and his fellow directors to the Ochrana authorities.[63] As the storm clouds of the First World War approached, concern about German spies intensified and Manasevich-Manuilov turned his attention to supplying lists of suspects. With growing tensions between the two countries, naval contracts dwindled and eventually petered out altogether. Thankfully for Reilly, the clouds of war on the horizon were to have a substantial silver lining.

SIX

THE HONEY POT

While Reilly and Nadezhda Massino were holidaying at St Raphael on the French Riviera,[1] a Bosnian Serb student named Gabriel Princip assassinated the heir to the throne of the Austro-Hungarian Empire, Archduke Francis Ferdinand, in Sarajevo on 28 June 1914. This set off a chain reaction that within six weeks would envelop the great powers in a world war. On 5 July Germany declared its support for Austria, who in turn issued an ultimatum to Serbia that was purposely designed to make acceptance impossible. As the great powers squared up to each other, Reilly hastily departed for St Petersburg, leaving Nadezhda to continue the holiday alone.

On his arrival back in the Russian capital, he soon learned from his contacts that Russia had resolved to take military action against Austria if Serbia was attacked. On 28 July Austria declared war on the Serbs and Tsar Nicholas mobilised Russian forces the following day. Germany's declaration of war on Russia on 1 August found the Russians ill prepared. What would turn out to be a catastrophe for Russia, and the Tsar in particular, would provide Reilly's big chance, not only to make the millions he dreamed of, but also to make his mark on history.

As the hostilities commenced, a small army of contractors and brokers set off to secure the guns, ammunition, powder and general military equipment that the Russian war effort would need in abundance. Within days of war being declared, Reilly had been commissioned by Abram L. Zhivotovsky of the Russo-Asiatic Bank and the Russian Army to acquire munitions for the Russian Army.[2] Before departing for Tokyo in early August he wrote to both Margaret and Nadezhda.[3] For Margaret it would be the last letter she would receive from him until the war was over. Once in Tokyo, Reilly successfully secured a large powder deal with Taka Kawada and Todoa Kamiya of Aboshi Powder Company,[4] and the contract was then put in the hands of Reilly's agent in Japan, William Gill.

While Reilly was in Tokyo, Samuel M. Vauclain, vice president of the Baldwin Locomotive Works of Philadelphia, arrived in St Petersburg seeking contracts for narrow gauge locomotives and munitions.[5] Although Reilly was absent from St Petersburg, Vauclain found that his main competitor for the munitions contract was Reilly. It was obvious to him that Reilly had tremendous political backing in Russia which emanated from the office of the Tsar's cousin, the Grand Duke Alexander Mikhailovich, a contact Reilly had made at the time of the Russo-Japanese War through Moisei Ginsburg. The grand duke showed Vauclain a telegram from Reilly, sent through his London office, in which he had cut his contract price.[6] However, on this occasion, Vauclain won the contract, and took back an order for 100,000 military rifles, converted to use Russian cartridges, to be manufactured by the Remington Arms Company. Not long after, Vauclain shrewdly converted the Baldwin plant at Eddystone, Pennsylvania, which was running two thirds below capacity, to manufacture arms and munitions.

Before the war was over, the United States would manufacture over a third of all Russia's war munitions and equipment. American industry quickly saw the opportunity that beckoned, as indeed did brokers such as Reilly. Having concluded the powder deal in Tokyo, Reilly booked a passage on the SS *Persia*, which sailed from Yokohama Docks bound for San Francisco on 29 December 1914.

It arrived in San Francisco on 13 January 1915.[7] On arrival he declared to US Immigration that he was a forty-one-year-old merchant of British nationality, born in Clonmel, Ireland. He further declared that this was his first visit to the United States, that his journey had started in St Petersburg and that he had a through ticket to his final destination, New York City.[8] Apart from his claim to have been born in Clonmel, the rest of the information he gave was true. From San Francisco he travelled to New York by train, where he took an apartment at 260 West 76 Street.[9]

Through the Russo-Asiatic Bank he was introduced to Hoyt A. Moore, an attorney specialising in import and export matters. Moore not only provided advice to the new arrival but also recommended an acquaintance, thirty-year-old Dale Upton Thomas, whom Reilly took on as his office manager. Hays, Hershfield and Wolf, at 115 Broadway, another Moore introduction, became Reilly's legal representatives. A short walk away, with its classical arched entrance and grand marbled lobby, was the Equitable Building, at 120 Broadway, which Reilly chose as his New York base. He took 2722, a prestigious high-floor suite overlooking the downtown financial district of Manhattan, from where he and Thomas were to operate for the next three years.[10] The Equitable Insurance Company was well established in Russia[11] and its Broadway building was already home to a number of Russian tenants, a good number of whom were dealing in wartime munitions contracts in America. It was also through Hoyt Moore that Reilly met Samuel McRoberts, vice president of the National City Bank, who was also keen to profit from the honey pot that the war in Europe promised to deliver. To this end he procured Reilly's appointment as managing officer of the Allied Machinery Company, which was also based at 120 Broadway.[12] It has been suggested that Allied Machinery was a Reilly front company, when in fact it had been established since 1911. McRoberts was elected to the board of directors the following year, from which position he was able to introduce Reilly into the company. Company records indicate that Reilly was neither a shareholder nor a director, and was purely an employee, albeit a senior one.[13] The purpose of the company was to 'manufacture, produce, buy, sell, export, lease, exchange, hire, let, invest in, mortgage, pledge, trade and deal in, and otherwise acquire and dispose of machinery, machine-tools and accessories, machinery products and parts and goods, wares and merchandise of every kind and description'. In other words, it had an extremely wide remit and was ideal for trading within the new munitions marketplace.

While it is clear that Reilly used his exceptional networking skills to their full advantage and no doubt made the acquaintance of a large number of businessmen in New York, these often tenuous relationships have been used to associate Reilly with a range of events with which he had no connection whatsoever. His rivalry with J. Pierpont Morgan, the Anglophile American financial magnate, is a prime example. Morgan, best remembered today for his ownership of the White Star Line and its ill-fated flagship the RMS *Titanic*, was the main player in the allied quest for munitions in the United States. His desire to monopolise the arms trade on behalf of the Allied powers alienated him from the small army of independent brokers, like Reilly, who sensed they would be squeezed out of the munitions marketplace if Morgan succeeded in his aims. The very month that Reilly arrived in New York, Morgan had signed an agreement with the British Commercial Agency that made him the sole agent in the USA for munitions purchases. As part of this deal, Morgan made his ambitions clear so far as the Russian market was concerned, by offering Russia a $12 million credit on the proviso that his company acted as agent for all contracts signed as a result.[14]

On 3 February 1915 an explosion rocked the DuPont Powder Plant in DuPont, near Tacoma, Washington. According to the *Tacoma Daily News* (an afternoon publication):

> With a detonation that was heard for miles, the black powder plant of the DuPont company at DuPont, near Tacoma, exploded at 9.30 this

morning, demolishing the building, killing Henry P. Wilson, thirty-five, unmarried, and seriously injuring Harry West, married. As Wilson and West were the only men in the vicinity at the time officers of the company said the exact cause could not be given. The roof was lifted off the building and the sides blown to pieces, corrugated iron being scattered for a radius of 200ft. The building was one of a chain and was known as the 'press' building, where the powder is pressed into cakes. Wilson's body was blown about 50ft from the building. West was thrown about 150ft.[15]

Richard Spence has speculated that Reilly's hidden hand was behind the explosion, as DuPont had opted to do business with Pierpont Morgan rather than Reilly.[16] Spence believes that German saboteur Kurt Jahnke executed the deed on Reilly's instructions, drawing attention to Jahnke's supposed later admission to his German superiors that he was responsible. The more likely scenario was that Jahnke was seeking to take credit for something that was none of his doing, and was, in all likelihood, a complete accident. Indeed, the official verdict remains, in the absence of any compelling evidence to the contrary, that it was an accident. According to former DuPont employees, explosions at the DuPont Works were not unusual. They did not happen often, but when they did they were usually due to accidental causes.

Furthermore, Reilly had been in America for less than three weeks when the explosion occurred. It would have been somewhat difficult for him to have sought a powder contract with DuPont, to have been rebuffed by the company, and then to have planned and executed such a response, all within the space of some nineteen days. In short, there is no tangible evidence to connect Reilly with either Jahnke or this tragic accident.

Since his departure from St Raphael back in July 1914, Reilly and Nadezhda had been exchanging letters. Her divorce, which had recently been granted, meant that they could now marry. Although there is no doubt that she was in love with him and that he was very fond of her, doubt remains as to whether he actually wished to marry her. Although in his letters to her he promised to send for her as soon as he arrived in New York, she could well have had reason to doubt him. The fact that throughout their three-year relationship she had been married and latterly awaiting a divorce meant that the issue of marriage had not been a consideration. Once the divorce came through in 1914, he may well have had second thoughts, being perfectly content for her to remain as his mistress. If this was not the case and he really did have every intention of marrying her, there would have been absolutely no need for the Machiavellian scheme Nadezhda now embarked upon.

At her own expense she purchased a ticket in the name of Nadine Zalessky at Le Havre and took the SS *Rochambeau* to New York. As the liner neared New York she cabled Reilly to notify him of her arrival in order that he might meet her at the pier. She also cabled the New York police, informing them that Reilly was importing a woman into the state for immoral purposes – a criminal offence under the Mann Act.[17] When her ship docked on 15 February,[18] Reilly was there to meet her and so too were the police. The police arrested Reilly and, despite his insistence that she was his fiancée, informed him that he could only avoid prosecution and possible imprisonment if he married her immediately. As he had already promised to marry her and she had stated that this was the purpose of her journey, he did not have a leg to stand on. It was the first day of Lent under the Orthodox calendar, however, and Orthodox weddings do not, by custom, take place during the first week of Lent. Reilly, therefore, had to appeal to the head of the Russian Orthodox Church in America, Metropolitan Platon, to give special dispensation for the wedding to take place.[19] As luck would have it, for Nadine at any rate, Platon gave his permission, and the wedding took place the next day at St Nicholas's Cathedral in Manhattan.[20] Nadine claimed in the marriage register that she was the twenty-seven-year-old daughter of Pierre and Barbara Massino, residing at the Ritz Carlton Hotel, at 313 East 63rd Street. She was, in fact, twenty-nine years

Reilly's marriage on 16 February 1915 almost certainly saved him from arrest by the New York Police Department.

old. Reilly stated that he was a forty-one-year-old bachelor, the son of George and Pauline Reilly of Clonmel, Ireland, residing at 260 Riverside Drive, an address that did not exist until 1925. Petr Rutskii from the Russian Consulate was one of the witnesses.

G.L. Owen[21] believes that the Reillys left New York shortly after their wedding and undertook a visit to Petrograd. The timing of this visit may seem incidental, but it is of crucial importance in terms of authenticating a claim by Owen that the Reillys sailed back to New York on the same ship as a prominent German spy. Franz Von Rintelen was sent to America by German intelligence to co-ordinate a campaign of sabotage and disruption that would hopefully stem the flow of munitions to the Allies. Von Rintelen arrived in New York on 3 April aboard the SS *Kristianiafjord*, travelling on a Swiss passport under the name of Emil V. Gasche.[22] A search of the passenger list, however, reveals no Sidney or Nadine Reilly on board, nor indeed any male passenger fitting

Reilly's general physical description (around 5ft 9 or 10ins tall, brown eyes, dark hair, in the region of forty years of age). This is purely and simply because the Reillys had been in New York all the time. They did not, in fact, leave the city until 27 April, when they boarded the SS *Kursk* bound for Archangel.[23]

Arriving in the north Russian port on 11 May, they proceeded immediately to Petrograd. While Nadine spent some time with her family, Reilly entered into negotiations with the Russian Red Cross, with a view to securing, on their behalf, ambulances and automobiles from Newman Erb and the Haskell and Barker Car companies.[24] He also met with the Tsar's cousin, Grand Duke Alexander Mikhailovich. The grand duke had been head of the Directorate of Commercial Navigation and Ports during the war, and worked closely with Ginsburg in organising coal supplies to Vladivostok. A keen photography enthusiast, Alexander Mikhailovich was no doubt much impressed by the American automatic camera Reilly brought with him.[25] According to G.L. Owen, the Reillys were in Petrograd between June/July and September of 1915, a view shared by Richard Spence.[26] Although originally intending to leave Archangel on 13 June,[27] their departure was postponed until 26 June, when they headed back on board the SS *Czar*.

The delayed departure was more than likely caused by the attentions of the Ochrana, who were taking a close interest in Reilly and the war materials he was trading in. Before going aboard the SS *Czar*, he was searched on the orders of Col. Globachev, head of the St Petersburg Ochrana. Nothing incriminating was found on him or in his trunks and he was allowed to proceed on his way.[28] One such deal that attracted Globachev's interest concerned a consignment of nickel ore ordered through Reilly by the Russian government. The consignment was duly shipped to Russia via Sweden in a deal Reilly brokered through the Swedish Russo-Asiatic Company. All had proceeded smoothly until a routine check indicated that the weight of the ore unloaded in Petrograd was somewhat less than the amount loaded in New York.[29] This immediately lead to rumours that the missing ore had been appropriated in Sweden and sold on to Germany. A more likely scenario, however, was that the Russian government had been short-changed in New York by a sleight of hand on the paperwork. It would not have been the first time that a Reilly consignment was loaded underweight but the customer invoiced for the full cargo.

Reilly's postponed departure lead to a rumour reaching the Russian General Staff that the Ochrana had detained him. Maj.-Gen. Leontyev of the Quartermaster-General's Office immediately sent a cable on 24 June[30] to the staff of the commander-in-chief of the 6th Army, instructing that urgent enquiries be made to establish what had happened to Reilly. In a reply from Maj.-Gen. Bazhenov, Leontyev was assured that Reilly had not been detained and that he had been allowed to depart unhindered.[31]

Arriving in New York on 10 July,[32] Reilly returned to his desk at 120 Broadway. It did not take him long to work out that the main problem being encountered by American companies was not in securing munitions contracts *per se*, but in ensuring that the order, once manufactured, was actually accepted on delivery. Russian inspectors, whose job it was to ensure that shells, for example, were up to standard, were exceptionally careful about passing them. In the first six months of the war it was found, to the great cost of those at the battlefront, that some shell deliveries were not compatible with Russian guns and could not be fired. The result of this was a more vigorous system of quality control. This inspection system applied to all munitions including rifles, which had to be specially converted to take Russian cartridges. This presented an opportunity for Reilly, who had a close relationship with those issuing the surety bonds necessary before the Russian government would accept the consignment. On 19 April 1915, for example, Reilly signed a deal whereby he would, 'assist in the performance of the said contract and in particular in reaching an understanding with the Russian Government as to the assurances required… that the contract will be performed'.[33] In other words, Remington Union would pay Reilly a large sum of money to ensure that their rifles successfully passed through the quality control process and were accepted by the Russian government. Over three years later, Samuel Prior, who had signed the agreement with Reilly on behalf of the Remington Union Company, quite accurately described the deal as a 'hold-up'[34] on Reilly's part, for unless he was given a commission on the deal, the implication was that he would use his influence to frustrate their ability to get the rifles accepted.

In late 1915 the Russian government sent an official purchasing supply committee to New York headed by Gen. A.V. Sapozhnikov, another old Reilly acquaintance from St Petersburg. Whilst the committee was an understandable attempt to rationalise Russia's munitions purchases in America, it was dogged with scandal almost from the day its members arrived. Although, as usual, Reilly had a personal motive for writing to Lt-Gen. Eduard Germonius on 21 December 1915, he was essentially correct in drawing attention to the disorganised and over-optimistic state of affairs concerning Russian munitions purchases in America. In his report he stated that:

In the last eight months the chief Artillery Administration in Petrograd and the Russian Artillery Commission in America have been holding talks with dozens of factories and endless different suppliers, banks, 'groups' or just 'representatives' about ordering from them 1,000,000 to 2,000,000 rifles and corresponding quantity of cartridges. The offers exceeded the demand many times over and if they were all added up it would appear that in these eight months Russia has been offered rifles and cartridges in quantities that may be expressed only in 'astronomical' figures. Understandably, there is nothing surprising about the fact that so many offers have been forthcoming: the example of Allison, who secured a contract for shells worth $86,000,000 is still fresh in everybody's memory. What one cannot understand is that all these offers have been examined in detail, thorough talks have taken place, a huge amount of time and money has been spent on correspondence and telegrams, inspectors have been ordered to look round factories, legal consultants have been given the job of drawing up contracts, in many cases draft, preliminary or even final agreements have been signed (and then torn up) – but these orders for rifles and cartridges have still not been placed.

The reason for this is that the Chief Artillery Administration does not know enough about the real state of the rifle and cartridge trade in America. Petrograd, as optimistic as the entrepreneurs themselves, is not giving up and continues to hunt for the grain of corn in all the paper-litter put out by Jones, Hough, Zeretelli, Morny, Wilsey, Bradley, Garland, Empire Rifle Company, American Arms Company, Atlantic Rifle Company et al., and is evidently ignoring the actual state of affairs.[35]

Reilly went on to draw attention to the fact that the allied countries had placed orders in America for approximately 7.5 million rifles, 3,500 million cartridges and about 1.5 million gun barrels. His conclusion was that in their haste to take advantage of these large Russian contracts, many American firms had seriously overreached themselves and were highly unlikely to be able to deliver on schedule.

This eventually turned out to be the case, although the situation was not helped by the over-enthusiastic quality-control system. Before too long the system began to have serious repercussions on Russia's ability to fight the war. The problem now was not the quality of the munitions they were receiving, but the fact that the inspection system was slowing the delivery process down to such an extent that the Russian Army at the battlefront was virtually out of shells to fire at the enemy. When Gen. Germonius became head of the Russian Purchasing Commission in America, this issue was one that was very much to the fore.

Again, Reilly saw a golden opportunity to exploit this opportunity. According to Vladimir Krymov he visited the plants that were contracted to manufacture shells and were experiencing difficulties in getting them passed, and proposed that in exchange for a commission he could ensure that the inspectors would pass the finished munitions.[36] It is not surprising that the companies were initially sceptical to say the least, as he was not the first person who had approached them with this proposal. He told the companies, however, that he and Gen. Germonius were related and that through the general he could not only ensure the successful acceptance of their current orders but could also secure new orders for them. As proof he persuaded the managing directors of two companies to have lunch at the Coq d'Or, a country restaurant outside New York, and told them they would see him, his wife and Gen. Germonius having lunch together. The directors knew that Germonius never went anywhere, let alone had lunch with middlemen or suppliers. Nadine persuaded Germonius to have lunch with them at the Coq d'Or, and Reilly was thus able to show off the unsuspecting general to the directors. On 7 January 1916, an agreement was signed between Reilly and Samuel M. Vauclain, John T. Sykes and Andrew Fletcher on behalf of the Eddystone Ammunition Corporation. The agreement gave Reilly 25 cents commission on every round of three-inch shrapnel shell that was accepted.[37]

Within a very short space of time the orders were accepted and Reilly collected a healthy commission. What the companies did not know was that before approaching them, Reilly had heard that fresh instructions were shortly to be issued to the inspectors to be less circumspect as the Russian army was virtually out of shells. The companies, however, were sure that Reilly was responsible for this miracle.

On 16 July 1916 Reilly was reunited with Alexandre Weinstein, who arrived in New York aboard the liner the St Louis. Having already made a small fortune in London on munitions commissions, Weinstein now no doubt hoped to get a share of the American honey pot Reilly had often boasted about. Having secured himself a desk in Reilly's office suite at 120 Broadway, he enthusiastically threw himself into the murky but lucrative world of US munitions deals, as did Moisei Ginsburg, who arrived from

Petrograd shortly after Weinstein. Corrupt practice was not the only difficulty the Russian Purchasing Commission had to contend with. In 1916 Col. Sergei Nekrassov, the chief inspector of the Russian Purchasing Commission's Artillery Department, was accused by George Lurich, an Estonian linked to a pro-Allied intelligence ring, of being a German spy.[38] In particular he accused Nekrassov of obstructing munitions production and of diverting supplies to Germany. This was a very serious allegation, and Lurich took the matter up with the commission, but the allegation was dismissed. Lurich then took the matter to Capt. Guy Gaunt of British Naval Intelligence, who passed it on to Maj. Norman Thwaites of SIS to investigate.[39] The depth to which Thwaites looked into this matter is unknown, although we do know that he spoke to Reilly to elicit his opinion of Nekrassov. Thwaites, not for the first time, gave a different account of this matter in his autobiography to that which appears on the official record. According to a US Bureau of Investigation report written some two years later, Thwaites 'had lunched with both Reilly and Weinstein and they had aroused his suspicions in their efforts to get Nekarossov out of trouble'.[40] In his 1932 autobiography, *Velvet and Vinegar*, however, Thwaites recalls:

> I had been asked to investigate certain charges brought against the Russian War Mission in New York. Reilly knew them and gave a clean bill of health. I came to the conclusion that our Russian friends were giving themselves a good time in the hospitable city on the Hudson, but I could find no evidence either of graft or of enemy contacts.[41]

He makes no reference to Lurich or Nekrassov by name or indeed anyone else apart from Reilly and Weinstein in this account. He also gives the impression that his enquiry was not concerned solely with Nekrassov, and refers to a young girl who had apparently given testimony 'against them'. The impression one gains is that she herself had close associations with the Austrian and German Consulates.

The Nekrassov affair is seen by some as a further validation of the view that Reilly was a German agent, or was at least in league with them. It is more likely, however, that Reilly was seeking to shield Nekrassov purely for his commercial value. Bearing in mind that Reilly had already made over $1million from munitions deals, a good number of which resulted from his ability to 'assist' in the inspections process, it would be hardly surprising if he had sought to defend one of his key contacts in the inspections network.

So far, talk of German sabotage and disruption was confined to the type of activities alleged by Lurich. This was about to change abruptly. At 2.08 a.m. on Sunday 30 July 1916, New York City was rocked by a thunderous explosion caused by the ignition of munitions on nearby Black Tom Island. The ground shook and flaming rockets and screeching shells filled the night sky. Shock waves caused thousands of windows in the Manhattan skyscrapers to shatter, sending a deadly shower of glass raining down on the streets below. Water mains burst, the telephone system went dead and panic gripped motorists on the Brooklyn Bridge as the mighty structure shuddered and swayed. Almost immediately New York was alive with people as thousands took to the streets in bewilderment. Looting was reported on 5th Avenue and the police were thrown into a state of confusion as burglar alarms triggered by the blast sounded off all over the city. Some twenty minutes later a second huge blast shook the city, sending more shells and rockets into the night sky. More than 13,000 tons of explosives had been ignited by the two separate blasts, one in a rail wagon and the other in a barge moored at a nearby pier.[42]

Richard Spence believes Reilly again played 'a critical role'[43] in the destruction of the Black Tom munitions terminal, supposedly for two reasons. Firstly, Spence draws attention to the fact that most of the munitions orders on Black Tom, waiting for dispatch by ship to Europe, were 'the fruits of Morgan inspired contracts',[44] and secondly that Reilly was aware of the 'contents, security and layout' and could 'arrange easy access to the site for the team of saboteurs led by Jahnke'.[45] The charge that Reilly had background knowledge of the Black Tom Terminal seems to centre on the fact that Allied Machinery was one of a number of companies that had an office on the Black Tom site. The reality, however, was that the perpetrators would not have needed someone like Reilly to guide them through the intricacies of Black Tom's security. As official investigations have clearly demonstrated, security at Black Tom was, in practice, virtually non-existent.[46]

Security at the terminal was the responsibility of two private agencies. The Lehigh Valley Railroad Company, who owned the terminal, employed their own force. In addition, the British authorities had contracted the Dougherty Detective Agency to undertake patrols. In spite of this, police and federal investigators noted that there was no gate separating the Black Tom Terminal from adjacent land. Although still referred to at this time as Black Tom Island, a landfill scheme had linked it to the mainland some years before. Those who worked the barges came and went at will and were never challenged or stopped by patrols or security officers. Critical areas of the terminal's perimeter were unlit. In terms of the waterside boundary it was revealed that no river patrols of any kind were undertaken beyond the occasional passing coast guard or New York City Police boat. Again, lack of lighting on the river side of the terminal would have made it exceptionally difficult for such passing boats to observe any untoward goings on. In fact, the most likely scenario was that saboteurs Franz Jahnke and Lothar Witzke entered the terminal by a small rowboat, while Michael Kristoff made his way in from the land side.

Spence further develops his theory by suggesting a scenario whereby Reilly, Jahnke and Sir William Wiseman, SIS representative in New York, are effectively involved in a loose-knit plot to entice the then neutral United States into the war on the Allied side. Jahnke, it is argued, was more than likely a double agent working for SIS.[47] According to Spence:

Wiseman could see that [President] Wilson and America would not join the war unless their moral indignation was aroused sufficiently against Germany. Acts of German sabotage, real and imagined, had moved American sentiment in the 'right' direction, and Wiseman could logically assume that further outrages would continue this trend.[48]

Further outrages did indeed occur. Within six months of Black Tom, residents of New York City once again heard the thunderous roar of exploding munitions. On the afternoon of 11 January 1917, 500,000 three-inch shells ignited at the Canadian Car & Foundry Company's shell assembly plant in Kingsland, New Jersey, some ten miles from New York Harbour. Thankfully, the shells were not primed with detonating fuses and none of the 1,400 workforce was killed or injured. However, for some four hours those living in northern New Jersey and New York listened to the ongoing explosions as fire engulfed the entire Kingsland plant.[49]

Spence asserts that Jahnke led the German sabotage team responsible for the Kingsland explosion, and states 'again, Reilly could provide the means to breach the plant's security'.[50] As investigation records clearly demonstrate, however, there was no need for anyone to covertly effect an entry into the plant. The official verdict was that one Fiodor Wozniak, who was working in Building 30 where the blaze began, was responsible for starting the fire that led to the plant's destruction. Indeed, the foreman in Building 30, Morris Chester Musson, later testified that 'Wozniak had quite a large collection of rags and that the blaze started in these rags. I also noticed that he had spilled his pan of alcohol all over the table just preceding that time'.[51] Wozniak was questioned during an internal company enquiry, and although he denied any involvement, he did admit that he was not Russian, as he had stated when he entered the company's employment, but was instead Austrian. He further revealed that he had served in the Austrian army and police force. After questioning he was shadowed by private detectives, but disappeared without trace.

Three months after Kingsland, on 10 April 1917, an explosion occurred at the Eddystone Works in Pennsylvania, killing 132 men at the plant. Richard Spence draws attention to the fact that some weeks before the explosion, managing director Samuel Vauclain had been in negotiation to sell the plant to the US government. Reilly, in Spence's words, was 'cut out completely'[52] from the deal. Was the explosion, asks Spence, Reilly's revenge?[53] Again, not a shred of evidence was produced to connect Reilly or indeed anyone else with the catastrophe at Eddystone. Indeed, while Spence rightly states that sabotage was suspected, it was, in fact, never proven or established.

The whole thesis is somewhat fanciful and an example of the conspiracy theory at its worst. Reilly was without doubt a ruthless man who would stop at little to meet his ends. The foundations which support this theory are somewhat shaky, however. The earlier meetings and coincidental journeys by train and ship clearly could not have taken place. As for the acts of sabotage themselves, it seems evident that some were quite simply tragic accidents. Others, such as Black Tom and Kingsland, did not require the kind of covert role attributed to Reilly – poor security and a lack of employee vetting is explanation enough for the ease with which German saboteurs were able to carry out their objectives unhindered.

By 1917, Reilly's cumulative earnings from war munitions contracts were well over $3 million.[54] He was now occupying an entire suite at one of New York's most expensive and luxurious hotels, the Saint Regis on 5th Avenue and East 55th Street. While his fortunes had never looked better, back on the Eastern Front the tide of the war was turning against Russia. Two and a half years of conflict had confirmed that Russia was neither strong enough militarily or economically to meet the challenge of all-out war. Heavy defeats quickly made conditions worse at home, triggering a wave of strikes. These developed into a general strike which began on 9 March.[55] Two days later the Tsar mobilised army units, but they sided with the strikers. On 15 March, under pressure from all sides, Tsar Nicholas abdicated on behalf of himself and his son and a Provisional Government took power.

Closer to home, a telegram from the German Foreign Minister to the German Ambassador in Washington was intercepted and decoded by British Naval Intelligence. The telegram instructed the ambassador to approach the President of Mexico with a view to them joining the war on Germany's side and launching an invasion of the United States. When the story became public, President Wilson frantically tried to find an alternative to war, but the Germans sealed their own fate by commencing a policy of unrestricted submarine warfare in March. After three American merchant ships had been sunk, Wilson asked the Congress for a Declaration of War on 2 April, and got it four days later. America's entry into the war would, in due course, turn its direction decisively in the Allies' favour.

As these dramatic events unfolded on the world stage, Reilly was, according to virtually everyone who has ever written about him, working behind German lines as a British agent. According to Pepita Bobadilla, who Reilly would later marry, he:

> …undertook the difficult and hazardous task of entering Germany (usually by aeroplane via the front line) in quest of military information. His services in this direction were of the utmost value and his exploits in Germany have become legendary.[56]

Reilly told his first wife, Margaret, a similar story.[57] Robin Bruce Lockhart asserts that Reilly enlisted in the German Army and, disguising himself as a colonel, bluffed his way into the head-quarters of the German High Command and sat in on a briefing attended by the Kaiser.[58] In the 1992 revised edition of *Ace of Spies*, Lockhart challenged John Major's Conservative government to 'open a window on the past' in order that Reilly's 'amazing' exploits in Germany could be made known.[59] The Official Secrets Act aside, no government could do this, for the reality is that Reilly's work behind enemy lines was nothing more than a fanciful fabrication on his part. Throughout the Allied offensives at Messines, Passchendaele and Ypres, Reilly was comfortably billeted at the Saint Regis Hotel on 5th Avenue. The only action he saw on the Western Front was in the newsreels shown in Manhattan's picture palaces.

With America now at war with Germany, the US Bureau of Investigation was charged with the responsibility of tracking down and apprehending any American citizen or alien who might be an enemy spy. Aided and abetted by the Office for Naval Intelligence and the Military Intelligence Division, they avidly set about investigating possible enemy agents and sympathisers. Within days of America's declaration of war, Roger Welles, director of Naval Intelligence, received a report from Agent Perkins of the US Bureau of Investigation concerning an individual suspected of enemy sympathies.[60] As a result of reading the report, he immediately ordered an investigation into the subject of Perkins' report, one Sidney George Reilly.

SEVEN

CONFIDENCE MEN

Those regarded as dangerous aliens had always been the responsibility of the Labor Department's Immigration Bureau, but in early 1917 the US Congress introduced new immigration legislation making it easier to deport undesirables. The Immigration Bureau now found it had neither the time, the manpower, nor the resources to conduct the investigations that would be prompted by the new law.

Two competing civil agencies, the Secret Service, which came under the US Treasury Department, and the US Bureau of Investigation, which came under the Justice Department, carried out domestic security investigations. As America entered the war they were also joined in this endeavour by the Military Intelligence Division and the American Protective League. The APL was a voluntary association of patriotic citizens created on 22 March 1917 as an auxiliary to the Bureau of Investigation.

In addition to assigning his own men to the investigation of Sidney Reilly, Roger Welles sent a copy of the Perkins' memorandum[1] to Maj. Ralph Van Deman of the US Military Intelligence Division, as it clearly had military implications:

From: Agent L.S. Perkins, New York City   3 April 1917
In Re: SIDNEY G. REILLY: NEUTRALITY MATTER

According to Winfield S. Proskey, consulting engineer for Flint & Co., 120 Broadway, close watch should be kept upon Sidney G. Reilly, Room 2721, Equitable Building, 120 Broadway. Col. Proskey says he has it from Capt. Gaunt of the British Consulate here that Reilly was a spy for the Japanese during the Russo-Japanese war, and is now an enemy of the Allies. Therefore, the conspicuous advocacy of the scheme to present 300,000 discarded Krag-Jorgensen rifles to the Russian army, which has attracted some attention to Reilly, as he seems to be the originator of it, should be looked upon with suspicion. In spite of his name, Reilly is of Semitic origin says Col. Proskey, and is of Oriental appearance. He is denounced by a prominent Russian, Peralstrauss, of 42 Broadway, as a pro-German.

The US Army had discarded the Krag-Jorgensen rifles back in early 1915. At the time it was believed that Franz Von Rintelen, the German intelligence agent, was seeking to purchase the rifles through an intermediary. It was thought that he intended, in turn, to supply them to the supporters of former Mexican President Gen. Victoriano Huerta to aid his restoration to power. Alternatively, his motive could simply have been to deprive the Allied powers of the opportunity to acquire them. At any rate, it seemed to Van Deman that here was a possible link between Reilly and a German attempt to purchase arms. Reilly was, by repute, a British citizen and Van Deman therefore wrote, on 7 July, to Sir William Wiseman requesting any information the British might have on Reilly.[2] Wiseman, who was based in New York City, was nominally part of the British munitions purchasing operation and responsible for British propaganda. In reality, the thirty-two-year-old Baronet was head of SIS in the United States. On 9 July Wiseman replied that Sidney Reilly:[3]

... claims to be a British subject, but doubt has been cast on this and it has been said that he is in reality a Russian Jew. In any case he is married to a Russian Jewess. For the last two years he has been mixed up with various scandals in connection with the purchase of Russian munitions here and his reputation is a bad one. He is said to do a certain amount of honest company promoting, but his chief line of business is collecting brokerages in more or less dishonest ways on any contract that he can possibly have something to do with. Reilly is said to have been at Port Arthur in 1903, where he was suspected by the Russians of acting as a spy for the Japanese. While in this country, during the present war, he has been mixed up with various undesirable characters and it would not be in the least surprising if he was employed by enemy agents in propaganda or other activities.

This letter no doubt spurred Van Deman to extend the investigation further in order to identify the 'various undesirable characters' referred to by Wiseman. The investigation itself was deputed to APL agents Hollis H. Hunnewell and Abel Smith, who worked under the supervision of McGregor Bond of the Office of Naval Intelligence. He in turn sent copies of all reports and memorandums to Lt-Col. Townsend Irving of the Military Intelligence Division. Not being experienced professional investigators, Hunnewell and Smith soon found themselves sinking into the mire of Reilly's complex personal and business relationships. One suspicious character seemed to open the door to several others. Before too long the investigation was taking on a momentum of its own. This may be one reason why it went on for so long. Neither were the investigators helped by the fact that within six months of Agent Perkins' memorandum, Reilly left New York and proceeded to Toronto to join the RFC. He was therefore absent for the remainder of the war and indeed for the remainder of the investigation. While it is clear that Hunnewell and Smith were certainly more than successful in tracking down a large number of individuals who were able to supply information, they seemed unable to successfully interpret what they found or discriminate in favour of what was relevant and meaningful. A seasoned investigator would no doubt have done a more circumspect job, but would not have committed to paper the same wealth of detail and trivia as Hunnewell and

Smith. To them we should be eternally grateful for inadvertently documenting, in such depth, the many dimensions of Reilly's life in New York.

Indeed, there seemed to be no shortage of people who were willing to come forward and testify against Reilly, which is not surprising given his ruthless approach to business. During the two and a half years he had been in New York he had undoubtedly crossed, or more to the point, double-crossed, a good many people. Norbert Rodkinson was one such person. Described in the reports as an Englishman,[4] Rodkinson is very much an enigma. He had lived in Russia for many years and now worked in New York for the brokerage firm Wagner & Company of 33 New Street. He told the investigators that Reilly's reputation as a spy and scoundrel was well established in Petrograd. He also commented on Reilly's marriage to Nadine, stating that it must be bigamous, as Reilly already had a wife and two children who had until recently been living in Port Arthur.[5] He further added that Reilly had sent them to Petrograd in 1916 where they had been left in 'dire straits'. The English colony in Petrograd had apparently taken up a collection for the family 'so that they could exist'. An Englishman by the name of Fred Hill is named in the testimony as being responsible for the money that was donated.[6] Rodkinson also confirmed his belief that Reilly had not been born in Ireland but in the town of Bendzine in Poland and claimed that both Reilly and Alexandre Weinstein asked him to transact business for them when he arrived in New York in 1916, but knowing of their 'evil reputation' he refused.

Col. Proskey, a consulting engineer for Flint and Company, the man who had sparked off the enquiry in the first place, told the investigators that he considered Reilly, 'one of the most astute and dangerous international spies now at large'.[7] It was well known, he said, that Reilly was a crook and an enemy of the Allies. He restated his earlier charge that he had spied for Japan and introduced the investigators to John F. Cordley, also from Flint and Company. Cordley identified Alexandre Weinstein as

Reilly's right-hand man and described the pair as 'dangerous'. In his view they would 'do anything for the almighty dollar'.[8] Cordley believed that Reilly had been educated at the University of Berlin, and stated that in 1914 he had visited Japan, but not 'as a member of the Russian Purchasing Commission'.[9] He further ventured that Reilly was said to be an officer of the Allied Machinery Company, and had made $1 million in Russian contracts.[10]

The Bureau's enquiries indicated that Weinstein was born in Kiev, Ukraine, in 1873,[11] where his father was a prominent banker. However, he was believed to have run a brothel there and served a prison sentence for bribery. Maj. Norman Thwaites, Wiseman's SIS deputy, was approached and permitted Hunneman and Smith sight of MI5 material on Weinstein, which indicated that he was viewed as an undesirable character during the eighteen months he spent in London. He was also reputed to have done business with German firms during this time in London. Another report from Thwaites stated that 'Weinstein claims to be a Russian and professes strong pro-British and pro-Ally sentiments but assurances have been received on good authority that he is in touch with prominent Germans'.[12] Known to be a gambler and womaniser, he resided at 60 St James's Street in Mayfair and had a reputation as an extravagant spender. This was hardly surprising, given that he had earned some £800,000 in commissions during the time he was in London.[13]

As the investigation gathered pace, the Bureau began to suspect that Weinstein was involved in business deals with those under suspicion of being German agents. The Elliot Bay Shipbuilding Company, for example, alleged that Weinstein had been involved in a recent, questionable shipbuilding transaction and that he possessed plans and specifications belonging to the company which must have been stolen.[14] He had apparently been introduced to them by Nicholas Kousnetzoff, who was involved in a wireless contract backed by Germany in 1917. It was noted that he had employed as his valet a German, Frederick Herron, who was apparently connected with Louis Miller, a saloonkeeper

on West 30 Street, who had been charged with being an anti-
American propagandist.[15]

Antoine Jahalsky, alias Tony Farraway, was an even greater
concern to the investigators. He, too, was referred to as a womaniser and gambler. They believed him to be the author of a
pamphlet entitled 'Why Poland Should Stand By Germany'.[16] He
claimed to have been born in Russian Poland, although Hunneman
and Smith suspected that he was in fact Austrian, and may have been
connected with the sale of Russian military documents to the
Austro-German consuls-general in New York.[17] Their suspicion
appears to have been kindled by a statement from the actress Clare
Kimball Young, who related that he had told her on one occasion
that he had a brother who was an officer in the Austrian army.[18]
She firmly believed that he was an Austrian and added that she
knew him as Tony Farraway. The actress Nita Naldi, a former
mistress, also mentioned that he had told her about his brother, who
had served in the Austrian army.[19]

The statement of another female acquaintance of Jahalsky only
added to the suspicion that he was a German spy. Former chorus
girl and actress Peggy Marsh had met Weinstein in London in 1915,
where she said he had a great reputation as a spender and was
constantly showering money and presents on the chorus girls. She
said that few women liked Weinstein because of his appearance (he
apparently had very prominent teeth), but were willing to accept
his friendship because of his extravagant generosity.[20] Marsh's
testimony also asserted that her friend and fellow chorus girl Gertie
Millar had been Weinstein's mistress before he left for America.
When she herself returned to New York a short while later, she
had met Weinstein again. He had introduced her to Jahalsky, with
whom she had an affair, and who had in turn introduced her to
Sidney and Nadine Reilly. In 1916 she had travelled with him
from New York to the west coast. In her opinion Jahalsky gave every
impression of being a German spy[21] – he had apparently asked her
to mix with officers and businessmen and get as much information from them as possible. She said he was interested in the study

of maps and had taken photographs, one apparently of the Roosevelt Dam, with a 'remarkable camera'. She recalled that he had made a mysterious visit to the mining country outside Phoenix, Arizona, to visit a Polish miner he had known 'in the old country'. She eventually left him in California and returned to New York.[22]

At the time Jahalsky made the Phoenix trip, Kurt Jahnke was co-ordinating a desperate, half-baked plan to slow down US troop movements to France by creating trouble for the US on the Mexican border.[23] German agents were to foment a wave of strikes among Arizona's copper miners with the connivance of the radical Industrial Workers of the World (IWW). These mines had a history of militancy, and it was hoped the strikes would soon lead to violence. In conjunction with inducing mutiny among black army units in Arizona and attacks on US border posts, Jahnke hoped this cocktail would send US troops rushing south. It was also noted that the British Secret Service had stated that Jahalsky was a 'most dangerous German spy', and was acquainted with Col. Nekrassoff of the Russian Commission.[24]

The third associate, former Russian naval lieutenant T.N. Agapeef, came to New York in 1917, taking an apartment at 29 West 52nd Street. The Russian Navy Department had purchased a converted yacht for use as a patrol vessel in the White Sea. Although commissioned under the Russian flag it had not left New York due to the 'present conditions in Russia'. According to the report:

> The commander of the ship, Lt T.N. Agapeef, was instructed to put the ship out of commission, send the crew to Russia and deliver to the representative of the Russian Admiralty the letter of credit which he had received in his capacity as commanding officer for the expenses during the voyage to Russia. Lt Agapeef did not comply with the order to return the letter of credit and disappeared from his post. Investigations showed that all the money of the letter of credit had been drawn.[25]

Agapeef had clearly thought better than to return to a country in the midst of revolutionary turmoil and could not resist the temptation to redeem the letter of credit, valued at $40,000. The Russian Embassy had requested his arrest, but this had been refused by the US State Department because of 'the present Russian situation'. He soon joined Weinstein in Reilly's office suite, where he also sought out commissions on war contracts.

Beatrice Madeline Tremaine, Reilly's twenty-eight-year-old mistress, lived with her mother at 140 Wadsworth Avenue, New York. Sometimes referred to as Reilly's 'ward', he had first met her at 'Lucille's', a dressmaking establishment in the spring of 1916, where she worked as a model. Shortly thereafter Reilly had taken her from Lucille's, sent her to a finishing school in Orange, New Jersey, and paid her an allowance of $200 per month.[26] She had then entered the 'moving picture' industry and was clearly making some headway. According to her testimony, Reilly had stated that Nadine intended to divorce him, and as a result she and Reilly were to marry on his return to New York.

Beatrice Madeline Tremaine also corroborated the fact that Reilly had been forced by the Mann Act to marry Nadine. Her account was supported by two former acquaintances at Lucille's, Madame Paul, the head of millinery and Madamoiselle Chauson, a salesperson. Madamoiselle Chauson also stated, however, that Miss Tremaine was a 'most skilled and dangerous liar'.[27] It was from Chauson that the investigators got the name and address of Norbert Rodkinson, who they were told knew a great deal about Reilly and Weinstein. Investigators later spoke with Beatrice's friend Delores Rose, an English chorus girl in the Follies show. Miss Rose is described as 'not of the best reputation, but loyal to her country'.[28] She worked at Lucille's at the time Beatrice had been a model there, and said it was an open secret among the models that Reilly had taken a liking to her. She also corroborated Beatrice's claim that Reilly had asked her to marry him, and related how she had told Beatrice of Norbert Rodkinson's claim that Reilly had deserted a family in Russia.[29] Denying that this was true, Beatrice had become angry and almost slapped her face. At the instigation of the investigators, Miss Rose met Beatrice again at her apartment and engaged her in conversation on several topics the investigators were interested in. Beatrice said that she did not believe that Reilly was in anyway disloyal to his own country. She confirmed that she was still receiving the monthly allowance from Reilly, even though he had not returned in June as she had expected.[30]

She was then interviewed for the third and final time, when it was reported that, 'in spite of careful questioning, Tremaine professed not to know any more about Reilly and his affairs than she had already related on the two previous occasions'.[31] It was concluded that her attitude was 'not altogether frank', and doubt was expressed that she was telling the whole truth. Quite possibly because of the investigation, which Delores Rose reported had 'greatly disturbed' her, Beatrice decided to leave New York and spend the winter in Florida, as she had been 'working hard in moving pictures and needed a rest'.[32]

The investigators never questioned Nadine herself, although it is clear that she was kept under very close observation. Enquiries suggested that she was aware of Reilly's attachment to Beatrice Tremaine and was very jealous. The investigators had, so they thought, good grounds for believing that in Reilly's absence Nadine had affairs with Weinstein and Jahalsky. Her maid Alice Todd had described Weinstein as her constant companion. However, although it was 'generally understood about the club that Mrs Reilly and Weinstein are intimate',[33] Alice Todd denied this, saying that while there was no doubt that a strong friendship existed she had never seen anything in their relations that might be interpreted to prove any immorality. The nearest the investigators got to an incriminating statement was an admission from Miss Todd that Weinstein 'is in the bungalow late at night'.[34]

It is clear that they fared much better when they questioned a man named Murray, the superintendent of the apartment block where Jahalsky lived. At the time they met Murray, Jahalsky was away in Texas. Murray volunteered that he did not like Jahalsky and was able to recall a number of women who had visited him. He had been particularly intimate with Gertrude Grimes and the actress Nita Naldi before he left for Texas. To the astonishment of the investigators, Murray stated that Nadine Reilly had come to Jahalsky's apartment at around 11 p.m. one night shortly after Reilly had left for Canada. He thought she had stayed all night, as the maid had seen her leave the following morning.[35]

At the time of the investigation Nadine was living alone in a bungalow in the grounds of the Allenhurst Club, in New Jersey. Thomas Harrison, the clerk of the Allenhurst Club, described as a 'loyal American', had assisted the investigators and stated that Russians of good standing at the club would have nothing to do with either Weinstein or the Reillys.[36]

While Weinstein was staying at the club he handed in a business suit to be pressed. In it were found four papers, including 'an elaborate type-written description, on a single piece of paper, of a new machine gun'.[37] Thomas Harrison showed the papers to another guest at the club, Alfred Johnson, City Chamberlain in New York, suggesting that Weinstein should be investigated as the matter seemed suspicious. Suspicious or not, this, like much else in the investigation, failed to lead to anything concrete.

Turning again to the British authorities, the investigators made an appointment with Col. F.W. Abbott at 165 Broadway, who was responsible for Russian contracts on behalf of the British government. He confirmed that he had met Reilly when the British Mission took over the management of Russian munitions contracts. Reilly had given him a great deal of trouble and implied that he had held up production to demonstrate that nothing could be done unless it went through him first. Abbott's conclusion was that Reilly was 'a clever schemer',[38] who was probably dishonest, although proof was so far lacking.

In search of that elusive proof, the decision was made to make a search of Reilly's office in the hope of at last unearthing some hard evidence. The search was carried out by agents Hunnewell and Smith, accompanied by two Russian translators. They opened a large portmanteau (a leather travelling trunk) that Reilly had brought with him from Japan. Inside they found a bag concealed within a compartment, which contained two packets of letters. These were clearly exchanges of correspondence between him and Nadine dating back to when she was in the south of France and he was in Russia, Japan and New York. She signed her letters 'Kisenka', meaning kitten in Russian. The two bundles of letters were shown to the interpreters, who concluded that they were merely love letters and of little consequence.[39] Hunnewell and Smith were, however, puzzled by her frequent references in the letters to his 'system' and how she hoped it would be successful. There was no indication anywhere to suggest what she meant or what the system was.[40] Richard Spence has claimed that Reilly's 'system' was an approach to business dealing gleaned from the arms dealer Basil Zaharoff.[41] To Zaharoff, '*le systeme*' was essentially the strategy of playing all sides off against each other in order to maximise profit. As we have already noted in Chapter Five, there is no concrete evidence that Reilly and Zaharoff ever met, let alone knew each other. His assertion must therefore remain at best speculation.

Hunnewell and Smith next turned their attention to Reilly's safe, which was opened and the contents searched. What they found confirmed that he did indeed have 'tremendous political backing in Russia'.[42] They also found many ammunition contracts made by Reilly on behalf of the Imperial Russian government for 'vast amounts'.[43] Of particular interest were the records of cheques issued by Reilly and by office manager Upton Dale Thomas on Reilly's behalf. Several had been written to the New York Club, where Reilly was a member. A cheque written to a Carl Lowie caught their eye as this showed that Reilly was transacting business with 'someone who apparently has a German name'.[44] Thomas, who had issued the cheque, volunteered that Lowie was in fact Danish. Also of interest were several large cheques, one for $6,000 made out to Weinstein and another for $2,000 made out to Jahalsky. Thomas stated that Weinstein's cheque was in part settlement of a shipping commission, while Jahalsky's was in part payment of money he had loaned to Reilly. A search of Weinstein's desk was equally fruitless.

Thomas was questioned about his knowledge of Reilly, Weinstein and Jahalsky. He told them that he knew very little about Reilly's or Weinstein's affairs and confirmed that he was also representing Jahalsky while he was away in Texas. The investigators found Thomas convincing and referred to him in their report as a 'loyal American'.[45] With little to show from their search at 120 Broadway, the investigators had to face the fact that their enquiry was running out of steam and out of time. The war in Europe was now drawing to its bloody conclusion as thousands of fresh American troops flooded into France, tipping the scales in favour of the Allies.

Of the three individuals the investigators initially focused upon, Reilly, Weinstein and Jahalsky, very little of worth was found that corroborated the view that they were either in sympathy with Germany or that they had aided or abetted the enemy in any way. Of the three, only Jahalsky would seem to have warranted any real cause for suspicion, although this in itself was founded on the flimsiest of circumstantial grounds. He was later arrested and closely questioned in Texas, but was released through lack of evidence.

The investigation's inconclusive result also calls into question the reliability of those who testified against Reilly. To a greater or lesser extent, a good number were themselves up to their necks in the murky pool of war profiteering. Some, like Vauclain, would later justify their actions by claiming their involvement was motivated purely by a desire to shorten the war, or in the earlier days of the conflict to 'keep America out'.[46] Some had lost out to Reilly in the scramble for contracts, while others had been double-crossed or conned by him. Reilly's perceived permissive lifestyle would equally have made him a marked man among the 'respectable' business community.

The allegations made by Norbert Rodkinson are the most significant, as they again raise the possibility that Reilly had married bigamously during the period 1904–1909, before he met Nadine. He could, of course, have heard about Margaret's earlier appearance in St Petersburg while living in the city. There is also a possibility that Margaret was actually in St Petersburg at some point in 1916. She herself referred to having been in Russia for a period of time during the course of the war, a claim given some credence by Foreign Office records indicating that she was issued with a passport in January 1916.[47] If she was there, her presence might be explained by her work for the Red Cross or in order to take up a position as a nanny in the city's large English colony.[48] The latter scenario could also explain how children might have made their way into Rodkinson's story of the 'deserted family'.

Rodkinson is also important in that he seems to be the direct source for the claims about Reilly's past which were later recycled by others and which resurface in a number of intelligence files, including those of SIS. When subjected to scrutiny, Rodkinson hardly emerges as a particularly savoury or reliable witness. Although the investigators believed him to be an Englishman, he was certainly not born in Britain. In fact, he later claimed to be an American. A memorandum from the Office of the Counselor at the US State Department, shortly after the war had ended, casts Rodkinson in an entirely new light:[49]

26 November 1918
Copy to: ONI, MID, Justice Department
Subject: Norbert Mortimer Rodkinson, Care Renskorff, Lyon & Co.

From the information on file in this office it appears that he is a native American citizen, born at Baton Rouge, of Russian-Jewish and French-Creole parentage. He has no birth certificate but says it was destroyed in a fire. His wife's maiden name was Polens and she was English of German parentage and doubtful morals.[50] He is a man of pleasing personality and apparently some ability – a linguist, with intimate knowledge of Russian life and affairs. His business reputation is doubtful. When, in January 1918, he obtained a passport to visit the United States, it was marked 'No Return' by the British authorities, but a protest from Rodkinson caused this decision to be reversed – as he was, at that time, apparently connected with the Ministry of Information. On reaching America he applied for a position under the

State Department, giving five references. Of these, only one vouches for him without reserve. Another can give no definite information about him. Two of the remaining three believe him to have been born in Germany, neither believe him to be on the square, and one says he would hesitate in employing him in a government position.

As for his private life – he has been married twice and was once stabbed by a '*fille-de-joie*'[51] while visiting in Berlin. He asserts he has been employed by the British Intelligence Department. Of this there is no record.

More revealing is a Bureau of Investigation memorandum, written some three months earlier, based upon information supplied by Col. Proskey, who sparked off the Reilly investigation in April 1917. Agent R.W. Finch of the Bureau's New York City office states that:

> Col. Proskey, of Flint & Co., 120 Broadway, NY, very confidential informant of this office, advises that he has been informed that a man by the name of Rodkinson, formerly employed by Flint & Co., desires to go on the proposed Russian Commission to Russia. He desires a letter of recommendation from Flint & Co. It is said that Rodkinson recently saw Senator J. Hamilton Lewis, who has promised to secure Rodkinson an audience with President Wilson.[52]

Proskey goes on to relate that Rodkinson had formerly represented Flint & Co. in Petrograd, during which period his house had been raided twice by the police. He also refers to Rodkinson's ability to speak German and Russian and states that after his 'troubles in Russia' he returned to the US and joined the firm of Renskorff, Lyon & Co. What lay behind his troubles in Russia is not known for sure. There was certainly a great deal of substance to the concerns outlined by the US State Department and Bureau of Investigation. For example, in the 14th US Census held in 1920, Rodkinson appears at 159 West 78th Street, New York City, living with Corinne, his English-born wife, and their English maid, Maud Peddar. He declared in his Census return that he was born in Louisiana. However, there is no record in Louisiana of anyone of that name or similar being born in or around 1874, his declared year of birth.[53]

He first appears in US Immigration records on arrival in New York on 10 June 1903 aboard the Kaiser Wilhelm der Grosse, which sailed from Bremen, Germany. Over the next two decades he, his first wife Susanne and second wife Corinne, crop up repeatedly, criss-crossing the Atlantic. Prior to the First World War, all journeys to New York began in Germany. Although he always described himself as a US citizen, as we have seen, he was never able to prove that he was born in the USA. While his general statements about Reilly's character are very much along the lines of a good many other people who knew him, his claim about Reilly being born in Bendzine and allegedly deserting his family in 1916 are very different matters. Whether Rodkinson's statements were true or not, he was certainly not an unblemished witness.

The result of the investigation was, to put it kindly, inconclusive. Roger Welles, the director of Naval Intelligence, who had initiated the enquiry back in April 1917, probably best summed it up, when, two months after the end of the war, he wrote to the director of the Bureau of Investigation, Bruce Bielaski, enclosing a copy of the file containing the results of the investigation:

> While the investigation disclosed nothing definite, there is a mass of interesting data that might be of use to your department should any of the individuals in question come under your observation. This office believes that these men are international confidence men of the highest class.[54]

On that rather resigned note, Welles signed off. In spite of everything he now knew about Reilly's nefarious disposition, even he would have found it hard to comprehend that within months of joining the RFC, the 'international confidence man' would be walking into the London headquarters of SIS for a personal audience with C, the service's legendary chief.

Eight

Code Name ST1

When Col. Abbott of the British Mission in New York first heard that Reilly had been seen wearing the uniform of a British officer he was 'astonished'.[1] Knowing of Reilly's dubious form, he could not understand how such a blackguard had been permitted to join the British Army, let alone be awarded a commission. Another officer, Col. Gifford, had spoken with the equally incredulous Maj. Thwaites, who implied he would be making clear his views to London in no uncertain terms.[2] Gifford assumed from this that Reilly would be recalled and probably asked to resign. In fact, nothing of the sort happened. Thwaites' attitude is somewhat strange to say the least in light of the following passage from his 1932 autobiography:

> In 1917 as a man of about thirty-eight he [Reilly] came to me in New York with the request that I should get him into the service. He felt that he ought to be doing his bit in the war… Reilly expressed the desire to join the Royal Air Force. I sent him to Toronto to the officer in command and he was promptly given a commission. But he was too valuable a find to be wasted as an Equipment Officer, to which department he was assigned. I reported to HQ at home that here was a man who not only knew Russia and Germany, but could speak almost perfectly at least four languages. His German was indeed flawless, and his Russian hardly less fluent.[3]

Thwaites goes on to relate how, as a result of his report to London, Reilly was summoned for an interview with C, 'the mysterious chief of hush-hush work', and then assigned work firstly in the Baltic and then East Prussia before being dispatched to Russia. It is no exaggeration to describe the comparison between this 1932 account and the reality of 1917 as breathtaking. Weinstein, who in 1932 is described as 'one of the nicest Russians I know',[4] was at the time referred to as an undesirable character and former brothel keeper who was fraternising with the enemy.[5] Reilly, who is also referred to in the most complimentary of terms in 1932 was, of course, given an even blacker report back in 1917.

Neither, it must be said, does Thwaites' version of recruiting Reilly sit comfortably with the account given within the telegrams exchanged between SIS headquarters in London and the SIS New York station during February and March 1918. With Reilly dead and Thwaites' original reports and telegrams safely out of the public domain, he probably saw little harm in taking credit for the recruitment of Reilly, who in 1932 was on the crest of a posthumous wave of celebrity as the great 'Master Spy', featured in strip cartoons and serials in England and on the continent.

Contrary to claims made by countless Reilly writers, there had been no relationship whatsoever between Reilly and SIS before 1918. This is made clear by C's personal diary, which indicates that Reilly had been proposed as someone who could be helpful to the department by Maj. John Scale, latterly of the SIS station in Petrograd.[6] C's diary further reveals Scale to have been liaising with the British Army in Canada and preparing agents with Russian backgrounds or experience for work in Russia.[7] Reilly had been brought to Scale's attention shortly after his enlistment by Maj. Strubell, the officer who had dealt with his commission and to whom he had volunteered his services for work in Russia.

While it seems evident that Reilly offered his services as opposed to being approached, his motive for doing so is far from clear. To believe that he wished to leave his wife, his mistress and his comfortable life of prosperity in New York to 'do his bit'[8] in the war, as suggested by Thwaites, is naïve in the extreme. After all, Reilly had shown not the slightest interest in doing 'his bit' before. Time and again it has been demonstrated that he was not someone who was in any way motivated by patriotism or ideology, but was driven purely by greed and self-interest.

Richard Spence has suggested that Reilly's departure from New York was a direct consequence of his supposed involvement in the sabotage campaign of Kurt Jahnke,[9] and that his subsequent RFC enlistment in Toronto was somewhat earlier than indicated by his Military Service Record.[10] From this, and Thwaites' statement that Reilly 'undertook work in Russia when Kerensky was dropping to his doom',[11] Spence develops the theory that Reilly went to Russia before the Bolshevik Revolution not after it. He pinpoints Reilly's arrival in Russia as being in early August 1917, when a special RFC training wing arrived there. Although unable to locate a personnel roster, he clearly believes that Reilly was a member of this unit:

> Reilly's disappearance [from New York] neatly coincides with the arrival in Russia during early August of a special RFC training wing. This unit was attached to the existing British military equipment mission under Gen. F.C. Poole. Reilly's service record lists him as an equipment officer, and he and Poole were to cross paths in Russia in 1918 and 1919.[12]

However, Air Mechanic Ibbertson recorded in his diary a full list of officers and other ranks who served with him in this unit and Reilly's name is conspicuous by its absence.[13] Bearing in mind the fact that the Jahnke sabotage theory is at best built on a foundation of sand, it has to be said that the wider hypothesis put forward by Spence is not substantiated by hard evidence. On the contrary, recently discovered correspondence between Reilly and his mistress Beatrice Tremaine clearly indicates that during the period July–December 1917, Reilly was in fact resident in the city of Toronto, at the King Edward Hotel. Situated on King Street

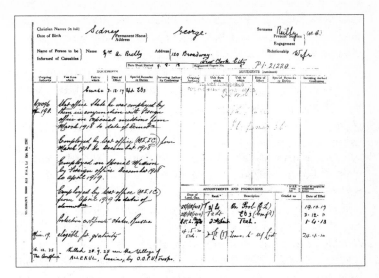

Reilly's RAF service record (note next of kin 'Mrs A. Reilly').

East, the hotel was not only Toronto's most luxurious, but was situated close to the Royal Flying Corps No. 4 School of Military Aeronautics at the University of Toronto, where Reilly trained prior to his departure for England in December 1917.[14]

If one is looking for persuasive coincidences, then surely the revolutionary events that were being played out in Russia during October and November 1917 are far worthier of consideration? Reilly initially enlisted with the RFC in Toronto on 19 October 1917, and was placed 'on probation' pending confirmation of a commission.[15] Several weeks before, the Bolsheviks had achieved majorities in both the Moscow and Petrograd Soviets, thus heightening speculation that an armed insurrection might be on the cards. When the Bolshevik takeover actually took place on 7 November that year,[16] Reilly was already undergoing training at the School of Military Aeronautics.[17]

Bearing in mind what we already know of his motivations and priorities, what personal reasons might he have had for wanting to

return to Russia in such haste? Once the Bolsheviks had taken
power it would not have been easy for a non-Russian civilian (as
'Sidney Reilly' officially was) to gain entry.

It is most likely that in 1914 Reilly's plan was to go to New
York to make as much money as he could from war contracts while
the conflict lasted. Britain was not alone in thinking the war would
be 'over by Christmas', and he no doubt wanted to make his mark
before it ended. It is equally likely that most of his possessions and
valuables remained behind in St Petersburg pending his return.
The abdication of the Tsar in March 1917 would not have
particularly unnerved him for the Provisional Government was
resolved to continue the war against Germany as an ally of France
and Britain, and many assumed that the Tsar's overthrow would
actually restore Russia's fortunes on the battlefield. Furthermore,
the Provisional Government's assumption of power would not
have had any adverse effects on his ability to re-enter the country
or to retrieve money or property lodged there. The threat of a
Bolshevik seizure of power was something entirely different. If
successful, there was a strong possibility that they would seal off
the country to foreigners, and there was no telling what might
happen in such revolutionary upheaval to any valuables he had
secreted away.

If he actually had a wife and children in Petrograd, as
Rodkinson alleged, he may well have wanted to get out to them
now that they were effectively trapped. In support of this theory
it should be noted that when, in November 1911, Reilly had
briefly been under surveillance from Russian counter-
intelligence, letters addressed to him had been intercepted from
his 'wife'. She was referred to in the surveillance report as, 'the
daughter of a Russian general living abroad'.[18] This wife could not
be Margaret, who, although living abroad, was not the daughter of
a Russian general. Neither could she be Nadine, the daughter
of a colonel, who in 1911 was living in St Petersburg with her
husband Petr at 2 Admiralty Quay, several blocks away from
Reilly's apartment at 22 Novo Isaakievskaya. As another intriguing

aside, the *Alphabetical Directory of the Inhabitants of the City of St Petersburg*, contains the name of one Anna Reile, who appears in the editions for 1913, 1914 and 1916.[19] In addition, it has already been noted in Chapter Three that on enlistment Reilly had to declare the name of the person to be informed in the event of him becoming a casualty of war. That person is recorded as 'Mrs A. Reilly of 120 Broadway, New York City'. The address was, of course, Reilly's office, then managed by two reliable associates, Dale Upton Thomas and Alexandre Weinstein. Nadine was then living outside New York and was well provided for by bank accounts he had set up before departing. If Mrs A. Reilly was Anna, the reason she was to be specially taken care of may well have been the children. While his motives for volunteering remain somewhat open to question, the months between his enlistment in Toronto and his return to Russia are vividly, and at times amusingly, recounted in the annals of SIS and MI5.

Thirteen days after the confirmation of his commission as a second lieutenant in the RFC, Reilly's name appears on a Canadian roster, dated 3 December 1917,[20] of officers who would shortly be posted overseas. In Reilly's case this meant England, where he arrived on a chilly New Year's Day and booked into suite 32 at the Savoy Hotel,[21] with lieutenants H.A. Kelly and M. Marks. After a week Kelly was posted to France and Marks to 39 Squadron in Shropshire. Reilly, though, ventured but a short distance to lodgings at 22 Ryder Street, St James.

On 13 January he met Maj. Scale, who had arrived in London from Petrograd on 9 January.[22] Scale briefed him on the formalities that must be dispensed with before his application could be taken further. These formalities clearly included the submission of testimonials and supporting documentation, for on 19 January he wrote to Col. Byron at the War Office, as directed by Scale:

Sir,

I have the honour to present:

1. A letter from Mr Owens-Thurston, a director of Vickers Ltd.

2. The original and translation of a certificate issued to me by the General Quarter Master of the Russian Army.

3. I have seen Gen. Germonius, chief of the Russian Mission and he will be pleased to reply to any enquiry made about me.

4. May I also refer you to Maj. J.F.G. Strubell RFC (Room 240, Air Board Offices, Hotel Cecil. Tel. Regent 8000, ext. 1240), who is the officer who recruited me for the RFC in Canada, and who could give full information about my circumstances and standing in New York.

Trusting that the above may be sufficient for the purpose you have in view.

I have the honour to be,

Sir

Your obedient servant

S.G. Reilly, 2/Lt RFC[23]

Attached, on Vickers headed notepaper, was the following testimonial:

To Whom it May Concern:

I have pleasure in stating that I have known Mr Sidney G. Reilly for thirteen years, and during that time I have had many opportunities of ascertaining his great abilities as a linguist. He was to my knowledge in Petrograd engaged in a great deal of Russian government business, and his knowledge of Russia always appeared to me to be extensive and accurate, and Russians of high official standing have testified to me as to the good work he did and his extensive knowledge of Russian affairs. I can only testify to his ability as a diplomatic businessman, whether the matter in hand is great or small, and during the thirteen years I have known Mr Reilly I have never heard anything disparaging to his character.

T.H. Owens-Thurston[24]

If Owens-Thurston had really never heard anything disparaging about Reilly he must have been one of the few who had not. On the other hand, the letter does dispel the view ventured by Richard Deacon that Reilly was the great adversary of Vickers. Whilst very much batting for Blohm & Voss, Reilly was careful to cultivate contacts and acquaintances wherever he could, particularly in rival firms such as Vickers.

The Russian military certificate Reilly enclosed was dated 8 August 1914 and issued by Maj.-Gen. Erdeli:

> By order of the Chief of Staff of the Army, I request that the bearers of the present: the British subject Sidney George Reilly and the Russian subject I.T. Giratovsky be given assistance for the purpose of expeditious and unhindered passage over the frontier.
>
> The above mentioned persons are commissioned by the Chief of the Artillery Department to acquire material and articles of armament for the needs of our Army.[25]

On 30 January SIS sent a standard enquiry form to MI5, with Reilly's the only name listed:

> Have you any objection to the following being employed by the Intelligence Department?
> Sidney G. Reilly, RFC Club, Bruton Street and 22 Ryder Street, St James.[26]

On 2 February MI5 likewise responded to SIS on their standard form of clearance:

> We have nothing recorded against the above. Nothing is known to the prejudice of any of the above by the police.[27]

There was one MI5 officer, however, who knew more than most about Reilly and would have been able to give chapter and verse about his mysterious background and clandestine activities – if only he had been able. Whether William Melville's insight would have prejudiced Reilly's application in any way was, by 2 February, of little or no consequence. Discharged from duty the previous September with kidney disease, Melville died in Bolingbroke Hospital, Battersea, on 1 February 1918,[28] the day before the MI5 memo giving Reilly the all-clear was sent to SIS.

By March 1918, MI5's investigation into Reilly's background was making little headway.

As a result, an appointment was made for Reilly to attend an interview with C on 15 March at SIS headquarters. While MI5 found nothing detrimental on Reilly, C clearly felt that he needed to know more about the mysterious Mr Reilly. On 28 February he sent a telegram to the SIS station in New York,[29] informing them of the task he had in mind for Reilly and asking for full particulars on his reputation and background. None of these enquiries would, of course, have been necessary if Reilly had been a known quantity.

At 10.00 a.m. on 4 March a cable was received at SIS Headquarters from Norman G. Thwaites (NG) in New York, replying to C's enquiry:

With reference to your telegram No. 206 of the 28th; SYDNEY REILLY is a British subject married to a RUSSIAN JEWESS who has made money since the beginning of the war through influence with corrupted members of the Russian purchasing commissions. He is believed to have been in PORT ARTHUR in 1903 as a spy for Japan. We kept him under observation in 1916. We consider him untrustworthy and unsuitable to work suggested.

NG[30]

Not to be deterred by this damning reply, C sent another telegram to New York the following day seeking further clarification. In the meantime, MI5 were also asked to keep a tab on Reilly pending the progress of his application. On 9 March they reported that despite placing him under surveillance for three days, 'nothing was discovered about his movements, owing to the fact that he usually moved about in taxis and it was nearly always impossible to get another cab'.[31] Conjuring up visions of a Keystone Cops chase, the 'tailers' were reduced to catching buses to the destinations Reilly was thought to be heading for – usually the Savoy Hotel. On one occasion they did actually manage to hail down a cab, only to be told by the driver that Reilly's cab had a more powerful engine and was not worth his while following!

The watch on his Ryder Street lodgings and interviews with others at the address led MI5 to report that he was 'very respectable,

SECRET

Information has been received from a reliable source that one, Sydney G. REILLY is reported to be one of a gang of confidence men of an international character. Believed to have been born in Russian Poland but claims to be a British Subject and his wife lives in United States. Working on war contracts in U.S. At time of war between Russia and Japan was spying for latter in Port Arthur. In December 1917 he joined the R.F.C. and was sent abroad in January 1918. He afterwards worked for the British Consul General at Moscow. May have consorted with suspected spies of names of Alexander (Weir?), Takeaway, Jahalsky, bears a very bad character. Said to be well off, banking with National Guarantee Trust. It is reported that he was held in suspicion by Major Thwaites in New York.

MI5 received a wealth of reports on Reilly's unsavoury past.

```
                  COPY.


Telephone Nos.                   St. James Palace Chambers.
                                     22 Ryder Street.
     Regent.1332                   St. James, S.W.
             1333

                                 19th Jan. 1918.



To Col. Byron, War Office
From 2/Lt. S.G. Reilly, R.F.C.

Sir,

            I have the honour to present,
(1) A letter from Mr. Owens-Thurston, a Director of Vickers, Ltd,
(2) The original and translation of a certificate issued to me
by the General Quarter Master of the Russian Army,
(3) I have seen Gen. Hermonias, Chief of the Russian Mission,
and he will be pleased to reply to any enquiry made about me.
(4) May I also refer you to Major J.F.G.          , R.F.C., (Room
240, Air Board Offices, Hotel Cecil. Tel: Regent 8000;Ext: 1240).
who is the officer who recruited me for the R.F.C. in Canada,
and who could give full information about my circumstances and
standing in New York.

            Trusting that the above may be sufficient for the purpose
you have in view,

            I have the honour to be,

                 Sir,

                 Your obedient Servant,

                       S.G. Reilly, 2/Lt.R.F.C.
```

When Reilly made an application to the War Office for intelligence work in January 1918, he was careful to submit glowing testimonials and references.

pays bills quite regularly, lunches and dines at the Savoy and Berkeley Hotels and is always in by midnight'.[32]

At 2.20 p.m. on 14 March, New York's reply to C's second cable was received at Whitehall Court:

Your telegram No. 210 of 5th:

Official of National Powder Bank has given us the following confidential statement on man in question whom he has known for several years: A shrewd businessman of undoubted ability but without patriotism or principles and therefore not to be recommended for any position which requires loyalty as he would not hesitate to use it to further his own commercial interests. He has been connected with Government contracts in RUSSIAN–JAPANESE and present wars and has undeniably excellent knowledge of those countries.

Above opinion precisely confirmed by our own estimate of man.

NG[33]

The following day, with no knowledge of the cables that had been criss-crossing the Atlantic on his behalf, Reilly presented himself at 2 Whitehall Court to keep his appointment with 'C'.[34] Meeting 'the Chief' was a formality that all potential agents had to undertake, and Reilly was no exception. Paul Dukes, a future friend and SIS colleague of Reilly, gave a rare and unique account of this no doubt awesome experience in his book, *Red Dusk and the Morrow*. On arrival at Whitehall Court, Dukes was met by a nameless colonel and escorted to C's office:

```
                          7th March, 1918.


     R E I L L Y,  2nd Lieut.


             In company with A.L.W., I kept observation
     on 22, Ryder Street commencing at 9.a.m.
     The above came out at 1.25.p.m. proceeded to a
     taxi in the centre of the road in St. James' Street,
     and disappeared in the direction of Pall Mall.
     Whilst I kept observation on this taxi, A.L.W.
     proceeded to one drawn up close to the curb higher
     up the Street.  The driver informed A.L.W., that
     as his was only a two cylinder and the one REILLY
     was in was a four cylinder it was useless for
     him to try and catch him.   We took up observation
     again on 22, RYDER STREET,  REILLY returned at
     3.40.p.m. and as he did not reappear by 8.15.p.m.
     the observation was withdrawn.


     P.                                        P.A.W.
```

MI5's surveillance of Reilly proved no easy task.

We entered the building and the lift whisked us up to the top floor. Leaving the lift my guide led me up one flight of steps so narrow a corpulent man would have stuck tight, round unexpected corners, and again up a flight of steps.

'The sanctum of the Chief' was 'a low dark chamber at the extreme top of the building'. The colonel knocked, entered, and stood at attention. A nervous Dukes followed. He recalled:

The writing desk was so placed with the window behind it that on entering everything appeared only in silhouette. It was some seconds before I could distinguish things. A row of half a dozen extending telephones stood at the left of a big desk littered with papers. On a side table were numerous maps and drawings, with models of aeroplanes, submarines and mechanised devices, while a row of bottles of various colours and a distilling outfit with a rack of test tubes bore witness to chemical experiments and operations. These evidences of scientific investigation only served to intensify an already overpowering atmosphere of strangeness and mystery. But it was not these things that engaged my attention as I stood nervously waiting. My eyes fixed themselves on the figure at the writing table. This extraordinary man was short of stature, thick set, with grey hair covering a well-rounded head. His mouth was stern, an eagle eye, full of vivacity, glanced – or glared, as the case might be – piercingly through a gold-rimmed monocle. The coat that hung over the back of the chair was that of a naval officer.[35]

Quite what impression C, Mansfield Cumming, made on Reilly is unknown. Cumming himself briefly recorded his impressions of Reilly in his diary for 15 March:

Scale introduced Mr Reilly who is willing to go to Russia for us. Very clever – very doubtful – has been everywhere and done everything. Will take out £500 in notes and £750 in diamonds which are at a premium. I must agree tho' it is a great gamble as he will visit all our men in Vologda, Kief, Moscow etc.[36]

The impression that Reilly was 'very doubtful' could only have been reinforced by the arrival of the final cable from New York at 2.25 p.m. on 21 March:

> Further my telegram No. 201 of 13th:
> MACROBERTS reports he likes Reilly personally but knows little of him. Another official of the bank gives me the following information from a man who has known REILLY for years: R is GREEK Jew: very clever: entirely unscrupulous. Present war has made about two million dollars on Russian contracts. Has connections in almost every country including Germany, Japan and Russia. ENDS. In connection with the above may I point out that there must be a strong motive for REILLY leaving profitable business here and wife of whom he is said to be very jealous, to work for you.
> NG[37]

C had a reputation as a risk taker who was willing to go against the grain. There could be no greater demonstration of this than his decision to give Reilly a chance in spite of the volumes of negative feedback he had so far received. The risk, in C's mind, must have been far outweighed by the vital operational need for reliable Russian intelligence. Negotiations between the Bolsheviks and the Germans had been taking place at Brest Litovsk, on and off, since 22 December 1917, and it was becoming increasingly apparent that matters were now coming to a head. While C was still exchanging cables with New York, the two sides finally signed the Treaty of Brest Litovsk on 3 March. It was a bitter pill for the Russians to swallow, involving a great loss of land and swingeing reparation payments. Lenin, however, was determined to pull out of the war, as he knew his infant regime's survival depended upon it. For the Germans it meant they could now throw their full weight against the Allies on the Western Front.

The War Cabinet in London, and the Allies collectively, now had two potential choices; they could either make a renewed attempt to entice the Bolsheviks back into the war against

Germany, or they could intervene in Russia in the hope that the Bolsheviks could be toppled in favour of a pro-war government. Either way, the need for good intelligence sources in Russia was now more important than ever.

On 22 March, the day after the final cable from 'NG' was received, C and SIS colleague Col. Claude Dansey visited a diamond dealer in the City of London by the name of Schuyler and purchased diamonds to the value of £750[38] for Reilly to take to Moscow.

That same day MI5 were beginning what they thought would be a routine enquiry to confirm the biographical details Reilly had given on his application. Their memorandum, under Reilly's name, addressed to the headquarters of Irish Command at Parkgate, Dublin, states:

> We should be glad to know if a man of the above name is registered as having been born at Clonmel on 24 March 1874, and any partic-ulars you can let us have concerning his parents. Will you kindly let us have an answer as soon as possible, as the matter is urgent.[39]

By 30 March, with no sign of a reply, MI5 sent a reminder memo. This clearly did the trick, for the following day Irish Command responded:

> Reference your 267275/D of 22 and 30 March, the Police Department report that there is no record in the register of this man's birth in Clonmel. Further enquiries are being made.
> (for) Major I.H. Price[40]

It was a further three days before MI5 alerted Maj. Kendall of SIS to the fact that C's new agent was not all that he claimed. By this point, the die had already been cast, for Reilly, or ST1[41] as he was now code-named, was aboard the Danish Merchant ship *Queen Mary*, steaming towards the Russian port of Archangel.

NINE

THE REILLY PLOT

Four days after his departure, C sent a cable to the British mission in Vologda, alerting them of Reilly's arrival:

> On 25 March, Sydney George Reilli, lieutenant in the RFC, leaves for Archangel from England. Jewish-Jap type, brown eyes very protruding, deeply lined sallow face, may be bearded, height five foot nine inches. He will report during April. Carries code message of identification. On arrival will go to Consul and ask for British passport officer. Ask him what his business is and he will answer 'Diamond Buying'. He has sixteen diamonds value £640 7s 2d as most useful currency. Should you be short of funds he has orders to divide with you. He will be at your disposal, utilise him to join up your organisation if necessary as he should travel freely. Return him to Stockholm end of June. More to follow.[1]

Instead of following orders and disembarking at Archangel, Reilly left the ship at Murmansk. The port itself was in the hands of a company of British marines, who had been sent in on 6 March to guard Allied war materials thought to be at risk since the Bolshevik's treaty with Germany. On leaving the merchant ship *Queen Mary*, Reilly was stopped for a routine inspection of documents and promptly arrested. He was confined aboard HMS *Glory*, where Maj.

Stephen Alley of SIS, who was on his way back to London, was summoned by Admiral Kemp to examine him. 'His passport was very doubtful, and his name was spelt REILLI. This, together with the fact that he was obviously not an Irishman, caused his arrest', said Alley.[2]

Within days of his interview with C, Reilly had made contact with Litvinov, the Russian Plenipotentiary, who had a small office at 82 Victoria Street, Westminster. Making an appointment to see Litvinov proved easier said than done. After two unsuccessful attempts, Reilly's third telegram finally managed to secure an interview on 23 March:

> Regret not having heard from you in reply to my second wire. Will you kindly wire me when and where I can see you tomorrow Saturday morning. I shall wait for your telephone message to Regent 1332 from eight till ten thirty o'clock tomorrow morning.[3]

As a result of the meeting, Reilly, or rather 'Sidney George Reilli', was issued with travel documents that permitted him to enter Soviet territory. Whether Litvinov had misspelled the name or whether this was the name by which Reilly identified himself to Litvinov is open to question.[4] A list of persons who had been issued with visas by Litvinov would certainly have been sent back to Russia on a regular basis, and Reilly may not have wished to encourage any comparison between himself and the Reilly of St Petersburg who had had such close connections with the Tsarist regime.

As soon as Alley appeared, Reilly produced a microscopic coded message from under the cork of a bottle of aspirins. Alley immediately recognised this as an SIS code and Reilly was quickly released.[5] Interestingly, Cumming's telegram also reveals that it was originally intended that Reilly would return in late June, as indeed Beatrice Tremaine had told US investigators he would.[6]

The reason Reilly was sent to Archangel seems quite clear, in that from there he could catch an express train directly to Moscow via Vologda. It seems equally apparent that he never had any intention of going straight to Moscow as ordered. One possible reason for leaving the ship at Murmansk might have been the fact that he could get a direct rail connection to Petrograd from there, which he could not have done had he gone on to Archangel.

As it turned out, he spent the best part of four weeks in Petrograd before finally journeying to Moscow. If the purpose of his return to Russia had some connection with the family referred to by Norbert Rodkinson, or to possessions of his located somewhere in the city, this could well explain the delay.[7] Whatever it was that was occupying him in Petrograd, he found the time to send C a detailed report on 16 April, outlining his own home-grown solutions to the situation he found himself in the midst of:

> Every source of information leads to definite conclusions that today BOLSHEVIKS only real power in RUSSIA. At the same time opposition in country constantly growing and if suitably supported will finally lead to overthrow of BOLSHEVIKS. Our action must therefore be in two parallel directions. Firstly with the BOLSHEVIKS for accomplishment of immediate practical objects; secondly with the opposition for gradual re-establishment of order and national defence.
>
> Immediate definite aims are safeguarding MURMAN; securing ARCHANGEL; evacuation of enormous quantities of metals, ammunition and artillery from PETROGRAD which liable to fall to Germans within month; preventing Baltic Fleet from passing to Germans by their destruction or rendering it unserviceable; and possibly substitution of moratorium for final repudiation of foreign loans. All above objects can be accomplished only by immediate agreement with BOLSHEVIKS. For minor ones, such as MURMAN-ARCHANGEL a sort of semi-acknowledgement of their Government, better treatment of their ambassadors in Allied countries may be sufficient.[8]

Building up to the point of his communication, Reilly states that the most potent factor in the equation is money. Only hard cash could effectively deliver all the other objects. Attributing German successes to their preparedness to use money, he coolly proposes to C that:

...this may mean an expenditure of possibly one million pounds and part of this may have to be expended without any real guarantee of ultimate success. Work must be commenced in this direction immediately and it is possibly already too late. If outlined policy should be agreed to, you must be prepared to meet obligations at any moment and at shortest notice. As regards opposition, imminent question is whether support to them comes from the Germans or from us.[9]

Almost without batting an eyelid and with ten out of ten for sheer audacity, Reilly was effectively asking for at least one million pounds in cash, to be sent to him personally, post haste, without any guarantee that such action would actually achieve its objective. Needless to say, the canny C was having none it. Although Reilly was to be entrusted with funds later on, they were for specifically targeted objectives and certainly not in the region of the sums that Reilly was asking for here. What would have happened to the £1 million had C been gullible enough to agree is best left to the imagination.

In almost prophetic terms, Reilly concludes his report by saying that, 'in any case, we have arrived at critical moment when we must either act or immediately and effectively abandon entire position for good and all'. As it would turn out, he took his own advice too literally.

On 7 May he arrived in Moscow in full dress uniform and headed immediately for the Kremlin. On reaching the main gates he informed the sentries that he was an emissary from the British Prime Minister, David Lloyd George, and demanded to see Lenin personally. Remarkably he was actually admitted, although he got no further than Lenin's aide Vladimir Bonch Bruevich. Reilly explained that he had been sent to the Kremlin as the Prime Minister wanted first-hand news concerning the aims and objectives of the Bolshevik government. He also claimed that the British government was dissatisfied with the reports that he had been receiving from Robert Bruce Lockhart, the head of the British Mission in Moscow, and had instructed him with making good this defect. It would seem that Reilly's interview was a very brief

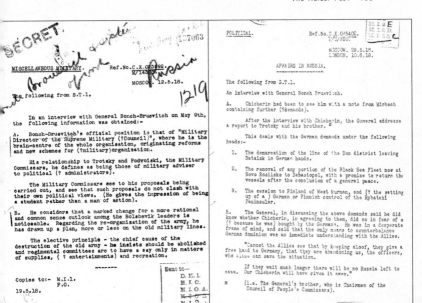

Two of Reilly's 'top secret' reports from Moscow, commenting on Russia's intentions towards Germany.

one. At 6 p.m. Robert Bruce Lockhart received a telephone call asking him to come over to the Kremlin.[10] On arrival he was asked if a man called 'Relli' was really a British officer or an impostor. Lockhart was incredulous when told the story of Relli's visit that afternoon. He had never heard the name Relli, and diplomatically said that he would need to look into the matter and get back in due course.

On leaving the Kremlin Lockhart immediately sent for Ernest Boyce, the head of SIS in Moscow, and angrily demanded an explanation.[11] Boyce confirmed that Reilly was a new agent sent out from London, but had no knowledge of his dramatic debut at the Kremlin. Boyce said he would send Reilly to Lockhart the following day to offer a personal explanation. Unsurprisingly, Reilly denied everything apart from the fact that he had been at the Kremlin on the afternoon of the seventh. Lockhart did not believe a word of Reilly's account but said many years later that his excuses were so ingenious that he had ended up laughing. It is unlikely that Reilly took any great heed of Lockhart's threat to have him sent home and merrily carried on going his own way. It is also clear from this event that Lockhart had not had sight of Cumming's telegram and was essentially in the dark about what was going on in London. Although Reilly's story was a bold bluff, he was actually correct about London's view of Lockhart, who the Foreign Office considered was providing inconsistent and ill-judged advice.[12]

While the story of Reilly marching up to the Kremlin gates is vividly recited by several Reilly biographers,[13] the impression given is that this was his first and last attempt to deal directly with the Bolshevik authorities before going underground. A series of telegrams to London marked 'Secret' tell a very different story, however. They reveal that the day after his dressing down by Lockhart, he was, in fact, back at the Kremlin for what turned out to be one of several in-depth meetings with Vladimir Bonch Bruevich's brother, Gen. Mikhail Bonch Bruevich. In a report headed 'Miscellaneous Military', Reilly referred in particular to two aspects of the meeting which had taken place on 9 May:

A. Bonch Bruevich's official position is that of 'Military Director of the Supreme Military (?Council)', where he is the brain centre of the whole organisation, originating reforms and new schemes for (?military) organisation.

His relationship to Trotsky and Podvoiski, the Military Commissars, he defines as being those of military adviser to political (?administrator).

The Military Commissars see to his proposals being carried out, and see that such proposals do not clash with their own political views. (He gives the impression of being a student rather than a man of action.)

B. He considers that a marked change for a more rational and common sense outlook among Bolshevik leaders is noticeable. Regarding the reorganisation of the army, he has drawn up a plan, more or less on the old military lines.

The elective principle – the chief cause of the destruction of the old army – he insists should be abolished and regimental committees are to have a say only in matters of supplies, (?entertainments) and recreation.[14]

1 The London & Paris Hotel in Newhaven, the scene of Hugh Thomas's murder in March 1898.

2 Rosenblum family portraits, most likely taken at various times during the 1880s (Grigory, Paulina, Elena and Marie).

3 Boris Rosenblum as a teenager.

4 Salomon Rosenblum as a teenager.

5 Ethel Voynich, writer of the Victorian classic
The Gadfly.

6 Sigmund Rosenblum *c.*1899.

7 Upper Westbourne Terrace, Paddington, in around the late 1890s, home to both Hugh Thomas and then Reilly (No. 6 is third on the right).

8 The offices of Ginsburg & Company in Port Arthur where Reilly based his activities. The picture was taken during the siege of Port Arthur shortly after it had been hit by a Japanese shell.

9 The foot of the grand staircase at the Hotel Cecil, the very spot where Louisa Lewis was last seen before her disappearance, talking to a man fitting Reilly's description.

10 97 Fleet Street, London; Reilly's patent medicine company operated on the first floor between 1908 and 1910.

11 Col. Petr Massino, Nadezhda's father, at the time of his court martial.

12 Nadine Massino married Reilly at St Nicholas' Cathedral, New York City, on 15 February 1916, blissfully unaware that he already had two other wives.

13 Reilly among a group of aviators and businessmen at the 1911 St Petersburg Flying Week (standing, left to right: Dyatlinov, Rayevsky, Reilly, Smith; sitting, left to right: Kuzminsky, Yefimov, Vasilyev, Volkov and Lebedev).

14 *Left*: Reilly in the uniform of an RAF Lieutenant, painted in around 1919. Contrary to his own account, he saw no active service whatsoever during the First World War.

15 *Below left*: Sidney Reilly, alias Konstantin Massino, 1918.

16 *Below right*: Major J.D. Scale, code name STO, who recruited Reilly to the Secret Intelligence Service in March 1918.

17 Mansfield Cumming, alias C, the head of the Secret Intelligence Service 1909–1923, portrait by SIS officer H.F. Crowther Smith 1918.

18 'Captain Reilly dares the Red Terror'. From the *Evening Standard*'s 'Master Spy' serial, 17 May 1931.

19 Reilly, disguised as a member of the Cheka, bluffs his way through a Red Army checkpoint. From the *Evening Standard*'s 'Master Spy' serial, 15 May 1931.

20 Reilly hides under a railway carriage as Red Army guards make their way down the station platform examining identity passes. From the *Evening Standard*'s 'Master Spy' serial, 14 May 1931.

21 *Top left*: Elizaveta Otten, Reilly's mistress, was arrested by the Cheka in a dawn raid on her flat, following the failure of the plot to overthrow Lenin.

22 *Top right*: Capt. George Hill aided Reilly's escape from Russia by providing him with a passport in the name of George Bergmann, a German art dealer.

23 *Bottom right*: Photograph from the German passport of George Bergmann (AKA Sidney Reilly), September 1918.

24 *Top left*: Caryll Houselander, nearly thirty years his junior, met Reilly through their mutual interest in art. Within months of their first meeting she became his mistress.

25 *Above*: Nelly Burton (Pepita Bobadilla) performing in the show *Houp-La*, 1916.

26 *Left*: Under the name Cita Bobadilla, Pepita's sister Alice Menzies made an unsuccessful attempt to follow her sister onto the stage.

27 Sidney and Pepita Reilly at their Savoy Hotel wedding reception, 18 May 1923. The bride was unaware that Reilly had just committed bigamy for the third time.

28 Adelphi Terrace, Reilly's London home at the time of his bigamous marriage to Pepita Bobadilla (No. 5 is situated mid-terrace).

29 One of the last photographs ever taken of Reilly, found in his OGPU File.

30 A none too flattering picture of Reilly from 1924, later used by Pepita in the ghostwritten book *Britain's Master Spy*, withdrawn from sale in Britain after the threat of legal action.

31 Another picture from the OGPU's comprehensive file on Reilly and his mysterious past.

32 OGPU temptress Maria Shultz was instrumental in luring Reilly to his fate.

33 Artur Artuzov, Head of KRO and the mastermind behind Operation Trust which ensnared Sidney Reilly in September 1925.

34 On first meeting Reilly, OGPU undercover agent Alexander Yakushev was struck by his bulging eyes, which he described as 'biting and cruel'.

35 'Dear Ernest, best wishes from beautiful Moscow' – minutes after Reilly posted this card, handcuffs were snapped on his wrists and he was taken under close arrest to the dreaded Lubyanka.

36 The transcript of Reilly's interogation carried out by Vladimir Styrne, deputy head of KRO, the OGPU's counter-intelligence division.

37 The dacha at Malakhovka where Reilly met the Trust's leaders and outlined his plan to rob Russian museums of their art treasures.

38 Vladimir Styrne, Reilly's interogator, reminded him that he was already under sentence of death.

39 George Syroezhkin, the OGPU agent who fired the final and fatal shot into Reilly's chest.

40 Boris Gudz joined the OGPU as a twenty-year-old. Now aged 101, he is the only person alive who took part in Operation Trust.

41 Grigory Feduleev, the OGPU officer who supervised Reilly's execution on 5 November 1925.

42 Sidney Reilly was shot dead by OGPU officers some thirty paces from this spot in Sokolniki Park, Moscow.

43 Reilly's final resting place – a burial pit situated in the Lubyanka's Inner Yard.

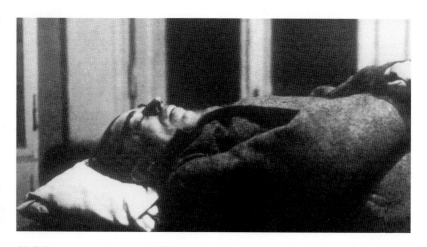

44 Reilly's corpse was taken to the OGPU Medical Unit, where it was laid out to be photographed on the night of 5 November 1925.

Despite the Brest-Litovsk Treaty, the report clearly confirms that all was not well between the Bolsheviks and the Germans. This is further amplified by Reilly's report of 29 May in which he relates details of a meeting between Bonch Bruevich and Georgi Chicherin, the People's Commissar for Foreign Affairs, at which new demands made by the German Ambassador Count Mirbach were discussed. The Germans wanted, in particular, three things:

1. The demarcation of the line of the Don district leaving Bataisk in German hands.

2. The removal of any portion of the Black Sea Fleet at Novo Rosiisko to Sebastopol, with the promise to return the vessels after the conclusion of a general peace.

3. The cession to Finland of West Murman, and German/Finnish control of the Rybatchi Peninsula.[15]

Bonch Bruevich was very much opposed to the proposals Chicherin had already conceded, and apparently told Reilly that he did not know whether Chicherin, 'in agreeing to them, did so in fear of or because he was bought by the Germans'.[16] Bonch Bruevich concluded that the only way to counter-balance the Germans was for an immediate understanding with the Allies. Reilly quotes him as exclaiming, 'cannot the Allies see that by keeping aloof, they give a free hand to Germany... if they wait much longer there will be no Russia to save. Our Chicherin will have given it away'.

By the time Reilly met with Bonch Bruevich again on 31 May, the Bolsheviks had formulated some response to the situation. In particular, Reilly refers to a decision that has been made to 'issue a proclamation to the people calling for a massed rising against the Germans'. The chief points of the proclamation are reported to be that:

1. Every German crossing the frontier is liable to be shot.

2. Population of localities invaded by the Germans must conceal or destroy all food stuffs, metal etc., break up roads, blow up bridges etc.

Reilly claims Bonch Bruevich asked him for his own views as to other steps that could be taken, to which he proposed 'a circular telegram to be sent to military directors in the provinces ordering them to mobilise their resources and prepare troops and population for struggle with Germany'. Bonch Bruevich then, according to the report, telephoned Trotsky in Reilly's presence and read him the proposals, which were apparently approved on the spot. Bonch Bruevich told Reilly that, 'the time was fast approaching when the Commissars would begin to realise that that the only safeguard for the Soviet government was open war with Germany'.[17]

Whatever the perceived direction of Bolshevik policy towards Germany was, Reilly himself seems to have already taken the view that the regime was vulnerable from within and no doubt saw opportunities for himself in such a situation. Without any official guidance or instructions on the matter, he promptly shed the identity of Lt Reilli of the RFC, and went underground, simultaneously adopting two new guises. In Moscow he became Mr Constantine, a Greek businessman, living at 3 Sheremet'evsky Lane, where he shared the apartment of actress Dagmara Karozus.[18] Contrary to the views expressed by Robin Bruce Lockhart and Edward Van Der Rhoer (who refers to her as Dagmara Otten), it was not with her that Reilly formed a romantic attachment, but her flatmate Elizaveta Emilyevna Otten.

Elizaveta was a twenty-two-year-old blonde with a lifelong ambition to be an actress. However, her father, a manager at the tea company Gubin & Kuznetsov, had forbidden it and encouraged her to consider becoming a mathematician instead. He died just as she was about to leave school, and she therefore entered the First Arts Theatre Studio unhindered, making her acting debut in the play *A Green Ring* in December 1916. Apart from her obvious beauty, she could also speak English, German and French, making her ideal for the type of work Reilly had in mind.[19] According to Elizaveta's later testimony, he moved into the apartment in late June and left on 7 August.[20]

In Petrograd he became Konstantin Markovich Massino, a Turkish merchant, sharing an apartment with Elena Mikhailovna Boyuzhovskaya, a pre-war acquaintance, at 10 Torgovaya Street. Reilly had also used another old contact, the former judge Vladimir Orlov,[21] to obtain identity papers in the name of Sigmund Rellinsky, which identified him as a member of the Cheka's criminal investigation department. (The Cheka was the secret police organisation created, on the orders of Lenin, by Felix Dzerzhinsky in December 1917. 'Cheka' stood for the All Russian Extraordinary Commission for Combating Counter Revolution and Sabotage, and later became the KGB.) The stage was now set for a plot that Reilly may well have been planning for some time.

The so-called 'Lockhart Plot', or to be more accurate the Reilly Plot, has raised much controversy over the years. Did the Allied powers really hatch a plot to overthrow the Bolsheviks? If so, was it really the case that the Cheka discovered the conspiracy at the eleventh hour or had they penetrated it from the very outset? Some have even suggested a development of this theory, namely that the Cheka had stage managed the whole thing from beginning to end, and that Reilly was really a Bolshevik *agent provocateur.*[22]

From mid-May Lockhart had convened several meetings with Boris Savinkov's Union for the Defence of the Fatherland and Freedom (UDFF) organisation. Savinkov, a Social Revolutionary, had been War Minister in the Provisional Government, and was now one of the Bolsheviks' most vociferous opponents. A former member of the Social Revolutionary Party, he had now formed his own underground movement, the UDFF, for which he claimed a fighting force of some 2,000 men. In July, Lockhart was reporting on contacts with an anti-Bolshevik group called 'the Centre', who had links with both Savinkov and the Volunteer Army of Gen. A.V. Alekseev in the south of Russia. Lockhart followed up these contacts with large sums of money and became more deeply involved in fermenting and encouraging anti-Bolshevik groups. Contacts were also being developed with Fernand Grenard, the French Consul General, De Witt

C. Poole, the US Consul General, and their respective intelligence functionaries, Col. Henri de Vertement and Xenophon Kalamatiano.

In June two Chekists by the names of Jan Buikis and Jan Sprogis, both ex-Latvian army officers, began the process of infiltrating themselves into opposition circles in Petrograd. Posing as disaffected Letts, it did not take long for them to come across Capt. Cromie, the British Naval Attaché and 'Mr Constantine'. As a result of this positive development and the possibility that the Lett Regiments might be open to revolting against the Bolsheviks, Reilly arranged for Schmidkhen and Bredis to meet Lockhart at the British Mission in Moscow in August. The Letts were seen as the Bolsheviks' praetorian guard and were entrusted with the security of the Kremlin and other centres of government. It could now be argued that Lockhart was thus entering realms for which he had little if any official clearance. If this were so, then Reilly, who had already gone well beyond his brief, was now, in effect, seeking to trump Lockhart by planning a coup d'état.

His longstanding idolisation of Napoleon and his borderline megalomania had convinced him that the time was now ripe for a strong man to emerge, just as it had been for Napoleon Bonaparte a little over a century before. It is doubtful whether C had ever intended Reilly to become directly involved in any covert actions against the Bolshevik regime, let alone in actually taking the initiative and attempting to install a new regime into power! Reilly had already begun the process of drawing up a list of 'shadow ministers' who would be ready at a moment's notice to assume responsibility for their portfolios on the fall of the Bolshevik government. Among those on Reilly's list was Gen. Nikolai Yudenich, who was to be Minister of War, and several old cronies such as: Alexander Grammatikov, Internal Affairs; Vladimir Orlov, Minister of Justice; and Vladimir Shubersky, Minister of Communications.

On 4 July Reilly attended the meeting of the 5th Congress of Soviets at the Bolshoi Theatre, along with Robert Bruce Lockhart and other Allied representatives. It was during a break from the proceedings that he first noticed Olga Dmitrievna Starzhevskaya in the theatre lobby. Olga was an attractive twenty-five-year-old typist who worked for the VTsIK (Vserossyiskiy Tsentralniy Ispolnitelniy Komitet – the All Russia Central Executive Committee). According to Edward Van Der Rhoer, Reilly introduced himself to her as Konstantin Georgievich Rellinsky of the People's Commissariat for Foreign Affairs and brought her a glass of Georgian champagne.[23] Her own recollections of the meeting are somewhat different in that she knew him as Konstantin Markovich Massino who worked for an unspecified Soviet organisation. An affair began shortly after their first meeting, and 'Massino' gave her 20,000 roubles to buy an apart-ment and furniture and they began living together there.[24] The third day of the Congress also marked the outbreak of a brief rebellion by the left wing of the Social-Revolutionary Party, who assassinated the German Ambassador, Count Wilhelm von Mirbach, in the hope of sabotaging the Treaty of Brest-Litovsk. The Letts were sent in to crush the revolt and cordoned off the Bolshoi Theatre, the Kremlin and other important locations. Fearing a search, Reilly apparently tore up several compromising documents he had in his possession and swallowed them. No search, however, took place and he was eventually able to leave the building unhindered.

While his plans for a coup were taking shape, an Allied force had landed at Archangel on 4 August. Its objectives were not to actually lock horns with the Bolsheviks, but to prevent the Germans from obtaining unused Allied military supplies that were stored in the area. Besides, this token force of 5,000 men was far too small to actually take offensive action. When the Bolsheviks learned the true size of the force they must have breathed a huge sigh of relief. This did not, however, stop them from raiding and closing the British and French diplomatic missions on 5 August as an act of retaliation.

This would mean that the meeting which Reilly arranged between the Letts and Lockhart at the British Mission must have taken place during the first four days of August, as the mission was closed after the Cheka raid on 5 August. Lockhart, although sceptical, was certainly intrigued by this development and asked to be introduced to a Latvian commander. The Cheka therefore arranged for Lt-Col. E.P. Berzin, the commander of the Special Light Artillery, who guarded the Kremlin, to make contact with Lockhart. Berzin was not a Chekist, but was known to be a loyal supporter of the Bolsheviks.

Buikis, Sprogis and Berzin therefore presented themselves at Lockhart's apartment at the Hotel Elite on 14 August.[25] Lockhart, still somewhat unsure about becoming involved in a Lettish rebellion, discussed his meeting with the French and American Consuls later that day. The following day he met Berzin again, only this time 'Mr Constantine' and the French Consul, Grenard, were in attendance. It was at this meeting that the fateful decision was made to entrust all further liaison with Berzin to 'Mr Constantine'. This effectively meant that Reilly was now in the driving seat of the plot. Berzin raised the matter of other Lettish regiments, who he believed could be recruited to assist the Allies in liberating Latvia. This, he estimated would cost something in the region of 4 million roubles. Lockhart and his colleagues promised to consider this.[26]

On 17 August[27] the first of several meetings between Reilly and Col. Berzin took place. Reilly informed Berzin that the requested funding had been approved and would be paid to him in several instalments, the first being 700,000 roubles which Reilly handed over there and then. Reilly then proposed something that had never been raised before by Allied representatives. Why, he asked, could there not be a Lettish rebellion staged in Moscow to coincide with further Allied intervention? Achieving his own ends by exploiting his role as an intermediary was a tactic Reilly had used successfully time and again in business.[28]

According to Lockhart, Reilly reported that his negotiations with the Letts were going smoothly, and suggested that he might be able, with the Letts, to stage a counter-revolution in Moscow. Lockhart, in his book, *Memoirs of a British Agent*, states that he consulted Gen. Lavergne and the French Consul Grenard, which resulted in Reilly being told in no uncertain terms to have nothing to do with 'so dangerous and doubtful a move'.[29] A detailed memorandum written to Foreign Secretary Balfour on 5 November 1918,[30] seeking to set the record straight on the 'alleged Allied conspiracy against the Soviet Government', however, makes no reference to so instructing Reilly. In this version, Reilly is merely told that, 'there was nothing to be gained by such action', which could hardly be described in anyone's language as a veto.

At this point Reilly promptly disappeared, not to be seen again by Lockhart until they met up again in England some months later. Liaising with Capt. George Hill, another British intelligence operative who was also working underground,[31] a series of meetings was held between Reilly and Berzin, at which two further instalments of 200,000 and 300,000 roubles were handed over. It was also agreed that the coup itself would be staged on 6 September during a joint meeting of the Executive Council of the Sovnarkom (Council of People's Commissars) and the Moscow Soviet at the Bolshoi Theatre. Reilly's plan was that Lenin and Trotsky would be humiliated rather than shot, by being led through the streets without their trousers. In a further example of Cheka provocation, Berzin now proposed that both Lenin and Trotsky should be shot. Although Reilly objected to this on the grounds that it would make martyrs of them, official Soviet accounts of the 'Lockhart Plot' have asserted that Reilly's plan was indeed to have them shot immediately on arrest.[32]

On 25 August, the French journalist René Marchand accompanied the French Consul Grenard to a meeting at the US Consulate. The meeting had been convened by Consuls Poole and Grenard to bring together their respective intelligence contacts – Reilly, Kalamatiano and de Vertement. Marchand, who was later exposed as a Bolshevik sympathiser, passed on an account of what he had heard to the Cheka. To preserve Marchand's cover it was suggested to him by Dzerzhinsky that he write a letter to French President Raymond Poincare, describing the conspiratorial discussions he had witnessed. Before this could be posted, the

Cheka would search his room and find the letter. This discovery would then act as the pretext for uncovering the plot.

Matters were pre-empted in a dramatic and totally unforeseen way, when, on 30 August, Leonid Kannegiser, a Workers' Popular Socialist Party activist, shot dead Moisei Uritsky, head of the Petrograd Cheka. That same day, in a completely unconnected incident, Fanya Kaplan, a member of the Social Revolutionary Party, shot Lenin as he left a meeting at the Michelson factory in Moscow. Lenin survived, but only just. Of the two shots fired at point-blank range, one missed his heart by less than an inch and the other missed his jugular vein by a similar margin.

These unconnected events were now knitted together by the Cheka to implicate and link Bolshevism's many opponents into one giant conspiracy that warranted the unleashing of a full retaliatory response. The 'Red Terror', as it came to be known, resulted in over a thousand political opponents being summarily rounded up and shot. The Cheka raid on the British Embassy in Petrograd resulted in the death of Cromie, who apparently put up resistance. Using a list supplied by Berzin, the Cheka also rounded up those who were involved in the 'Lockhart Plot' and more besides. Lockhart was arrested, although later released in an exchange for Litvinov, who had been arrested in London in reprisal. Elizaveta Otten, Reilly's lover and chief courier, was also arrested, along with his other mistress Olga Starzheskaya. Maria Fride, one of Kalamatiano's couriers, was also arrested at Otten's flat with a set of papers she had brought for Reilly. Olga later related the story of her arrest in a petition to the Red Cross Committee for the Aid of Political Prisoners:

I was arrested at VTsIK where I had worked at the Administrational Section since May. A day before, at night, my flat was searched but nothing was confiscated, and nobody was arrested. The reason for my arrest is known to me and is as follows: my groom Konstantin Markovich Massino, who I deeply loved and intended to share my life with, proved to be Englishman Reilly, who participated in the

Anglo–French plot. Throughout our acquaintance he gave himself out for a Russian, and it was shortly before his disappearance that he told me who he really was. Until that moment I had no doubts he was Russian. I believed him and loved him, regarding him as an honest, noble, interesting and exclusively clever man, and in the deep of my heart I was very proud of his love. Therefore I was horrified by what I discovered about him during the interrogation. There proved to be two completely different persons. The deception, dirt and mean behaviour of this man pained me enormously. I have learnt about this ploy only from the papers. He never told me anything about it. Moreover, he seemed to me to be a supporter of Soviet power, though we never had any serious political discussions, as I was exclusively engaged in the settlement of my personal life, a new flat, household and work matters. My interest in politics was merely superficial. Throughout my stay in Moscow, and before that, I was never involved in any illegal organisations and made no statements against the existing order; moreover, I always supported Bolshevism and Communism as I understood it, and all those who knew me used to call me a Bolshevik.[33]

Elizaveta Otten also petitioned the committee:

I was arrested on 1 September for my acquaintance with British officer Sidney Reilly, who was involved in the Anglo–French plot. I had known Reilly over four months, as from the very beginning of our acquaintance he could bind me to himself. He never talked to me about his political motives, I only knew that he served at the British Legation. He shared a flat with us and when repression against the British officers began, he left us saying he would depart from Russia forever. Shortly before his leave he asked me to do him a favour and pass on to him any letters that may arrive at his former address while he was staying in Moscow. I promised to do that being unaware that these letters may have political meaning, otherwise I would not have agreed to do that, as I had never been involved in politics. At the interrogation I discovered that Reilly had been foully deceiving me for his own political purposes, taking advantage of my exclusively good

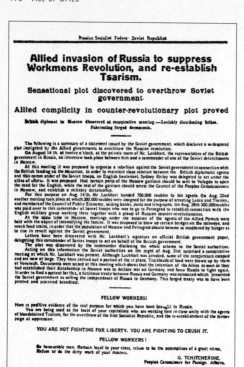

Russian Socialist Federal Soviet Republic

Allied invasion of Russia to suppress Workmens Revolution, and re-establish Tsarism.

Sensational plot discovered to overthrow Soviet government.

Allied complicity in counter-revolutionary plot proved

British diplomat in Moscow discovered at conspirative meeting.—Lavishly distributing bribes. Fabricating forged documents.

The following is a summary of a statement issued by the Soviet government, which discloses a widespread plot instigated by the Allied governments to overthrow the Russian revolution.

On August 14th, at twelve o'clock, at the private room of Mr. Lockhart, the representative of the British government in Russia, an interview took place between him and a commander of one of the Soviet detatchments in Moscow.

At this meeting it was proposed to organise a rebellion against the Soviet government in connection with the British landing on the Mourman. In order to maintain close relation between the British diplomatic agents and this comm ander of the Soviet troops, an English lieutenant, Sydney Riesley was delegated to act under the allias of «Rei». It was proposed that certain parts of the Moscow garrison should be sent to Vologda to open the road for the English, while the rest of the garrison should arrest the Council of the Peoples Commissioners in Moscow, and establish a military dictatorship.

For this purpose on Aug. 14th. Mr. Lockhart handed 700,000 roubles to his agents. On Aug. 22nd another meeting took place at which 200,000 roubles were assigned for the purpose of arresting Lenin and Trotsky, and members of the Council of Public Economy, seizing banks, posts and telegraphs. On Aug. 28th 300,000 roubles was paid over to this commander of Soviet troops who was to go to Petrograd to establish connection with the English military group working there together with a group of Russian counter-revolutionaries.

At the same time in Moscow, meetings under the auspices of the Allied Powers were held with the object of intensifying the famine. It was proposed to blow up certain bridges on the railways, and wreck food trains, in order that the population of Moscow and Petrograd should become so maddened by hunger as to rise in revolt against the Soviet government.

Letters have been discovered with Mr. Lockhart's signature on official British government paper, delegating this commander of Soviet troops to act on behalf of the British government.

The plot was discovered by the commander disclosing the whole scheme to the Soviet authorities.

Acting on this information the Soviet authorities on the night of Aug. 31st surprised a conspirative meeting at which Mr. Lockhart was present. Although Lockhart was arrested, some of the conspirators escaped and are now at large. They have carried out a portion of their plans. Trainloads of food were blown up by them at Voronezh. Documents were seized at this meeting which shows that the intention of the Allies as soon as they had established their dictatorship in Moscow was to declare war on Germany and force Russia to fight again. In order to find a pretext for this, a fictitious treaty between Russia and Germany was concocted which presented the Soviet government as selling the independance of Russia to Germany. This forged treaty was to have been printed and scattered broadcast.

FELLOW WORKERS!

Here is positive evidence of the real purpose for which you have been brought to Russia.

You are being used as the tools of your capitalists who are working here in close unity with the agents of bloodstained Tzarism, for the overthrow of the first Socialist Republic, and the re-establishment of the former reign of oppression.

YOU ARE NOT FIGHTING FOR LIBERTY. YOU ARE FIGHTING TO CRUSH IT.

FELLOW WORKERS !

Be honourable men. Remain loyal to your class, refuse to be the accomplices of a great crime, **Refuse** to do the dirty work of your masters.

G. TCHITCHERINE,
Peoples Commissary for Foreign Affairs.

A Russian propaganda leaflet issued to Allied troops in Murmansk, naming Reilly as a conspirator in the plot to 'overthrow the Russian Revolution'.

attitude to him, and by his seeming departure from Moscow he wanted to veil a change of his attitude towards me, intending to move to one divorced lady[34] he had promised to marry.[35]

Although both statements should be read with a pinch of salt in terms of their exaggerated naïvety concerning Reilly's actions, they do reflect the genuine shock both women felt on learning of his nefarious and duplicitous exploitation of them on a personal level.

On 3 September, details of the 'Lockhart Plot' were sensationally published in the Russian press.[36] Reilly was named as one of the principal plotters and a dragnet was put out for him. The Cheka raided his flat, but once again Reilly had, in the nick of time, vanished into thin air.

TEN

FOR DISTINGUISHED SERVICE

With Cheka raids taking place throughout Petrograd, Capt. George Hill sent Lockhart a message using SIS 'dictionary' code: 'I have', he reported, 'been over the network of our organisation and found everything intact'. 'There was undoubtedly a fair amount of nervousness among some of the agents', however.[1] Hill, under the impression that Reilly had been arrested by the Cheka, assured Lockhart that, 'I have got all of Lt Reilly's affairs under my control, and provided I can get money it would be possible to carry on'.[2] Lockhart was never to receive the message, for when Hill's courier arrived at Lockhart's flat, she found that it had shortly before been raided and Lockhart arrested. The message was therefore diverted to Lockhart's assistant, Capt. Will Hicks. Hicks replied that it was important to lie low for some days to come, and that to the best of his knowledge there would be no more money for Hill as the source for obtaining it had completely dried up. Hicks too was of the view that Reilly had been arrested, although he had no news to confirm this. On receipt, Hill sent a further message to Gen. Poole informing him of the day's events in Moscow.

At midday on 4 September, 'a girl of Lt Reilly's' brought Hill a message to say that he was safe in Moscow, having travelled by train in a first-class compartment from Petrograd. On arrival at the Nicolai Station in Moscow, he had been informed that his chief courier and mistress, Elizaveta Otten, had been arrested. Hill immediately went to see Reilly, who was now in hiding, occupying two rooms in a flat 'at the back end of town'.[3] When Hill arrived there he found that Reilly had changed his name but was not going out during the day or even at night, as he had no identity papers to match the new name he was using. Reilly wanted a passport, some new clothes and another place to stay, as his present abode was 'entirely unsuitable'.[4] Although Hill makes no direct reference to whose flat this was, the transcript of the so-called 'Lockhart Trials' reveals testimony by Olga Starzhevskaya, who states that Reilly stayed with her between 3 and 4 September, which coincides exactly with the two days he spent at 'the back end of town'.[5]

When Hill proposed that Reilly should make his escape by the safest route, heading westwards via the Ukraine, using a network of agents in that area for safe houses and assistance, Reilly refused. This route, he felt, would take far too long, and instead chose the more dangerous option of travelling north to Finland, from where he hoped to make his way to a neutral port. In the meantime, Hill moved Reilly to new accommodation the following day, 5 September. Intriguingly, although Hill was not specific as to the location, it would seem from his report that this was an office of some description.[6] His dramatised version of these events, published in 1932, however, gives a slightly different account. According to this, Hill lodged Reilly with a prostitute who 'was in the last stages of the disease which so often curses members of her profession'. Hill claimed that Reilly 'was the most fastidious of men and while being caught by the Bolsheviks had little terror for him, he could hardly bring himself to spend the night on the couch in her room'.[7] In another clue that suggests that he spent 3 and 4 September with Olga Starzhevskaya, Hill states that Reilly's change of apartment was a good thing, 'for the place where he had spent the previous night was raided by the Cheka the next evening'.[8] This would therefore be the night of 5 September, the

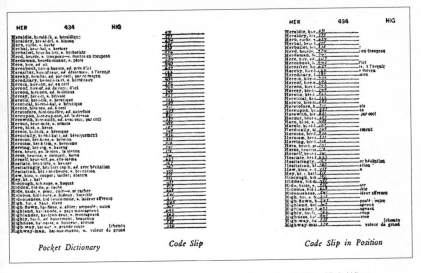

| Pocket Dictionary | Code Slip | Code Slip in Position |

The key to the SIS dictionary code used by Reilly and Hill to communicate with each other while in hiding.

date of Olga's arrest. That same evening six or seven of Hill's couriers were arrested and summarily executed by the Cheka.

As Hill was not suspected of involvement in the Lockhart Plot, Capt. Hicks decided that he should drop his cover of George Bergmann, resume the identity of Capt. George Hill, and leave Russia with the British Mission, who had been given clearance to leave by the Bolshevik authorities. This was most fortuitous for Reilly, for Hill was now able to give him the George Bergmann identity papers that would enable him to make his escape. According to Hill's report, Reilly left Moscow aboard a sleeper train bound for Petrograd on Sunday 8 September,[9] although Reilly's own recollection some seven years later was that the date was Wednesday 11 September.[10] Hill's account, being recorded at the time, is more likely to be the correct one. The date of his departure aside, the chronology of Reilly's recollections coincide pretty much with accounts given by other participants. Reilly's account states:

Having finished the liquidation of my affairs in Moscow, on 11 September, I departed for Petrograd in a railway car of the international society in a compartment reserved for the German Embassy, accompanied by one of their legation secretaries and using the passport of a Baltic German. I spent about ten days in Petrograd, hiding in various places, to liquidate my network there and also search for a way to cross the Finnish border – I wanted to escape to Finland. I was not able to do this, so I then decided to go through Revel [now Tallinn]. I departed Petrograd for Kronstadt, after receiving a 'Protection Certificate', which was issued to natives of the Baltic. I had, in addition to this document for exiting Petrograd for Kronstadt, a pass issued to one of the Petrograd workers committees in a Russian name. There was a launch with a Finnish captain already waiting for me at Kronstadt, on which I spent the night. I set off for Revel… In Revel I took up residence in the Hotel Petrograd using the name of George Bergmann, an antiquarian who had left Russia after a misunderstanding with the Soviet authorities… After ten days I departed secretly on the launch for Helsingfors, and from there to Stockholm and London, where I arrived on 8 November.[11]

Passing through Revel before crossing the Gulf of Finland to Helsingfors was not an option without risk, for Estonia was then under German occupation and the port was a major naval base teeming with officers and ratings of the German Baltic fleet. Fortunately, on disembarking, the Germans found 'Herr Bergmann's' identity papers to be in order and he was able to walk away unhindered. At the hotel in Harju Street he mixed freely with the German officers staying there and dined with them on several occasions, as well as with the captain and his wife.

It was probably with some relief on Reilly's part that the little boat eventually left Revel for Helsingfors a few days later. On arrival he bade the captain farewell and gave him a sealed, handwritten letter (in German):

I feel that after everything you have done for me, I must not leave you here clothed in all the lies I had to use, and that I owe it to you to say who I really am. I am neither Bergmann nor an art dealer. I am an English officer, Lt Sidney Reilly, RFC, and have been for about six months on a special mission in Russia, and have been accused by the Bolsheviks of being the military organiser of a great plot in Moscow... I believe it is not necessary to stress that I consider it my duty towards you not to interest myself in anything military here, and not to pump the officers who were introduced to me. I believe that I played the role of the art dealer Herr Bergmann quite well, only once or twice did I catch myself using an English expression; for the rest, I imagine your lady wife was a little suspicious of me! It would be useless to offer you my gratitude – it is too big.[12]

Despite the self-created myths of daring missions behind German lines, this was his only genuine encounter with German personnel during wartime. That aside, it should equally be acknowledged that he was taking no risks at Revel. Had he been exposed as a fleeing British spy, he would certainly have faced a firing squad.

While Reilly was on his way back to London from Helsingfors, the US Consul, De Witt Poole, en route to America, called into the British Embassy in Christiania (now Oslo) on 30 September. His interview with the British Ambassador resulted in a 'personal and most secret' telegram to the Foreign Office in London from Ambassador Sir Mansfeldt Findlay:

There is strong suspicion that an agent named Reilly, whose wife appears to be living in New York, has either compromised Lockhart, who employed him in propaganda among Letts, by exceeding his instructions and endeavouring to provoke a revolt against the Bolsheviks, or has even betrayed him.

Reilly advocated encouraging a revolt, but Lockhart, after consulting the United States Consul General and the French Consul General, refused to do so, and instructed Reilly to limit his efforts to propaganda with a view to deterring the Letts soldiers from resisting Allied forces. It appears that Reilly was in communication with a certain Russian strongly suspected of being an *agent provocateur*, to whom he had given an address at which he still remained some days ago. Lockhart is now arrested. Neither Reilly nor the Russian has been arrested, and they are still at large. Hence suspicion.[13]

The telegram clearly caused quite a stir when it was decoded in London on 1 October. The Foreign Secretary, Arthur Balfour, appears to have concurred with the cautious advice from his Department of Political Intelligence. The DPI's Rex Leeper advised Balfour that he had seen several reports from Reilly and had found them satisfactory. He further pointed out that Poole's account at least cleared Lockhart of the charges levelled at him by the Bolsheviks. The FO's Russia Department also assured Balfour that Reilly would be, 'closely interrogated' on his return. The matter was then passed over to Maj.-Gen. George Macdonogh, the Director of Military Intelligence at the War Office. Macdonogh in turn sent a copy to Lt-Col. C.N. French, the War Office liaison with SIS, who contacted C for his response. The response to French was used to compose a reply to Sir Ronald Graham at the Foreign Office on 10 October:

Reilly is an officer who was sent to Russia as a military agent last March. In June, it became apparent that his utility as a military agent was being impaired by the fact that he was in touch with Mr Lockhart, who was using him for some political purpose. Reilly had been warned most specifically that he was not to get into any official position, or to get mixed up with politics; therefore when it became apparent that he was doing so, a wire was sent ordering him to proceed to Siberia to report on German prisoner-of-war camps – this with the idea of getting him away from the political atmosphere, in which he was being involved. He apparently never went there; perhaps he was ordered not to by Mr Lockhart. He certainly had no business to be doing propaganda, which he apparently was instructed to do by Mr Lockhart. MI1c [SIS] have all the details of this man's career, and I suggest that it is advisable to wire to Sir M. Findlay to advise him and Mr Poole that they should not raise a hue and cry about Reilly until we know more about the circumstances. We have had one report that it was a Lettish officer who gave the plot away; and because it has failed, it does not seem right or just that the blame should be cast on this man who should properly have never been employed on such work. Presumably the clue to which the United States Consul General refers, is the fact that Reilly's wife is in America. MI1c have her address, and incidentally some of Reilly's valuables and his Will.[14]

Reilly arrived back in England on 8 November and immediately reported to C to give a personal account of himself. Whether C confronted him about his background check or opted to let sleeping dogs lie is not known. Clearly concerns were raised by Poole's cable and the fact that his cover had been blown. Reference to Reilly in the Russian press had been picked up by journalists in England and on the continent, resulting in a measure of unwelcome publicity for the novice agent.

This had other unfortunate repercussions for Reilly, as it would appear that one avid reader of the 'Lockhart' story in the Brussels press was none other than his estranged wife Margaret, who, as a result, had presented herself at the Netherlands Legation (British Section) on 15 October seeking news of her husband. Two days later she followed up her visit with a letter:

Dear Sir,

Referring to the interview I had with your bureau last Tuesday 15 instant, it was only after I came away from the Rue de la Science, that I remembered that I omitted to leave you my address. Since giving up my house in the Rue Montoyer I have been staying with friends (Mr and Mrs Wary) 13 Rue de Linthout.

It has been announced a few days ago in the Dutch papers that Colonel Lockhart the English agent had arrived at the Swedish frontier coming from Russia. Colonel Lockhart will have been accompanied by a number of other Englishmen. It is possible that my husband Mr Reilly may have been among the number. At all events it is certain that Colonel Lockhart will be able to give direct news of him.

I ask you earnestly Mr van Kattendyke, to try and get me into communication with my husband as soon as possible. I feel and know that I cannot hold out much longer.

In hopeful anticipation, I remain yours truly,

Margaret Reilly[15]

A month passed and with no news presenting itself as a result of her letter, she wrote directly to the War Office in London on 16 November 1918:

Gentlemen,

I write to ask for news of my husband, Sidney George Reilly, who I have reason to believe has been actively working against the Bolshevist government in Russia.

In various papers published here in the first weeks of September of this year there were accounts of a Franco-English programme to capture Lenin, Trotsky and company and to establish a military dictatorship in Moscow. The names of the American and French Consuls POOL [sic] and GRONARD were mentioned. Also the French general Lavergne. The leader of the movement, however, seems to have been the English colonel Lockhart who was actively seconded by the English agent Lt Reilly.

In reading these reports I was forced to the conclusion that the agent in question [Reilly] could be no other than my husband as he knows Russian extremely well having been a well-known naval agent and shipbroker in St Petersburg before the war. As I have been totally without news of my husband since 28 July 1914 you will understand Gentlemen how anxious I am to know if he is alive and to able [sic] to get word to him. Pray be so good as to let me have a reply as soon as possible.

Yours very truly

Margaret Reilly[16]

An unsigned copy letter in reply advises her that, 'If you will send him a letter at the above address same will be forwarded by first opportunity'. The carbon copy gives no clue to 'the above address', but it is fair to assume that it was the Air Board, under whom all RAF personnel came. Officially, Reilly was an RAF lieutenant, and any enquiries from family concerning the whereabouts of service personnel were dealt with in a like manner. Not unsurprisingly, it would appear that Reilly made no reply to Margaret's letter, and as a result she wrote on 4 January 1919 directly to the Air Board:

Gentlemen,

I ask you urgently for news of my husband Sidney G. Reilly who I am told is captain in the Royal Flying Corps. Since the outbreak of war I am absolutely without a word or message of any kind from him. I, having been surprised by the war here in Belgium whilst my husband was in St Petersburg where he had an important business as naval agent and ship-broker.

Friends met him in London in April 1918. He was wearing the uniform of a captain in the Royal Flying Corps and was staying at 22 Ryder Street, St James's. He mentioned to the friends in question that he would very shortly be going abroad; though he did not say where he was going.

The British Minister here, Sir Francis Villiers, received a despatch from the Foreign Office stating that Mr Reilly had been working against the Bolsheviks and, being compromised, escaped into Finland.

It was Sir Francis who advised me to write to you. Will you not have pity for me gentlemen, and let me know as soon as possible what has become of my dear husband? If you can communicate with him please let him know that in health I am well but that I desire ardently to hear from him. My financial situation is also rather strained. I enclose a photograph of Mr Reilly. Thanking you in anticipation for a word in reply,

I remain yours truly

Margaret Reilly[17]

One cannot help suspecting that the main motive for wanting to trace her estranged husband was the 'strained financial position' she refers to. It would seem that Margaret had been experiencing a difficult time financially during the war when she lost contact with Reilly. In fact, there is strong evidence to suggest that her financial problems extended somewhat further back. On 15 May 1914 she made a Will naming the sole beneficiary as one Joseph Wary of The Villa Charlotte in Zellick, Belgium, 'as evidence of my gratitude for the financial help which he gave me'.[18]

Little did Margaret know, as she sat down to write to the Air Board on 4 January, that her 'dear husband' was at that moment several thousand miles away back in Russia, lunching with Boris Suvorin in Ekaterinodar, Ukraine. As an acknowledgement of C's confidence he had, within weeks, been assigned another mission, this time in the company of Capt. George Hill, whose acquaintance he had made in Moscow.

A few days after arriving back in London on 11 November, the day the war finally came to an end, Hill was summoned to SIS headquarters by C to report personally on the work he had undertaken in Russia.[19] At the end of the interview Hill was given one month's leave. 'Alas', recalls Hill, 'less than a week had passed before I was summoned back to his office once again'.[20] On arrival, he found none other than Reilly in C's room. Reilly's presence was no doubt the result of his intense lobbying to return to Russia at the first opportunity. On 25 November, for example, he had written to Lockhart to solicit his help and support:

I have told C (and I am anxious that you should know it too) that I consider that there is a very earnest obligation upon me to continue to serve – if my services can be made use of in the question of Russia and Bolshevism. I feel that I have no right to go back to the making of dollars until I have discharged my obligations. I also venture to think that the state should not lose my services. If a halfway decent job would be offered me I would chuck business altogether and devote the rest of my wicked life to this kind of work. C promised to see the FO about all this.[21]

Five days later, on 30 November, the Foreign Office agreed that two agents should be sent out to the south of Russia under the cover of the British Trade Corporation. Reilly, it was decided, should go, 'with an assistant of his own choosing',[22] hence Hill's summons to Whitehall Court. With both Reilly and Hill now before him, C explained that 'certain important information about the Black Sea coast and South Russia was wanted for the Peace Conference that was to assemble in Paris at the end of the year'. Not only was Hill asked to volunteer to accompany Reilly on this mission to Russia, thereby forfeiting his leave, but was also informed that the Southampton train from Waterloo was departing in two hours time. After some coaxing from C, Hill agreed to go. Reilly had apparently had his passport issued and been briefed on the mission two days before where he 'got final instructions' and was told that he would, 'leave on 12th'.[23] Why Hill was called in at such short notice is not clear. His claim to have only been a week into his leave when summoned back may have been in error, however, as according to Reilly's diary their meeting with C occurred on 12 December.

Several days before the meeting with C, the *Izvestia* newspaper had reported in Moscow that both Reilly and Lockhart had been sentenced to death in their absence by a Revolutionary Tribunal for their roles in the attempted coup, and that their sentence would be carried out immediately should either of them ever be apprehended on Soviet soil in the future.

Clearly unperturbed by this, no mention appears in Reilly's diary. The diary does, however, corroborate the fact that Hill was somewhat less than enthusiastic to go. Hill recalls that as they left Whitehall Court that afternoon, 'Reilly could not bear the leisurely way in which I left the building with him',[24] and quotes him as saying, 'Hill, I don't believe you want to catch that train. I bet you fifty pounds you won't be on it'. As it turned out, Hill caught the train with only seconds to spare. Arriving on the platform he saw Reilly, 'hanging out the window' of a first-class compartment halfway up the train. Apparently he 'paid up like the sportsman he was'. Reilly himself simply recorded in his diary that day, 'Left at 4.30 p.m. Hill just managed catch train'.

According to Hill, Reilly was 'extremely keen on the trip'. This may have been down to revelling in his new role as 'gentleman spy', or could have been for other reasons. If there was any truth to the story that he had been secreting away a wife and two children in Port Arthur, and then in Petrograd, where better to have moved them than to Odessa? He had maintained close personal and business ties with the city, which was not only free from Bolshevik control, but was an international port and a gateway to other destinations should a further move be necessary.

Arriving in Paris the following day they dined at La Rue in the Boulevard de la Madeleine, the proprietor of which was none other than the former chef at the Café de Paris (known as Kiuba's) in St Petersburg. Hill recalls they had, 'a great welcome and a great dinner, with marvellous wine and the oldest brandies served as brandy should be served, in crystal goblets'.[25] They then proceeded to the Gare de Lyon to catch the 8 p.m. train to Marseilles. Although occupying a first-class compartment, Reilly records that he had a 'horrible night'.[26] This is hardly surprising, for according to Hill, 'we were packed liked sardines in a first-class carriage with people sitting on the floor and along the entire length of the corridor outside the coupes'. The train was not only overcrowded with ordinary passengers but with 'scores of badly wounded French soldiers on their way from hospital to their homes in the south'.[27]

Finally arriving in Marseilles at 11 a.m. the next morning they met up with John Picton Bagge, who was returning to his post as Consul-General in Odessa, and John Waite, the former Consul-General in Helsingfors. As merchants, accredited by the Board of Trade, Hill and Reilly, along with Bagge and Waite, boarded the Greek warship *Isonzo*, bound for Malta. Hill notes that this was not a strange arrangement, as Greek naval ships often carried traders. The *Isonzo* docked at Valetta at noon on 17 December, where the party stayed overnight. Reilly spent his time in Valetta 'making purchases'[28] and writing to Nadine in New York. At 3 p.m. the following day they set sail for Constantinople on board the *Rowan*, provoking complaints from Reilly that it was, 'the dirtiest ship [I] ever saw'.[29] After a near miss with a floating mine off the coast of Gallipoli on 22 December, they finally arrived in Constantinople at 8 a.m. the next day, which Reilly described as 'a lovely sight'.[30] After lunch aboard HMS *Lord Nelson*, as guests of Admiral Calthorpe, commander-in-chief of the Mediterranean Fleet, the final stretch of the journey to Sevastapol was made on the minesweeper *Larne*. The *Larne*'s skipper, Cmdr Hilton, clearly struck up a good rapport with Reilly, who found him to be a 'tremendous chap'.[31] They finally stepped ashore on Christmas Eve, and immediately set about arranging meetings.

Reilly and Hill had arrived at a particularly crucial time, for the British government had resolved on 13 November to aid the anti-Bolshevik forces, or Whites as they were known, led by Gen. Anton Denikin. Based in the south of Russia, the hope was that his Volunteer Army might defeat the Bolsheviks by pressing up through the Ukraine and into the heart of Russia, where another White Army, led by Admiral Alexander Kolchak, was advancing from the east.

Christmas Day was, according to Reilly, a very quiet affair, as were the New Year celebrations at the Kuban Club in Ekaterinodar.[32] In complete contrast, however, Hill recalls that they celebrated New Year at the Palace Hotel in Rostov, and refers in graphic detail to:

> ...a large ballroom which had a balcony round it, divided into boxes. In the centre of the ballroom a beautiful fountain played. The tables were thronged by queerly assorted, oddly dressed men and women. Beautiful women wore threadbare blouses, down-at-heel shoes, yet on their fingers displayed rings or on their necks colliers that would have made even a Cartier's assistant's mouth water. Others, with the air of duchesses, wore luxurious fur coats, which as a rule they took good care to keep fastened, for in most cases anything worn beneath was

scanty and painfully shabby. One girl I especially remember was particularly well dressed, yet she wore hand-knitted socks and bark sandals.[33]

Reilly and Hill were apparently decked out in full evening dress. Everyone, to Hill's recollection, seemed to be enjoying themselves although Reilly particularly disliked the 'old regime formalities', such as the band's impromptu habit of striking up numerous national anthems, which obliged all present to stand rigidly to attention. After one such rendition, Hill observed Reilly with interest 'as he sipped Turkish coffee, took an occasional drink of iced water, and with precision smoked one Russian cigarette after another'.[34]

Many hours and drinks later, Hill recalls feeling 'desperately tired', and making his way to his bedroom where he got into his pyjamas. Faintly, from below, he heard the band playing. Responding to the strains of *The Old Hunters' March*, he put on his dressing gown and went downstairs, where 'something' possessed him to lead the band and a crowd of revellers on a march 'up and down the corridors and stairs, into the attics and through the kitchens of the Palace Hotel'.[35]

Which is the correct recollection? How could they each be in two separate locations, celebrating New Year, when the one thing they do agree on is that they celebrated New Year together? Although an initially perplexing conundrum, the answer is a very simple one. Until the Bolsheviks took power, Russia was using a calendar that was thirteen days behind that used in Britain and indeed most other places in the world. The Bolsheviks decreed that Russia should fall into line with everyone else. The Whites, who controlled the zone Reilly and Hill were in, opposed everything the Bolsheviks did on principle, and stubbornly carried on with the old Russian calendar. Reilly had a small English Letts pocket diary, and recorded all the events which took place while he was in Southern Russia on a daily basis, following on from their departure from London. Rather like the man who does not adjust his watch when moving from one time zone to another,

Reilly had simply carried on regardless. Hill, by contrast, was going by the calendar in use in the area at the time, and so a thirteen–day time gap exists between the two sets of recollections. Proof of this theory is to be found in Reilly's diary, where on the 13 January he refers to 'great NY celebrations, everyone getting horribly drunk – Hill leading band in dressing gown. Old regime all over'.[36]

It is equally clear from his diary that Reilly set about his task of collecting information about the Black Sea coast and South Russia with enthusiasm, arranging a whole series of meetings with political and military leaders in the area in order to draft his dispatches. On 27 December he had met Denikin's Minister for War, Gen. Lukomsky, and had 'a long conversation' with him. From his very first report Reilly nailed his colours firmly to Denikin's mast, stating that 'the Volunteer Army represents the only concrete dependable force and living symbol of Russian unity' whose success or failure would be determined by the extent of Allied support.[37] On New Year's Eve he sent off the report along with a letter to Nadine. The New Year celebrations were noted as being very tame.

By the time of his second dispatch it was noted that 'the prevailing atmosphere is not a healthy one, neither for the political stability of the Kuban territory nor for the Volunteer Army which is still greatly dependent upon the territory's resources and upon its support in men'.[38] On 5 January he met with Gen. Poole, who had recently returned from the battle front, and noted that 'our ideas are practically in agreement'.[39]

Those ideas formed the nucleus of his next despatch, which advised that:

> … the military situation of the Volunteer Army is extremely serious, the question of its equipments, provisioning, armaments and of its technical means cannot be characterised otherwise than appalling (I am borrowing this definition from a conversation with Gen. Poole); the question of the urgency of Allied assistance becomes therefore more important than the question of its extent.[40]

It also mentions arms to carry on the fight, 'Whippet tanks, and bombing planes', as well as clothing.[41] Reilly estimated that the Red Army would be quite a formidable force by the spring of 1919 with more than a million men in the field. He expressed the view, however, that the task of overcoming them would be 'a comparatively easy one'. He believed that 'Bolshevik armies will not stand up to regular troops', and that this would be even more the case 'if the latter are technically equipped', and stated that he thought that 'it will be fateful for Russia and probably Europe if this task is not accomplished by next summer'. As painful experience would show, however, Denikin and his army would find overcoming the Bolshevik troops to be anything but easy.

In terms of political analysis, Reilly claimed that the reformist objectives of the National Centre were in harmony with Denikin's ultimate objectives. 'Although in the main lines the political tendencies of the commander-in-chief and his council are identical with those of the National Centre, still monarchist aspirations are strong in some political coteries close to the commander-in-chief'. This was typical of a good number of statements made by Reilly. Like the Delphic Oracle of Ancient Greece, he often couched his pronouncements with qualifications and get-out clauses. In this case he identified generals Lukomsky and Dragomirov as 'convinced monarchists', both of whom held sway with Denikin in political matters. Reilly concluded his second dispatch almost prophetically, asserting that 'there can only be one opinion on the urgent necessity of worldwide propaganda against Bolshevism as the greatest danger that ever threatened civilisation'.[42] Clearly feeling 'very pleased at the success of number 2',[43] Reilly got to meet Denikin and his key advisors on 10 January. The following day he was to quote Denikin's views directly:

People think that in order to pacify Russia, all one has to do is to take Moscow. To hear again the sound of the Kremlin bells would, of course be pleasant, but we cannot save Russia through Moscow. Russia has to be reconquered as a whole, and to do this we have to carry out a very wide-sweeping movement from the south, moving right across Russia. We cannot do this alone. We must have the assistance of the Allies. Equipment and armament alone are not sufficient; we must have Allied troops which will move behind us, holding territories which we will reconquer, by garrisoning the towns, policing the country and protecting our lines of communication.[44]

It is worth noting that Denikin uses the word reconquer as opposed to liberate in this interview with Reilly, which is an indication in itself of his outlook. It also highlights one of the main reasons for his ultimate failure to win widespread trust and support among the general population.

Whether or not this sentiment caused him any concern is not recorded in either Reilly's dispatches or in his diary. He could not fail but notice the general disenchantment among the people, however, and warned that workers were being 'driven into the arms of the Bolsheviks by the suppression of every kind of labour association',[45] and that all sections of society were outraged by the reactionary character and abuse of power by the regime of Cossack leader Peter Krasnov. Reilly was certainly correct in believing that Krasnov's recent alliance with Denikin could not be relied upon, nor could Krasnov be trusted to respect Denikin's authority.[46] Proof of Reilly's concerns about Krasnov were confirmed when the Cossack 'flared up' in a 'rather aggressive way'[47] during a meeting between the two. Krasnov stridently put forward the view that Denikin's Volunteer Army command was only 'thinking of grasping the maximum amount of power'.[48] He also felt that the formation of Denikin's government was 'still in the experimental stages'. By contrast, he asserted that his own government had 'a fully organised apparatus to take charge not only of the military but also of the economical tasks'.[49]

On a personal note, Reilly noted disapprovingly that Gen. Poole was still 'fooling around' with two women.[50] It is not clear, however, whether his displeasure was incurred by the 'fooling around' or that they were 'such ugly women'.[51] Reilly felt that this made a very 'bad impression'!

On 22 January Reilly and Hill received news that, on C's recommendation, they were to receive the Military Cross 'for distinguished services rendered in connection with Military operations in the Field'.[52] That evening Reilly treated everyone to champagne, but noted in his diary that Col. Terence Keyes had refused to drink and was behaving 'like a cad and fool'.[53] Keyes and Reilly had taken an immediate dislike to each other on first meeting. Reilly's diary is punctuated with a number of remarks about Keyes' caddish behaviour. For his part, Reilly seems to have taken some delight in 'annoying him immensely'.[54]

On 3 February Reilly and Hill arrived in Odessa on the last leg of their mission together. The next day Hill was due to return to England and at Reilly's behest they spent part of the day strolling around the city. While walking along Alexandrovsky Prospect, Reilly's steps began to falter, his face went white and he fell to the ground. After some minutes he recovered but refused to discuss what had happened. Hill assumed that this was the result of an emotional crisis, possibly triggered by childhood memories or the like.[55] This incident occurred outside house No. 15, and for this reason Hill theorised that Reilly may possibly have lived there as a child. While it is most likely that Reilly's 'emotional crisis' was in fact a mild epileptic fit of the type he was prone to have at times of acute stress, the story is an intriguing one. Was it coincidental that his collapse occurred at this particular spot or was there perhaps, as Hill thought, something there that might have brought it about?

During the 1880s and '90s, No. 15 was owned by one Filuring Leon Solomonovich.[56] There are no indications that anyone by the name of Rosenblum owned the property at any time during Reilly's lifetime. His family could, of course, have been tenants, although following up such a theory is next to impossible due to the destruction of records for this particular period during the Second World War. However, one further possibility has since come to light as a result of research into Rosenblum family records. Five houses from the spot where Reilly fell stands 27 Alexandrovsky Prospect, the home of the late Mikhail Rosenblum, occupied in 1919 by his daughter Elena Rosenblum.[57]

Late the following day Reilly accompanied Hill to Constanza Station to see him off on his long journey home. For reasons not apparent or explained, Reilly records in his diary 'saw Hill off; were shot at'.[58] This is a most puzzling reference, for it does not appear in Hill's recollection of his departure. Although it is possible that this incident happened to Reilly after Hill's train had departed, the circumstances surrounding the incident remain a mystery.

The very same day that Hill departed from Odessa, Margaret Reilly arrived in London from Brussels. Having heard nothing from her husband as a result of her recent letters, Margaret had crossed the Channel, booked into the Buckingham Hotel off the Strand, and made a beeline for the Air Ministry. There she met one G.E. Pennington, who later wrote a brief minute of their meeting:

> These wives of Reilly are rather tiresome. About two months ago one came to the Air Ministry and asked for his address. I passed her on to Carrington. She gave an address at Brixton Hill, 2 Maplestead Road. However, I don't think it will do the Bolsheviks or the Germans any good to let MI1c's man have a little licence.[59]

She was, however, given the address of Capt. Spencer at the War Office, to whom she wrote on 4 February:

> Dear Sir,
> I have been advised at the Air Ministry – by Capt. Talbot, room 443 – to address myself to you by letter in order to have information of my husband, Lt S.G. Reilly, technical air officer. I appeal to you most earnestly to let me know where he is and how I can communicate with him.

When the war broke out my husband was in Petrograd where he was established as Naval Agent and Ship Broker. The outbreak of hostilities surprised me in Brussels where I remained on hoping to receive a message there from Mr Reilly. None came, and eventually it was impossible to communicate with my husband. Trusting in your courtesy and kindness for an early reply,

I remain dear Sir

Yours truly

Margaret Reilly[60]

This, at last seemed to do the trick. Capt. Talbot had clearly established who Reilly was and noted that he was seconded to SIS. He therefore gave her the name of Capt. Spencer, a non-existent officer, whose name was used by senior SIS personnel when dealing with persons outside the department. As a result, a letter was sent to Reilly in Odessa. Whatever Margaret said to him in the letter it had the desired effect. Within days of receipt he cabled SIS in London as follows:

19 February 1919

Please pay Mrs REILLY from my account £100. Please inform her that I shall [group indecipherable] further provision when I return.[61]

This reply was written at the London Hotel, Odessa, where he had checked in on 9 February. Now operating alone, his final dispatches were chiefly about the situation he found in Odessa. Southern Russia was divided into two Allied operational zones, the eastern zone British, the western zone French. The city of Odessa therefore had a French garrison of some 60,000 men, whom Reilly criticised for their 'decidedly unfriendly' attitude towards the Volunteer Army. He was particularly critical of Col. Henri Freydenberg, who he accused of deliberately obstructing the Volunteers' efforts to supply, mobilise and operate their own forces. In particular he accused the French of 'treating Russian staff officers with a total lack of elementary courtesy and even with insulting rudeness', and of converting Odessa 'into one of the worst administered and least safe cities in the world'.[62]

On 21 February Reilly requested, 'that I be ordered to return home as my further stay here is a waste of time and only verbal reports can elucidate this intricate situation'.[63] By 10 March he was in Constantinople for a conference with John Picton Bagge and the Assistant British High Commissioner to Constantinople, Rear Admiral Richard Webb. Reilly's reports were described by Webb as 'disquieting' and he immediately arranged for Reilly to leave for London so that he could give a full personal account at the Foreign Office. Walford Selby of the FO's Russian Department concluded that Reilly's reports contained 'a fund of useful information on the subject of the whole situation in South Russia'.[64] He also marked a copy of Reilly's dispatch 13, concerning the state of affairs in Odessa, 'Circulated to the king and War Cabinet'.

In comparison to his first Russian mission the previous year, one might be tempted to conclude that he took a comparatively passive, indeed neutral, reporting role in the south of Russia. In reality he used his position in a very proactive way in support of Denikin, whose role as prime Bolshevik challenger he promoted unashamedly in his reports. As we shall see in the following chapter, true to form, he was also using the opportunity to make personal contacts and obtain commercial information that he would shortly seek to make capital out of in more ways than one.

Having briefed the Foreign Office, Reilly was now reunited with Hill for a further short assignment. Hill recalled:

Suddenly, I was instructed to go to Paris, and Reilly, who had by now returned from Odessa, was to go with me. We were to hold ourselves in readiness to give expert information should it be required, to observe what was happening in Paris, particularly in connection with Russian affairs, and possibly to act as liaison officers with the newly formed Council of Ambassadors.[65]

From London Reilly and Hill travelled with a party of Admiralty officials and Sir William Bull, Conservative MP for Hammersmith South and a close friend of C. The party booked into the Hotel Majestic, where Bull introduced them to the Secretary of State for War, Winston Churchill, his aide Sir Archibald Sinclair, and Lord Northcliffe, the proprietor of the *Daily Mail*.

After a few days at the hotel, Reilly and Hill were compelled to leave and move to the Hotel Mercedes, as the Foreign Office felt it was not appropriate for them to be staying at the same hotel as members of the official British delegation.[66] At the Mercedes they found that the Greek Prime Minister, Eleutherios Venizelos, and his delegation were occupying two floors of the hotel. Hill was already acquainted with Venizelos, having met him on an earlier intelligence mission to Salonica in 1916, shortly after the Greeks entered the war on the Allied side. As a result of this and several rounds of late night drinks, Reilly and Hill learnt of Venizelos' territorial ambitions for Greece,[67] which they passed on to the Foreign Office. It was also here that they picked up a rumour that the Soviet government might, after all, be recognised and invited to send a delegation to the Paris Peace Conference. At lunch with a journalist by the name of Guglielmo, they were told that two envoys, William Bullitt and Lincoln Steffens, had been sent to Moscow by the American delegation to parley with the Bolsheviks. Bullitt had apparently telegraphed the text of the Bolsheviks' proposals for potential recognition to President Wilson, who was supposedly much impressed. The next day, 25 March, Reilly and Hill breakfasted with Foreign Office officials Walford Selby and Harold Nicolson at a hotel in the Rue St Roque, which Reilly took great delight in volunteering had been Napoleon's headquarters in 1795.[68] Having been appraised of the 'recognition' rumours, Selby and Nicolson were then apparently treated to an encyclopaedic rendition by Reilly of almost every building in Paris which had any historic link to Napoleon.

According to Hill they were later joined at the table by 'an acquaintance on the staff of the American military delegation', who told them that Bullitt 'would be breakfasting with Mr Lloyd George the following morning'.[69] What happened next is not so clear, as both Reilly and Hill claimed sole responsibility for taking the story to Henry Wickham Steed, the editor of the *Daily Mail*, who was in Paris at the time.[70] The following day, 26 March, the *Mail* ran a sensationalist exposé of the proposal to recognise the Bolsheviks, under the headline 'Peace with Honour'. In it, Wickham Steed attacked anyone in the Allied camp who would 'directly or indirectly, accredit an evil thing known as Bolshevism'.[71] As a result, Lloyd George backed away from the American proposal, and the possibility of recognition was scuppered, for the time being at least.

Following the *Daily Mail* exposé, Hill was sent back to South Russia and Reilly returned to London, where he was briefly reunited with Nadine, who had left New York for London on 26 March on the SS *Baltic*. It had been eighteen long months since he had last seen her, during which time their lives had both moved on. It could not have taken him long after arriving back in London to realise that his relationship with Nadine had changed irrevocably. Months of separation and a host of mutual infidelities had undoubtedly taken their toll. The fact that within a fortnight of their reunion, Reilly journeyed alone to Southampton, where on 15 April he boarded the New York-bound SS *Olympic*, would seem to reaffirm this assumption.

Eleven

Final Curtain

Instead of heading for New York as scheduled, the captain of the SS *Olympic* docked at Halifax, Nova Scotia, on 21 April, due to propeller trouble.[1] Although most Olympic passengers completed their journey by transferring to the SS *Adriatic*, Reilly was in no mood to wait and took a train to New York's Pennsylvania Station via Boston.[2]

The object of his visit was to meet Samuel MacRoberts and as many other bankers as he could, in order to persuade them of the virtues of his latest 'grand plan'. Working as an intermediary for Polish banker Karol Jaroszynsky,[4] an old acquaintance from his pre-war St Petersburg days, Reilly was clearly seeking to lay the foundations for an Anglo-American syndicate to invest in a post-Bolshevik economy.

Confirmation of his intentions are to be found in a cable dated 10 May to John Picton Bagge at the Department of Overseas Trade, in which he emphasised his belief that American business was looking for new export markets and saw Russia as a place of some potential.[5] In Reilly's view, MacRoberts in particular was keen to form a syndicate involving American and British interests to exploit the opportunities that a Denikin victory might bring. In an echo of the rivalry over munitions contracts during the war years, MacRoberts was keen to press ahead in order to gain an advantage over J. Pierrpont Morgan. On 15 May Reilly departed for England on board the White Star Line's SS *Baltic*.[6] Arriving in Liverpool on 25 May, he stayed overnight at the Adelphi Hotel before heading back to London.

Bagge also saw the potential of the Jaroszynsky proposals, recognising that their success would not only bring about new market places for British-made goods, but might eventually lead to economic and political control of Russia. Ultimately, however, British banks like Lloyds, the London County and Westminster Bank and the National and Provincial Bank were reluctant to make major commitments while the success of the White forces was still in the balance. Indecisiveness and the snail-like progress of discussions within the Foreign Office, the Treasury and the Department of Overseas Trade meant that by the time consensus appeared to have been reached, it was a matter of 'too little, too late' to be of any benefit to Denikin.

Despite the fact that Reilly's assignment to South Russia had ended in March, this did not stop him from continuing to correspond with the likes of Rex Leeper and John Picton Bagge on a personal basis, sending them a stream of memorandums and handwritten missives from his Albany apartment in London's exclusive Piccadilly. Someone else high on Reilly's address list was Churchill's aide Sir Archibald Sinclair, MP, who he had first met the previous month at the Hotel Majestic in Paris. Reilly seems to have used the same tried and tested methods of achieving access and influence in British circles as he had utilised so effectively in St Petersburg a decade earlier. This was essentially done by cultivating the aides and associates of the influential, who once secured as acquaintances could then act as a pipeline to their lords and masters. By this method he had forged an association with Admiral Gregorovitch, the Minister for Marine, through his aide Lt Petr Zalessky. In like manner, he now went to considerable trouble to befriend and cultivate Archibald Sinclair.

One can only guess at how Reilly's extra-curricular activities were viewed by SIS top brass. By October 1919, the first tell-tale

signs that Reilly had blotted his copybook were becoming
apparent. Having only recently become the recipient of the Military
Cross, it would seem that Reilly felt that his 'distinguished service'
should be further acknowledged by promotion. On enlistment in
November 1917 he had been commissioned as a second
lieutenant,[7] but now, over a year later, clearly felt that he was
more than due for further recognition. After all, George Hill, who
had enlisted as a lieutenant, was now a captain, and to Reilly, a
superior officer. Reilly therefore took his case to Maj. D.J.F.
Morton, head of SIS Production Section[8] and his immediate
superior. As a consequence, Morton wrote on 3 October 1919 to
Col. Stewart Menzies, head of SIS Section II, which dealt with
military matters:

> Would you consider forwarding the name of Lt Reilly for an honorary
> commission as major. At present he holds a temporary commission as
> lieutenant in the Air Force. He is now engaged on important work for the
> Foreign Office which necessitates his conferring with soldiers and civilians
> of high rank, and finds his low rank a great hindrance. I am certain the
> Foreign Office would back this up, and if you will consider the matter, I
> would try and obtain a written statement from them to that effect.[9]

Replying on 16 October, Menzies wasted few words in rejecting
the matter out of hand:

> Lt Reilly is in the Air Force so how can we help? In any case the WO
> [War Office] are adamant in their refusal to give even honorary
> promotion as in the event of this officer becoming a casualty, 'finance'
> are responsible for paying the widow a pension etc. There is, however,
> no harm in first sounding the Air Ministry.[10]

While Menzies' offhand response was a correct reflection of War
Office policy, it is equally the case that had he wished to assist in
getting Reilly promotion, he most certainly could have done. The
rebuff was a sign that while Morton might be behind him for the

time being, others in SIS were most certainly not, either seeing Reilly as an overrated upstart or as a loose cannon. Never being one to accept no for an answer, Reilly seems to have opted for unilateral action. From here on it would appear that to those outside the service he referred to himself as 'Captain Reilly', and has been styled as such by Winfried Ludeke,[11] Pepita Bobadilla (later Reilly),[12] and a host of other writers down the years. By 1932, even his old adversary Norman Thwaites referred to him as 'Captain Sidney Reilly MC' in his autobiography.[13]

Five months after his New York trip, Reilly was still working hard to push his Russian banking scheme. It is clear from a memorandum to Picton Bagge, dated 10 October, that he had now set his sights on enticing French bankers and had been sufficiently encouraged by their response:

My dear Bagge

In confirmation of my memorandum of the 8th instant, I now enclose the prospectus of the SOCIETE COMMERCIALE, INDUSTRIELLE ET FINANCIERE LA RUSSIE, which has been formed recently in Paris.

It is the Banking Combine of which M. YAROSHINSKY told us, and in which some of his banks are interested. You will see from this that the French bankers proved very much more receptive than our friends in the City. In connection with this French Banking Combine, I have received the following information from Paris. Last week a meeting took place at the French Ministry of Commerce and Industry, under the presidency of Gen. MANGIN, the Chief of the Economic Mission to Russia which was to leave on the 8th of this month. Besides the representatives of the Ministry and the French banks and industries, there were also present representatives of the Russian government and of Russian banks and industries.

Resolutions were passed urging the necessity of resuming trade relations on a large scale with Russia, and the dispatch of an Economic Mission to Russia was welcomed. Furthermore, the formation of the above named company with a capital of 50 million francs, was approved and government support in the matter of credits and tonnage was promised. Of the 50 million francs, 20 million francs are being subscribed by French banks, and 15 million francs by French industrialists, and 15 million francs are reserved for Russian banks, and the Russian banks and Russian industrialists. It is stated that a credit of 400 million francs will be accorded to this company by the French banks. The Russian banks have stipulated that although they are participating in the formation of this company they reserve to themselves the liberty of action and participation in similar combinations formed in other countries.[14]

Three days after the memorandum's composition, the city of Orel finally fell to Denikin's forces. Now only 200 miles south of Moscow, the Whites and their sympathisers could be forgiven for seeing victory within their grasp. The territory Denikin controlled had gradually inflated over the past months to total some 600,000 square miles. However, within a week the Red Army had turned the tables and had retaken Orel. Having overstretched his supply lines to breaking point, Denikin was now forced into an unbroken retreat that would ultimately lead all the way back to the Black Sea where his campaign started. Along with the collapse of Denikin's offensive went Reilly's ambition of playing a pivotal role in the rebuilding of Russia's economy. Had Denikin succeeded in ultimately taking Moscow and ousting the Bolsheviks, Reilly would no doubt have played a major role in the economic reconstruction of the country. The money he had made to date from munitions deals would have been a mere drop in the ocean compared to the rewards that would have been his for the taking in a Bolshevik free Russia.

Not one to be discouraged for long, Reilly set about composing a nineteen-page memorandum entitled *The Russian Problem*,[15] in which he set out his views on bringing about the downfall of the Bolsheviks. In conclusion he stated that:

The policies and proposals outlined in this memorandum can be summarised as follows:

1. Abolition of the Bolshevik government – by force, as no other effective means are available or conceivable.

2. The necessary force to be supplied by the military co-operation of the Russian National Armies with the armies of Finland, Poland and the Border States.

3. To obtain this co-operation an agreement must be effected between Denikin and the other states in the matter of their political and territorial differences at a special Inter-State Conference.

4. The conditions for effecting this agreement and for rendering it of sufficient duration for the attainment of the main object are:

4.1. Agreement between the Allied governments as to the definite terms to be proposed to the Inter-State Conference.

4.2. Readiness of the Allied governments to impose these terms upon the parties by moral and if necessary economic pressure, and on the other hand to give the parties all the necessary support immediately the terms have been accepted.

4.3. Certain changes in the personnel and policy of the Polish government and the Denikin government.

5. Elimination of Germany's harmful influence by an attempt at an economic understanding with regard to Russia. For this it is necessary:

5.1. To prepare the ground in France for acquiescence to or participation in such understanding.

5.2. To induce a group of British financiers to take the initiative in forming a British-German pool for the control of Russian Bank Stock.

5.3. To carry out all those measures (some of which have been indicated here) which are necessary for retaining the control in this pool in British or British-French hands.

As a self-appointed expert on Russia and one of the few people in intelligence circles who had actually been there during this critical period, Reilly took every opportunity he could to hawk his views to anyone of influence who might be receptive. An indication of his success in this direction can be seen from a note sent by Sir Archibald Sinclair to Winston Churchill on 15 December 1919.[16] Reilly had apparently met Sinclair some days previously in order to give him a copy of *The Russian Problem*. While discussing it, he had allowed Sinclair sight of a letter recently received from the *Daily Mail* proprietor Lord Northcliffe, to whom he had also sent a copy. This resulted, as Reilly had hoped, in Sinclair sending the memorandum to Churchill with a covering note in which he remarked, 'I have seen a very cordial note to Reilly from Northcliffe saying that he had "read every word" of the memorandum "to the end"'.[17] This again exemplifies another of Reilly's tactics, namely establishing influence by association. Despite the mutual suspicion that existed between Northcliffe and Churchill, Reilly knew that Churchill would be keen to see anything that Northcliffe had expressed an interest in.

While Reilly's mind was clearly fixed on grandiose schemes, SIS was far more concerned with bread-and-butter issues, namely intrigues between pro-German Russians and German militarist elements in Berlin. As a result of information volunteered to the Foreign Office by the daughter of Chaikovsky, a member of the White Russian delegation in Paris, SIS in London sent a cable on 30 January to the SIS station in Paris:

> With reference to your telegram CXP.583 of today, enclosed please find particulars of the German-Russian reactionary conspiracy report. This information was obtained from the daughter of Chaikovsky, to whom we have given your private address and told her to write you and fix up an appointment, and she will keep you in touch with any fresh movements she gets wind of... It would be as well to get in touch with Reilly and show him the enclosed report, and ask him to give you all the assistance he can.[18]

The report stated that:

Information has been received regarding a conspiracy which is being hatched by German and Russian reactionaries. The headquarters is in Berlin, and there are important branches in Paris and the Crimea. The first step in the conspiracy is to be a coup d'etat in the south of Russian Volunteer Army, which is to eliminate the leading pro-Entente elements including DENIKIN unless the latter is willing to fall into line with the plans of the pro-Germans. After this coup d'etat, the Volunteer Army under instructions from Germany, will conclude an armistice with the Bolsheviks.

The report asserts that:

… the centre of these intrigues is in Berlin under the direction of Gen. Ludendorff. Gen. Ludendorff has an agent in Paris whose name is unknown to me, who has received strict instructions from Gen. Ludendorff to have nothing to do with the official representative of the German government in Paris, as his organisation in Berlin is hostile to the German government and intends ultimately to overthrow it.[19]

Investigations ensued and cables passed back and forth between London and Paris. In a detailed report from Paris on 23 March, Reilly perceptively told C that:

Without wishing in any way to minimise the dangerous possibilities of the so-called 'German-Russian Plot' I am inclined to believe that under the present circumstances one is liable to attach to it more importance than it can in reality have. I have no faith from experience in the capabilities of the Russian Monarchists and I cannot imagine that the Germans can consider them as valuable associates.[20]

The report is also noteworthy in drawing attention to a prophetic view expressed by Nicolai Koreivo that:

Russia has nothing to expect from the Allies who have been all along pursuing a selfish policy towards her, and who have fooled and betrayed KOLTCHAK, DENIKIN and YUDENITCH for their own ends. An alliance between the German military party and the Bolsheviks would be the most satisfactory policy so far as Russian national interests are concerned. The League of Nations is a dream which is fortunately dissipating owing to America's abstention, and it is therefore all the more necessary to adopt a 'Realpolitik' in which Russia and Germany will play a major part, and which promises the quickest political and economical recovery of these countries.[21]

This is more or less what came to pass two years later in April 1922 when Germany and Russia signed the Rapallo Treaty, recognising each other's regimes and giving up all financial claims against each other. It was an inevitable recognition by the two nations of their mutual self interest.

Another inevitable recognition of mutual self interest was the decision by Sidney and Nadine Reilly to seek a divorce. Although they were not legally married, Nadine did not know this, and they had therefore to go through the motions of divorce in order that he could keep up the pretence. As such, they journeyed to Paris on 4 March 1920 in order to start the legal process. Reilly and Nadine called into the SIS office in Adam Street to be issued with a passport and travel tickets, although no prior arrangement seems to have been made. This was made apparent the following day when C received a note from Section H: 'Reilly and wife No. 2 called at Adam Street yesterday for passport and passage to Paris. As you were away, I told Crowley verbally to get on with it, but I know nothing about the journey nor whether it is to be at our expense or not'.[22]

Not for the first time Reilly was combining his private business with that of SIS. Having made contact with the lawyers who were to attend to the divorce, he wrote two letters to Sir Robert Nathan at the Foreign Office from the Hotel Lotti in Rue de Castiglione, where he and Nadine were staying. From these letters dated 13 and 14 March it is clear that he had met Baranoff and Burtsev[23] in connection with the unrest in Germany.[24] On returning to London, Reilly wasted little time in typing up two more memorandums on Russian policy, sending copies to Archibald Sinclair, to ask for his view on them, before submitting them to the Foreign Office and the Department of Overseas Trade. Sinclair, as Reilly had hoped, immediately sent them on to Churchill, along with a brief letter dated 24 June:

> Secretary of State
>
> I hope you will find time to read these two short memoranda by my remarkable MI1c friend Reilly. They contain a concrete proposal for bringing about the downfall of the Soviet government by economic means and for putting us in a position at the earliest possible moment to obtain food and raw materials from Soviet Russia. He is very anxious to obtain 'my' opinion on them before pressing his views on the FO and DOT.
>
> Reilly is reputed to possess an expert knowledge of finance, which would seem to be borne out by his personal prosperity and the authority which he enjoys among Russian financiers such as M. Jarascynski. For knowledge of Russia, grip of Russian problems, insight into the tendencies of political and economic forces and powers of prophecy which have been constantly tested throughout the last year, he is without a rival among my Russian and Anglo-Russian visitors. Picton Bagge would concur in this opinion, and so I have reason to believe would 'C' from the Intelligence point of view.[25]

Reilly's proposals hinged on three points of attack from within Russia: persuading the Red Army leaders to make a deal with Denikin to overthrow the Bolsheviks; positively enrolling the help and support of the Orthodox Church; and persuading the Ukrainians to link up with Denikin against the Bolsheviks. Although Reilly's memorandum was favourably received by Rex Leeper in the Political Intelligence Department, Sir Ronald Graham of the Russian Department was distinctly cool about it. The Foreign Secretary, Lord Curzon, was more inclined to back Graham's view than Leeper's and the proposals were therefore scotched.

That same month Nadine and Reilly parted for the last time when she returned to New York.[26] Within a year, Reilly was to strike up a new relationship, this time with a girl nearly thirty years his junior. Caryll Houselander[27] had recently left St John's Wood Art School, and was introduced to Reilly by another former student, Della Clifford, who had met him through friends in the Russian émigré community. Della showed Reilly Caryll's sketches as she was 'too shy, and despised her drawings too much to take them to him herself'.[28] Caryll was fascinated by religion, art, mysticism and Russia, and found herself immediately attracted to a man who seemed to embody all these. Being a devout Catholic, she found herself struggling to reconcile her feelings and her religious beliefs. In her 1955 autobiography she recalled this inner turmoil:

> I was driving myself to a dangerous state of psychological, as well as spiritual starvation, and becoming more and more driven by my own emotions. I had emptied myself of almost everything that was essential to me, and now felt the necessity of filling that emptiness. I did not define this, but obviously it added a fierce intensity to every natural temptation and complicated all my emotional relationships with other people.[29]

Eventually Caryll succumbed to temptation and began a two-year affair with Reilly:

> In spite of my infidelity I still regarded myself as a Catholic and still regarded my sins as being sins… now I was tempted to turn my back on the Church once and for all, and to take what happiness life seemed to offer me outside it… the simple truth was that I was being swept by temptation as dry grass is swept by a flame of fire.[30]

As with Beatrice Tremaine, Reilly was content to support Caryll and have her at his beck and call. Unlike Beatrice and the other women he had known, however, she had comparatively simple tastes. As Dermot Morrah recalled, 'I myself knew Caryll from 1919 and saw her constantly… she was living as the mistress of a man… who made her a weekly allowance, small but quite adequate to her simple manner of life'.[31] True to form he seems to have regaled her with his usual 'Master Spy' stories, including an account of his 'friend' Rasputin. In 1950 Caryll recalled that:

> …a man who was a very great friend of mine and who was… at one time a spy… became a friend of Rasputin's and, strange as it is, really did have mixed feelings for him, part loathing and part liking. At all events he lived with him for about a year, travelling about Russia with him, and Rasputin confided his own spiritual history to him, and told him that he had formerly and of his own choice surrendered his soul to the devil and from that time had been able to work many more cures.[32]

While Reilly certainly had connections and contacts with Rasputin and his circle, his claim to have lived and travelled with him for a year is easily refuted by Ochrana records. Rasputin's activities and associations were probably the best documented of anyone in Russia bar the Tsar himself. Reilly's name is nowhere to be found in the Ochrana's vast record of Rasputin and his movements.

Another friend of Caryll's from her days at the St John's Wood Art School was Eleanor Toye.[33] Eleanor became Reilly's secretary for approximately two years, and later confided to Jean Bruce Lockhart (Robert Bruce Lockhart's wife) her experiences of the darker side of his compelling personality. Reilly, she said, 'suffered from severe mental crises amounting to mental delusions. Once he thought he was Jesus Christ'.[34]

On the business front, Reilly was far from idle. Recognising a kindred spirit in Leonid Krasin, the corrupt head of the newly established Soviet Economic Mission in London, he suggested a scheme of mutual benefit, whereby the Soviet government and Marconi signed a deal for the supply of a wireless service in

Russia.[35] Reilly and Krasin were to work together on a number of other deals from which they were to line their own pockets. Some months after the Marconi deal, for example, Krasin was involved in smuggling a hoard of diamonds out of Russia to be secretly sold in the West. Lenin's government was in dire need of foreign currency and such covert deals were one of the ways in which foreign trade missions obtained it. This was, however, to be a deal with a difference. According to Georgi Solomon, a Russian colleague of Krasin's, the diamonds were sold by Krasin at below the best obtainable market price to a third party, the proceeds of which went back to Moscow. The third party then had them recut and resold in Paris for a significantly higher price with Moscow none the wiser. This windfall was then, no doubt, shared with Krasin. In 1930, Solomon recalled that the third party with the Parisian connections was a British officer of the rank of captain who was an Anglicised Russian Jew.[36]

According to Reilly's SIS file, other allegations about his conduct were also coming out of Paris at this time. On 3 September SIS received a note from the Naval Intelligence Division:

Sidney Reilly, Paris

This man is reported from a reliable source to be wearing naval uniform in Paris and his conduct is not satisfactory. Is he still working for C?[37]

C replied to the DNI on 7 September in his usual bluff manner:

With reference to the attached report, Mr Sidney Reilly is employed by me and is engaged at present on a highly important and confidential mission. Will you cause further enquiries to be made from the reliable source as to the precise respect in which this ex-officer's conduct is not satisfactory. I feel confident that the statement that he has been wearing naval uniform is not correct and I think it, therefore, at least possible that the accusation as to his conduct is also incorrect.[38]

The DNI replied that the source was a Russian who had left Paris two weeks previously and had stated that Reilly had been boasting of being in close touch with the Secretary of State for War, and confirmed that Reilly had indeed been wearing naval uniform.[39] C wrote a dismissive note boldly across the bottom of the page – 'The further information does not give anything sufficiently definite to bear out the original accusation'.[40] This incident, while a minor one, was no doubt remembered unfavourably by the Director of Naval Intelligence, Admiral Sir Hugh Sinclair. Within three years he would suceed Cumming as chief of MI1c, and would not prove to be so tolerant of Reilly and his antics as Cumming had been.

After a brief respite in London following his return from Paris, Reilly was called in by C to be briefed about a new mission. While the Treaty of Versailles had redrawn the map of Europe, there was still a good deal of unfinished business to be settled in Paris. Poland's frontier with Russia was a prime case in point. The Poles themselves favoured the frontier of 1772, while the Council of Ambassadors in Paris proposed on 8 December 1919 a border closely resembling the old eastern frontier of Poland when she had been part of the Russian Empire.

The matter was ultimately settled not by negotiation in Paris, but by the Russo-Polish War which broke out in April 1920, following Polish incursions into the Ukraine. While the war initially ran in the Russians' favour, the Poles took the upper hand following their victory at the Battle of Vistula in August 1920.

With talk of an armistice between the Poles and Russians in the air, first-hand intelligence was required about the possible outcome of a settlement and the implications this might have for Gen. Wrangel, Denikin's successor as commander-in-chief of the White Volunteer Army in the south.

On 21 October 1920 Reilly left for Poland[41] where he and ST25 (Sir Paul Dukes) linked up. On 29 October Reilly was able to send a cable through the British First Secretary in Warsaw, Sir Percy Loraine:

Armistice concluded on the 25th at Bolsheviks' request between Ukrainians and Bolsheviks must be regarded for the present only as cessation of military operations till latest 7 November. It involves neither military restrictions nor political clauses. Was in first instance called forth by independent action of several Bolshevik divisions anxious for rest.[42]

By sending the cable through Sir Percy, Reilly had clearly ruffled feathers at the Foreign Office. As a result of a Foreign Office letter to SIS on 3 November,[43] a rather terse but polite cable was sent to Reilly by Section G2 on 8 November, pointing out that while 'no real harm has been done in the matter' he should not in future use this open means of communication.[44] Reilly's papers also show that this was not the only example of his misusing embassy facilities, for included in his correspondence are a number of letters written on embassy notepaper.

Although these minor transgressions hardly endeared him to senior SIS officers, it was his growing association with Boris Savinkov, whom he regarded as Russia's Napoleonic saviour, which would ultimately put the most strain on his relationship with the Service.

A perfect case in point was Reilly's visit to Savinkov's headquarters in Warsaw. From here Col. Sergei Pavlovsky was leading regular guerrilla raids into Soviet territory, attacking Red Army camps and derailing troop trains. Not content with gathering intelligence, Reilly (not for the first or last time) exceeded his remit by becoming actively involved:

At the end of 1920, having become a rather close intimate of Savinkov's, I went to Warsaw, where Savinkov was then organising a foray into Byelorussia. I personally took part in the operation and was inside Soviet Russia. Ordered to return, I went back to London.[45]

Whether Reilly actually bore arms or was merely observing the attack is unknown. Whatever role he ultimately played, he certainly had no authority to cross the Soviet border or become involved, hence C's order for him to return.

A peace treaty was signed between Russia and Poland on 18 March 1921, which resulted in the Poles eventually succumbing to Russian pressure to withdraw the facility for Savinkov to use Warsaw as a base for his operations. In the autumn of that year he was forced to leave and go to Prague, where he found a less than enthusiastic welcome from the Czech government. Funding was another major problem as his main benefactor was Reilly, whose finances were now somewhat stretched.

Despite filing a law suit against the Baldwin Locomotive Company for an unpaid munitions commission of $542,825, Reilly no doubt realised that the claim could take a considerable time to get to court (as indeed it did). Confronted with the additional pressure of having to prop up Savinkov, he now faced the very real prospect of financial ruin. As unpalatable as it was, there seemed only one way out of the rut – selling the treasured Napoleonic collection that had taken some twenty-five years to build up. He therefore made the momentous decision to put the collection up for sale in New York, where he sensed he would get the best return. Not unsurprisingly, the sale attracted great attention. It was not everyday that such a major collection was put on the open market. The *New York Times* reported that the:

> ... notable collection of Sidney G. Reilly of New York and London, consisting of literary, artistic and historical properties illustrative of the life of Napoleon Bonaparte, will be sold at the American Art Gallery on 4 and 5 May. It is one of the finest gatherings of material on this interesting subject that has ever been brought together by a private collector and sold in America. It contains some of the most important items illustrative of the life and times of the great Emperor from his first appearance as a factor in the military life of France, through the eventful days following, down to the final stages of his career and death on St Helena.[46]

The proceeds of the sale, a little under $100,000, do not appear to have lasted long. In June 1921 Savinkov convened the first meeting of the Anti-Bolshevik Congress, which met in Warsaw between 13 and 16 June. The initiative was one more attempt to try and weld together the disparate groups opposed to Lenin's regime. Apart from overcoming the mutual suspicion of the various groups, it was obvious that lack of funds was the main obstacle to putting their plans into action. After the congress had ended, Reilly received a letter from Savinkov's aide Dmitry Filosofoff:

> I will tell you frankly that I felt ashamed to associate with people who had come to attend and would return to Russia full of hope and would risk their lives in their work – whereas we were unable to give them help to continue the struggle.
>
> I repeat for the um-teenth [sic] time that it all depends on money. The press is ready, the peasants await liberation, but without a fully planned organisation, it is hopeless. Our chief trouble is that it may not be possible to prevent abortive or premature riots. This applies especially to Petrograd from whence we received detailed intelligence (after your departure). From this we see that riots can be expected at any moment and, if they cannot be supported, it is possible that they will be suppressed. Even Boris Savinkov will not be able to go there owing to insufficient financial aid. In other words – money, money, money![47]

With renewed energy Reilly responded to Filosofoff's call for funds, pulling out all the stops he could think of. A letter to the Air Board, written on Reilly's behalf by one H.F. Pougher, is indicative of the lengths Reilly went to:

> Dear Sir
> Pardon the liberty but Lt Sidney G. Reilly late RAF gave me your name with a view to having his promotion gazetted which entitles him to arrears from 2nd to that of lieutenant, and arrears of gratuity. He mentioned in letter you understood his case copy of same I enclose. I

should esteem it a great favour if you would hasten same.

Thanking you

H.F. Pougher[48]

When the letter was referred to SIS for their comments, Reilly was clearly embarrassed at being seen to be chasing money, and with mock disdain claimed that 'Pougher is a small clerk at Holt's [Bank] whom I have assisted financially from time to time. I promised him any arrears of pay or gratuity he can recover'.[49]

He also continued lobbying through all channels in Savinkov's favour and began to put plans in place to bring Savinkov over to England to drum up support for his cause. In submitting a report on Savinkov to SIS, he asked that it be gone over and polished up:

> … and when ship-shape have it roneo'ed and put in circulation in the ordinary way. As Savinkov is coming over with me to London, I am very anxious that the people who count and whom he will probably see, should get it well in advance (say – Winston Ch; Leeper. The PM's secretary Sir Edw. Grigg and anybody you think useful).[50]

His plans for Savinkov's visit very quickly ran into the opposition of the Foreign Office, however, when it refused to grant him an entry visa. Not to be deterred by this, Reilly approached C directly and requested that he ignore the Foreign Office and instruct the Paris Passport Control Officer[51] to issue a visa regardless. Not unsurprisingly, C refused. Never able to accept no for an answer, Reilly went straight back to Paris to appeal to the Passport Control Office to issue the visa directly. Maj. Thomas Langton was the Passport Control Officer in Paris, but it is more likely that Reilly made a beeline for his deputy, Maj. William 'Robbie' Field Robinson, who was a close friend of his. Whatever persuasion he used, the upshot was that a British entry visa was issued to Savinkov by the Paris PCO.[52] Not surprisingly, this incident caused major fallout within SIS and indeed in wider government circles. It is perhaps no coincidence that by early

1922 SIS had, to all intents and purposes, officially severed its links with Reilly.

In a revealing letter to an SIS colleague dated 23 January 1922, Reilly ends by saying, 'I am not calling at the office; as Morton may perhaps have told you, just now it is healthier for me to keep out of the way for a while'.[53]

C's position is made even clearer by a cable from SIS headquarters in London to the Vienna station, dated 1 February 1922, who were clearly seeking clarification about Reilly's status:

In reply to your letter about Reilly, I wired you yesterday to say that you should give him no more information than was absolutely necessary.

To be quite frank I rather share your views and am of the opinion that he knows far too much about our organisation. Owing to his unofficial connection with us he knows such a lot that it would hardly do to quarrel with him, or, in fact, to let him see that he is receiving different treatment to that which he has become accustomed.

He worked for this office during the war in Russia and he then undoubtedly rendered us considerable service. Since the Armistice he has kept in touch with us and I think that, on the whole, we have received a great deal more information from him than he has obtained from us, although we have been able in many cases to give him facilities which he would otherwise not have enjoyed.

You no doubt know that he is Boris Savinkov's right-hand man, and it is probably Reilly who is financing the whole movement and he can therefore be looked upon as being of some considerable importance.

He is exceedingly clever, certainly not anti-British and is genuinely working against the Bolsheviks as much as he is able.

I think the above will give you the cue as to how to deal with him; you should certainly not appear to be hiding anything from him or show a want of frankness, but at the same time be careful not to tell him anything of real importance.

It just strikes me that he may ask you to give facilities for two individuals, with whom he is in touch and who are two of Savinkov's principal assistants, to proceed to Constantinople. Naturally any such request must be forwarded to the competent authorities, as the last thing in the world we should wish is to become embroiled in any way with Savinkov, although of course we are not adverse to hearing all about the gentleman and his plans.

Yours sincerely

BM[54]

If Reilly's position was in any doubt, an SIS cable to the New York Passport Control Officer the following July was even more succinct:

S.G. Reilly worked for us during and after the war in Russia, and knows a certain amount about our organisation as it was then constituted. He is apparently familiar with your name as he asked for a letter of introduction to you personally, in case he had difficulty with his passports. We avoided giving him any letter, as although he probably thinks Passport Control is cover for this department, it is just as well that he should not be certain. In fact, if he puts any questions, it will be as well for you to say that your work is entirely Passport Control and that you know nothing of any other work as the organisation is now completely altered. As Reilly travels on a British passport, there is no reason why he should worry you at all, but in case he rolls up this is just to warn you that he has now nothing to do with us.[55]

Reilly's departure from SIS was not, of course, an isolated one. SIS were at this time shedding a good number of operatives who had initially been recruited during the war. George Hill and William Field Robinson also left SIS in 1922. With the onset of peace, rapprochement with Russia, and government budget cuts, the service could no longer maintain its establishment at previous levels. Reilly apparently took the decision to dispense with his services rather badly and appealed to C to reconsider.

The appeals evidently fell on deaf ears. For Reilly there were to be no more second chances – the final curtain had indeed fallen on his brief but highly eventful SIS career.

TWELVE

A CHANGE OF BAIT

Reilly's relationship with SIS was not the only one that hit the rocks in 1922. In the early months of the previous year he had struck up a business association with Brig. Sir Edward Spears, who had left the army the previous year. Whilst Spears had good connections that he had built up in the army, he lacked, by his own admission, business experience.[1] He proposed to make good this deficiency by taking on Reilly as a partner in the tobacco business they set up in the Czech capital Prague. Their biggest venture was, however, an attempt to commercially market Czech radium, to which end they founded the Radium Corporation Ltd.

Spears' first impression of Reilly was 'rather seedy but really quite nice'.[2] Throughout their tempestuous business relationship Spears, like Lockhart and C before him, seems caught between these two opposing sides of Reilly's character. Often frustrated, and at times angered by his methods, he can never bring himself to dislike Reilly on a personal level.

In July 1921 Reilly met Lockhart again while on a business trip to Prague with Spears. Lockhart, who was now commercial secretary at the British Legation in Prague, was involved in 'smoothing the way for the revival of Central European banks'.[3] Spears and Reilly lunched with Lockhart, and discussed with him the situation concerning commercial opportunities and the banking negotiations that he was involved in. Reilly was, as usual, mixing business with pleasure, and seems to have taken Spears on a hectic round of socialising during their stay. The same day as their lunch with Lockhart, Spears recorded in his diary:

> … with Reilly to a Russian Charity Fête – very popular and hot – did not like it. R[eilly] made great friends with some Russian singers. Poor people they are having a bad time. Lost children… one of them, a colonel in Russian army former ADC to an Archduke and a friend of Polovtsoffs. R[eilly] dragged me to dine at the place they play at. They sang gipsy songs to us… overcome by R[eilly]'s generosity.[4]

By the following month, Reilly's unreliability was becoming apparent to Spears; who wrote:

> Reilly was to have seen Guedalla[5] at 3 did not turn up, absorbed in Russian business, I rather annoyed… Guedalla and Guy[6] gave me the impression they are not at all keen on Reilly – saw R[eilly] at the Albany[7] – he delighted as he saw Churchill who wants him to see L[loyd]G[eorge].[8]

The atmosphere was hardly improved when Spears received what he considered to be a 'rude' telegram from Reilly two weeks later. 'I won't stand cheek',[9] Spears recorded in his diary that day. Within months, however, their relationship had taken an even greater turn for the worse. What had started out as misgivings about reliability and protocol now focused on Reilly's honesty in his dealings with the company. Suspicions had apparently been raised as to the amount of money Reilly was taking from company funds and receiving in expenses.[10] Matters came to a head on the morning of 25 October when Spears arrived at the office and was outraged to find that the phone had been cut off 'owing to Reilly not having paid'.[11] After a row over an inflated expenses claim, Reilly appears to have placated Spears with yet

another of his 'get-rich-quick' schemes, for as Spears' diary
records, on 22 November he and Reilly proceeded to the British
and North European Bank 'to see Rheiar re a Bulgarian egg
scheme'. The following week Spears was again lecturing Reilly:

> ...on the danger of dealing with shady people and mixing politics
> with business – for R[eilly] has I fear compromised his position in
> Prague by identifying himself too much with Savinkov who is now
> out of favour there. R[eilly]'s great danger is his associates before he
> worked with us, he is not careful enough.[12]

If 1921 had seen its ups and downs so far as the Spears/Reilly
relationship was concerned, then 1922 was downhill all the way.
On 20 April another Reilly 'get-rich-quick' scheme hit the dust.
Held out as another sure-fire winner, the 'big Moravian scheme',
in Spears' own words, 'went fut'.[13] Following another row over
Reilly's business methods in June,[14] Spears no doubt decided that
he had no other option but to terminate his business relationship
with him. On 2 August over lunch, he 'very pleasantly' severed his
connection with Reilly.

This was a further blow to Reilly's already depleted bank
balance, which was still bearing the brunt of funding Savinkov's
activities. His chance meeting in Berlin with the wealthy widow
Pepita Bobadilla, some four months after parting company with
Spears, can therefore be seen as a somewhat fortuitous lifeline.

Like Reilly, much mystery has surrounded Pepita Ferdinanda
Bobadilla's true identity, nationality, parentage and origins. Many
have claimed that she was born in Latin America and came over
to England, where she found celebrity as an actress. According to
an interview Pepita gave to *The Tatler* magazine in October 1918,
she was born in Equador.[15] On various other occasions over the
years she claimed to have been born in Argentina and Chile.
Reilly himself told a number of friends and acquaintances that she
had an Equadorian mother and an Irish father,[16] although it is not
clear whether he actually believed this himself or was simply a

willing accomplice in perpetuating the myth. She herself also did much to encourage and perpetuate this myth. The truth, however, is somewhat less exotic and very much more down to earth. Her mother, Isobel, was born in 1862 in Lancaster, the daughter of a flour warehouseman.[17] On 5 June 1888 Isobel arrived in Hamburg, and registered at the British Consulate where she informed them she was looking for a job as a servant.[18] It would seem that Isobel had met Franz Brueckmann in England and on his return to Germany had followed him. One month after her arrival in Hamburg, on 5 July, she gave birth to a son, Franz Kurt Burton.[19] Although Franz Kurt's record of birth does not indicate the name of his father, he was almost certainly Brueckmann. In fact, Isobel moved into an apartment owned by Brueckmann shortly after Franz Kurt's birth.

Her second child, Nelly Louise Burton, was also born in Hamburg on 20 January 1891.[20] Again, no father's name appears on the record. Isobel was still living at the apartment owned by Brueckmann at the time, and Brueckmann may possibly have fathered the child too. On 27 April 1892, Isobel returned to England with her two young children in tow.[21] Two years later, Isobel gave birth to her third and last child, a daughter named Alice. Again, no father is indicated on any records.[22]

In 1910 Nelly made her modest entry into show business as a dancer and in 1912 was engaged by the Bal du Moulin Rouge, in the Pigalle district of Paris.[23] The Moulin was reputedly the centre of Parisian sinfulness and was famous for having first commercialised the cancan in the 1890s. It was here that she adopted the stage name of Josefina Bobadilla.[24] In 1915 the Moulin burnt down and Nelly returned to England. The war had provided a great stimulus to all forms of entertainment, and the theatre in particular. Musicals proved a popular form of escapism, and were packed out by servicemen wanting to make the most of their brief period of leave. Nelly's initial break in London was with Charles B. Cochran, who recruited her as a chorus girl after an audition in spring 1916.

With more productions and performances came the demand for more actors and actresses. This was good news for chorus girls like Nelly, as the chorus line was a ready source for promoters to tap into. In November 1916 she was given her first acting role by Cochran, who cast her as Gladys in *Houp-La*, which was to be the first production staged at his new theatre, the St Martin's, which was due to open in December. *Houp-La*, described by Cochran as 'a comedy set to music',[25] starred Gertie Millar and George Graves. Gertie Millar, eleven years Nelly's senior, was an old hand and had been on stage since the age of thirteen. She had been the mistress of a Russian businessman, who had only recently left London for New York, by the name of Alexandre Weinstein.[26]

The London stage was a honey pot for rich 'playboys' like Weinstein and Reilly, and it was some three years later in January 1920, after a performance of *Daddies*, at the Haymarket Theatre that Nelly was first introduced to Reilly. It would also seem that Reilly had met her wealthy brother-in-law, Stephen Menzies, during his time in New York. By all accounts, Alice and Stephen Menzies had a very 'open' marriage, and it was rumoured that she and Reilly had been more than acquaintances on his return to London. Alice, the more extrovert of the two sisters, threw herself headfirst into the 'Roaring Twenties', as an emancipated Flapper, dancing the Charleston till dawn and maintaining her own apartment at Pembroke Mews in Belgravia.[27]

In October 1920, Pepita married the sixty-year-old playwright Charles Haddon Chambers, thirty-one years her senior.[28] The marriage was a great surprise to everyone, not least the forty-year-old widow engaged to Haddon Chambers, who only learned that her intended had deserted her when she picked up the *Evening Standard* the following day.[29] Pepita, like her sister, had now found herself a husband of substance and, like Alice, maintained her own apartment, at 35 Three Kings Yard in Mayfair.[30] The adjective that could most accurately describe their marriage would have to be 'short', for five months later Haddon Chambers died of a stroke at the Bath Club, leaving the newly wed Pepita the not insubstantial sum of £9,195.[31]

Although she had first met Reilly in 1920, her 1931 book tells of a 'love at first sight' encounter with 'Master Spy' Reilly the year after Haddon Chambers' death:

> My first meeting with Sidney Reilly took place at the Hotel Adlon in Berlin. It was in the December of 1922, and the Reparations Commission was in session in the German capital. I was staying there with my mother and sister and among the acquaintances we made was an English delegate on the Commission.[32]

This delegate apparently regaled Mrs Burton and her two daughters with tales of Britain's Master Spy and his daring exploits. That same evening at dinner, Pepita claims to have had her first glimpse of Reilly:

> When raising my eyes from my coffee I found them looking straight into a pair of brown ones at the other side of the room. For a moment his eyes held mine and I felt a delicious thrill running through me. The owner of the eyes presented a well-groomed and well-tailored figure, with a lean, rather sombre face, which conveyed an impression of unusual strength of resolution and character. The eyes were steady, kindly and rather sad. And with it all there was an expression, which might almost have been sardonic, the expression of a man, who not once but many times had laughed in the face of death.[33]

In this romantically charged account, Reilly gets a member of the British delegation to introduce him to Pepita, and by the end of the week they have become secretly engaged. History again repeated itself when they married the following May, and Caryll Houselander discovered almost at the last moment that the man she was devoted to was about to marry another. Devastated by Reilly's marriage, she was never really able to recover emotionally or fill the void he left. In 1947 she confided to a friend:

> I know what it can feel like to part from a man whom one is in love with, for I too have done so, years and years ago... A few years of grief on earth are nothing compared to being together in eternity in God's presence.[34]

Reilly was not alone in being secretive about their engagement; Pepita, too, kept it hidden from those closest to her: 'Our engagement was a secret one and I carefully kept it from my mother and my sister during the short time we were together'.

By 9 January 1923 Reilly was back in London and wrote to his 'sweet little pal', who was still in Berlin,[35] letting her know that due to the ongoing legal dispute with Baldwin Locomotives, he would be unable to visit her on 15 January. He hoped, however, that she would be able to come to London to meet him instead. Although containing little of importance, the letter is significant in that it is one of the few personal letters he wrote to a wife or lover that has survived. The final part of the letter is particularly telling in that it typifies his 'affectionate' charm:

> I need not tell you what it will mean to me to see you here. But again, considering your dependence on Cita,[36] I beg you not to violate any of your plans on my account. Thank you many times for your sweet letters. They have been to me like a caress from your lovely little hand. With infinite tenderness, yours Sidney[37]

For a couple who had, supposedly, only just met a few weeks before, and had spent a little over a week together, a great deal of detailed knowledge about each other's affairs is evident from this letter. Their marriage took place on 18 May 1923 at the St Martin Register Office in London.[38] The witnesses were George Hill and Stephen Alley, formerly of SIS, and Pepita's sister Alice. A lavish reception at the Savoy Hotel was attended by many theatrical acquaintances of Pepita's and a smaller number of Reilly's former SIS colleagues. A number of those present on the groom's side knew or suspected that this was a bigamous marriage, but said nothing. In fact, it was his second if not third bigamous union. Although she would be blissfully unaware of this for ten years, the realities of the world Reilly moved in dawned on Pepita much quicker:

> Gradually I was initiated into those strange proceedings which were going on behind the scenes of European politics. I learned how beneath the surface of every capital in Europe was simmering the conspiracy of the exiles of Russia against the present tyrants of their country… in this whole movement Sidney was intensely interested and was devoting much time and money to the cause.[39]

So too were the Bolsheviks. On 6 February 1922 the Cheka had been disbanded and the State Political Directorate (GPU) created in its place. When the Soviet Union came into being later that year the GPU was renamed the Unified State Political Directorate (OGPU). Having established an iron-like grip on internal dissent, the organisation now began to focus on dissidents and opposition leaders outside the Soviet Union who it perceived to be a threat to the Bolshevik regime. The ultimate eradication of such opponents was now given top priority.

To this end the OGPU was to perpetrate one of the biggest and most successful hoaxes in the history of counter-espionage. Perfecting an old Ochrana tactic, the OGPU's Counter-Intelligence Department (KRO) set up an organisation called the Monarchist Organisation of Central Russia, whose cover was a trust based in Paris by the name of the Moscow Municipal Credit Association. The Trust was a deception operation devised to entice counter-revolutionary exiles back into Russia where they could be executed or imprisoned. Its ostensible purpose was to offer support to anti-Bolsheviks, and by so doing could infiltrate KRO agents into exile groups. This not only gave KRO impeccable first-hand knowledge of what was being planned, but also enabled it to directly influence events in groups where agents had been able to infiltrate the inner circles and take up posts of responsibility.

One of KRO's top targets was Boris Savinkov, who they aimed to lure back to Russia through a similar deception operation code-named 'Syndicate II'. When in July 1923 Sidney and Pepita visited him at the Chatham Hotel in Paris, they found him closeted by bodyguards, who were clearly taking the possibility of OGPU abduction very seriously. While Reilly himself greatly admired the 'Napoleonic' Savinkov, his actress wife knew a ham performance when she saw one and was not the least bit impressed by 'the portly little man who strutted in with the most amusing air of self assurance and self esteem'.[40] Pepita could hardly contain her disdain as Savinkov 'posed in front of the mantelpiece' thrusting his hand 'into his breast in the approved Napoleonic manner'.[41]

The main subject under discussion in Paris was the growing realisation that funding for Savinkov's cause was running thin, due to the recent decisions of the French, Czech and Polish governments to cease their contributions. Like many other European governments, they were slowly coming to the con-clusion that despite the dedicated efforts of the Russian opposition, the Bolsheviks were not to be budged from power. The net result was that Reilly was left as the main source of income for Savinkov's organisation.

In addition to this burden, Margaret was still hovering in the background exerting her mysterious hold over him. Their last meeting occurred just prior to Reilly's departure from France, and no doubt involved a further plea from Margaret for money.[42] Her own fortunes had shown little sign of improvement over the years. There seems little she would not do for money when in a tight corner, and could well have supplied information about her estranged husband to the Baldwin Locomotive Company, who were in the process of preparing their defence against his claim for outstanding munitions commission.[43]

Despite Pepita's money, Reilly was intent upon restoring his own fortunes. Ever a creature of habit he again returned to the world of patent medicine as a means of making money. With

The only true statement Reilly made about himself in the Marriage Register was his address; everything else from his name, age, former rank and the status of his father, was a complete fabrication.

Hugh Coward and long-time associate Alexandre Weinstein he set up Modern Medicine Ltd, with £5,000 capital.[44] The three founder directors were joined shortly afterwards by William Barclay Calder, who had been a partner in the Ozone Preparations Company.[45] Reilly had high hopes for the company and placed particular faith in a preparation known as Humagsolen,[46] which he intended to market in America. To this end he and Pepita planned to visit America in July, where Reilly also hoped to further pursue his legal claim against the Baldwin Locomotive Company, which seemed to have become bogged down in the legal mire of claim and counter claim.[47] Shortly before he was due to depart he called in at the London office of his friend Maj. 'Robbie' Field Robinson in the Strand, and pleaded to him, 'Robbie, I am broke. My credit in London is finished. I must get over to New York to fight my case. It is my last chance. Will you help?'[48] Field Robinson immediately went to the bank and withdrew two £100 notes which he gave to Reilly in exchange for an IOU. This enabled Reilly to book their passage. 'Of course, I never saw the money again', Field Robinson told George Hill twelve years later when he was assisting Hill in researching his Reilly biography.[49]

It would seem that Reilly was viewed by some acquaintances as akin to a naughty child that you could never remain angry with for too long. On this basis, Reilly was often able to return to people he had previously crossed or dropped into hot water, like

Lockhart, C and Field Robinson, for small favours. Edward Spears would appear to be a further example, for the week after he had procured £200 from Field Robinson, Reilly approached Spears for letters of introduction to two of his American business contacts in Chicago. On 19 July Spears wrote to Reilly:

> Herewith the introductions promised... your best introduction to Mr Borden is through Mr Hertz. If he is interested, the fact that you have a direct introduction to Mr Borden will be an additional advantage, but nothing will have such an effect as Mr Hertz's recommendation, as Mr Borden has great faith in him. Wishing you all good luck on your journey.[50]

According to Spears' introduction, the Modern Medicine Company Ltd had 'a brilliant future before it'.[51] Sadly, when Reilly arrived in Chicago, he was unable to interest Messrs Borden and Hertz in the wonders of Humagsolen. Modern Medicine's brilliant future failed to materialise and the company eventually went bankrupt.[52] Neither was Reilly to find any joy concerning the other purpose of his American visit. The Baldwin Locomotive Company was to remain resolute that it was not legally obliged to pay him a cent in commission.

Returning empty handed to England in January 1924, the failures of the past year were clearly beginning to take their toll on his health. When advised by his doctor that he was on the verge of a breakdown due to business worries, he reluctantly agreed to follow the doctor's advice and take a long holiday in the south of France for a complete rest and change of surroundings.

With their hotel reservations and railway passage booked, the Reillys were ready to depart from London during the third week of January 1924, when an unannounced visitor called at their home. In her ghostwritten book, *Britain's Master Spy*, published a decade later, Pepita refers to the mysterious bearded visitor as 'Mr Warner' and gives a dramatic account of the events that unfolded during the week following his appearance on their doorstep.[53]

According to *Britain's Master Spy*, Mr Warner was, in fact, an anti-Bolshevik Russian whose real name was Drebkoff. Having been invited into their sitting room, he proceeded to explain that he had been delegated by anti-Bolsheviks in Russia to visit Reilly and beseech him to return and lead them to power. Appealing to Reilly's vanity, he is quoted by Pepita as telling Reilly, 'We want a man in Russia… a man who can command and get things done, whose commands there are no disputing… a man who will be master'. As 'excitement was surging up within him' Reilly found it hard not to be seduced by the call as Drebkoff told him 'we still have no leader… with one accord they all, Balkoff, Opperput, Alvendorff, Vorislavsky and the others, call for you – we are ready to strike – we wait for your hand to guide us'.[54]

Drebkoff produced documentation that seemed to substantiate his claims and invited Reilly to lunch at the Savoy. Clearly moved by this turn of events, Reilly took up the offer and consequently decided to postpone the French holiday for a week in order that he could 'learn fully… the prospects of our friends in Russia'.[55] Barely able to resist the temptation to return, Reilly finally resolved that due to ill health he could not accept, but promised Drebkoff that once he had recovered they could count on him.

After accompanying a disappointed Drebkoff to the station to see him off on his journey back to Russia, Reilly returned home to find the house empty. Within minutes a stranger appeared at the door to tell him that Pepita had been knocked down by a car and was in hospital. Just as he was about to leave for the hospital, Pepita telephoned to tell him that shortly after he left for the station, a man called to tell her that he had been knocked down by a car and had been taken to hospital. On being offered a lift to the hospital, she readily agreed, but was drugged in the car by a hypodermic needle, and came to in a chemist's shop where she had been left by the occupants of the car. Reilly concluded immediately that this was an attempt to kidnap him and take him back to Russia.

This cloak and dagger story of Pepita's has understandably met with much cynicism over the years and is certainly typical of the highly dramatised stories included in her book. Before dismissing the account out of hand, however, a passage from a letter written on 25 January 1924 by Pepita to her sister Alice, who was holidaying in Cannes, should be considered: 'after yesterday's events it would seem there are no lengths to which Sidney's enemies will not go'.[56]

Whether the attempted kidnapping was a reality, an embellishment or a fantasy, it seems clear that something sinister occurred during their last week in England.

By the following week they had joined Pepita's sister Alice at the Hotel de la Terrasse in Theoule, a short distance from Cannes. Despite the fact that he was supposed to be taking things easy, Reilly's correspondence indicates that he was in almost daily communication with both political and business contacts.

In letters to Savinkov, for example, Reilly frequently refers to his perilous financial state. While his finances were indeed far from satisfactory, his repeated references to the lack of ready cash could well be a ploy, for by this stage he was more than likely tiring of his role as Savinkov's principal coffer: 'I am unable to send you even 500 francs. I am waiting for a few pounds from London, but have not received them yet'. After seven weeks in the south of France, Reilly was now desperate to get back to New York in pursuit of his Baldwins claim:

Made up my mind to leave this imaginary paradise and get back to the austere reality. Nothing to live upon. Staying here would be like letting grass grow under my feet... Wrote letters to a few friends who owe me about £200 in total... the situation with my creditors in London is that at any minute I can be declared insolvent. To successfully finish my lawsuit in New York, I need to be present there personally, but have not the slightest chance to go there. To buy a return ticket I need at least £200, which is similar to dreaming about mines on the moon.[57]

Despite this plea of poverty, Reilly's mine on the moon clearly came up trumps, for after spending a month tidying up his affairs in London, he and Pepita booked a passage on the SS *New Amsterdam*, which sailed for New York on 7 May.[58]

While Reilly was closeted with lawyers in New York, the OGPU were putting the final touches to their plan to entrap Savinkov. Having infiltrated a number of OGPU agents into Savinkov's inner circle, moves were set in hand to persuade him to return to Russia. After several weeks of soul-searching, he finally succumbed to temptation, despite advice to the contrary from Reilly, who now travelled back across the Atlantic aboard the SS *Paris* to bid him farewell.

On 10 August Savinkov left Paris for Berlin, where he was met by Syndicate II agents Alexander Yakushev and Eduard Opperput. They provided him with a Russian passport in the name of V.I. Stepanov and arranged his passage to the Byelorussian border, which he crossed on 20 August. He was barely fifteen miles inside Soviet territory when Roman Pilar of the OGPU placed him under arrest as he sat down for breakfast in a forester's hut just outside Minsk.

When news of Savinkov's arrest and trial were announced by *Izvestia* on 29 August, Reilly at first refused to believe it. On 3 September *The Times* published an account of the trial, and Reilly immediately wrote a letter to the *Morning Post* (and a copy to Winston Churchill) asserting that reports of Savinkov's capture and trial was Bolshevik propaganda, and that in all likelihood Savinkov had been killed crossing the border.[59] His letter was published in full on 8 September, but was very shortly to be proven erroneous by new information published by *The Times*. On learning the truth, Reilly reacted angrily, sending a further letter to the *Morning Post*, which was published on 15 September:

Sir

I once more take the liberty of claiming your indulgence and your space. This time for a twofold purpose, first to express my deep appreciation of your fairness in inserting (in your issue of 8th inst.) my letter in defence of Boris Savinkov when all the information at your disposal tended to show that I am in error; secondly, to perform a duty, in this case a most painful duty, and to acknowledge the error into which my loyalty to Savinkov has induced me.

The detailed and in many instances stenographic press reports of Savinkov's trial, supported by the testimony of reliable and impartial eyewitnesses, have established Savinkov's treachery beyond all possibility of doubt. He has not only betrayed his friends, his organisation, and his cause, but he has also deliberately and completely gone over to his former enemies. He has connived with his captors to deal the heaviest possible blow at the anti-Bolshevik movement and to provide them with an outstanding political triumph both for internal and external use. By this act Savinkov has erased forever his name from the scroll of honour of the anti-Communist movement.

His former friends and followers grieve over his terrible and inglorious downfall, but those amongst them who under no circumstances will practise with the enemies of mankind are dismayed. The moral suicide of their former leader is for them an added incentive to close ranks and carry on.

Yours

Sidney Reilly[60]

Churchill, on reading the *Morning Post*, sent a copy of his earlier letter to Archibald Sinclair and a word of support to Reilly:

Dear Mr Reilly

I am very interested in your letter. The event has turned out as I myself expected at the very first. I do not think that you should judge Savinkov too harshly. He was placed in a terrible position; and only those who have sustained successfully such an ordeal have a full right to pronounce censure. At any rate I shall wait to hear the end of the story before changing my view of Savinkov.

Yours very truly

W.S. Churchill[61]

Sir Archibald Sinclair's reply to Churchill on 23 September further reinforces this view in quoting the Finnish financier Brunstron, whose comments on Savinkov's behaviour are said to be 'more merciful, and I think, shrewder than Reilly's, whose judgement is no doubt affected by the bitter disappointment he must have felt at the failure of his plans'.[62]

Despite the writing on the wall, Reilly continued to push his legal claim, which was eventually lost in the New York Supreme Court. Not unsurprisingly, Baldwin's lawyers White and Case had done a great deal of homework on Reilly and his less than salubrious past.[63] The recital of this in court caused Reilly to lose his temper and was probably the final nail in the coffin of a case that was legally tenuous to say the least.

While the verdict was a bitter blow, Reilly resolved to remain in New York and rebuild his fortunes. In December 1924 he, Upton Dale Thomas and several other old associates from his munitions days, set up Trading Ventures Incorporated at 25 Broadway, New York City.[64] In a letter to Edward Spears dated 22 January 1925 Reilly explained that:

> I am now permanently established in New York. I am president of the above company [Trading Ventures Inc.], which I have formed and in which I own a large interest. I have unfortunately lost my big lawsuit and as the times seem to be extremely prosperous here I thought it is the wisest thing to make use of my very extended connections here.

Reilly went on to disclose the main activities of his new company:

> … generally speaking the type of business which I am doing here is the same as we were doing in our former association with Brunstrom. The most fashionable business here at the present moment is bond issues for foreign municipalities and foreign industries.[65]

Finally getting to the point of his letter, Reilly remarked that if Spears 'should come across anything of this kind' he would be 'very glad to undertake it'. 'I would', he goes on, 'also be very much interested in anything in the way of export and import between Great Britain and the United States, as well as in the placing and financing of British inventions and processes here'.[66]

From company records[67] it is clear that major injections of capital were going to be necessary if his ambitions for Trading Ventures were to amount to anything. To this end Reilly was clearly hunting for new business opportunities that might bring this about. However, he was also only too keenly aware that hunting of another kind was being conducted in New York and that he was more than likely the prey.

THIRTEEN
PRISONER 73

Despite the Syndicate II operation and the controversy surrounding Savinkov's arrest, the good intentions of 'The Trust' had not been questioned in the West. The organisation's support, influence and capability were, however, very much the talking point of Western intelligence agencies. Cmdr Ernest Boyce, head of the SIS station in Helsingfors, from where Russian operations were now directed, apparently wished to establish whether the Trust had, or was likely to have, the capability to take power in Russia. Boyce therefore resolved that the best way of finding out was to send his former colleague Reilly. To send one of his own agents would have involved risk, and in all likelihood would not have been sanctioned by C.

Without any consultation with SIS in London, he wrote to Reilly on 24 January 1925:

Dear Sidney

There may call on you in Paris from me two persons named Krasnoshtanov, man and wife, they will say they have a communication from California and hand you a note consisting of a verse from Omar Kahyam which you will remember. If you wish to go further into their business you must ask them to remain. If the business is of no interest you will say 'thank you very much, good day'.

Now as to their business. They are representatives of a concern which in all probability has a big influence in the future on the European and American markets. They do not anticipate that their business will fully develop for two years, but circumstances may arise which will give them the desired impetus in the near future. It is a very big business and one which it does not do to talk about as others who have a suspicion that the concession is obtainable, would give their ears to know all about who is at the back of it and why they themselves cannot make any headway. There are especially two parties very much interested. One, a strong international group, would like to upset the whole concern as they fear their own financial interest in the event of the enterprise being brought to a satisfactory conclusion. The other, a German group, would like very much to come in, but originators represented by the two persons mentioned above, through whom it is important that arrangements for future communication be made, and who have worked hard on the preliminary work ever since they left Russia, will have nothing to do with them as they fear this particular group would want to take too much into their own hands. They have therefore connected up with a smaller, French, group consisting of less ambitious persons. The undertaking is so large, however, that they fear this group will not be able to handle it alone. They are therefore wanting to enter into negotiations with an English group who would be willing to work in with the French group. It is to be thoroughly understood, however, by anyone coming in that when the enterprise is firmly established the board will be composed from those who have done the spade work. They refuse at present to disclose to anyone the name of the man at the back of this enterprise. I can tell you this much – that some of the chief persons interested are members of the opposition groups. You can therefore fully understand the necessity for secrecy.

A talk with the representatives will enable you to form your own judgement as to the feasibility of their ideas.

I am introducing this scheme to you thinking it might perhaps replace the other big scheme you were working on but which fell through in such disastrous manner. Incidentally, you would help me considerably by taking the matter up. The only thing I ask is that you keep our connection with this business from the knowledge of my department as, being a government official, I am not supposed to be connected with any such enterprise. I know your interest in such business where patience and perseverance against all sorts of intrigues and opposition are required and I know also you will look after my interests without my having to make some special agreement with you. Please let me know where to address letters to you in the future.

Kindest regards and best of luck. Please also remember me to your wife.[1]

'California', according to Pepita Reilly, 'stands for Russia, the verse from Omar Kahyam (sic) for a cipher message: the big scheme which fell through disastrously was the Savinkov affair. The letter means in fact that there is in operation a strong anti-Bolshevik group, having at its head some of the members of the Bolshevik government'.

Clearly intrigued by this unexpected letter, Reilly replied to Boyce from his office at 25 Broadway, New York:

I am kicking myself for not being in Paris, and thereby missing the Californian couple. You must understand that although I am here I am not losing touch with the situation at all and am in constant correspondence with the different manufacturing groups in the various countries.

I fully realise the possible importance of the scheme which the Californian promoters have in hand. Since the failure of the big scheme on which I was working, and especially since the recent fight for share control which has been going on in the board of directors, I have finally convinced myself that the initiative must come direct from the present minority interests. I believe that the time is gradually getting ripe for the minority interests to realise that the whole business will go to wreck and ruin unless they make up their minds to sacrifice a good portion of their original ideas and come down to earth in a manner which will be acceptable both to the internal and international market. Whether minority interests have already reached this mental attitude or not it has been impossible for me to discover in any definite form, and, therefore, I regret so intensely missing the Californians.

After treating Boyce to a long and drawn-out discourse on how the 'Californians' should proceed, he turns to the 'minority interests', who he states are:

> ...fully acquainted with the internal market; they know exactly what is required, and they know how and by what means the business can be reorganised, but what they probably lack is, first – money, and secondly – an understanding with the leading personalities in the international market.

In conclusion, Reilly states that:

> ...as regards a closer understanding with the international market, I think that to start with only one man is really important, and that is the irrepressible Marlborough. I have always remained on good terms with him and last year, after the disaster of my big scheme, I had a very interesting correspondence with him on the subject. His ear would always be open to something really sound, especially if it is emanated from the minority interests. He said as much in one of his very private and confidential letters to me.

Clearly now hooked, he ended the letter by confirming that:

> I would welcome it very much if the Californian promoters would get in touch with me, either by coming here or by correspondence. I am sure that it will be of mutual benefit, not only to the whole situation but to each of us individually.
> Very sincerely yours
> Sidney G. Reilly[2]

As a result of Reilly's positive response, Boyce put him in contact with one of his Helsingfors-based agents, Nikolai Bunakov, code name ST28. On 27 March Reilly wrote a revealing letter to Bunakov, in which he outlined his thinking on anti-Soviet strategy. The letter would later be quoted in the Russian and foreign Communist press as evidence of the West's hostile intentions towards the Soviet state and of their perception of Reilly as a terrorist. Whether the letter constitutes a genuine plan of action on Reilly's part or is simply another example of his 'Walter Mitty' bravado is very much open to debate. Although he may well have taken part in one of Savinkov's guerrilla raids into Belorussia in December 1920, there is little if any evidence that Reilly had any realistic plans to use terror as a vehicle for achieving the overthrow of the Soviet state. As we shall see later in this chapter, his objectives were somewhat more materialistic.

According to the letter, Reilly saw terror as a measure without which a solution (in terms of ousting the Bolsheviks) was not possible. He also set out for Bunakov a justification for this point of view:

> Terror should be directed from a central point, but carried out by small independent groups or persons against individual prominent representatives of the Soviet government. The aim of terror is always a double one. The first and less important is the removal of dangerous persons. The second and more important is to bring the morass into the movement, to put an end to lethargy, to destroy the legend of the invulnerability of the authority. If there is no terror it means there is no spirit in the movement.[3]

Going on to anticipate objections to the practicality of his proposal, Reilly continued:

> You may say that it is easy to speak of terror when one is safe abroad, but I tell you that I know people who have expended tremendous energy in its preparation (suitable to the present situation and the latest technical improvements) and are prepared to begin immediately the necessary means are placed at their disposal.[4]

After several further exchanges of correspondence, Reilly wrote to Boyce on 4 April to confirm that:

> I fully agree with the board that the simplest and most effective way to gather all the necessary data and to arrive at a complete understanding as to the future operations and improvements of manufacture is for me to come out and to inspect the factory personally.
>
> I am not only willing but anxious to do so and am prepared to come out as soon as I have arranged my affairs here. Of course, I would undertake this tour of inspection only after very thorough consultation with you and Engineer B. Whilst there is no limit to which I am not prepared to go in order to help in putting this new process on the market, I would naturally hate to provide a Roman holiday for the competitors. I think that I am not exaggerating in presuming that a successful inspection of the factory by me and the presentation of a fully substantiated technical report would produce a considerable impression in the interested quarters and generally facilitate to realisation of the scheme.
>
> I am looking forward to your more definite advices which ought to reach me about the 20th inst. And in the meantime I shall do all to make myself free for a quick departure.[5]

Arrangements were made to sail from New York on 26 August in order to arrive in Paris on 3 September. Reilly and Pepita were met at the Gare du Nord by Boyce, with whom they dined that evening. The following day Pepita left for a few days in Ostend to visit her mother whom she had not seen for over a year. While she was away Reilly met a number of underground contacts and pronounced that he was 'convinced of the sincerity and potentiality' of the Trust organisation.

On Pepita's return they dined with Gen. Kutyepov, who was keen for Reilly to meet the Trust representatives, but went to great lengths to implore him not to cross the Russian border under any circumstances. Pepita quotes Kutyepov as advising Reilly 'let them come to you – the arrangement has been made most definitely with the people from Moscow centre that they are to come to Helsingfors to see you there'.[6] The following day they took a train to Cologne where they had agreed to separate. He was to head for Helsingfors via Berlin, as it was felt his arrival there would be less circumspect if he was alone. Pepita was to head for Hamburg, where she was to await his return. As the Berlin train arrived and Reilly stepped aboard, Pepita had a feeling of foreboding:

> A whistle shrilled. I felt Sidney suddenly lift me into his arms. Then he set me down and stepped into the train. I saw his hand waving out of infinite blackness. A lump rose in my throat. I suddenly wanted to cry. Slowly the train gathered speed. I saw the hand waving through the tear mists rapidly receding into the distance. Then it was gone.[7]

Once in Helsingfors, Reilly sent Pepita a long letter dated Tuesday 22 September:

> My Sweetheart,
>
> I had a rotten trip. Sunday we had very bad weather and the little steamer did everything to make the passage very uncomfortable. I was not seasick but felt very headachey [sic] and congested. Yesterday about noon we stopped for a short while at Revel and I could gaze from the deck of the steamer upon the scene of my former exploits... We arrived here about 5 p.m. It was very fortunate that I had wired for a room from Paris. I got the one and only free. I got in touch with E's assistant (a very intelligent youngster, keen as mustard and most anxious to serve me in every possible way).[8]

Reilly had by now met his initial contact Nikolai Bunakov (ST28), the former Tsarist naval officer who worked under Boyce and had been, in turn, introduced to the Shultzes (the 'Californian' couple). They struck him as:

> ... a most extraordinary couple. He is just a boy, probably a very fine and undoubtedly a very brave boy, but of the type which you characterise as

'nincompoop'. She is the head of the concern, and her very long skirt cannot disguise the trousers which she is wearing – she is of the American school-marm type, which, strangely enough, is not uncommon in Russia, very plain and unattractive, but full of character and personality.[9]

Vyborg, close to the border with Russia, was the rendezvous point where it had been arranged that Reilly would meet the Trust representatives. It was here that he was introduced to two undercover OGPU agents: Alexander Yakushev, supposedly a senior Trust representative from Moscow; and George Syroezhkin. The task now was to entice him over the border and to begin the process of debriefing him.

Yakushev gave Reilly an impressive account of the Trust's power and influence within the organs of government and sought his guidance on the attitude a Trust government should take on a range of domestic issues. Yakushev later recalled that:

The first impression of him was unpleasant. His bulging dark eyes expressed something biting and cruel; his lower lip drooped deeply and he was too slick – the neat black hair, the demonstratively elegant suit. Everything in his manner expressed something haughtily indifferent to his surroundings. He took a seat in an armchair, carefully adjusted the crease in his trousers, then showed off his new yellow shoes and silk stockings. He began the conversation with world-weary seriousness and a superior tone by announcing that he found it impossible at the moment to travel to us.[10]

Yakushev asked Reilly how many days he had, retorting that it was a great shame that he had travelled all the way from America, only to stop at the very threshold which he dare not step across. This intended slight to Reilly's courage had the desired effect. According to Yakushev's report:

Reilly thought hard for a moment, then said, 'You've persuaded me. It's decided, I'm going with you.' He immediately became alive.[11]

Although now resolved to cross the border, Reilly still had nagging doubts. This is clear from reading between the lines of a letter he wrote to Pepita shortly before he left Vyborg with the Trust representatives. He entrusted the letter to one of Boyce's agents, Nikolai Bunakov, under strict instructions to send it to Pepita only in the event that he did not return as planned on 28 September. Bunakov in turn gave the letter to another SIS agent, Harry Carr, who locked it in his safe:

My most beloved, my sweetheart,

It is absolutely necessary that I should go for three days to St Petersburg and Moscow. I am now leaving tonight and will be back here on Tuesday morning. I want you to know that I would not have undertaken this trip unless it was absolutely essential, and if I was not convinced that there is practically no risk attached to it. I am writing this letter only for the most improbable case of a mishap befalling me. Should this happen, then you must not take any steps; they will help little but may finally lead to giving the alarm to the Bolshies and to disclosing my identity. If by any chance I should be arrested in Russia, it could be only on some minor, insignificant charge and my new friends are powerful enough to obtain my prompt liberation. I cannot imagine any circumstance under which the Bolshies could tumble to my identity provided nothing is done from your side. Therefore, if I should have some trouble, it would only mean a very short delay in my return to Europe – I should say a fortnight at the most. Knowing you I am certain you will rise to the occasion, keep your head, and do all that is necessary to keep the fort as regards my business affairs.

Naturally none of these people must get an inkling where I am and what has happened to me, and remember that every noise, etc, may give me away to the Bolshies.

My dearest darling, I am doing what I must do and I am doing it with the absolute inner assurance that, if you were with me, you would approve. You are in my thoughts always and your love will protect me. God bless you ever and ever. I love you beyond all words.

Sidney[12]

In order to undertake the journey, Reilly was given a Soviet passport in the name of Nikolas Nikolaivich Sternberg. The border crossing was to be made just south of Vyborg by wading across the Sister River, and passing through a 'blind spot' on the Russian side of the river that would avoid the border patrols. Having changed out of his American outfit into a less conspicuous suit, Reilly set off with Yakushev, who later recalled in his report:

> We walked slowly, ears tuned to every little whisper. Reilly's new boots squeaked so we made him wet his soles in a puddle then dug little holes in them with a knife. Moving with stealth and in total silence we reached the banks of the Sister River. Crossing the river took considerable time because Reilly, in addition to undressing and dressing, had to unwind and then rewind the elastic bandages he wore for the enlarged veins in his legs. In pouring rain we approached Peschanoi Station, got out and walked the rest of the way. Then we took the first train to Leningrad.[13]

It was here, at Syroezhkin's apartment, that Reilly was introduced to Vladimir Styrne, the Deputy Head of the KRO, the OGPU's counter-intelligence section, who represented himself as a member of the Moscow City Council. Styrne took the opportunity to fill in a few gaps in the OGPU's knowledge of Reilly by subtly questioning him from the point of view of a fellow conspirator. That same evening Reilly, Yakushev and a White guard (Mukalov-Mikhaylov) left for Moscow by international sleeping car. After some initial doubts, Reilly now seemed more at ease and back to his old gregarious and arrogant self. From Yakushev's report, it would seem that the conversation was dominated by talk of Savinkov, who Reilly, with no sense of irony, slated for his poor judgement of people, and for being too fond of women, gambling and comfort. Savinkov's mistress, Madame Derental, was uncharitably referred to as a 'stinking Jewess, with a shiny face, fat hands and thighs' in an echo of Reilly's earlier scathing remarks about Gen. Poole's mistress in South Russia.

Pressed for his views on matters of state policy, Reilly was only too happy to oblige. The views recalled by Yakushev are most revealing if not somewhat shocking. As a Jew, albeit one in denial of his roots, he advised that a pogrom was unavoidable, but counselled that the Trust government should not associate itself directly, but call such measures 'an expression of national feeling'. He advised them to control the Orthodox Church and profit from its inflence rather than trying to abolish it altogether.[14]

The next morning when the train arrived in Moscow they were met at the station and driven to a dacha in Malakhovka where he met the Trust's leaders over lunch. After the meal they went to a nearby forest clearing for reasons of security, where a discussion took place concerning the Trust's funding. Reilly told them that 'no government will give you money. Today, everyone's house is on fire. Churchill believes, as I do, in the speedy over-throw of Soviet power, but he is not in a position to supply funds'.[15] Instead, Reilly proposed to them a plan to raise money that was, in his own words, 'crude and will probably repel you'.

The plan was essentially to mount a campaign of raids on Russia's museums, aimed at robbing them of art treasures, which would then be smuggled to the West and sold by Reilly. This does not appear to have been an 'off the cuff' suggestion, as Reilly apparently produced a detailed list which included French masters, Rembrandts, antique coins, engravings and miniatures. Yakushev was less than impressed and voiced grave misgivings about Reilly's scheme, protesting that this would 'ruin' the organisation's reputation. Reilly merely brushed this off, telling Yakushev that 'for the sake of money, a reputation may have to be sacrificed'.[16] He also promised to supply Yakushev with $50,000 to finance the appropriation scheme as well as an introduction to Churchill, should Yakushev be able to visit England.

As dusk gathered Reilly said his goodbyes and got into the car he thought was taking him to Moscow's October Station to catch the night train back to Leningrad. As the car entered Moscow Reilly asked if he could be taken to a safe-house in order that he could write and post a letter to his English contact (Ernest Boyce) to confirm that he had actually been in Moscow. This was agreed and they went to the apartment of Eduard Opperput. As soon as Reilly had posted the letter and returned to the car, handcuffs were snapped onto his wrists and the car sped off not to the railway station but the OGPU's feared Lubyanka building. Before the Revolution, the palatial Lubyanka had been the headquarters of the All Russian Insurance Company. One of the building's apparent attractions for the Cheka was its cavernous cellars. From the subterranean world below street level no one on the outside could hear the firing squads that during the 'Red Terror' had often worked around the clock.

On arrival Reilly was taken to the office of Roman Pilar, who had arrested Savinkov the previous year. Pilar reminded Reilly that he was still effectively under sentence of death from the 1918 tribunal, and counselled that full co-operation was his best policy. By all accounts Reilly kept his composure throughout and other than confirming his own identity refused to answer any questions about the identities of other British spies in Russia. Reilly was also searched, and according to Mikhail Trilliser, head of the OGPU's Foreign Intelligence Department, found to be in possession of unspecified 'valuables' that had apparently been 'hidden in Leningrad'.[17] He was then taken to cell 73 and from then on would be referred to as 'Prisoner 73', or simply '73'.

The next day, 28 September, the OGPU staged an incident on the border at the very time and location where Reilly and his companions were due to cross back into Finland.

Villagers in Vanha Alakyla heard several volleys of rifle fire. In full view of the Finnish border guards on the other side of the river, a truck arrived and two apparently dead bodies were loaded into the back of the van which then drove away. A meeting of the Trust's Council was convened in Moscow and was informed that Reilly was one of the two dead. The OGPU was clearly banking on word getting out from this meeting, via the genuine White Russian conspirators involved, back to their contacts in

Helsingfors. Pepita, meanwhile, was trying to contact her husband at the Hotel Andrea in Vyborg, where he should have arrived that evening. When he failed to arrive she sent Boyce a telegram on 30 September: 'No news from Sidney since twenty-fifth. Should have returned today. Hotel Andrea Vyborg expected him yesterday, but wired has not arrived. What steps shall I take? Wire if you have news – very anxious'. Boyce sent a short to the point reply, 'Have had no news whatever, have telegraphed'.[18] The next day he sent Pepita a letter:

Dear Mrs Reilly

I have heard from no one as to Sidney's condition. In fact I have had no news from that part of the world since I left. Judging from your telegram he has apparently undergone the operation after all. This is rather a surprise to me as I thought the doctors in Paris considered it unnecessary. I suppose further complications must have set in which decided him to have the operation. As I understood it the operation was a simple one but his recovery might take a little longer than was expected. We must not get panicky. I am sure he is in safe hands and everything will be done to make his recovery as speedy as possible. It will not help us to send frantic telegrams. We shall hear as soon as he is able to get about again.[19]

As Reilly reflected on his predicament in cell 73, he may well have hoped that on learning of his capture, the British government would take steps to have him extradited, or swapped as they had done with Lockhart back in 1918. In this belief he clearly adopted the view that his best chance of survival was to play for time.

FOURTEEN

A LONELY PLACE TO DIE

Contrary to popular opinion, Reilly was not tortured or subjected to any physical maltreatment by the OGPU. Seventy-seven years later, Boris Gudz, then a twenty-three-year-old OGPU liaison officer attached to Vladimir Styrne, recalled that, 'no physical methods were used, I can guarantee that'.[1] From the very start their approach was clearly one of respect for someone they considered a worthy adversary. Although he made several statements about himself, his background and his activities since he was last in Russia, he would not be drawn on any of the matters the OGPU most wanted to know about. Vladimir Styrne, credited with being one of the OGPU's best interrogators, duly noted the results of his initial interviews with Reilly:

> 7 October 1925
>
> I, Deputy Head of KRO OGPU, Styrne, questioned the accused citizen Reilly, Sidney George, born 1874, Clonmel (Ireland), British subject, father, captain in the navy. Permanent residence, London and more recently New York. Captain in the British Army. Wife abroad. Education: university; studied at Heidelberg in the faculty of philosophy; in London, the Royal Institute of Mines, specialising in chemistry. Party: active Conservative. Was tried in

November 1918 by the supreme tribunal of the RSFSR, the Lockhart case (*in absentia*).[2]

The following is the full, unedited version of the statement which Reilly made to Styrne, taken from his OGPU file:

During the 1914 war, I joined the army as a volunteer in 1916, until 1915 I lived in New York where I was engaged in military supplies, including supplies to the Russian government. After joining the British Army as a volunteer, I was appointed to serve in the Royal Flying Corps (from 1910 I was engaged in aviation and can regard myself as one of the aviation pioneers in Russia; I was one of the founders of 'Krylia', the first aviation society in Russia), where I worked until January 1918. In January 1918 I joined a secret political service, where I worked until 1921, after which I set up a private business of a financial nature (loans, stock companies and so on). During my service in the Royal Flying Corps I had no occasion to come to Russia... In March 1918, being on 'Secret Service', I was sent to Russia as a member of the British mission as an expert to report on the current situation (I held the rank of lieutenant at the time). I arrived in Petrograd through Murmansk, then proceeded to Vologda, and subsequently came to Moscow, where I stayed until 11 September 1918, spending most of my time on numerous trips between Moscow, Petrograd and Vologda.

From passive intelligence work, I, like other members of the British mission, gradually switched to a more-or-less active fight against Soviet power, which I did for the following reasons:

The signing of the Brest-Litovsk peace treaty on terms very profitable to Germany naturally aroused concerns about joint actions the Soviet powers and the Germans would take against the Allied powers, to which I should add the existence of numerous reports (which ultimately proved to be mendacious) on the movement of German prisoners from Russia back to Germany, and finally, the anger caused by the oppression of the Allied missions by the Soviet power. I believe that the Soviet government at that time pursued the wrong policy towards at least the British mission, for Lockhart, up to the end of June, in his reports to the British government, recommended that it should pursue a soft line towards the Soviet power. At that time, as far as I remember, the Soviet Government was especially concerned about establishing a regular army, and Trotsky many times discussed this issue with Lockhart, stressing the importance of sympathies for this cause on the part of the Allied governments. The situation radically changed after Mirback's arrival and the continuous concessions of the Soviet power to his demands (the demands of the German government).

Mirbach's death triggered an immediate repression against us. We had anticipated that the Germans, apart from other claims, would demand the expulsion of all Allied missions, which did actually happen. Right after that, searches were made of the consulates and some mission members were arrested, but soon released. Also, the order was made banning all Allied officers to travel. From this very moment, I started my fight against Soviet power, which manifested itself mostly in military and political intelligence and in identification of the active elements that could be used in the fight against the Soviet government. For this purpose, I went underground and obtained documents from various persons; for some period of time, for example, I was a commissar in charge of transporting spare vehicle parts during the evacuation from Petrograd, which provided me with a good opportunity to travel between Moscow and Petrograd without any restrictions, even in the commissar's coach. At this time, I resided mostly in Moscow, changing flats nearly every day. The culmination of my work was my talks with Colonel Burzin, whom I met at Lockhart's. The essence of the matter you would know from the proceedings records. At the time I passed on to the patriarch a considerable amount of money allocated for the needs of the clergy which was in distressful circumstances then. I want to stress that I never discussed with the patriarch or his entourage any counter-revolutionary affairs, and my intentions were unknown to the patriarch and to his inner circle. The money was allocated from the funds I had received; I had in my possession considerable amounts of money, which, in view of my special status (total financial independence and exclusive confidence due to my ties with highly placed persons) were provided me unaccountably. These very funds I spent on my fight against Soviet power.

I believe that the persons that were brought to the Lockhart trial had nothing to do with me, or in some cases, had a very remote relation to me; as for those who were closely associated with me, they fled to the Ukraine after the discovery of the plot. Meanwhile, I had a very vast net of informers, which I also immediately dissolved right after the discovery of the Lockhart case. I financed their flee to the Ukraine.

Reilly then related the story of his escape from Petrograd (reproduced in Chapter Ten), before moving on to recount:

I was then appointed a political officer in the south of Russia and left for Denikin's headquarters in the Crimea, in the south-east and in Odessa. In Odessa I stayed until the end of March 1919, and by the order of the British High Commissioner in Constantinople, I was dispatched to make a report on the current situation on the Denikin front and the political situation in the south to officials in London and to Britain's representatives at the Peace Conference in Paris. In the course of the Peace Conference, I was a liaison in charge of Russian affairs with different departments in London and Paris; during that time, I met B.V. Savinkov. Through 1919 and 1920, I had close relations with different representatives of the Russian émigré parties (the SRs in Prague, the Savinkov organisation, commercial and industrial circles and so on). At that time, I was pressing my comprehensive plan through the British Government concerning support of Russian commercial and industrial circles, headed by Yaroshinsky, Bark and others. All this time, I served the secret service, my main responsibility being to make reports on Russian affairs for Britain's higher echelon.

At the end of 1920, having become a rather close intimate of Savinkov's, I went to Warsaw, where Savinkov was then organising a foray into Belorussia. I personally took part in the operation and was inside Soviet Russia. Ordered to return, I went back to London. In 1921 I continued to provide active support to Savinkov, took him to

London and introduced him to government circles. The same year I took him to Prague, where I introduced him to government contacts. I also arranged his secret flight to Warsaw.

In 1922 my strategy changed. I was disappointed with intervention. I became increasingly inclined to the opinion that the most appropriate way of struggle would be to reach an agreement with the Soviet power such that would throw open the gates of British commerce and business to Russia. At that time I proposed a project for the establishment of an enormous international consortuim for the restoration of Russian currency and industry, this project was accepted by some in government circles. In charge of this project were the Marconi Company or, to be exact, Godfrey Isaacs, the company's chairman and the brother of the Viceroy of India. This project was discussed with Krasin and eventually dropped, yet nearly all the elements of this project were taken as a base for the proposed international consortium that was established at the time the Genoa conference was held.

In 1923 and 1924 I was primarily preoccupied with my personal affairs. As for my fight against the Soviet power, I was less active here, although I wrote much about it in the papers (British) and supported Savinkov, consulting influential circles in England and America on Russian affairs.

In 1925 I resided in New York. In late September 1925 I illegally crossed the Finnish border and arrived in Leningrad and subsequently Moscow where I was arrested.

[signed] Sidney Reilly[3]

Two days after making this statement, on 9 October, Reilly volunteered that:

I arrived in Soviet Russia on my own initiative, hearing from Bunakov of the existence of an apparently important anti-soviet group. I have always been actively engaged in anti-Bolshevik matters and to these I have given much time and my personal funds. I can state that the years 1920–24, for instance, cost me at a very minimum calculation £15,000–£20,000.[4]

Some weeks later Pepita received a further letter from Boyce in Helsingfors, dated 18 October, in which he broke the news to her that things had definitely gone wrong:

> I am on my way to Paris via London and hope to be with you on Thursday or latest Friday. The position I am sorry to say is much worse than I had hoped from the information previously received. It appears that at the last moment just before they hoped to complete the whole business a party of four of them were prospecting in the forests near by and were suddenly attacked by brigands. They put up a fight with the result that two were killed outright. Mutt[5] was seriously wounded and the fourth was taken captive.[6]

Promising to meet her in Paris when he would hopefully have more precise and up-to-date news, Boyce signed off. At this point it is clear that Pepita considered the possibility that Boyce might be an OGPU double agent who had entrapped her husband.[7] This would not be the last time that such suspicions were to fall on Boyce.

From the OGPU interrogation records, it would appear that the information Reilly had thus far given about himself was as far as he was willing to go in terms of volunteering the information they were demanding. On 13 October Reilly responded to Styrne's ultimatum, to co-operate fully or face the consequences, by categorically stating, 'I am unable to agree'.[8] On 17 October he again wrote to Styrne, emphasising that he would not provide the 'detailed information' they were seeking.[9] Psychological methods were therefore brought to bear on him, which ultimately succeeded in persuading him to co-operate. Even when this point was reached on 30 October, it is clear that Reilly did his best to drag things out.

How then was he persuaded to talk and what did he tell them? Reilly himself left a trail of clues in the form of daily notes he made during his last week in cell 73. Using a pencil he made tiny handwritten notes on cigarette papers. These he hid in his clothing, in his bed and in cracks in the plasterwork of the cell walls. They were later found when the cell was searched, and photographic enhancements made by OGPU technicians.[10] The handwriting in the daily diary is clearly identifiable as Reilly's. The constructions, grammar and use of abbreviations are not only in keeping with his general written style, but are consistent with other examples of earlier diaries he kept.

In 1992 Robin Bruce Lockhart called into question the diary's authenticity in a revised edition of his *Ace of Spies* book,[11] dismissing it as 'Soviet disinformation'. If it was an OGPU fabrication, however, created solely to mislead the West, why was it never used at any time during the following sixty-six years of Communist rule in the Soviet Union? On the contrary, it remained classified at the highest level and was kept securely in the archives of the OGPU and its successor organisations.

Why he wrote the diary is another question altogether. The most likely scenario is that he assumed, or at best hoped, that he would eventually be released to the British authorities. Had this happened, he would, no doubt, have tried to smuggle the diary out with him. Like the postcard he posted to Ernest Boyce shortly before his arrest, it was a testament or boast to the fact that he had entered the lion's den and returned to tell the story. It was also a record of OGPU interrogation techniques, which he was sure would be of interest to SIS. The diary itself contains many abbreviations, and the following account reproduces only the text of which the meaning is clear and incontrovertible –

Friday 30 October 1925[12]

Additional interrogation in late afternoon. Change into work clothes. All personal clothes taken away. Managed to conceal a second blanket. When called from sleep was ordered to take coat and cap. Room downstairs near bath. Always had premonition about this iron door. Present in the room are Styrne and his colleague, assistant warder, young fellow from Vladimir gubernia, executioner[13] and possibly somebody else. Styrne's colleague in chair. Informed that GPU

Collegium had reconsidered sentence and that unless I agree to co-operate the execution will take place immediately. Said that this does not surprise me, that my decision remains the same and that I am ready to die. Was asked by Styrne whether I wished time for reflection. Answered that this is their affair. They gave me one hour. Taken back to cell by young man and assistant warder. Prayed inwardly for Pita,[14] made small package of my personal things, smoked a couple of cigarettes and after fifteen to twenty minutes said I was ready. Executioner who was outside cell was sent to announce decision. Was kept in cell for full hour. Brought back to the same room. Styrne, his colleague and young fellow. In adjoining room executioner and assistant all heavily armed. Announced again my decision and asked to make written declaration in this spirit that I am glad I can show them how an Englishman and a Christian understands his duty.[15] Refusal. Asked to have things sent to Pita. Refused. They said that no one will ever know about it after my death. Then began lengthy conversation – persuasion – same as usual. After three-quarters of an hour wrangling, a heated conversation for five minutes. Silence, then Styrne and colleague called the executioner and departed. Immediately handcuffed. Kept waiting about five minutes during which distinct loading of weapons in outer rooms and other preparations. Then led out to car. Inside were the executioner, his warder, young fellow, chauffeur and guard. Short drive to garage. During drive soldier squeezed his filthy hand between handcuffs and my wrist. Rain. Drizzle. Very cold. Endless wait in garage courtyard while executioner went into shed – guards filthy talk and jokes. Chauffeur said something wrong with radiator and pottered about. Finally start, short drive and arrival GPU by north – Styrne and colleague – informed post-ponement twenty hours was communicated. Terrible night. Nightmares.

According to OGPU reports, Reilly spent the night alternately crying and praying before a small picture of Pepita. It seemed that the classic 'mock execution' technique had finally shaken his resolve. The scenario he describes, the endless waiting, the uncertainty, followed by a postponement of the execution is typical of this psychological method of interrogation and no doubt induced the nightmares to which he refers.

Much controversy surrounds a letter written on the same date as the 'mock execution', 30 October. The full text of the letter, which is contained in the OGPU file on Reilly, is as follows:

To the Chairman of the OGPU
F.E. Dzerzhinsky

After the discussions that have taken place with V.A. Styrne, I express my agreement to co-operate in sincerely providing full evidence and information answering the questions of interest to the OGPU relating to the organisation and personnel of the British intelligence service and as far as it is known to me what information I have relating to the American intelligence and likewise about those persons in the Russian émigré organisations with whom I had dealings.
Moscow, the Inner Prison,
30 October 1925
[signed] Sidney Reilly[16]

Again, there have been suggestions that this too was an 'OGPU fabrication'. Gordon Brook Shepherd, for example, asserts that:

… it is inconceivable that Reilly, who had throughout displayed defiance, would have failed to mention [in the diary] such a volte-face. It seems all the more probable therefore that the document was produced by the OGPU's diligent factory of lies and forgery to make things look neat and pretty in their files.[17]

Edward Gazur, the FBI counter-intelligence officer who debriefed Alexander Orlov after his defection to the US, was even more emphatic: 'there is no doubt in my mind that Orlov did not know of the existence of such a letter when he died in 1973 as he would have certainly addressed the matter with me'.[18] He is firmly of the view that 'the letter was a fabrication conceived and floated

On 30 October 1925, Reilly wrote to Cheka boss Felix Dzerzhinsky, in a last ditch effort to buy himself more time.

by the KGB [sic]'.[19] Gazur takes his argument further by reasoning that 'had Reilly confessed, he would have likewise been placed on trial if only for the Soviets to reap an extraordinarily bountiful harvest of propaganda'.[20]

This scenario is a most unlikely one, however. There is no evidence that the Bolsheviks ever had any intention of subjecting Reilly to a show trail. Not only had he already been tried *in absentia* in 1918, and been sentenced to death, they had already announced his death via the Moscow Trust Council meeting within days of his arrest. Clearly, they would have found it a little difficult to then bring him back to life in order to place him on trial. Furthermore, Reilly's letter can in no way be described as a 'confession'. It is purely a statement of intention that he is prepared to co-operate. Savinkov, on the other hand, certainly did 'confess' in every sense of the word, and the statement he made was a clear recanting of his opposition to the Bolsheviks:

I unconditionally recognise your right to govern Russia. I do not ask your mercy. I ask only to let your revolutionary conscience judge a man who has never sought anything for himself and who has devoted his whole life to the cause of the Russian people.[21]

Reilly, on the other hand, no doubt hoped that the letter would save his life or at least buy him time. In fact, his own handwritten notes testify to the fact that during the following five days he did exactly what he said he would do in the Dzerzhinsky letter. It is also clear, however, that what he told them was generally low-grade information, much of which they already knew. The one thing they were keen to learn more about, the identity of SIS agents currently working in Russia, he was unable to tell them, as he had had no connection with SIS for over four years.

Saturday 31 October 1925
Next morning called at 11. Spend day in Room 176 with Sergei Ivanovich and Dr Kushner.[22] Apparently Styrne much impressed with his report – increased attention. At 8 p.m. drive dressed in GPU uniform. Walk in country at night. – Arrival Moscow apartment. Great spread. Tea. Ibrahim. Then conversation alone with Styrne – that protocole [sic] expressing my agreement. Ignorance of any agents here – object my trip. Appraisal of Winston Churchill and Spears. My unexpected decision in Wyborg. Styrne went with protocol to Dzerzhinsky, returned half an hour later. Informed sentence stopped and agreed in principle my plan. Return to cell slept, four solid hours, after Veronal.[23] – Unfortunately my turn get up early. – Called at 11. Uniform, precautions that I not be seen. Devised programme with Styrne – 1) 1918, 2) SIS, 3) Political spheres England, 4) American Secret Service, 5) Politics and banks USA, 6) Russian émigrés. Source for information regarding 1918 – Main object German identification, scene at American Consulate[24] – Cut off supplies untruth[25] – Accused of provocation – 2a) Savinkov's changed attitude, distrust, my conviction proven. My intentions if Savinkov returned. Rest. Ask whether knew Stark,[26] Kurtz.[27] Story of Operput,[28] Yakushev.[29] Then

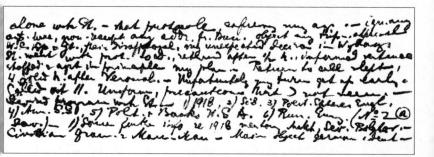

The last week of Reilly's life is recorded in the diary he wrote on cigarette papers in cell 73.

began on Number 2 – SIS. Only introduction. – finished 5 p.m. Retired to room 176. Rest, dinner. At 7 p.m. dictated Numbers 4 and 5. Then cell. Veronal did not act.

Sunday 1 November 1925

During interrogation tremendous stress laid whether Hodgson[30] has any agents and whether any inside agents anywhere in Comintern. – Questions regards Dukes,[31] Kurtz, Lifland, Peshkov.[32] – Questions regarding Litseintsy.[33] Told story of Gniloryboff[34] and other case attempted escape. Asked whether any agents are in Petrograd. Lots of talk about my wife – offers any money or position – Sergei Ivanovich Kheidulin.[35] Feduleev[36] and guard with glasses was with me in cell. No work. Drive in afternoon. Corrected American report.

Monday 2 November 1925

Called 10 a.m. SIS continued – general organisational details.[37] Repeatedly asked regarding agents here[38] Burberry, Norwegian Ebsen,[39] Hudson[40] in Denmark and others. Explained why agents here impossible – none since Dukes.[41] Returned to my mission in 1918. Kemp,[42] misunderstanding with Lockhart.[43] Conversation with Artur Khristianovich Artuzov.[44] Zinoviev's letter.[45] Doctor dissatisfied with my state. Styrne hopes to finish Wednesday – doubt it. Slept very badly this night. Reading till 3 a.m. Getting very weak.

Tuesday 3 November 1925

Hungry all day. Frunze's funeral.[46] Called about 9 in the evening. Styrne's letter and message through Feduleev. Six questions, the German's work, our collaboration: what kind of materials we have concerning USSR and Comintern. China. Duke's agents. My conversation with Feduleev. Short letter to Styrne. Veronal. Slept well.

Wednesday 4 November 1925

Very weak. Called at 11 a.m. – Apology from Styrne – Friendliness. Work to 5 – later dinner. Later drive, walk. Work to 2 a.m. Slept without Veronal. Styrne gave previous protocol to sign. Began about Scotland Yard – Childs,[47] Carter[48] – Executive work. Basil Thompson.[49] Boris Seid.[50] Thoughts on Krasin.[51] Law regarding foreigners… Paris. Bunakov travelled to Paris. Long conversation about his trip. Protocol – My thoughts about Amtorg[52] and Arcos.[53] Wise.[54] Broker, Urquhart.[55] Possibility of agreement/terms – Russian bondholders. Divide and rule.[56] My idea concerning an agreement with England Churchill, Baldwin, Birkenhead, Chamberlain, McKenna. Petroleum groups, Balfour, Marconi, financing of debts in USA – English unrest.[57] Questions – again Hudson, Zhitkov, Ferson, Abaza.[58] Questions about Persia. – Military attaché US Faymonville,[59] China, makes use of young English agent as an envoy in Russia. Very attentive about Berens. Existence of agents in Arcos and mixed companies… Feel at ease about my death. I see great developments ahead.

His sentence about 'feeling at ease' in the context of his death, is not easily translated into English and can therefore be interpreted in at least two different ways. It could mean that he was now recon-ciled to his death, or it could mean that as a result of the past five days of co-operation and the absence of any further talk about carry-ing out his sentence, he was no longer so concerned about the threat.

It should also be acknowledged that whatever conclusions one draws from his 'diary' and the OGPU's corresponding records, Reilly undoubtedly acted with courageous stubbornness during the weeks he was incarcerated at the Lubyanka. Whatever else one could say about his actions and motivations during his life, his final weeks were a credit to his personal courage and resolve. The fact that his resolve was gradually eroded by the effective psychological techniques applied by the OGPU should not detract from this.

By 4 November the OGPU had concluded that Reilly had no more to tell. Equally, there was also the risk that the longer matters progressed, the greater the chance that the border shooting story would be exposed as a sham. Some of those involved in the Trust sting were of the view that Reilly should not have been arrested, as by doing so the whole operation risked immediate exposure. However, the decision to arrest Reilly and ultimately carry out his death sentence was almost certainly taken by Stalin himself.

Boris Gudz remembers that 'Stalin insisted that the Politburo's line was that under no circumstances was he to be released. He had to be shot, and quickly, because otherwise, eventually, rumours would start doing the rounds that we had him under arrest, foreign governments would find out about the whole thing, there would be all kind of diplomatic problems.' Stalin foresaw all these difficulties and said: We have to put an end to him once and for all – execute him!'.[60] Although the decision to carry out the sentence was an irreversible one made at the highest level, it would seem that the OGPU officers on the ground did, in fact, exercise a degree of discretion in how it was done. Boris Gudz was personally acquainted with the four officers deputed to carry out the order, and believes that:

There was something quite humane about the way they went about it. Reilly was driven out for walks in the open air of Sokolniki Park quite often, so this particular trip was just another one of his regular outings so far as he was concerned. Maybe he suspected something, because there were a lot of people there that day. Anyway, it was done in such a way that the end came suddenly. I know that for a fact – it was very sudden.[61]

Grigory Feduleev, the OGPU agent who was in charge of the execution party, described in some detail the events which took place on the evening of 5 November 1925:

For the Deputy Head of KRO OGPU Comrade Styrne
REPORT
I write to inform you that in accordance with the instruction received from you, Comrades Dukis, Syroezhkin, myself and Ibrahim drove out of the GPU yard with No. 73 at precisely 8.00 p.m. on 5 November 1925. We set out in the direction of Bogorodsk. We arrived at the spot between 8.30 and 8.45. It was agreed that the driver, when we got to the spot, would repair a fault in the car, which he did. When the car stopped I asked the driver what was the matter. He replied that there was a blockage and it would take 5–10 minutes to put right. I then proposed to No. 73 that we stretch our legs. Once out of the car I walked on the right-hand side and Ibrahim on the left-hand side of No. 73, and Comrade Syroezhkin on the right hand side about ten paces from us. When we had gone thirty to forty paces from the car, Ibrahim, who had dropped back from us, fired a shot at No. 73, who let out a deep breath and fell to the ground without uttering a cry. In view of the fact that his pulse was still beating, Comrade Syroezhkin fired a shot into his chest. After waiting a little longer, ten to fifteen minutes, during which time the pulse finally stopped beating, we carried him to the car and drove straight to the medical unit, where Comrade Kushner and the photographer were already waiting. At the medical unit the four of us – myself, Dukis, Ibrahim and a medical orderly – carried No. 73 into the building indicated by Comrade Kushner. We told the orderly that this person had been hit by a tram, in any case his face could not be seen as the head was in a sack, and put him on the dissecting table. We then proceeded to take photographs. He was photographed down to the waist in a greatcoat,[62] then naked down to the waist so that the wounds could be seen, then naked full length. After this he was placed in a sack and taken to the morgue attached to the Medical Unit, where he was put in a coffin and we all went home. The whole operation was completed by 11.00 p.m. on 5 November.

No. 73 was collected from the morgue of the OGPU medical unit by Com. Dukis at 8.30 p.m. on 9 November 1925 and driven to the prepared burial pit in the walking yard of the OGPU inner prison, where he was put in a sack so that the 3 Red Army men burying it could not see his face.[63]

Authorised agent of 4th section of the KRO OGPU Feduleev.

It is significant that Reilly's body was put in a sack so as to avoid anyone not involved in the operation from identifying him. Clearly they were still concerned with word getting out that Reilly had not in fact died on 28 September after all. The fact that he had been shot unawares, rather than by firing squad, as would have been the case had the sentence been carried out in 1918, can be seen as dispensation or even as a mark of respect.

This aside, the way of his death should not obscure the ultimate question of why he found himself entrapped in the OGPU's snare in the first place. Was Reilly's death ultimately brought about by his own vanity and lack of judgement? Had the king of the confidence men finally met his match, or were more sinister forces at play?

On 12 August 2001 the *Sunday Times* reported on the imminent publication of a new book by Edward Gazur under the headline, 'Double Agent may have sent Ace of Spies to his Death'. According to the report, 'Gazur contends that Orlov told him that Cmdr Ernest Boyce, an MI6 officer and colleague of Reilly's, played the key role in entrapping the spy. Boyce was a long-term double agent working for the Russians and was motivated solely by hard cash, said Gazur'.

The spy writer Nigel West was also quoted by the *Sunday Times* as saying, 'The reason why this hasn't come out until now is that Orlov, who was not debriefed by British intelligence, never told anybody but Edward Gazur'. It is therefore puzzling to read in Gazur's book that:

In 1972, while Orlov and I were going over the Reilly affair, I was not concerned with the identity of the British intelligence officer who had been compromised by the KGB [sic] as it was of no particular intelligence significance in the modern sense and consequently I never thought to ask the name of this individual. To the best of my recollection, Orlov never mentioned or volunteered the man's identity or if he did it is now long forgotten.[64]

If this is so, on what evidence is the charge against Boyce made? According to Gazur,

…based on additional facts that Orlov provided at the time combined with independent documentation, I was able to deduce the identity of this key player. Insomuch as Orlov never directly furnished this identity, I originally felt it prudent to do likewise; however, on further reflection I realised that SIS was already aware of the man's identity and so, as this information was historically relevant, there remained no valid reason to stay silent.[65]

Gazur gives no details of what these 'additional facts' are or to the relevance of the 'independent documentation', however. In the absence of such hard and fast evidence, the case against Boyce must remain no more than educated guesswork. This is not to say that the OGPU did not have the co-operation of SIS or former SIS operatives in their quest for Reilly. Before the entrapment operation could begin, a great deal of background research on Reilly must have been carried out. This is clear from OGPU documentation held on him. While a large proportion of the information on Reilly's personal background is erroneous, it seems clear that this could only be because he himself was the indirect source. It would seem a strong possibility that the information was obtained from an SIS or former SIS colleague, based in part on what Reilly had told that individual or individuals. It should also be borne in mind that these sources may not even have been aware that they were assisting the OGPU, as such background information could well have been sought through cover organisations like the Trust and its supposed anti-Bolshevik agents.

Neither is it likely that Reilly himself volunteered this information about his alter-ego 'Rosenblum' during his interrogation, for as we have already seen, he maintained to the very end that he was an 'Englishman and Christian' by the name of Sidney George Reilly. To have done anything else would have destroyed what little hope he had of being extradited or swapped on the initiative of the British authorities. Where then could this erroneous information about his Rosenblum background have come from? A key clue lies in the following passage from his OGPU file:

> His father was Mark Rosenblum, a doctor who worked as a broker and subsequently as a shipping agent. His mother was *née* Massino of impoverished noble stock. The Rosenblum family resided at house No. 15 on Alexsandrovsky Prospect.[66]

The view that 15 Alexandrovsky Prospect was Reilly's childhood home was the theory of one man, George Hill, who had witnessed Reilly breaking down, as a result of what he believed was an 'emotional crisis', outside this house in February 1919. The document also contains most of the other old chestnuts Reilly told Hill about his past. Would it therefore be fair to conclude that Hill was knowingly or unknowingly an OGPU source? Notes written by Vladimir Styrne suggest that Hill, who by 1925 was no longer employed by SIS, may have been collaborating with the OGPU.[67] During the Second World War, Hill was seconded to the Special Operations Executive, and posted, at Moscow's request, to the Russian capital to act as a liaison officer to the NKVD. He later came under suspicion following the 1963 defection of Kim Philby,[68] although nothing conclusive appears to have come of this.

In addition to claims that Reilly's death was a result of betrayal, it has to be said that not everyone accepted that he was dead. Pepita never really came to terms with his death and continued to believe that he was being kept a prisoner.[69] Neither in fact did his first wife Margaret believe in his death.[70] Whilst their sentiments might be put down to wishful thinking, others have also refused to believe he died for very different reasons. Robin Bruce Lockhart,[71] Edward Van Der Rhoer[72] and Richard Spence[73] have all articulated the view that Reilly defected to the Soviets in 1925 and that his death was a 'put-up job' to cover his traces. Indeed, Lockhart devoted a whole book to propounding the thesis, although very little of the book actually relates directly to Reilly himself.[74]

The whole theory of Reilly's supposed defection rests entirely on one proposition, however – that he did not die at the hands of the OGPU on 5 November 1925. According to the account of Feduleev, Reilly's corpse was photographed in the sick bay of the OGPU's headquarters. This book contains one of the photographs taken that evening. Robin Bruce Lockhart declared that this picture is 'clearly of someone other than Reilly' and that the 'whole story suggests a faked death'.[75] He later told this author that the OGPU photographs were clearly fakes as they showed a man, 'who if not a Chinaman had Asiatic blood'.[76] However, this is virtually the same description of Reilly that C himself gave in his cable to SIS Vologda on 29 March 1918,[77] when he described his appearance as that of a 'Jewish-Jap type'. Other official descriptions have also referred to his 'oriental appearance'.[78] Since Lockhart's dismissal of the mortuary photograph's authenticity, it has been subjected to forensic analysis by Kenneth Linge, a Fellow of the British Institute of Professional Photography and Head of Photography at Essex Police Headquarters. A veteran of over 200 operational 'scenes of crime' cases, Linge has been called upon to give expert testimony in criminal cases throughout the country, and has carried out extensive research into facial identification techniques.

Asked by the author to examine the OGPU photograph of Reilly's corpse, he compared it with other pictures taken of Reilly over a fifteen-year period, and concluded that 'the likelihood of the same feature layout and feature form being repeated in another person's face is so remote as to be virtually negligible. I therefore believe that the person shown on the image, the deceased, is the person shown on the other images'.[79] The proposition that the body lying in the Lubyanka Sick Bay is someone other than Sidney Reilly can no longer be sustained.

Reilly's life ended, as indeed it had begun, shrouded in mystery. He may not, in the words of Robin Bruce Lockhart, have been the 'greatest spy in history',[80] or even, in the conventional sense, a spy at all. He was, however, certainly one of the greatest confidence men of his time. It is a testimony to his skills of deception that his 'Master Spy' myth has outlived him by more than eighty years. In the final analysis, the confidence man's motto – 'you can't cheat an honest man' – came back to haunt him. Reilly's own inherent dishonesty had allowed the OGPU to set him up and ultimately to cheat him of his life.

To SGR Killed in Russia, by Caryll Houselander —[81]

Pure Beauty, ever-risen Lord!
In wind and sea I have adored
Thy living splendour and confessed
Thy resurrection manifest.
Not now in sun and hill and wood,
But lifted on this bitter rood
Of man's sad heart, I worship Thee
Uplifted once again for me.

For now the Jews cast lots again
On thy raiment, mock Thy pain,
And make Thy torments manifold,
Selling Thee again for gold.
I bow to Thee in this new shrine,
This later calvary of thine;
And in the soul of this man slain
I see Thee, deathless, rise again.

APPENDICES

REILLY MYTHS

Over the years a number of myths about Reilly have gained circulation and passed into folklore. Some were fabricated by Reilly himself and blindly perpetuated by friends, colleagues, journalists and writers. Others have subsequently arisen since his death through wishful thinking and flawed research.

It is tempting to think that a longer book could be written about the person Reilly was not and the things he did not do, as opposed to who he really was and what he actually did. The following six appendices typically illustrate how such myths have arisen over the last century.

Appendix One

The Gadfly

> He was not at all angry when she later published a novel, much praised by the critics, which was largely inspired by his early life.
> *Ace of Spies* by Robin Bruce Lockhart[1]

Published in 1897, *The Gadfly* was a great success in Britain and the United States, where it was actually first published, due to Heinemann's fear that it might attract adverse public reaction due to the inflammatory emotions they believed it contained. The *Daily Graphic* reviewer said that 'One does not often come across a story of as notable power and originality as *The Gadfly*', while the *Daily Chronicle* hailed it as 'a novel of distinct power and originality'.[2] It was in Russia, however, that *The Gadfly* had its biggest success. Its anti-clerical and revolutionary theme appealed enormously to those who were opposed to the Tsarist regime and who later supported the Bolshevik revolution. It was subsequently translated into thirty languages worldwide. A dramatic version was staged in Moscow for many years from 1920, taking on a *Mousetrap*-like run. The Russians produced two full-length film versions of the book, the first in 1928 and the second, in colour in 1955, which won an award at the Cannes Film Festival. There have also been at least three operatic versions produced. By the time of Ethel Voynich's death in 1960, at the age of ninety-six, the book had sold well over 5 million copies in Russia alone and over a million copies in China and Eastern Europe.

The Gadfly is set in Italy in the first half of the nineteenth century and tells the story of Arthur Burton who, unbeknown to himself, is the illegitimate son of Montanelli, an Italian priest, and Gladys Burton, an English woman. It bears a striking resemblance to the 'Georgi' story Sidney Reilly told George

Hill and others in the 1920s. Before the death of his mother, Arthur like Georgi is under the spiritual care of his real father, who is in charge of a seminary in Pisa. The young man is gentle and devout and even has thoughts of entering the priesthood until he becomes involved in a conspiratorial group called the Young Italy Society, devoted to freeing Italy from Austrian rule. In Reilly's story, Georgi is at university under the care of Dr Rosenblum, where he, likewise, becomes involved in the 'League of Enlightenment', a radical political group.

After Montanelli is elevated to a bishopric, Arthur confesses his association with the Young Italy Society to his father's successor Father Cardi, who immediately betrays him to the authorities. He is imprisoned, and when released is shattered to learn for the first time that Montanelli is his real father. Reeling from the shock, he fakes suicide by throwing his hat into the water at the docks and stows away on a ship bound for Buenos Aires. Georgi, also reeling from the shock of being revealed as a bastard, fakes his suicide in Odessa Harbour and stows away on a ship bound for South America. Once in South America, Arthur wanders about aimlessly, his heart filled with hatred for everything and everybody. He allows himself to be maimed and mutilated and to suffer all kinds of indignity; stuttering horribly, he ends up as a hunchback in a travelling circus, a pathetic figure of tortured ridicule. He spends thirteen years in South America before returning not just to free Italy, which was his boyhood desire, but to rid her of priests in general whilst undertaking a vendetta against Montanelli in particular. Now involved in violent action he changes his name to Felice Rivarez. He is eventually arrested and finally confronts Montanelli, now a cardinal. Arthur tells Montanelli who he really is and presses him to choose between him and God. Montanelli chooses the latter, as he must, and Arthur is condemned to be shot.[3] The whole affair, however, unhinges the cardinal's mind and while carrying the host in solemn procession, he raises it then smashes it to the ground in a symbolic identification of himself with God the Father, sacrificing his only begotten son for the salvation of mankind.

Since the publication of Lockhart's *Ace of Spies* in 1967, other authors and journalists have taken his assertions about *The Gadfly* as sacrosanct and have repeated them as received fact.[4] First off the mark was Tibor Szamuely's *Spectator* article,[5] which appeared some months after the publication of *Ace of Spies*. 'Is it possible to imagine', asked Szamuely, 'anything more weird than the fact that Soviet Russia's most revered literary hero [Arthur Burton] being based upon the real-life character of their greatest enemy?'

Szamuely was not alone in being unable to resist this line in Cold War irony. The BBC World Service dedicated one of its Russian language programmes to *The Gadfly*.[6] Not only did it feature the 'sensation' that the prototype of Ethel Voynich's *The Gadfly* was none other than the famous spy Sidney Reilly, lynchpin of so many anti-Soviet plots, but went one step further. Reminding listeners that *The Gadfly* was the inspiration for the deeds of Pavka Korchagin, the hero of Nikolai Ostrovsky's classic Civil War epic *How the Steel Tempered*, it took great delight in raising the spectre of the young fighter for the Soviet Republic in reality following the bitter enemy of Soviet power.

Desmond McHale's 1985 biography of Ethel's father, George Boole,[7] also unquestioningly adopted the Lockhart line, although he did concede that Voynich never admitted any Reilly connection with the book or its central character.[8] Tibor Szamuely, however, casts a shadow of doubt on the matter by implying that she had deliberately remained tight lipped on the issue of who Arthur Burton's prototype was. He relates an episode in 1955 when a delegation of Soviet journalists was in New York for the first time since the onset of the Cold War. One morning a Russian diplomat burst into the hotel room of journalist Boris Polevoi. Almost incoherent with excitement he related that he had, that very morning, seen Ethel Voynich, assumed by the Russians to be long dead. The journalists commandeered a car and raced off to her home at 450 West 24th Street. Arriving unannounced on her doorstep, they proceeded to interview her about *The Gadfly* and the inspiration for Arthur Burton. Szamuely quotes her response to the Burton question as being, 'No, I'm afraid I can't remember... it was all so long ago'.

Szamuely's source for this answer is unclear, as the quote certainly does not appear in Russian press stories which followed the 1955 publicity. In fact, both Boris Polevoi and Eugenia Taratuta corresponded at length with Ethel after the 1955 meeting in New York. Taratuta's correspondence and interviews with her were a major contribution to her biography of Ethel Voynich,[9] the only one to be published to date. As a result of the 1968 BBC broadcast, both Polevoi and Taratuta published their correspondence with Ethel Voynich in a rebuttal article published in *Izvestia* on the subject of Arthur Burton and the characters in *The Gadfly*.[10] For example, in a letter to Taratuta, dated 25 April 1956, Voynich elaborates on the conception of the book:

> For a long time in my youth I was imagining a man who voluntarily sacrificed himself to something. Partly, this image might have appeared under a strong impact of Mazzini's[11] life and activities. In autumn 1885, for the first time in my life I turned up in Paris and spent a few months there. In the Louvre's Square Salon I saw a well-known portrait of a young Italian known as *A Man in Black*, ascribed to Francia, Fracabijo and Rafael. This is how *The Gadfly* story somehow took shape in me.

In the same letter she refers again to characterisations:

> Gemma is the only true-life character in the novel. You can recognise in her
> more or less closely a portrait of my friend Charlotte Wilson whom I called
> Gemma when I was writing the book.

The following year, Voynich wrote on 14 January 1957 a letter to Boris
Polevoi, who had specifically asked her about the Arthur Burton character:
'You ask me whether the real prototype of Arthur ever existed… indeed, the
characters in the novel do not necessarily have, as prototypes, people who
actually existed'. She went on to say that 'The origin of Arthur's image comes
from my old interest in Mazzini and a portrait of an unknown young man in
black in the Louvre'.

Polevoi and Taratuta were not the only ones to dispute and challenge
Lockhart's theory. The actor Hugh Millar, a long-time friend, confidante and
neighbour of Ethel Voynich's in New York, wrote privately to Robin Bruce
Lockhart shortly after the publication of *Ace of Spies* in November 1967,
taking him to task over his claims. Lockhart's reply, dated 8 December 1967,[12]
is most revealing in more ways than one and has, to date, never been
published.

When asked by Millar about his source for the statement that Ethel was
Reilly's mistress and that Reilly was the inspiration for Arthur, Lockhart replied:

> …the original source of the 'affair' with Reilly was Reilly himself. This was
> checked later directly with Mrs Voynich herself before the last war by another
> author who had intended to write a book on Reilly but never got round to it
> as he did not have enough material.

Over and above the fact that Reilly is hardly the most reliable or truthful of
sources when it comes to his own past (or virtually any other matter come
to that), it seems certain that the 'other author' referred to by Lockhart was
none other than Reilly's SIS colleague George Hill. It is clear from the papers
Lockhart deposited with the Hoover Institution, that Hill was actively
researching his Reilly book in 1935.[13] In terms of Hill allegedly checking
Reilly's claim directly with Ethel Voynich, it has to be said that some
considerable doubt exists as to whether this was ever the case. There is no
record of Hill ever having written to Ethel Voynich, or indeed of her ever
having written to him. Bearing in mind that she lived in New York City
between 1920 and her death in 1960, Hill could, of course, have taken the
opportunity to visit New York to interview her. However, US immigration
records show no sign of Hill entering the United States at any time during
the inter-war period.[14]

Curiously, as a further justification for his view, Lockhart also stated in his letter to Hugh Millar: 'Incidentally, a point that I did not mention in my book was Reilly's stutter from which he suffered in his youth – a handicap also of the 'Gadfly'.

Of the countless people who knew or had recollections of Reilly over a considerable period of time, not one has ever mentioned a stutter. The only reference on record to any kind of peculiarity in Reilly's speech refers to his accent and pronunciation rather than to such an impediment.[15] It could be, of course, that Reilly told Hill that he had a stutter as a child in order to further authenticate his claim to be the inspiration for Arthur Burton.

Over and above the compelling evidence of Ethel Voynich's own statements and the gaping holes in Lockhart's theory, the fact remains that the chronology simply does not add up. Ethel Voynich conceived the idea of *The Gadfly* in 1885/86 and started writing it in 1889. How could Rosenblum, who was eleven or twelve years old at this time have possibly had any influence in the creation of the story? By the time Rosenblum arrived in England at the end of 1895 the book was virtually finished. It must therefore be concluded that Arthur Burton was not based on Sidney Reilly, but Sidney Reilly was based upon Arthur Burton. Whether he would so readily have adopted Arthur's mantle had he known he would ultimately share Arthur's fate is a moot point.

Although *The Gadfly* provided Reilly with the template for his fabricated life story, it does not explain where he got the fine detail about the years he allegedly spent in South America. We do not need to go too far along the library shelf for the answer, which is to be found in a later, lesser-known Ethel Voynich book, *An Interrupted Friendship*, published in 1910. The book attempts to recapture the success of *The Gadfly* by returning to the story of Arthur Burton, alias Felice Rivarez, and focuses on the period he was in South America.

In Ecuador a group of explorers, led by Col. Duprez, are deserted by their interpreter and seek a replacement, which turns out to be no easy task as the respectable interpreters are too scared to join them. They are inundated with applications from those who have no skill with languages. When Rivarez presents himself he is mistaken for a tramp.[16] It soon becomes apparent, however, that under the grime and dirt he is a gentleman and that his claim to be able to speak several languages is true. Col. Duprez therefore takes him on and they proceed with the expedition. When crossing a river, Rene, one of the explorers, falls in and gets his equipment wet so that when he is about to be attacked by a jaguar, his gun will not fire. Just as the jaguar cuts his arm with its claws, however, a shot rings out killing the animal – Rivarez has saved Rene's life. When the expedition is in danger from being attacked by a tribe of savages, Rivarez goes to the natives alone and successfully calms them. When he returns safely, Col. Duprez gives him a permanent contract and says that it is the only way he has at that time to show his gratitude to Rivarez for risking his life to save theirs. He adds that he will let all of France know about him when they return. Three years pass and they return to Europe.

Here then is the genesis of the Fothergill story. In this case it is at least chronologically possible that Rosenblum provided Voynich with some inspiration, although highly improbable. Again, it is more likely that he lifted the tale from her, rather than the other way around.

APPENDIX TWO

MISTAKEN IDENTITY

In July 1905, Reilly graduated from the Royal School of Mines with top
marks... he then went straight up to Trinity College Cambridge, to do
research into Civil Engineering.
Sidney Reilly – *The True Story* by Michael Kettle[1]

The evidence Kettle presents in support of this theory is, at first sight,
compelling and beyond doubt. According to Kettle, Reilly used the name
Stanislaus George Reilly to successfully make an application to study
electrical engineering at the Royal School of Mines in Exhibition Road,
Kensington, on 15 September 1904. On the form he refers to his experience
of railway, waterway and road construction work in India. At the top of the
form a college official has noted that Reilly produced a certificate
confirming that he had studied at Roorkee College in India and that his date
of birth was 24 April 1877.[2]

Kettle relates in his book how he set about trying to establish the claims
made on the application form by studying India Office Records in London
and initiating enquiries in India. He concludes that Reilly's claim to have
been educated at Roorkee is without foundation as indeed are his claims to
have been a civil engineer.[3] In his view, the whole story was a skilfully
constructed alibi, which Reilly 'carefully kept up to date all his life'[4] as a cover
for his spying activities. He produces no evidence to show that Sidney Reilly
ever used the name Stanislaus Reilly or used Stanislaus' curriculum vitae,
fictitious or otherwise, as a cover or alibi for himself, however. It is also
significant that not one of Sidney Reilly's friends, acquaintances or colleagues
ever heard or referred to this 'India story'.

In July 1905, Stanislaus Reilly's student records indicate that he completed his electrical engineering course with full marks and was then admitted to Trinity College, Cambridge, to do research in civil engineering in October 1905. Kettle speculates that Reilly lived at Jesus Lane with Margaret until 1907 or 1908. On his application he had stated that he had been educated at 'schools in India'. In establishing what seems the most conclusive piece of evidence, Kettle sought the opinion of John Conway, a Fellow of the British Academy of Forensic Sciences. He examined the handwriting on the college application forms from 1904 and 1905 with a letter written by Sidney Reilly to his wife Pepita on 25 September 1925. Conway concluded that the three samples were all written by the same hand.[5] Kettle also unearthed an application made by Stanislaus Reilly to join the Institute of Civil Engineers in May 1925, and found from the institute's archives that Stanislaus Reilly had remained on the institute's membership list until 1948, when Kettle presumes that SIS had his name removed.

When marshalled together, the pieces of evidence Kettle has assembled seem to establish almost beyond doubt that Stanislaus Reilly was a character whose background had been fabricated by Sidney Reilly in order to cover his past and to gain admission to the Royal School of Mines and to Trinity College, Cambridge. Subjected to closer examination, however, major faults are to be found running through his evidence.

Kettle's enquiries were apparently set in motion after reading in *Ace of Spies* that Reilly had claimed to be a graduate of the Royal Institute of Mines in London.[6] He therefore set about finding corroboration for this in the records of London University, eventually discovering an application form dated 5 September 1904, in the name of Stanislaus George Reilly. One can appreciate that the coincidence was uncanny. A person of a similar age to Sidney Reilly, with a Polish first name and an identical middle and family name, found at an institution Reilly himself had apparently claimed to have attended.

Sidney Reilly's claim was to have studied chemistry not electrical engineering, however. Furthermore, the application form unearthed by Kettle was not a Royal School of Mines application, it was for the adjacent City and Guilds Central Technical College, which later became part of Imperial College, along with the Royal School of Mines, in 1907.[7] At Trinity College, it is certainly the case that S.G. Reilly was admitted in October 1905 and lived at 8 Jesus Lane, Cambridge. However, he most certainly was not living at that address 'with his wife Margaret' for, as Cambridge City records affirm, the address was a lodging house offering single-room accommodation to individual students. The lodging house keeper during the time that S.G. Reilly lived there was Mrs L. Flatters.[8] College minute books also indicate that S.G. Reilly took a keen part in extra-curricular activities and joined the Trinity College Boat Club on 14 October 1905.[9] In terms of the hand-writing on the application forms allegedly matching that of Sidney Reilly's, one should appreciate that even among handwriting experts, such pronouncements are not viewed as an exact science. Equally, it must also be recorded that John Conway was not a handwriting expert, his field of expertise lay in establishing whether or not documents were authentic.

While Kettle quite properly checked the details of Stanislaus Reilly's birth, had he run a similar check on records of death he would have found that Stanislaus George Reilly died at the age of seventy-five, at Horton Hospital in Epsom, Surrey, on 13 June 1952.[10]

The death certificate is a key piece of evidence. It provides numerous leads to other documents concerning the administration of his estate, by which other family members can be traced. In this way, Stanislaus's daughter Aline and nephew Noel were both located. They were able to provide details of their family history and in particular an account of Stanislaus's life and career.[11] From this, a check was carried out of contemporary British and Indian records, which authenticated their recollections.[12] Indian residential records confirm that he was living in India until 1903, where he had worked as an overseer and an assistant engineer in Khandwah and Dharmpur. Due to the fact that he was in London and Cambridge between 1904 and 1907 he does not appear in the residential records during those years. On his return to India he married Aline's mother, Edith Anne, at Agra in 1909. Aline was born two years later in Dehra Dun, shortly after which he became engineer and manager of the Dehri Rohtus Light Railway.[13] On 11 June 1918 he was commissioned as second lieutenant in the Indian Army Reserve of Officers (Infantry), from where he was seconded to the Royal Engineers. A year later he was promoted to lieutenant and was promoted again to lieutenant-colonel before being released in 1920. The Reilly family returned to England before the outbreak of the Second World War, where Stanislaus was engaged as a civil engineer. Edith died in 1945[14] and Stanislaus's health, too, declined after the war. In fact, his resignation from the Royal Institute of Mines in 1948 was for reasons of ill health and was certainly not the result of SIS machinations. It is therefore clear that Stanislaus George Reilly was in fact a real and distinctly separate person from Sidney George Reilly, and not the fabrication of Sidney Reilly or SIS.

Appendix Three
The Factory Fireman

> The Kaiser was building a gigantic war machine.... but British intelligence
> had no idea what kind of weapons were being forged inside Germany's
> sprawling war plants. Reilly was sent to find out.
> *Spies* by Jay Robert Nash[1]

The story of how Reilly infiltrated the Krupps plant in Essen and made away
with plans of Germany's most secret weapons bears all the hallmarks of a
classic Reilly storyline, with the courageous and resourceful 'Master Spy'
triumphing against the odds. With a German foe, this story no doubt went
down well with colleagues and friends just after the First World War. When
first published in 1967, Robin Bruce Lockhart's *Ace of Spies* maintained that
this episode occurred in 1904. However, twenty years later, when he
published *Reilly: The First Man*, 1909 is given as the date[2] The story itself,
whether told by Lockhart, Nash or Van Der Rhoer[3] is at least consistent.

In true *Boys' Own* style, the tale opens with Reilly arriving in Essen in
the guise of a Baltic German shipyard worker by the name of Karl Hahn.[4]
Having scrupulously prepared his cover by spending time at a Sheffield
engineering firm learning the craft of a welder, he immediately secures a
position as a welder at the plant and joins the works fire brigade, which
enables him to move around at night without raising suspicion. The cunning
Reilly then persuades the foreman in charge of the fire brigade that a
complete set of plans of the plant are needed to indicate the position of fire
extinguishers and hydrants. The plans are duly lodged in the foreman's office
for members of the brigade to consult, and Reilly sets about locating the
secret plans.

In the dead of night, using lock-picks, he breaks into the office where they are kept but is disturbed by the foreman. Reilly throttles the man to death before completing the theft. In making his escape, he is intercepted by a night watchman, but knocks the man out and ties him up before walking out of the factory with the plans.

From Essen, Reilly took a train to Dortmund where he had a safe house, changed into his Savile Row suit and tore the plans into four pieces, mailing each one separately. If one was lost, the other three would still reveal the gist of the plan.

The fact that this tale is nothing more than an entertaining yarn can be clearly established by reference to the substantial archives of the Krupps Company in Essen. The index of files alone amounts to over 100 pages and indicates that comprehensive records have survived which cover the development of the plant and the personnel of the works fire brigade. After a disastrous fire in 1865 Alfred Krupp decided to found a fire brigade for his factory, which on foundation consisted of thirty-six men, organised in six companies of six.[5] It is clear from the records that the Krupps fire brigade was a professional fire brigade, and was not organised on the basis of the British model for works brigades that were made up from volunteers from among the workforce.[6] Reilly's story describes such a scenario whereby Hahn responds to a factory notice calling for volunteers to join the works brigade, hardly in keeping with the reality of a professional brigade.[7]

Service in the fire brigade was based on the principle that members lived on the factory site, or nearby, in houses provided by the Krupps Company. By 1900 a lack of space put this policy in jeopardy. The following year, however, measures were taken to ensure that housing for all members of the brigade was available. New accommodation in Altendorferstrasse, Bunsenstrasse and Harkortstrasse provided 214 flats by 1902.[8] There is no record of a Karl Hahn living in any Krupps property. Likewise, there are records of those who served on the brigade from 1873 up to 1915.[9] Again, the name Karl Hahn is noticeable by its absence.

Interestingly, it would seem that the fire brigade also acted as a security service for the plant.[10] Security records and correspondence for the period 1878–1915 again make no reference to a Karl Hahn. Could it therefore be that, although not a member of the fire brigade, a Karl Hahn was employed as a welder at the plant? The card index of employees[11] by the name of Karl Hahn working at the plant, from the turn of the century to the outbreak of the First World War, indicates the following persons:

Karl Hahn, born 16 June 1889 at Bielefeld, lathe operator (employed 1903–45)
Karl Hahn, born 10 November 1875 at Beuren, mason (employed 1912–36)

Karl Hahn, born 12 December 1887 at Demerath, machinist (employed 1912–27)

Karl Hahn, born 20 June 1878 at Schoeneberg, labourer (employed 1906–26)

Of the four, only one was actually working at the plant at the time Lockhart sets his account. More conclusively, all four workers were still employed at the plant when Reilly died in 1925, and by implication could not have disappeared one dark night in 1904 clutching secret company plans. Ironically, there is one brief reference to Sidney Reilly in the Krupps archive – a press clipping from the *Chattanooga Times*, dated 1 August 1981, reviewing Edward Van Der Rhoer's book *Master Spy!*

Appendix Four

The Battleship Blueprints

Reilly worked behind locked doors in his flat in Potchtamsky Street. He spent hours with a hot iron and layers of blotting paper, placing the blueprints between sheets of glass and making Photostat copies. For three vital years before the outbreak of the First World War, the British Admiralty were kept up to date with every new design or modification in the German fleet – tonnages, speeds, armament, crew and every detail down to cooking equipment.

Ace of Spies by Robin Bruce Lockhart[1]

The story of how Reilly supposedly made a fortune from Blohm & Voss warship contracts in 1911 through 'Medrochovich and Chubersky [sic]', while at the same time obtaining German warship blueprints, is pure fantasy.[2] According to this story, he used his position as agent for Blohm & Voss to request, on behalf of the Russian Ministry of Marine, design specifications of the latest German warships. Before passing them on to the ministry, Reilly photographed them and sent the copies to the Admiralty in London.

We already know that, despite his subsequent claims, Reilly had little connection with Mendrochowitz and Lubiensky, and was in no way responsible for their status as agents for Blohm & Voss. We also know now that he had no connection with SIS or NID before 1918. The diary of Mansfield Cumming (C) is understandably silent on Reilly before this date, for the two did not know each other or even meet until March 1918. C's diary is particularly helpful, however, in that it indicates how SIS were actually obtaining German naval designs at the very time Reilly claimed to be obtaining them in St Petersburg.

Hector Bywater, a British journalist and naval expert living in Germany, was recruited as an SIS agent in 1910.[3] He spent the best part of the next three and a half years penetrating German dockyards and the Berlin Navy Office.[4] Working with a small group of other agents he managed to obtain photographs, silhouette drawings and design details of virtually every German warship then in commission. Had Reilly actually been a British agent at this time, and obtained the blueprints as Lockhart said, there would have been little purpose in Bywater and his colleagues risking their lives. The most charitable view one can take of this story is that it was a device to explain away his seemingly intimate pre-war relationship with the Germans. Just after the First World War, when most of his story telling was done, would hardly have been the best of times to admit to such a close association with the old foe.

APPENDIX Five
RESCUING THE TSAR

In late 1917 and 1918, behind-the-scenes helpers such as Charles Crane, Karol Yaroshinsky the Polish-Russian banker and close friend of the Romanovs, as well as Sidney Reilly, the erstwhile Russian double agent, who was operating on Britain's behalf, were involved in the formulation and execution of various attempts to snatch both Russia and the family from the Bolsheviks.

The Plots to Rescue the Tsar by Shay McNeal[1]

The proposition that a successful and audacious rescue actually took place and has remained hushed up for over eighty years is, in this author's view, straining historical credibility almost to breaking point. Determining whether or not such an attempt was ever contemplated or pursued by the Allies is not, however, the purpose of this book; although Shay McNeal's claim that Sidney Reilly was at the heart of such a plot most certainly is. According to McNeal, Reilly was sent to Russia in early 1918 to undertake a special secret assignment, which involved rescuing the Tsar and his family.[2] So secret was this mission to be that all mention of it in official correspondence was apparently forbidden. An extract from a cable dated 28 May 1918 from Gen. MacDonough, the Director of Military Intelligence in London, to Brig.-Gen. Poole in Murmansk, is quoted in support of this view:

> The following two officers are engaged on special secret service and should not be mentioned in official correspondence or to other officers unless absolutely unavoidable, Lieutenants Mitchelson and Reilly.[3]

However, to assert that this quotation supports the rescue theory is to misunderstand the nature of the cable. To appreciate its context and meaning, one needs to see the cable it has been extracted from in its entirety:

Following for the information of Admiral and yourself: Regarding your Military Intelligence organisation, the following has been provisionally approved. Lieutenant-Colonel Thornhill will be in charge of all officers doing military intelligence in Russia except those on secret service, whose relations with him will be defined at some later date, but who should collaborate with him in every possible way for the present and should keep him informed of any military or political information they may obtain. The following two officers are engaged on special secret service and should not be mentioned in official correspondence or to other officers unless absolutely unavoidable, Lieutenants Mitchelson and Reilly.

With regard to officers doing official intelligence under Thornhill the following is provisional establishment: one General Staff Officer, 1st Grade viz; Thornhill, one General Staff Officer, 3rd Grade at Archangel, one General Staff Officer, 3rd Grade at Murmansk. Van Someren nominated for former place. Who would you and Thornhill like for Murmansk? Five attached officers Carstin, A.F. Hill, Tanplin, Hodson and Pitts to be distributed as Thornhill thinks best. He should send orders at once to three first named who are in Russia. Two clerks, one for the office in Murmansk, and one for Archangel. Is this arrangement suitable? Lockhart has been informed that in future all intelligence will be controlled by Thornhill. One officer, exclusive of above all, will be nominated from London to run all secret service. I should like to hear who Thornhill would like in this capacity. The following are suggested as possible, Maclaren, Lee or Boyce.[4]

Following the March 1918 landing of a British marine company at Murmansk under Brig.-Gen. Poole, MacDonough was responsible for overseeing the creation of a military intelligence network to complement Poole's operation. The reference in the second paragraph to 'official intelligence' is significant. Officers carrying out 'official intelligence' were those doing bona fide military intelligence work (i.e., those concerned with troop movements, logistics, weaponry and equipment, etc.), as opposed to those assigned to the Secret Intelligence Service and working under the umbrella of military intelligence for the purposes of cover only. For this reason, the Secret Intelligence Service operated under the War Office cover name of MI1c (later MI6). Their responsibilities, as today, were essentially to acquire political and economic intelligence (as opposed military matters). The cable therefore makes clear to Poole and Admiral Kemp (Commander of the British White Sea Fleet) that of the cohort of military intelligence officers assigned under Lt-Col. Thornhill, two – Reilly and Mitchelson, were in fact

SIS officers acting under the cover of military intelligence. It is this distinction that is significant or 'special' and which warrants confidentiality.

McNeal also points to Reilly's contact with the Russian Orthodox Church during the summer of 1918 as further evidence of his involvement in rescuing the Tsar. It is, she believes, 'safe to assume that the Church would have made its best efforts to assist the former head of the Church, as in the eyes of the Church the Tsar was God's representative on earth', and concludes that Reilly was, 'taking money to the Church to assist in hiding the family for a time before they were to be moved or restored.'[5]

'Plots to Rescue the Tsar' offers no tangible evidence that Reilly's liaisons with the Church had any connection with the fate of the Tsar. On the contrary, documentary evidence exists which points to the more logical scenario that recognising the mass support the Church still commanded among the general population, Reilly was keen to elicit its support for his self-initiated plans to overthrow the Bolshevik regime. Indeed, on 22 June 1918 Reilly had cabled London to report that as a result of a recent meeting with N.D. Kuznetsov, an Orthodox Church go-between, Patriarch Tikhon was prepared to endorse Allied intervention, at a price.[6]

In terms of Reilly's reports and cables generally, McNeal later states that there are 'irregularities' concerning Reilly's Secret Intelligence Service personnel file, which is, 'literally blank during the period from May to October 1918',[7] implying that this supports the view that he was involved in a secret mission that could not be formally recorded. The reality is somewhat different. Reilly, in fact, sent a series of cables to London during May and June 1918, but these were filed by the War Office and the Foreign Office[8] and thus do not appear on his personnel file. Equally, during the period July to September, as in April, he was effectively following his own inclinations, contrary to the orders and instructions he had been given by London not to interfere or to become politically involved,[9] and was not therefore filing regular reports. George Hill, who was working closely with Reilly, did keep a detailed account which refers to Reilly's activities and is notable for its lack of any reference to the Tsar or his captivity.[10]

Reilly's alleged association with the multi-millionaire banker Karol Jarosznsky during this period is also seen as a factor linking him to the escape plot. Jarosznsky was, according to McNeal, 'a close friend and benefactor of the Romanovs while they were in confinement',[11] and Reilly, in the words of Sir Archibald Sinclair, was 'his right-hand man'.[12] While it is legitimate to quote Sinclair, it should be pointed out again that as with so many other quotes, it is the context which is crucial. In this particular case, the quotation is taken from a letter written by Sinclair to Mr Tilden-Smith, a Board of Trade official, on 11 November 1919. This was not, however, a retrospective acknowledgement of Reilly's association with Jaroszynsky, but a comment on the position at the time of writing, in the context of the Board of Trade's interest in Jarosznsky. Indeed, Sinclair had only known Reilly since their March 1919 introduction at the Hotel Majestic in Paris. Although Reilly had been acquainted with Jaroszynsky in pre-war St Petersburg and was closely involved in his post-war banking schemes described in Chapter Eleven of this book, there is no evidence of any kind actively linking Reilly with Jaroszynsky's activities during the period of his first Russian mission for SIS (April–September 1918).

Despite the fact that the diary of Sir Mansfield-Cumming, the Chief of SIS, makes no reference to any matters remotely connected with the Tsar's family and their potential rescue, McNeal alludes to a claim made by James Smythe in a 1920 book on the same subject.[13] According to Smythe, the family were freed by British Intelligence agents through a newly constructed tunnel that led from the cellar of the Ipatiev House, where they were being held, to the nearby British Consulate.[14] However, no concrete evidence of such a tunnel has ever been produced to substantiate this, or indeed any of Smythe's other claims. The argument for Reilly's involvement is further reinforced, in McNeal's view, by an account of the Tsar's last days in captivity by Parfen Domnin, his personal attendant. In this document,[15] Domnin refers to an engineer by the name of Ilinsky. McNeal speculates that Ilinsky may have had something to do with the construction of the tunnel and that he and Reilly may be the same person, as this could be a typographical error for Relinsky, one of the aliases he used in Russia during this period.

All in all, the case for Reilly's involvement is as unconvincing as it is lacking in hard evidence.

THE ZINOVIEV LETTER

> The forging of the Zinoviev letter was the high water mark in Reilly's whole career.
> *Sidney Reilly – The True Story* by Michael Kettle[1]

Documents purporting to originate from the executive committee of the Communist International (Comintern) in Moscow had been appearing in anti-Communist circles in Paris for some months prior to the discovery of the so called 'Zinoviev letter' in October 1924. The letter, which was almost certainly a forgery, was supposedly written by Gregory Zinoviev, the president of Comintern. It called on British Communists to mobilise 'the group in the Labour Party sympathising with the treaty' to bring pressure to bear in support of its ratification. It further urged them to encourage 'agitation-propaganda' in the armed forces.[2]

At the 5th Congress of the Communist International in June and July, Zinoviev had clearly spoken out in favour of making Britain a priority for Comintern agitation and propaganda. The letter therefore fitted into an already established picture. The identity of the forger has never been satisfactorily established, although Michael Kettle has claimed proof positive for his theory that it was none other than Sidney Reilly. Kettle asserts that the letter 'was first deciphered as being in Reilly's handwriting by the present author [Kettle]'.[3] Kettle called on the services of John Conway to authenticate his Zinoviev theory, who declared that he was 'satisfied that from the quality of the writing – that is pen control and spacing, the letter formations and sizes and other characteristics – that they were written by the same person'.[4] Bearing in mind then Conway's flawed verdict on earlier Kettle theories (see Appendix 2), one has to be highly sceptical of his conclusion in this case.

It must also be borne in mind that the only piece of Reilly's handwriting Conway had from Kettle for the purposes of comparison was in English, taken from Pepita Reilly's *Britian's Master Spy* book.[5] As Conway himself concedes 'the fact that the texts are in languages with different alphabets makes for some difficulty in comparison'. In spite of this he concludes that 'the design and drawing of characters are the same'.[6] In order to carry out a more reliable comparison, a handwriting analyst would require a sample from Reilly that was actually written in Russian in order that he could compare like with like. This Conway did not have. Since Conway's analysis over thirty years ago, samples of Reilly's Russian letter formation have come to light[7] and add further weight to the view that Reilly was not the writer of the letter published in Kettle's book.

In view of Conway's questionable record and his inability to make a like comparison, his verdict can only be regarded as unsafe. Without this, Kettle's theory is supported by only the flimsiest of circumstantial threads, namely the diary of former MI5 officer Donald Im Thurn.[8] Im Thurn had a peripheral connection with events surrounding the letter's eventual publication in the *Daily Mail*, in that he allegedly sold a copy of it to Lord Younger, the then treasurer of the Conservative Party. On 8 October Im Thurn recorded in his diary that an individual he referred to as X had met him that day and given him a very brief verbal account of what would turn out to be the Zinoviev letter.[9] Clearly intrigued, Im Thurn asked X to find out more. On 13 October X asked for more time to 'dot the i's a bit more' and the following day alleged that Prime Minister Ramsay MacDonald was endeavouring to prevent news of the letter getting out.[10] With no more than the fact that Reilly had used a similar phrase in two letters of 25 and 30 March 1925 to former SIS colleague Ernest Boyce,[11] Kettle immediately concluded that here was proof that Reilly and X were the same person. Reilly, however, was on the other side of the Channel on 13 October, and therefore could not have simultaneously been in London meeting Im Thurn.[12]

Further doubt is cast on Kettle's theory by newly declassified government papers on the Zinoviev episode. These point to Col. Stewart Menzies, then deputy chief of SIS, as the person responsible for leaking the letter to the *Daily Mail*. His allegiance, 'lay firmly in the Conservative camp',[13] and he later admitted sending a copy of the letter to the paper's editor.[14] In April 1952, Menzies, who had risen from deputy chief to chief of SIS in 1939, wrote to the Foreign Office to say that there would be 'no harm whatsoever'[15] in destroying some of the papers concerning the Zinoviev episode. The Foreign

Office later conceded that 'perhaps some letters and papers have been destroyed in the past which ought to have been preserved under the Public Records Act'.[16] It is highly unlikely that SIS knew the true origin of the letter or that Reilly had any connection whatsoever with the episode.

Despite the fact that the *Daily Mail* published the letter only four days before the General Election, under the headline 'Civil War Plot by Socialists' Masters', it is highly questionable as to whether this in itself lost Labour the election. All the indicators were pointing to a Labour defeat well before the *Mail*'s revelation. Although Labour seats fell from 191 to 151, the party's vote actually rose by more than a million. The real losers of the 1924 election were the Liberal Party, whose seats fell from 159 to 40.

Abbreviations Used in Notes and Bibliography

BI   United States Bureau of
Investigation (now FBI)

BT   Board of Trade

CAB   Cabinet (UK)

CCAC   Churchill College Archives
Centre

FSB   Federalnaya Sluzhba
Bezopasnosti (Federal
Security Service)

FO   Foreign Office

GPU   Gosudarstvennoye
Politicheskoye Upravleniye
(State Political Directorate)

HO   Home Office

MID   Military Intelligence Division
(US)

MI1c   Military Intelligence 1c (see
SIS)

MI5   Military Intelligence 5 – the
Security Service

NID   Naval Intelligence
Department/Division (UK)

OGPU   Obyedinennoye
Gosudarstvennoye
Politicheskoye Upravleniye
(Unified State Political
Directorate)

ONI   Office of Naval Intelligence
(US)

PRO   Public Record Office, Kew
(now National Archives)

SIS   Secret Intelligence Service
(MI1c, now MI6)

WO   War Office

Notes

Introduction and Preface

1. *Ian Fleming, The Man Behind James Bond*, Andrew Lycett (Weidenfeld & Nicolson, 1995), pp.216–17.
2. *The Life of Ian Fleming, Creator of James Bond*, John Pearson (Jonathan Cape, 1966), p.189.
3. Leonard Mosley, a foreign correspondent and contemporary of Fleming's, who later became a successful espionage writer himself, recalled their conversation in a review of the book *Master Spy*, Edward Van Der Rhoer (Charles Scribner's, New York, 1981).
4. Ibid. (p.112).
5. *The Secret War of Charles Fraser-Smith*, Charles Fraser-Smith with Gerald McKnight and Sandy Lesberg (Michael Joseph, 1981), p.127ff.
6. *Ian Fleming, The Man Behind James Bond*, Andrew Lycett, pp.118 and 132.
7. *The Diaries of Sir Robert Bruce Lockhart*, volume 1: 1915–1938, Kenneth Young (ed.) (Macmillan, 1973), pp.153–54, 165.
8. *Ian Fleming, The Man Behind James Bond*, Andrew Lycett, p.223.

One – A Sudden Death

1. *Highways and Byways of Sussex*, E.V. Lucas (Macmillan & Company, 1904).
2. A biography of Hugh Thomas from records of the General Synod of the Church of England is held by the Anglesey County Records Office (WM/659); also Alumni Records (Magdalene College Archives, Cambridge, pp.152–53); Bangor Diocesan Records (B/P/1055).
3. The Ozone Preparations Company had its origins in Rosenblum & Co. Consultant Chemists, which was established in 1896 at 9 Bury Court, London EC. In 1897 the trading name was changed to Ozone and moved to Imperial

Chambers, 3 Cursitor Street, Holborn.

4. The first meeting between Sigmund Rosenblum and Margaret Thomas was described by Margaret in a transcript she left with Capt. William Isaac of the War Office on 11 November 1931. Isaac produced a brief summary which contained some typographical errors. The original manuscript stated that this first meeting occurred in 'the summer of 1897'. Isaac returned the original manuscript to Margaret and sent the summary to Col. Valentine Vivian, head of SIS Section V – Counter Intelligence (Sidney Reilly's SIS File CX 2616, henceforth referred to as *The Reilly Papers* CX 2616).

5. *Ace of Spies*, Robin Bruce Lockhart (Hodder and Stoughton, 1967), p.29.

6. *Ace of Spies*, Robin Bruce Lockhart (p.29); and *Master Spy*, Edward Van Der Rhoer, p.5.

7. Under passport regulations in force at the time (Foreign Office Regulations Respecting Passports, issued 15 July 1895), passports issued for travel on the continent were 'not limited in point of time, but available for any time, or for any number of journeys on the continent'. However, British subjects wishing to visit Russia would have needed to apply for a passport for travel to Russia and, furthermore, to seek a visa from the Russian Consulate. Although the Thomases already had valid passports for the continent, there is no record of them applying for passports to Russia in the Foreign Office (FO) 611/18 Passport Names Index.

8. The Foreign Office issued passports for the Continent and Egypt to Hugh Thomas on 30 December 1897 and to Margaret on 9 January 1898, FO 611/18 Passport Names Index.

9. Family Division of the High Court of Justice, Principal Probate Registry, 3 May 1898, No. 1456.

10. The sixty-two-year-old Alfred Lewis had been manager of the hotel since 1887. Ironically, he was to die of cardiac failure at the hotel three years later.

11. Entry 433, Register of Burials in the Parish of Llansadwrn; Anglesey County Records Office WPE/32/6. It is also noteworthy that the funeral took place one day before the death was officially registered on 17 March 1898.

12. *Sussex Express*, 19 March 1898, p.5.

13 Entry 316, 1898 Register of Deaths in the Registration District of Lewes in the Sub-district of Newhaven in the County of Sussex.

14 In the first edition of *Ace of Spies* by Robin Bruce Lockhart, published in 1967, a typed copy of Hugh Thomas's registration of death is reproduced. Issued by Somerset House on 19 September 1938, this copy certificate was almost certainly applied for by George Hill, who was researching a bi ography of Sidney Reilly during this period. According to this copy, the death was certified by 'S.W. Andrew MRCS'. By examining the original handwritten entry, however, it is clear that the typist has made a transcription error. The correct name is T.W. Andrew.

15. Dr Thomas Andrew was born in Perthshire in 1837 and qualified in

medicine in Edinburgh in 1861. He and his wife Margaret lived at Balkerach Villa, Doune, where he died on 21 January 1905. His obituary referred to the fact that he had never ventured outside of Scotland.

16. Louisa Lewis lived at the London & Paris Hotel. Her recollections of the weekend of 12/13 March 1898 may possibly have a significant role to play later in our story.

17. Letters dated 17 and 25 May 2001 from Diana Oxford of Kingsford Stacey Blackwell, Lincoln's Inn, London, to the author.

18. Why Rosenblum chose the name 'T.W. Andrew' is not entirely clear. It should, however, be noted that the names and identities he assumed over a period of years were almost always derived from people he had known or met. When living at 50 Albert Mansions, his immediate neigbour at no. 49 was named Andrews (Electoral Register 1896/97, Parliamentary, Country and Parochial Electors in Kennington, Vauxhall Ward, Polling District No. 5).

19. Entry 88, 1869 Register of Births in the Registration District of Clerkenwell in the Sub-district of Goswell Street in the County of Middlesex.

20 Foreign Office Passport Names Index, A. Luke, issued 13 December 1894, FO 611/17.

21. See note 4.

Two – THE MAN FROM NOWHERE

1. *Ace of Spies*, Robin Bruce Lockhart, p.22.

2. *Master Spy*, Edward Van Der Rhoer, p.4.

3. *Deadly Illusions*, John Costello & Oleg Tsarev (Century, 1993), p.22.

4 *Sidney Reilly – The True Story*, Michael Kettle (Corgi, 1983), p.12.

5. *Secret Service*, Christopher Andrew (William Heinemann, 1985), p.83.

6. *A History of the British Secret Service*, Richard Deacon (Frederick Muller, 1969), p.139.

7. For examples of these claims see foreword of *Britain's Master Spy – The Adventures of Sidney Reilly*. This is the US version of the book published by Harper Brothers, New York, in 1932. The earlier British version, *The Adventures of Sidney Reilly*, published by Elkin, Mathews & Marrot, had been withdrawn from sale the previous year due to legal proceedings initiated by Margaret Reilly; *Portraits of Unusual People*, Vladimir Krymov (Paris, 1971), p.70; *Ace of Spies*. Robin Bruce Lockhart, p.22; and letter/enclosure from Capt. William Isaac of the War Office to SIS, dated 17 November 1931 (*Reilly Papers* CX 2616).

8. Ibid.

9. Clonmel (US Immigration records referred to in note 15); Dublin (US Bureau of Investigation/ONI Memorandum of 23 August 1918), p.2, and Sonderfahndungsliste GB File, p.78, R-38 (Central Office for National Security – RHSA, Department IV (Gestapo) E4).

10. *A History of the British Secret Service*, Richard Deacon, p.140. A slightly different version of the quotation is given by Robin Bruce Lockhart: 'I came to Britain to work for the British. I had to have a British passport and needed a British place of birth and, you see, from Odessa it's a long, long way to Tipperary!', *Ace of Spies*, p.104. The source for this story is almost certainly Robert Bruce Lockhart who was Commercial Secretary at the Legation at the time of Reilly's visit. According to the *Diaries of Robert Bruce Lockhart* (p.55), his journal for 1921 is missing. However, Edward Spears' diary would suggest that the lunch took place on Sunday 17 July 1921 (Churchill College Archives Centre, Cambridge MSS SPRS 2/4).

11. *Britain's Master Spy – The Adventures of Sidney Reilly* (foreword, pp.ix and 7).

12. The manuscript of *The Adventures of Sidney Reilly* was serialised by the *Evening Standard* before it appeared in book form. Reference to Reilly's year of birth appears in the second instalment on 11 May 1931, p.26.

13. *Britain's Master Spy – The Adventures of Sidney Reilly*, foreword p.ix.

14. *Memoirs of a British Agent*, Robert Bruce Lockhart (Putnam, 1932), p.322.

15. When, as Sigmund Rosenblum, he married Margaret Thomas on 22 August 1898 (Entry 186, 1898 Register of Marriages in the District of Holborn in the County of London) he indicated his year of birth as 1873, as he did when he entered the United States in January 1915 (US Immigration, Port of San Francisco, Volume 7978, p.26, 13 January 1915), again in July 1915 (US Immigration, Port of New York, Volume 5587, p.103, 6 July 1915), and when he married on 16 February 1915 (State of New York, Certificate and Record of Marriage (No. 4199) between Sidney G. Reilly and Nadine Zalessky, Borough of Manhattan Bureau of Records).

16. When he married Pepita Haddon Chambers on 23 May 1923 (Entry 29, 1923 Register of Marriages in the District of St Martin, in the County of London) he indicated his year of birth as 1874, as he did when he entered the United States in 1924 (US Immigration, Port of New York, Volume 7978, p.26, 15 May 1924, and US Immigration, Port of New York, Volume 8155, p.5, 21 October 1924).

17. *History of the British Secret Service*, Richard Deacon, p.140, and *Sidney Reilly – The True Story*, Michael Kettle, p.13.

18. The only member of his family that he endeavoured to keep in touch with was his first cousin Felicia Rosenblum who lived in Warsaw. According to an 'Explanatory note' appended to Reilly's OGPU File No. 249856, written on 10 November 1925 by V.A. Styrne (now part of Trust File 302330, Vol. 37, Central Archives of the Federal Security Service, Moscow), 'He was extremely bothered by being a Jew and made every attempt to conceal his origin'.

19. Although marketed as being written by Sidney Reilly and his wife, the

book *Britain's Master Spy – The Adventures of Sidney Reilly* is not an autobiography. It was ghostwritten by journalist Stuart Atherley six years after Reilly's death on the instructions of Pepita Reilly.

20. Reports commissioned by the author dated 11 August 2000 and 12 October 2000 by Stepan Zhelyaskov, Vital Records Specialist at the State Archives of Odessa Region.

21. Report commissioned by the author dated 11 August 2000 by Gerda Rattay of Vienna City Archive (ref MA 8-A-1285/2000).

22. Reports commissioned by the author dated 4 September 2000 by Dr Juliane Mikoletzky of the Technical University of Vienna Archives and 3 September 2000 by Thomas Maisel of the University of Vienna Archives.

23. According to War Office records (The Army List), at the Public Record Office, only one Maj. Fothergill is to be found during the time period in question. Maj. Charles Fothergill was commissioned in 1855, retired in 1881 and went into business. He was never involved in any South American expeditions nor had he any intelligence connections. It is not beyond the bounds of possibility, however, that Charles Fothergill was known to Sidney Reilly, who was acquainted with his son Basil Fothergill.

24. It is likely that Abram was born before the 1821 Russian decree which required Jews in the Kingdom of Poland to take surnames. Furthermore, it was not until 1826 that separate civil registers were begun for recording births, deaths and marriages for each religious community (Roman Catholic, Jewish, Protestant and Russian Orthodox). It is not therefore possible to verify Abram's specific date of birth.

25. Gentile names are shown in brackets following the first mention of a Hebrew name. All future references use the goyish or gentile name used by that individual (goy is Hebrew for gentile).

26. Marriage Records 1840, town of Szczuczyn, province of Bialystok, Lomza Gubernia, Fond 264, Bialystok Archive, Poland, Jankiel Leyba Rosenblum and Hana Bramson.

27. There is no 'H' in the Cyrillic alphabet, and the Hebrew name Hersh therefore appears as Gersh when written in Russian.

28. University of Leeds Russian Archive, MS 1080/859, Family Tree of the Rosenblum, Neufeldt and Wolff families; MS 1080/322, letter from Vera Bramson to Sophia Wolff, 24 April 1928; Letter from Esfir Bramson to the author, 3 March 2003

29. Service File of Mikhail Abramovich Rosenblum; Fond 316, Inventory 64, Case 448, Russian State Military Historical Archives, Moscow.

30. Mikhail Rosenblum married Sophie Zonshein on 24 September 1889; Fond 39, Inventory 5, Case 46, p.106, State Archives of Odessa Region. Their son Boris was born in Odessa on 6 July 1890; Fond 39, Inventory 5, File 52, p.185, State Archives of Odessa Region.

31. A variety of versions of Rosenblum family photographs (p.26) have surfaced over the past four decades, including the one of a teenage Reilly (p.29). They were taken seperately on various occasions during the 1880s, and not taken contemporaneously in 1890 as implied by Michael Kettle (*Sidney Reilly – The True Story*, p.72).

32. To date no trace of a record of birth for Rosenblum has ever been found in any of the locations put forward as his place of birth within the former Russian Empire: Bedzin, Poland; Bielsk, Poland; Odessa, Ukraine; Kherson, Ukraine; St Petersburg, Russia. Ukrainian records in particular are incomplete due to the ravages of the Second World War.

33. The first Odessa General Census, XLVII, Table 24, pp.152–53.

34. OGPU File no. 249856.

35. Mikhail Rosenblum studied chemistry for two semesters in the physico-mathematical department of Novorossiysk University, before leaving to study medicine at the Imperial Medical Surgery Academy in St Petersburg. Reilly claimed to have studied in the same department for two semesters before leaving the university.

36. Extract from manuscript by Margaret Reilly dated 13 November 1931 (*Reilly Papers* CX 2616).

37. Box 182, XIIIh, files 7 and 10 (index cards), 1891-1895, Ochrana Collection, Hoover Institution Archives, Stanford, California.

38. *Sidney Reilly – The True Story*, Michael Kettle, p.14.

39. Ibid.

40. Felitsia Vladimirovna Neufeldt (*née* Rosenblum) was the daughter of Grigory Rosenblum's brother Vladimir. She lived in Warsaw from 1900 and was widowed in 1911. She, along with her sons Ira and Marek, and their respective families, were confined in the Warsaw ghetto by the Nazis during the Second World War and died in the Treblinka death camp between July 1942 and June 1943.

41. *Iron Maze*, Gordon Brook-Shepherd (Macmillan, 1998), p.15/16.

42. The unrest was sparked by a government decision concerning army conscription. Student opposition followed, accompanied by political demands.

43. Fond 2, Inventory 2, Case 1241, 'List of foreign passports issued (1892–1899)', Odessa City Governor's Office, contains a list of around 2,400 names. To obtain a passport to travel abroad, a Jew would need to obtain the following documents: ordinary citizen's identity card, certificate from the chief of police confirming that there was no objection to the applicant leaving the country, certification of regimentation with military enlistment registration office, or notice of completion of military service, and a Treasury certificate showing the payment of a passport application fee of fifteen roubles.

44. Reilly's Deuxième Bureau file 28779/25 was among French intelligence material taken by the Germans to Berlin after the fall of

France in 1940. The Russians, in turn, took the consignment to Moscow in 1945. Between December 1993 and May 1994 some 10,326 cartons of material weighing twenty tons were returned to the French by the Russians. The French maintained that 10,000 boxes of material, including file 28779/25, still remained in Russian hands. After a hiatus of five years the Russians returned a further 900 metres length of archives in 2000. A number of files, however, including 28779/25, remain in the still restricted Osobyi Archiv at the Russian State Military Archive, Moscow: Fond 7k, opis 2, delo 3047; Fond 7k, opis 1, delo 104, pp.256–64; Fond 198k, opis 2, delo 1057, p.68.

45. According to file F7 12894 (Police reports on Russian refugees in Paris) and F7 12904/7 (Anarchists in France and abroad – 1892/1923) in the National Archives, Paris, the 4th and 5th districts of Paris were the principal areas where Russian refugees, Jews and students resided during the 1890s. These two districts also feature in three other files, F7 12591/12596/12600 (Description sheets for aliens and suspects – 188/1907).

46. Arthur Abrahams was the son of Michael Abrahams, founder of the firm Michael Abrahams, Sons & Co. In London, Reilly used a number of lawyers including Michael Abrahams, Sons & Co., Willett & Sandford and Robert Carter. This ensured that no one lawyer had a complete awareness of his activities. Paris city records

for 1896 indicate that Abrahams had a Paris office and flat at 23 Rue Taitbout.

47. Albert Mansions and Victoria Mansions were both upmarket apartment blocks completed in 1894. Albert Mansions stood on the corner of Rosetta Street and South Lambeth Road. Rosenblum took over the tenancy of 50 Albert Mansions from William Gould. Although the postal address for No. 50 was Rosetta Street, the address on Rosenblum's notepaper was 'South Lambeth Road', which he clearly felt to be a more prestigious address. Adapting addresses in this manner was to be a trait of his.

48. 9 Bury Court, in the Parish of St Andrew Undershaft, in the City of London, was leased to Albert Adolph, who sub-let the premises to Rosenblum and three other occupiers (City of London Rates Valuation Lists 1891–1896, Section 13).

49. According to the 1897 List of Officers and Fellows of the Chemical Society, p.53, Rosenblum was elected a Fellow on 18 June 1896.

50. According to the 1898 Register of Fellows, Associates and Students of The Institute of Chemistry, p.85, Rosenblum was admitted a Fellow on 4 March 1897.

51. The Institute's charter (clause 5, p.15) states that it 'rests with the Council to determine in each case whether the candidate shall be required to pass either or both the intermediate or final examinations'. He would also have been required to produce a satisfactory certificate of moral

character. The certificate and identity of the person who perjured themself in providing it, is no longer in the archives of the Royal Society of Chemistry.

52. William Fox's place of business was 39 Mincing Lane in the City of London, in close vicinity of Rosenblum & Co. at Bury Court. Fox was also Rosenblum's neighbour at 52 Albert Mansions, Lambeth (Electoral Register 1896/1897, Parliamentary, County and Parochial Electors in Kennington, Vauxhall Ward, Polling District No. 5).

53. *Ace of Spies*, Robin Bruce Lockhart, p.27/28.

54. Ibid.

55. Lithuania State Historical Archives, Fond 1226, Schedule 1, File 167, (born Kovno 17 April 1869, Levi son of Mojsej Bramson and Leja daughter of Jakov).

56. Report by V Ratayev (Ochrana, Paris), to Department of Police, St Petersburg, 24 February 1903, Fond 102, Inventory 316, 1898, delo 1, chast 16, litera A, listy 84ob-85, State Archive of the Russian Federation, Moscow.

57. Interview between E L Voynich biographer Carol Spero and Winifred Gaye (Ethel Voynich's stepdaughter), Bath, Somerset, 1992

58. *Rare People and Rare Books*, E. Millicent Sowerby (Constable, 1967), p.21.

59. Rosenblum's letter of application, his character reference and records of his attendance are to be found in the British Museum Archives (Sigmund Georgjevich Rosenblum – ticket number A63702.12044). Four books in particular made available to Reilly suggest the nature of his research: Blagden, Sir Charles, *Some observations on ancient inks* (1787); Merrifield, Mary P., *Original treatises on the arts of painting*. 2 vol. (1849); *A Booke of secrets, shewing divers waies to make and prepare all sorts of Inke and Colours*, Trans. W.P. London (1596); William Linton, *Ancient and modern colours* (1852). It should also be noted that Wilfred Voynich held a reader's ticket (No. A53962 2897). British Museum records indicate that the ticket was obtained on the recommendation of Sergei Stepniak.

60. Police Orders for 10 April and 5 May 1893; PRO MEPO 7/55, pp.264 and 340.

61. PRO MEPO 4/342 (Register of Leavers) and MEPO 21/32 (Pension Register).

62. CID, *Behind the Scenes at Scotland Yard*, H.L. Adams, p.167.

63. Memorandum dated 28 April 1896 (The Melville Papers).

64. Sir Edward Bradford, chief commissioner to the Home Office, 28 April 1902, PRO HO 45/10254.

65. Vladimir Krymov, who knew Reilly in St Petersburg before the First World War, related in *Portraits of Unusual People*, that Reilly was dubbed 'the man who knew everything' due to his unique ability to keep his ear to the ground.

66. Arthur Wood of the *Daily Telegraph* and James Hogan of the *Daily Graphic* had rooms at 3 Cursitor Street in 1898.

67. 'The question as to the permissibility of advertising is one

which still agitates the minds of our members, notwithstanding that the censors gave a no uncertain pronouncement on the matter as long ago as 1893, and the attention of members was again drawn to it in December 1895. I am sorry that the expression of opinion is felt by some among us as forming a bar to the legitimate practice of their profession; a profession which a minority – and I trust a small minority – of our members would perhaps unconsciously reduce to the level of a trade. To my mind, to advertise or to tout for practice is degrading, and a virtual acknowledgement that he who does so cannot compete on equal terms with his fellows. In no other professions in this country are such practices tolerated' (the address of the president, Dr Thomas Stevenson, FRCP, to the 12th Annual General Meeting of the Institute of Chemistry, 1 March 1898, contained in the 1898 Proceedings, p.25).

68. Entry 379, Register of births in the District of Gorey in the County of Wexford, Ireland. Margaret Callaghan daughter of Edward and Anne Callaghan (née Noctor), 1 January 1874.

69. Entry 55, Register of Marriages in the District of Gorey in the County of Wexford, Ireland. Edward Callaghan, fisherman, and Anne Naughter, 27 February 1870 at the Catholic Chapel of St Michael.

70. Entry 385, Register of Births in the District of Gorey in the County of Wexford, Ireland. James Callaghan, son of Edward and Anne Callaghan (née Naughter),

24 February 1872. He died on 15 March 1930: Entry 248, Register of Deaths in the Registration District of Manchester South, Sub-district of Didsbury in the County of Manchester CB.

71. Entry 149, 1895 Register of Marriages in the District of Paddington in the County of London. Hugh Thomas and Margaret Callaghan, 19 February 1895.

72. Entry 186, 1898 Register of Marriages in the District of Holborn in the County of London. Sigmund Rosenblum and Margaret Thomas, 22 August 1898.

73. Entry 478, 1903 Register of Marriages in the District of Islington in the County of London. Joseph Bell and Violet Pannett, 4 June 1903. Entry 281, 1910 Register of Marriages in the District of Islington in the County of London. Charles Cross and Edith Pannett, 24 August 1910. Henry Freeman Pannett was a Royal Mail official who was an associate of William Melville from the late 1890s up to his retirement in 1908.

74. *Ace of Spies*, Robin Bruce Lockhart, p.32; *Sidney Reilly – The True Story*, Michael Kettle, p.15; *Memoirs of a British Agent*, Robert Bruce Lockhart, p.323; *Deadly Illusions*, John Costello and Oleg Tsarev, p.22; *Iron Maze*, Gordon Brook-Shepherd, p.18; *Spies*, Jay Robert Nash (M. Evans and Company, New York, 1997), p.411; *Master Spy*, Edward Van Der Rhoer, p.6.

75. Parish Register, Parish of Ballygarret, County of Wexford,

6 September 1845; Baptism of Edward Callaghan son of John and Elisa Callaghan (*née* Quinn) – sponsors Paul Byrne and Mary Callaghan (National Library of Ireland, Ballygarret Parish Register, Microfiche P4255).

76. Foreign Office Regulations Respecting Passports (3) – 'Naturalised British Subject', he will be so designated in his passport, which shall be issued subject to the qualification mentioned in the 7th clause of the Act 33 Vic; c.14.

77. Entry 17, Register of Births in the District of Belmullett in the County of Mayo, Ireland. Sidney Reilly son of Michael and Mary Reilly (*née* Barret), 1 February 1878.

78. Entry 48, Register of Marriages, St George's Catholic Church, St Saviour's, Southwark, Surrey, between William Melville and Catherine Reilly, 20 February 1879; according to the 1901 Census (Shragh, County Mayo, 145/DED Derryloughlin 9 1-5), Catherine's brother John and his family were still living in the area at the turn of the century.

79. Extract from manuscript dated 11 November 1931 (*Reilly Papers* CX 2616).

80. PRO FO 72/2048, Report dated 10 February 1897.

81. By liquidating, it must be assumed that Margaret was referring to a sale or disposal of the contents of the Manor House. According to Land Title MX80076 at the Harrow and District Land Registry, the property, which stood on the corner of Buck Lane and Kingsbury Road was owned by Edward Nelson Haxell, who from 1895 let the house to tenants. The house was legally known as Kingsbury House. There were, in fact, two properties known as Kingsbury House in the 1890s, the other being part of the Stud Farm complex on the opposite side of Kingsbury Green. With the confusion of two Kingsbury House names, Hugh Thomas used his own chosen name, The Manor House, when he became the tenant in 1897. The lease to the property was sold on 24 June 1898 to the Countess of Dundonald, who changed the name of the house to The Grange. Neither should this property be confused with Kingsbury Manor, which stands today in Roe Green Park. This latter property was built in 1899 for the Duchess of Sutherland. Its name changed from 'The Cottage' to Kingsbury Manor in 1932.

82. Rosenblum notified the Chemical Society and the Institute of Chemistry of his change of residence, giving them his new 'Hyde Park' address (IC Register of Fellows, Associates and Students, 1899–1900, p.85). His notepaper interestingly carries a small Russian double-headed eagle with the motto 'Mundo Nulla Fides' (No Faith in the World), which is literally interpreted to mean 'place not your faith in worldly things'. It is a clear invitation to place one's faith not in the worldly but in the divine, and was the motto of the Reverend Hugh Thomas (source – Rouge Dragon Pursuivant, College of Arms, London).

83. See note 79.

84. *Ace of Spies*, Robin Bruce Lockhart, p.31.

85. According to Land Title NGL446317 at the Harrow District Land Registry, the property belonged to the Church Commissioners for England, who owned the entire Paddington Estate of which Upper Westbourne Terrace was a part. Hugh Thomas took over the tenancy from Reuben Greatorex in 1891. Ormonde Crosse, previously the tenant at nearby 32 Delamere Terrace, took over the tenancy from Sigmund and Margaret Rosenblum in June 1899. The estate was sold by the commissioners on 30 August 1954 to the London County Council, who demolished it and built a council estate development. The LCC renamed Upper Westbourne Terrace 'Bourne Terrace', the name it bears today.

86. Passport Names Index, issued to S.G. Reilly, 2 June 1899, PRO FO 611/19.

87. PRO FO 372/2756, Nos 7096/7531.

88. *Sidney Reilly – The True Story*, Michael Kettle, p.15.

89. *Ace of Spies*, Robin Bruce Lockhart, pp.32–36. The 1901 Census indicates that no one by the name of Margaret Reilly or Rosenblum, born on 1 January 1874, was residing in the UK at this time.

90. There is no record of Reilly ever having had any connection with the Admiralty or NID. Joseph Bell, an Admiralty clerk, was a witness at Rosenblum's 1898 wedding. As best as can be established, he had no connection with the Naval

Intelligence Department. Admiralty records indicate that Bell was a second class assistant at the Nautical Almanac Office.

91. See note 79.

92. The chronology of this claim is in error. Sidney and Margaret Rosenblum took steps in 1899 to change their name to Reilly by Deed Poll, through solicitors Michael Abrahams Sons & Co. However, their hasty departure from England in June 1899 meant that the application was never completed let alone presented to the High Court. When Sidney eventually changed his name legally, a decade later, his High Court application (PRO/J18/95) referred to this earlier, aborted application. Whilst Margaret used the name Reilly from 1899 until her death in 1933, she never changed her name legally from Rosenblum.

93. Letter dated 17 April 1899 (The Melville Papers; Box 35, Index Vc, Folder 3, Ochrana Archive, Hoover Institution, Stanford, California); Service File of Fedor Gredinger (Fond 1405, Inventory 544, File 3314, Russian State Historical Archive, St Petersburg).

94. See note 56 and Polysulphin Company, PIP/Keynsham, No 231, Somerset Record Office.

95. Sigmund Rosenblum's name was placed on the Department of Police 'Wanted List', which was distributed to all police departments and border posts. (Circular No. 4900 – Rosenblum is No. 47 on the list; Fond 63, Inventory 23, File 11, sheets 190–93, State Archive of the Russian Federation, Moscow).

THREE – GAMBIT

1. Untitled synopsis by Margaret Reilly (as submitted to Cassell & Co. Ltd and Capt. William Isaac of the War Office, November 1931, *Reilly Papers* CX2616; also PRO HD 3/117, item 10; Mr White in Petrovsk, 16 July 1900.

2. Untitled synopsis by Margaret Reilly (see note 1).

3. *The Truth About Port Arthur*, E.K. Nozhin, p.927 (St Petersburg, 1907). Nozhin was a correspondent for the Port Arthur newspaper Novy Krai, which maintained close relations with the Port Arthur authorities.

4. *My Life At Russia's Service – Memoirs of the Grand Duke Kirill Vladimirovich* (reprint, St Petersburg, 1996), p.101.

5. *The Truth About Port Arthur*, E.K. Nozhin, p.933.

6. *Trade in Port Arthur*, a statistical report to Russia's finance minister S. Yu Witte, by Dmitry Matveyevich Pozdneyev (St Petersburg 1902); State Historical Archives of St Petersburg.

7. Ibid., Appendix 1, Report No. 97.

8. Ibid

9. Fond 104, op 1d 58, listy 122-124, d 60, list 17, Russian State Historical Archive, St Petersburg.

10. Fond 967, Inventory 2, File 153, sheets 77 and 83 reverse (Russian State Archive of the Navy, St Petersburg).

11. Document dated 11 January 1921, *The Reilly Papers* CX 2616; The Truth about Port Arthur, E.K. Nozhin, p.933.

12. US Immigration, Port of New York, Volume 6887, p.20, line 2

(16/9/21) refers to Margaret's 1903 entry.

13. *Secrets of Espionage: Tales of the Secret Service*, Winfried Ludecke (J.B. Lippincott, Philadelphia, 1929), p.106; and *History of the Japanese Secret Service*, Richard Deacon (Frederick Muller, 1982), p.48/49.

14. *Ace of Spies*, Robin Bruce Lockhart, p.35.

15. Letter from Professor Ian Nish to the author, dated 11 April 2001.

16. US Bureau of Investigation report written by Agent L. Perkins, 3 April 1917.

17. Guy Gaunt was nominally head of British intelligence in New York. However, he came under the Naval Intelligence Division, not SIS.

18. *The Yield of the Years*, Guy Gaunt (London 1940), pp.109–16.

19. 'Rakka ryusui' is the 1906 report of Col. Akashi Motojiro dealing with his secret co-operation with revolutionary movements within the Russian Empire during the Russo-Japanese War. The 1988 translation by Inaba Chiharu also includes relevant Japanese General Staff telegrams from 1904/05. Among Akashi's contacts were Felix Volkhovsky, who had succeeded Sergei Stepniak as the leading light in the 'Russia Free Press Campaign' in London.

20. *History of the Japanese Secret Service*, Richard Deacon, pp.49–50. The original copy of this letter, along with other Deacon source material pertaining to this book was destroyed. This was confirmed in a letter to the author by Deacon's widow, Eileen McCormick, dated 10 November 2000.

21. *History of the Development of the Directorate of Military Intelligence*, Lt-Col. William Isaac, PRO WO 106/6083, p.13.

22. Lt-Col. Joseph Newman retired from the army in 1892, having seen action during the Indian Mutiny 1857–58 and the Zulu Wars 1877–79, where he was mentioned in dispatches (The Army List 2031/2089, PR0).

23. Fond 846, Inventory 4, File 100 (Russian State Military Historical Archives, Moscow).

24. Fond 846, Inventory 4, File 77 (Russian State Military Historical Archives, Moscow).

25. Untitled synopsis by Margaret Reilly (as submitted to Cassell & Co. Ltd) November 1931.

26. *Portraits of Unusual People*, Vladimir Krymov (Paris, 1971), p.78.

27. *History of the Japanese Secret Service*, Richard Deacon, p.49; and *Secrets of Espionage; Tales of the Secret Service*, Winfried Ludecke, p.106.

28. Entry 255, 1870 Register of Births in the Sub-district of Penshurst in the Registration District of Sevenoaks in the County of Kent.

29. File of H.B. Collins, Fond 846, Inventory 4, File 92 (Russian State Military Historical Archives, Moscow).

30. Letters by and references to Anna Grigoryevna Collins are to be found in H.B. Collins' file (note 27 above).

31. *History of the Japanese Secret Service*, Richard Deacon, p.49; and Secrets of Espionage; *Tales of the Secret Service*, Winfried Ludecke, p.106.

32. Memorandum dated 6 June 1904 (Melville Papers).

33. *The Record of the Anglo-Iranian Oil Company Ltd*, Volume 1 (1901–18), pp.50–51 – BP Amoco Archive, University of Warwick.

34. Ibid., p.49.

35. *Ace of Spies*, Robin Bruce Lockhart, p.41.

36. London Post Office Directories (Kellys) 1904/18.

37. Entry 475, Register of Deaths in the Sub-district South West Battersea, Registration District of Wandsworth in the County of London, 1 February 1918.

38. Author of 'Counter-Espionage and Security in Great Britain during the First World War', *English Historical Review*, Volume 101 (1986), and 'British Internal Security in Wartime', *Intelligence and National Security*, Volume 1 (1986).

39. *The Origins of the Vigilant State*, Bernard Porter (Boydell Press, 1987), p.230.

40. The barrister Henry Curtis-Bennett KC (knighted in 1922 and elected MP for Chelmsford in 1924, succeeding E.G. Pretyman as Conservative candidate) was given an honorary commission in the RNVR when he joined MI5 in 1917; *Curtis: The Life of Sir Henry Curtis-Bennett*, Roland Wild and Derek Curtis-Bennett (Cassell, 1937), pp.66–79.

41. Memoir by William Melville MVO, MBE, PRO KV 1/8; *The Security Service 1908-1945*, The Official History, p50 (Public Record Office, 1999).

42. Ibid.

43. Rear-Admiral Esmond Slade, on retiring as director of the Naval Intelligence Division in 1909, reported to Prime Minister Herbert Asquith that 'It is impossible to draw a line between

the information which would be useful to one department or the other [Admiralty and War Office], so I endeavoured to establish a working agreement between the two offices'; PRO CAB 16/9B, p.195.

44. *Le Littoral*, 18 February 1904, p.1.

45. Melville had twice been honoured by the French government (*Police Review*, 17 May 1895, p.236; *Police Review*, 17 June 1903, p.344), and had also assisted the Ochrana in France (Ochrana Archive, Box 35, Index Vc, Folder 3).

46. As a Royal bodyguard he spoke several languages including French and Italian; I Guarded Kings, Harold Brust (Hillman Curl, 1936), p.44.

47. *The Record of the Anglo-Iranian Oil Company Ltd*, Volume 1 (1901–1918), p.52 – BP Amoco Archive, University of Warwick.

48. Ibid.

49. Ibid.

50. Letter from Sidney Reilly to Alexandre Weinstein, dated 30 June 1905 (Papers of Mrs A.C. Menzies).

51. *The Record of the Anglo-Iranian Oil Company Ltd*, Volume 1 (1901–1918), p.52 – BP Amoco Archive, University of Warwick.

52. Ibid.

53. Untitled synopsis by Margaret Reilly (as submitted to Cassell & Co. Ltd), November 1931.

54. Police Department Report, dated 21 February 1905, Fond 102, Inventory 316, File 19, Sheet 38, 1905 (State Archive of the Russian Federation, Moscow).

55. Ibid.

FOUR – THE BROKER

1. A decade later the US Bureau of Investigation, forerunner of the FBI, carried out extensive enquiries into Reilly's background during the First World War. Their files contain several references to the movements of his 'second wife' (US Bureau of Investigation Case Files, 1908–1922; Old German File 39368. Also Office of Naval Intelligence; Files on A. Jachalski, S. Reilly and A. Weinstein, National Archives, Washington DC (hereafter referred to as Bureau of Investigation/ONI). US Bureau of Investigation/ONI synopsis of names in the Weinstein Case, 23 August 1918, p.8). The Bureau's records concerning Reilly are examined in detail in Chapter Seven.

2. US Bureau of Investigation/ONI; 4 September 1918, Reilly, Weinstein, Jechalski Case: Synopsis of Persons involved, p.12.

3. Royal Air Force Record of Service; Sidney George Reilly MC (PRO, Pi 21220).

4. She eventually married a doctor, Ira Neufeldt, and moved to Warsaw where she was widowed in 1910.

5. Ochrana Surveillance Reports, S.G. Reilly, 11–29 September 1905, Fond 111, Inventory 1, Files 2960-2961, State Archive of the Russian Federation, Moscow.

6. File 1061 (Correspondence with Count T. Lubiensky and J. Mendrochowitz); File 1062 (Applications for Business Representation in Russia 1904–1919), Archives of Blohm & Voss GmbH, Hamburg State Archive.

7. *Ace of Spies*, Robin Bruce Lockhart, pp.52–53. Police records on the arrival of foreign citizens in St. Petersburg: Fond 102, Inventory 316, File 19, Sheet 38, 1905, State Archive of the Russian Federation, Moscow.

8. Ochrana Surveillance Reports, S.G. Reilly, 11–29 September 1905, Fond 111, Inventory 1, Files 2960-2961, State Archive of the Russian Federation, Moscow. Walford was managing clerk for a solicitor and a member of St Petersburg's 'English Colony'. He died in Dudley at the age of seventy-six (Entry 424, Register of Deaths in the Registration District of Dudley, 13 April 1934).

9. Telegram from J. Mendrochowitz to Blohm & Voss, 14 December 1908, File 1077, Archives of Blohm & Voss GmbH, Hamburg State Archive.

10. Letter to Hermann Frahm from Sidney Reilly, 13 April 1909; File 1077, Archives of Blohm & Voss GmbH, Hamburg State Archive.

11. Telegram from Hermann Frahm to Sidney Reilly, 14 April 1909, File 1077, Archives of Blohm & Voss GmbH, Hamburg State Archive.

12. Letter from J. Mendrochowitz to Blohm & Voss, 23 April 1909, File 1077, Archives of Blohm & Voss GmbH, Hamburg State Archive.

13. Telegram from Blohm & Voss to J. Mendrochowitz, 26 April 1909, File 1077, Archives of Blohm & Voss GmbH, Hamburg State Archive.

14. Letter from Blohm & Voss to Count T. Lubiensky and J. Mendrochowitz, 27 April 1909, File 1077, Archives of Blohm & Voss GmbH, Hamburg State Archive.

15. Letter from J. Mendrochowitz to Blohm & Voss, 27 April 1909, File 1077, Archives of Blohm & Voss GmbH, Hamburg State Archive.

16. Letter from J. Mendrochowitz to Blohm & Voss, 1 March 1909, File 1077, Archives of Blohm & Voss GmbH, Hamburg State Archive.

17. *Ace of Spies*, Robin Bruce Lockhart, pp.52–53.

18. Ibid. p.54.

19. File 1082 (Correspondence with Kurt Orbanowsky), Archives of Blohm & Voss GmbH, Hamburg State Archive.

20. Ibid.

21. Ibid.

22. *Portraits of Unusual People*, Vladimir Krymov, p.69.

23. File 1083 (Correspondence with various partners regarding rebuilding of the Russian Navy), Archives of Blohm & Voss GmbH, Hamburg State Archive.

24. *The Nanny with the Glass Eye*, Leon C. Messenger, 1985 (US National Archives, Washington).

25. *The Royal Flying Corps in France*, Ralph Barker (Constable, 1994), p.9.

26. *Ace of Spies*, Robin Bruce Lockhart, p.46. The Frankfurt International Air Show was held in 1909, not in 1910 as Lockhart asserts.

27. Ibid., pp.47–48.

28. Report commissioned by the author dated 11 April 2001, by Elmar Stracke of the Frankfurt Institute for Urban History.

29. Deed Poll Notification, High Court of Justice, 23 October 1908, PRO J18/95, pp.479–80.

30. *Ace of Spies*, Robin Bruce Lockhart, pp.45–46.

31. 97 Fleet Street, in the Parish of St Bride, was owned by

S.R. Cartwright. A jewellers, Saqui & Lawrence, occupied the ground floor and basement. The upper part of the premises were initially empty, but were let to the Ozone Preparations Company between 1908 and 1911 (City of London Quinquennial Rates Valuation List 1906–1911, Volume 2). The Ozone Preparations Company is listed in Kelly's London Directory, under 'patent medicine' for 1909, 1910 and 1911.

32. William Barclay Calder, among his many business interests, had, like Reilly, been a one-time timber merchant. He was associated with Reilly in a number of ventures, the last being another patent medicine scam, the Modern Medicine Company Ltd, founded in 1923. Calder himself died in 1958 (Entry 208, Register of Deaths in the Sub-district of Harrow in the Registration District of Harrow in the County of Middlesex, 28 January 1958.

33. *The Streets of London*, Benny Green (Pavillion, 1983), p.77.

34. Charles Fothergill died on 23 February 1919 (Entry 341, Register of Deaths in the Registration District of Kensington in the County of London). Basil Fothergill died ten years later on 6 August 1929 (Entry 317, Register of Deaths in the Registration District of Eton in the County of Buckinghamshire).

35. Letter from E.W.G. Tappley, general manager of the Hotel Cecil, to J.H. Lewis, the uncle of Louisa Lewis, dated 27 October 1908.

36. Donald McCormick used the *nom de plume* 'Richard Deacon' when writing espionage books. However, *Murder by Perfection* (John Long, 1970), was published under his own name.

37. Gregory was principally involved in the selling of honours scandal during the Lloyd George Administration (1916–22). After the fall of Lloyd George he continued to tout honours and was eventually prosecuted in 1933.

38. *Murder by Perfection*, Donald McCormick, pp.15–16.

39. *London County Council: Names of Streets and Places in the Administrative County of London* (4th edition, 1955).

40. Ordnance Survey Maps 1906–1919, 7–73 (HMSO), London Official and Commercial Directory 1908, 1909.

41. Chief Inspector Arthur Askew of Scotland Yard investigated the honours case of 1933 as well as the investigation of the death of Edith Rosse in the same year. He was convinced Gregory had poisoned Mrs Rosse but was never able to prove it. The decision not to prosecute was certainly not through any lack of effort on Askew's part. In fact, he probably carried out the most in-depth investigation into Gregory and his background ever attempted. Askew's conclusions on his investigations into Gregory are to be found in the *Sunday Dispatch* (12 September 1954, p.5).

Five – The Colonel's Daughter

1. *Ace of Spies*, Robin Bruce Lockhart, p.36.

2. Untitled synopsis by Margaret Reilly, submitted to the War Office and Cassell & Co. Ltd, November 1931.

3. *The Nanny with the Glass Eye*, Leon C. Messenger, Central Intelligence Agency, Studies in Intelligence (Winter 1985), p.31.

4. Ibid., p.31.

5. Ibid.

6. Wilson was HM Vice-Consul in Brussels.

7. Letter from D. Wilson to H. Tom (HM Consul General), 29 May 1931, Brussels Despatch No. 156 (PRO FO 372/2756).

8. *Ace of Spies*, Robin Bruce Lockhart, p.55.

9. Ibid.

10. In 1989 Robin Bruce Lockhart published *Reilly: The First Man* (Penguin, New York, 1987). It was only published in the US and Canada.

11. Ibid., p.6.

12. *Novoe Vremia*, 26 October 1912 (or 8 November 1912 by the Gregorian calendar), p.2 (State Public Library, St Petersburg).

13. Margaret Reilly's Red Cross File No. 45345.

14. *The Nanny with the Glass Eye*, Leon C Messenger, pp.26–27.

15. Ibid., p.27.

16. Service File of Petr Massino (Fond 400, Inventory 17, File 13135; Fond 400, Inventory 12, File 28672, Russian State Military Historical Archives, Moscow).

17. Ibid.

18. Service File of Petr Zalessky (Fond 406, Inventory 9, File 1410, Russian State Archives of the Navy, St Petersburg).

19. Directory of the Maritime Ministry 1911.

20. US Bureau of Investigation/ONI, Report from Operative 101 to H. Hunnewell, 6 September 1918.

21. Service File of Georgi Massino (Fond 400, Inventory 9, File 34550, Russian State Military Archives, Moscow).

22. 'Explanatory Note' appended to Reilly's OGPU File 249856, written on 10 November 1925 by V.A. Styrne, p.1 (now part of Trust File 302330, Vol 37, Central Archives of the Federal Security Service, Moscow).

23. See note 16.

24. The Trial of Petr Massino (Fond 801, Inventory 15, File 99, Russian State Military Historical Archives, Moscow).

25. In November 1927 the Bolsheviks published an edited version of the interrogations of leading Tsarist ministers to coincide with the tenth anniversary of the Revolution. In 1964 the Russian journal *Issues of History* published the 'Resolution' of the Extraordinary Commission Regarding the Activity of Rasputin and his Close Associates and their Influence over Nicholas II in the Area of State Governance' which, until then, had been held in a secret repository in the Archive of the October Revolution (now known as the State Archive of the Russian Federation).

26. *Rasputin – The Last Word*, Edvard Radzinsky (Weidenfeld & Nicolson, 2000), p.219.

27. *History of the Russian Secret Service*, Richard Deacon (Taplinger, New York, 1972), p.141.

28. Ozone Preparations Co., Handbill *c.*1910.

29. *Portraits of Unusual People*, Vladimir Krymov, p.69.

30. *Ace of Spies*, Robin Bruce Lockhart, p.49.

31. Ibid.

32. Membership list of the All-Russian Aviation Club (Fond 2000, Inventory 15, File 40091, Russian State Military Historical Archives, Moscow).

33. *A Documentary Story of Russian Aviator Nikolai Evgrafovich Popov*, V.N. Sashonko (Leningrad, 1983).

34. Department of Police Report to Interior Ministry re Krylia, 23 December 1910, Fond 102, 4 deloproizvodstvo, 1910, delo 106 litera B, tom 8, listy 19–23, State Archive of the Russian Federation, Moscow.

35. Vozdukhoplavatel, 1911, No. 8, p.424ff (State Public Library, St Petersburg).

36. Ibid.

37. The Komendantskoe Pole Aerodrome was closed in 1963 to make way for the building of apartment blocks. St Petersburg's airport is today located at Pulkovo.

38. *Portraits of Unusual People*, Vladimir Krymov, p.70.

39. Kratkie informatsionnye materially, p.94, State Public Library, St Petersburg.

40. Ibid.

41. *Portraits of Unusual People*, Vladimir Krymov, p.70.

42. Representation in the Ottoman Empire by Walter Berghaus, Volume 1 1903–1913, File 1118, Archives of Blohm & Voss GmbH, Hamburg State Archive; also Walter Berghaus File, Dahiliye Emniyey Collection, Basbakanlik Osmanli Arsivi, Cagaloglu, Istanbul, Turkey.

43. Ibid.

44. Ibid.

45. Ibid.

46. Ibid.

47. *Portraits of Unusual People*, Vladimir Krymov, p.71.

48. Gofman's death was reported in *Novoe Vremya* on 19 October 1911, p.1.

49. A report by the State Historical Archive, St Petersburg, on 'Kiuba's', dated 21 March 2001 (commissioned by the author).

50. According to Vienna Police records, 'Dr Sidney Reilly' (born St Petersburg 20 February 1872) stayed at the Hotel Bristol with his 'wife' Erna (Ernestine) Reilly (born 1886) prior to 2 March 1911 and again from 6 March 1911. During the intervening week he was staying at the Weiner Cottage Sanatorium (Meldearchiv, Antiquariat 'B', 1911, Vienna City Archive).

51. Records of the 'New English Club' (Central State Historical Archives of St Petersburg, Fond 1115, Inventory 1, Files 1–25).

52. Ibid.

53. Letter from Cecil Mackie to Consular Department, 10 December 1918, PRO FO 369/1025, item 7.

54. The name of the project was Nikoliev.

55. Count Thaddaeus Lubiensky.

56. Large cruiser.

57. Small cruiser.

58. Letter from Sidney Reilly to Kurt Orbanowsky, 25 April 1912, File 1083, Archives of Blohm & Voss GmbH, State Archive of Hamburg.

59. Letter from Sir Charles Ottley (St Petersburg) to London Office,

30 September 1912 (Rendel Papers 31/7595, Tyne & Wear Archives Service).

60. *Reilly: Ace of Spies*, Thames Television, 1983.

61. *History of the Russian Secret Service*, Richard Deacon, p.143ff.

62. Counter-intelligence surveillance report on Sidney G. Reilly, 28 November 1911, Fond 2000, Inventory 15, File 177, Russian State Military Historical Archive, Moscow.

63. Department of Police Report to the Interior Ministry re Krylia, 23 December 1910, Fond 102, 4 deloproizvodstvo, 1910, Inventory 106 litera B, tom 8, listy 19–23, State Archive of the Russian Federation, Moscow.

Six – The Honey Pot

1. US Bureau of Investigation/ONI, Report of 10 September 1918.

2. Reilly had first met Abram Zhivotovsky in the Far East, a decade earlier. *Portraits of Unusual People*, Vladimir Krymov, p.70.

3. Letter from Margaret Reilly to the War Office, dated 16 November 1918 refers to last receiving news from her husband on 28 July 1914 (*Reilly Papers* CX 2616). His letter to Nadezhda is noted in 'US Bureau of Investigation/ONI, Report of 10 September 1918'.

4. US Bureau of Investigation/ONI, Memorandum of 23 August 1918.

5. *Steaming Up!*, Samuel M. Vauclain with Earl Chapin May, p.236.

6. US Bureau of Investigation/ONI, Report of 11 October 1918. Reilly's 'London representative' was Alexandre Weinstein.

7. US Immigration, Port of San Francisco, Volume 7978, p.26, 13 January 1915.

8. Ibid.

9. New York Directory 1915.

10. Ibid.

11. *Russko-Amerikanskie ekonomicheskie otnosheniia, 1900–1917*, V.V. Lebedev, pp.142–44.

12. US Bureau of Investigation/ONI, Memorandum of 23 August 1918 (pp.1–3); and Memorandum of 10 September 1918, p.2.

13. Incorporation Certificate, Allied Machinery Company of America, 18 May 1911, Certificate and Report of Inspectors of Election of the Allied Machinery Company of America, Stockholders Meeting, 27 November 1916.

14. *J.P. Morgan Jr, 1867–1943*, John D. Forbes (University of Virginia Press, 1981), p.89.

15. *Tacoma Daily News*, 3 February 1915, p.1.

16. 'Sidney Reilly in America, 1914–1917' by Richard B. Spence, *Intelligence and National Security*, Volume 10, No. 1, January 1995, pp.98–99.

17. James R. Mann was a member of the US House of Representatives who authored and sponsored 'The Mann Act' of 1910. This forbade, under heavy penalties, the transportation of women from one state to another for immoral purposes.

18. US Immigration, Port of New York, Volume 5510, 15 February 1915.

19. *Portraits of Unusual People*, Vladimir Krymov, p.72.

20. Certificate of Marriage of Sidney G. Reilly and Nadine Zalessky, 16 February 1915, Marriage Register No. 4404–15, Borough of Manhattan.

21. *The Career of Sidney Reilly, 1895–1925: A Case Study in Circumstantial Evidence*, G.L. Owen (unpublished manuscript).

22. US Immigration, Port of New York, Volume 5500, 3 April 1915.

23. *New York Times*, 26 April 1915, SS *Kursk* sailed at 12 p.m. on 27 April 1915.

24. US Bureau of Investigation/ONI, Report of 10 September 1918 and Memorandum of 12 September 1918.

25. US Bureau of Investigation/ONI, Report of 10 September 1918.

26. 'Sidney Reilly in America, 1914–1917', Richard B. Spence, *Intelligence and National Security*, Volume 10, No. 1, January 1995, p.119, note 87.

27. Fond 1343, Inventory 8, File 269 (Russian State Military Historical Archive, Moscow).

28. Ibid.

29. US Bureau of Investigation/ONI, copy of Report on 'de Wyckoff' dated January 1917 from French Deuxieme Bureau to ONI).

30. Fond 1343, Inventory 8, File 269, Russian State Military Historical Archive, Moscow.

31. US Immigration, Port of New York, Volume 5587, 10 July 1915.

32. 'Sidney Reilly in America, 1914–1917', Richard B. Spence, *Intelligence and National Security*, Volume 10, No. 1, January 1995, pp.96–97.

33. US Bureau of Investigation/ONI, Memorandum of 31 August 1918.

34. US Bureau of Investigation/ONI, Memorandum of 12 September 1918.

35. Letter from Sidney Reilly to Gen. A.V. Germonius (Fond 6173, Inventory 1, File 25, State Archive of the Russian Federation, Moscow).

36. *Portraits of Unusual People*, Vladimir Krymov, pp.72–73.

37. US Bureau of Investigation/ONI, Report of 11 October 1918.

38. US Military Observer, Berlin to AC of S, G-2, US Army, Subject: Lurich, 3 November 1921 (UDS, File 800 11-381, Maj. W. Cowles to W. Hurley, Office of Under Secretary, Department of State, 10 December 1921).

39. *Velvet and Vinegar*, Norman G. Thwaites (Grayson and Grayson, 1932), pp.181–82.

40. US Bureau of Investigation/ONI, Memorandum of 23 August 1918.

41. *Velvet and Vinegar*, Norman G. Thwaites, p.181.

42. *The Brooklyn Daily Eagle*, 31 July 1916, p.1.

43. 'Sidney Reilly in America, 1914–1917', Richard B. Spence, Intelligence and National Security, Volume 10, No. 1, January 1995, p.105ff.

44. Ibid.

45. Ibid.

46. *Sabotage at Black Tom*, Jules Witcover (Algonquin Chapel Hill, 1989), p.160.

47. 'Sidney Reilly in America, 1914–1917', Richard B. Spence, *Intelligence and National Security*, Volume 10, No. 1, January 1995, pp.108–09. The theory that Jahnke was a double agent is dispelled in the US National Counterintelligence Center's *American Revolution to World War Two*, Frank J. Rafalko (ed.), Chapter Three, p.11 and note 152. British sources also reject the view that Jahnke had any connection with SIS.

48. Ibid.
49. *Spreading the Spy Net*, Henry Landau (Jarrolds, 1935), p.270.
50. 'Sidney Reilly in America, 1914–1917', Richard B. Spence, *Intelligence and National Security*, Volume 10, No. 1, January 1995, p.106.
51. *Spreading the Spy Net*, Henry Landau, p.272.
52. 'Sidney Reilly in America, 1914–1917', Richard B. Spence, *Intelligence and National Security*, Volume 10, No. 1, January 1995, p.111.
53. Ibid.
54. US Bureau of Investigation/ONI, Reports of 23 and 28 August, and 10 September 1918.
55. 9 March by the Gregorian calendar in use in the West. By the Julian still being used in Russia it was 24 February.
56. *Britain's Master Spy – The Adventures of Sidney Reilly*, foreword, p xii.
57. Unpublished synopsis by Margaret Reilly (November 1931); Reilly also told a mercantile agency in New York that he had 'served in the British Army in France during the period of the war' (YN 1215, 24 July 1925, *Reilly Papers* CX 2616).
58. *Ace of Spies*, Robin Bruce Lockhart, p.19ff.
59. *Ace of Spies* (1992 edition), Robin Bruce Lockhart, p.60.
60. Report of Agent L.S. Perkins of US Bureau of Investigation, 'Sidney G. Reilly – Neutrality Matter', 3 April 1917.

SEVEN – CONFIDENCE MEN

1. See Chapter Eight, note 55.
2. US War Department, General Staff, Military Intelligence Division (MID) Box 2506, File 9140–6073, Ralph Van Deman to William Wiseman, 7 July 1917.
3. Ibid., William Wiseman to Ralph Van Deman, 9 July 1917.
4. US Bureau of Investigation/ONI, Memorandum from Chief Yeoman Bond to Lt Irving; 'Names in the Weinstein Case'.
5. Ibid.
6. US Bureau of Investigation/ONI, Memorandums of 6 and 12 September 1918.
7. US Bureau of Investigation/ONI, Memorandum of 23 August 1918.
8. Ibid.
9. Ibid.
10. Ibid.
11. See note 4.
12. US Bureau of Investigation/ONI, Memorandum of 21 August 1918.
13. Ibid.
14. Ibid.
15. US Bureau of Investigation/ONI, Memorandum of 10 September 1918.
16. Bureau of Investigation/ONI, Reports of 6 June and 17 October 1918.
17. Ibid.
18. Ibid.
19. Ibid.
20. US Bureau of Investigation/ONI, Memorandum of 10 September 1918.
21. Ibid.
22. Ibid.
23. *American Revolution to World War II*, Frank J. Rafalko (ed.), Chapter Three, note 114 (US National Counterintelligence Center).
24. US Bureau of Investigation/ONI, 'Reilly, Weinstein, Jachalsky Case: Synopsis of (copy of card file) of

Persons Involved', 4 September
1918.

25. Ibid.

26. US Bureau of Investigation/ONI,
Reports of 10 and 12 September
1918. (In the spring of 1916
Nadine returned to Russia on
word that her father had been
taken ill. It would seem that
Reilly's relationship with Tremaine
began during her absence.
According to US Immigration
Records, Nadine returned to New
York on 18 June 1916. Her father
eventually died on 20 July 1917 –
Service Record of Petr Massino,
Fond 400, Inventory 17, File
13135; Inventory 12, File 28672,
Russian State Military Historical
Archives, Moscow).

27. US Bureau of Investigation/ONI,
ibid.

28. Ibid.

29. Ibid.

30. Ibid.

31. Ibid.

32. Ibid.

33. US Bureau of Investigation/ONI,
Reports of 21 August, 6 and 10
September 1918.

34. Ibid.

35. Ibid.

36. Ibid.

37. Ibid.

38. US Bureau of Investigation/ONI,
Report of 17 October 1918.

39. US Bureau of Investigation/ONI,
Report of 10 September 1918.

40. Ibid.

41. Trust No One, Richard Spence,
(Feral House, 2002), p25.

42. US Bureau of Investigation/ONI,
Report of 10 September 1918.

43. Ibid.

44. Ibid.

45. Ibid.

46. *Steaming Up!*, Samuel M. Vauclain
with Earl Chapin May (Brewer
and Warren, 1930), p.248.

47. Foreign Office Passport Names
Index (FO) 611/24, Mrs Margaret
Reilly, Passport No. 69238, issued
4 January 1916.

48. According to Leon C. Messenger
(*The Nanny with the Glass Eye*,
p.25), 'Mother explained that
Daisy (Margaret) had had many
years experience as a governess'.
We do not know when she first
undertook such a post, but it is
unlikely to have been before the
war. The first recorded post as a
governess is in 1922 for the
Wary family in Belgium (ibid.,
pp.25–26), although it is unlikely
that this was the first such post.
Working for an English family
in St Petersburg would be have
been a natural move in the
circumstances.

49. Department of State, Office of the
Counselor, Subject: Norbert
Mortimer Rodkinson',
26 November 1918 (National
Archives, Washington DC).

50. Entry 486, Register of Births in the
Sub-district of Brixton in the
Registration District of Lambeth
in the County of Surrey, Corinne
Elise Augusta Polens, 6 January
1881. Corinne was the daughter
of Otto Polens, a German
merchant and Corinne Knaggs, a
London music hall performer. Her
'doubtful morals' no doubt refers
to her alleged association with
prostitution.

51. French term for prostitute.

52. US Bureau of Investigation,
Memorandum by Agent R. W.
Finch (New York City), 2 August
1918, re.: 'One Rodkinson,

aspirant for position on Russian Commission'.

53. 14th Census of the United States: 8 January 1920 (Manhattan, Enumeration District No. 566, Sheet 8A).

54. ONI, letter from Rear-Admiral Roger Welles (director of Naval Intelligence) to A. Bruce Bielaski (chief, US Bureau of Investigation), 14 January 1919 (National Archives, Washington DC).

EIGHT – CODE NAME ST1

1. US Bureau of Investigation/ONI, report dated 17 October 1918, p.2; from Chief Yeoman Bond to Hollis Hunnewell.

2. Ibid.

3. Velvet and Vinegar, by Norman G. Thwaites, p.181.

4. Ibid.

5. US Bureau of Investigation/ONI, memorandum to Lt Irvine, dated 23 August 1918.

6. Diary of Mansfield Cumming, 15 March 1918 (quotations from the diary are taken from *The Quest for C* by Alan Judd); Army List and Indian Army List (PRO) indicates that John Dymoke Scale (born 27 December 1882) was an Indian Army career officer who had first been sent to Russia in December 1912. In June 1913 he qualified as a Russian interpreter first class before rejoining the 87th Punjabis in July 1914. At the outbreak of war he was transferred to France where he distinguished himself in the trenches, was promoted to major in May 1916 and awarded the DSO in April 1917. That same month he was

sent back to Russia and attached to the SIS station in Petrograd, which is also corroborated by *History of the British Intelligence Organisation*, M.K. Burge, p.7, Intelligence Corps Museum, Chicksands, Bedfordshire.

7. Diary of Mansfield Cumming, 17 March 1918.

8. *Velvet and Vinegar*, Norman G. Thwaites, p.181.

9. 'Sidney Reilly in America, 1914–1917', Richard Spence, *Intelligence and National Security*, Vol. 10, No. 1 (January 1995), p.111.

10. RAF Service Record of 2nd Lt Sidney G. Reilly (PRO Pi21220).

11. *Velvet and Vinegar*, Norman G. Thwaites, p.183.

12. 'Sidney Reilly in America, 1914–1917', Richard Spence, *Intelligence and National Security*, Vol. 10, No. 1 (January 1995), p.112.

13. Diary of Air Mechanic R.H. Ibbertson, ref DB340, RAF Museum, Hendon.

14. In 1919 Beatrice Tremaine met Douglas Rollins, son of former New Hampshire Governor Frank West Rollins, in Florida. They married in 1921 and lived in Europe until his death on 9 June 1932. On her death in 1986, her estate, including her letters and papers passed to her sons Douglas Jr and Gordon Rollins.

15. RAF Service Record of 2nd Lt Sidney G. Reilly (PRO Pi21220).

16. The Bolsheviks' seizure of power on 25 October 1917 (Julian calendar) is here and henceforth referred to as 7 November 1917 (Gregorian calendar).

17. Reilly refers to the School of Military Aeronautics in a

document dated 12 October 1921 concerning his claim for arrears of pay and gratuity (*Reilly Papers* CX 2616).

18. Counter-intelligence surveillance report on Sidney G. Reilly, 28 November 1911, Fond 2000, Inventory 15, File 177, Russian State Military Historical Archives, Moscow.

19. Alphabetical Directory of Inhabitants of the City of St Petersburg, State Public Library, St Petersburg, TsSB, S591 Len V-38.

20. Canadian Department of National Defense, Directorate of Military History, Special card index, '2nd Lt Sidney G. Reilly MC'.

21. Report dated 9 March 1918 (Sidney Reilly's MI5 File PF 864103). The Hotel Cecil next door to the Savoy had unfortunately been commandeered by the War Office for additional office space.

22. Passport of John Dymoke Scale No 173914 (The Papers of John Dymoke Scale)

23. Letter from Sidney Reilly to Col. Byron, War Office, dated 19 January 1918 (Sidney Reilly's MI5 File PF 864103).

24. Ibid. (attached to letter).

25. Ibid. (attached to letter).

26. Memorandum from SIS to MI5, dated 30 January 1918 (Sidney Reilly's MI5 File PF 864103).

27. Memorandum from MI5 to SIS, dated 2 February 1918 (Sidney Reilly's MI5 File PF 864103).

28. Entry No. 475, Register of Deaths in the Registration District of Wandsworth, in the Sub-district of South West Battersea, 1 February 1918.

29. Telegram No. 206 of 28 February 1918, from C to SIS New York.

30. Telegram CX 021744, CMX 188, received London 10.00 a.m. 4 March 1918 (*Reilly Papers* CX 2616).

31. Observation reports dated 6–9 March 1918 (Sidney Reilly's MI5 File PF 864103).

32. Report dated 9 March 1918 (Sidney Reilly's MI5 File PF 864103).

33. Telegram CX 023100, CMX 201, received London 2.20 p.m. 14 March 1918 (*Reilly Papers* CX 2616).

34. 2 Whitehall Court (today part of the Royal Horseguards Hotel) was designed by the architects Archer and Green and built in 1884. Conveniently situated opposite the War Office, it was, to all intents and purposes, a faceless apartment block. C had commandeered the top floor and rented it under the name of Capt. Spencer (Kelly's Post Office Directory 1918).

35. *Red Dusk and the Morrow*, Sir Paul Dukes (Williams and Norgate, 1923), p.9. In *Ace of Spies*, p.98, Robin Bruce Lockhart states that 'when Dukes was summoned for his first interview with the Secret Service chief, Reilly was present at the meeting and endorsed Cumming's selection'. However, it is clear from Dukes' own account that the interview took place in July 1918 when Reilly was in Russia (*The Story of ST25*, Sir Paul Dukes, Cassell, 1938, pp.28–29.

36. Diary of Mansfield Cumming – 15 March 1918.

37. Telegram CX 023996, CXM 212, received London 2.25 p.m. 21 March 1918 (*Reilly Papers* CX 2616).

38. Diary of Mansfield Cumming –
    22 March 1918.

39. Memorandum from MI5 to Irish
    Command, dated 22 March 1918
    (Sidney Reilly's MI5 File PF
    864103).

40. Memorandum from Irish Command
    to MI5, dated 31 March 1918
    (Sidney Reilly's MI5 File PF
    864103).

41. The prefix ST refers to the SIS
    station through which Reilly was
    reporting – Stockholm.

Nine – The Reilly Plot

1. Telegram CXM 159, dated 29
   March 1918 (*Reilly Papers* CX
   2616).

2. Letter from Stephen Alley to Robin
   Bruce Lockhart, dated 13 May
   1966, Box 6, Robert Bruce
   Lockhart Collection, Hoover
   Institution Archives, Stanford,
   California.

3. Telegram dated 22 March 1918, 5.25
   p.m. (Sidney Reilly's MI5 File PF
   864103/V1).

4. The fact that C also refers to Reilly
   as 'Reilli' in his telegram CXM
   159 of 29 March 1918 strongly
   suggests that this misspelling is
   intentional.

5. Ibid., note 34.

6. US Bureau of Investigation/ONI,
   Report dated 16 September 1918,
   p.1, from Chief Yeoman Bond to
   H. Hunnewell and A. Smith.

7. Gen. Edward Spears recalled Reilly
   telling him of 'a valuable
   collection of coins and
   Napoleonic relics' he wanted to
   retrieve. It is also apparent from
   Spears' letter that some or all of
   this collection was still in Russia
   in 1925 (letter to Robin Bruce

   Lockhart dated 2 January 1967,
   Box 6, Robert Bruce Lockhart
   Collection, Hoover Institution
   Archive, Stanford, California.

8. Telegram CX 027753, dated 16
   April 1918 (*Reilly papers* CX
   2616).

9. Ibid.

10. *Memoirs of a British Agent,* Robert
    Bruce Lockhart (p.276).

11. Ibid.

12. The following month Foreign
    Secretary Arthur Balfour cabled
    Lockhart castigating his judgement
    and advice: 'You have at different
    times advised against Allied
    intervention in any form; against it
    by the Japanese alone; against it
    with Japanese assistance; against it
    at Vladivostock; in favour of it at
    Murmansk; in favour of it with an
    invitation; in favour of it without
    an invitation since it was really
    desired by the Bolsheviks; in
    favour of it without invitation
    whether the Bolsheviks desired it
    or not'. 'Lockhart Plot or
    Dzerzhinskii Plot?', R.K. Debo,
    pp.426–427.

13. *Sidney Reilly – The True Story*,
    Michael Kettle, p.24; *Ace of Spies*,
    Robin Bruce Lockhart, pp.67–68;
    Master Spy, Edward Van Der
    Rhoer, pp.24–25.

14. Telegram CX 013592, sent from
    Moscow on 12 May 1918 (PRO
    WO 32/5669).

15. Telegram CX 035402, sent from
    Moscow on 29 May 1918 (PRO
    WO 32/5669).

16. Ibid.

17. Telegram CX 035176, sent from
    Moscow, 3 June 1918 (PRO WO
    32/5669).

18. Dagmara Genrikhovna Karozus was
    not, as suggested by previous

writers, a Russian. She was in fact German, and as such had been on Department of Police files since 1914 (Fond 102, 6 deloproizvodstvo, opis 174, delo 69, tom 30, listy 37-40, 1914, State Archive of the Russian Federation, Moscow).

19. Personal file of Elizaveta Emilyevna Otten, Inventory 6, edinitsa khranenija 120, Obraztsov State Academic Theatre, Moscow.

20. Account of the trial proceedings of the Supreme Tribunal, Moscow, of 29 November 1918, as reported in *Izvestia*, 1 December 1918.

21. Vladimir Grigoryevich Orlov (1882-1941), a former counter-intelligence officer in the First World War, who served in the Criminal Department of the Cheka in Petrograd. To conceal his real identity he adopted the name Boleslav Orlinsky. In September 1918 he fled to Finland and later served on Denikin's counter-intelligence staff in the Civil War. In 1920 he settled in Germany where he continued his fight against the Bolsheviks by publishing compromising material about them in the western press. He was thought to be the prime suspect in connection with the forged Zinoviev letter, although nothing was ever proven. He was shot by the Gestapo in 1941 for anti-Nazi activity.

22. *Master Spy*, Edward Van Der Rhoer, p.224ff; *History of the Russian Secret Service*, Richard Deacon, p.264ff; *Reilly – The First Man*, Robin Bruce Lockhart, p.55; 'The Terrorist and the Master Spy: The Political Partnership of Boris Savinkov and Sidney Reilly, 1918–25', Richard Spence, *Revolutionary Russia*, Vol. 4, No. 1, June 1991, p.120ff.

23. *Master Spy*, Edward Van Der Rhoer, p.47.

24. Account of the trial proceedings of the Supreme Tribunal, Moscow of 29 November 1918, as reported in *Izvestia*, 1 December 1918.

25. The Hotel Elite was situated at 2 Petrovka Street, ten minutes walk from the Bolshoi Theatre. It was later renamed the Hotel Aurora, after the battleship which fired on the Winter Palace during the Great October Revolution. It is known today as the Budapest Hotel.

26. *Memoirs of a British Agent*, Robert Bruce Lockhart, pp.314–16, 'Final Report of Robert Bruce Lockhart to Foreign Secretary Balfour', dated 7 November 1918 (PRO FO 371/3337/185499).

27. 'Final Report of Robert Bruce Lockhart', Ibid.; 'Report of Work Done in Russia' by Capt. George Hill (PRO FO 371/3350/79980).

28. Reilly's tactic of 'divide and rule', referred to by Nadine as his 'system' (US Bureau of Investigation/ONI, Report from Chief Yeoman Bond to H. Hunnewell and A. Smith, dated 10 September 1918), is discussed in Chapter Seven in the context of his dealings with Blohm & Voss.

29. *Memoirs of a British Agent*, Robert Bruce Lockhart, p.316.

30. FO 371/3348, No. 190442, dated 5 November 1918.

31. George Hill was initially assigned to Military Intelligence after being discharged on 13 June 1915 as a

result of being wounded in France. He undertook assignments in the Balkans, Egypt and Russia for the director of Military Intelligence at the War Office, before being assigned to SIS in 1918. In his 1932 account of this period (*Go Spy the Land*) he refers to himself as Agent IK8 of the British Secret Service. However, 'IK' does not appear to be an SIS prefix and one must therefore assume that it was a code name given to him by Military Intelligence. While operating in Russia on behalf of SIS, Hill had an ST prefix like all other agents in this field of operation (Service File No. 51224, Capt. George A. Hill, Canadian Department of National Defense; Army Service Record of Capt. George A Hill (PRO Pi 15714)).

32. The allegation appeared in *Izvestia* on 3rd September 1918. George Hill refers to Reilly's objection to making martyrs of Lenin and Trotsky in his 'Report of Work Done in Russia' (PRO FO 371/3350/79980). Likewise, there is no reference to Reilly's alleged intention to have Lenin and Trotsky shot in either the report by K.A. Peterson (Political Commissar of the Latvian Rifle Division – State Archive of the Russian Federation, Fond 1235, Inventory 93, File 207) or in the 1924 memoirs of Jacob Peters (Deputy Chairman of the Cheka), the two most reliable Soviet sources who were actually involved in these events.

33. Petition to the Red Cross for the Aid of Political Prisoners from Citizen Olga Sarzhevskaya,

Butyrka Prison, Moscow, 11 November 1918 (Fond 8419, Inventory 1, File 356, sheets 355–356, State Archive of the Russian Federation, Moscow).

34. The 'divorced lady' is a reference to Olga Starzheskaya, born Stavropol 1893. She was divorced in 1915 (questioning of Olga Starzheskaya by Varlaam Avanesov (Fond 8419, Inventory 1, File 321, sheets 60–62, State Archive of the Russian Federation, Moscow).

35. Petition to the Red Cross for the Aid of Political Prisoners from Citizen Elizaveta Otten, Butyrka Prison, Moscow, 11 September 1918 (Fond 8419, Inventory 1, File 155, sheets 174–175, State Archive of the Russian Federation, Moscow).

36. *Izvestia*, 1 September 1918, and in a hand bill 'Sensational plot discovered to overthrow Soviet government' by G. Chicherin (People's Commissar for Foreign Affairs) distributed to Allied troops at Archangel.

TEN – FOR DISTINGUISHED SERVICE

1. 'Report of Work Done in Russia' by George Hill (PRO FO 371/3350/79980).

2. Ibid.

3. Ibid.

4. Ibid. Hill gave Reilly his passport, which was in the name of George Bergmann, and Reilly replaced the photograph with his own. Hill had chosen the name for himself as he 'hated giving up the name of Hill, and finally decided to get as near it as I could in German. That is why I chose Berg, the equivalent

for Hill, and tacked on 'mann' to make it quite certain I was of German descent'. *Go Spy the Land*, George Hill, Cassell, 1932, p.217.

5. Account of the trial proceedings of the Supreme Tribunal, Moscow, of 29 November 1918, as reported in *Izvestia*, 1 December 1918.

6. 'Report of Work Done in Russia' by George Hill (PRO FO 371/3350/79980).

7. *Go Spy the Land*, George Hill, p.245.

8. Ibid.

9. 'Report of Work Done in Russia' by George Hill (PRO FO 371/3350/79980).

10. 'Trust' File No. 302330, Vol. 37, p.241 (Central Archive of the Federal Security Service, Moscow).

11. Ibid. In this account he refers to the captain as Finnish. In fact Harry Van den Bosch was a Dutchman who lived in Revel and sailed to and from Petrograd. The reference to a Finn was no doubt to protect the identity of Van den Bosch from the OGPU.

12. Letter to Harry Van den Bosch from Sidney Reilly, dated 10 October 1918 as reproduced in *Sidney Reilly – The True Story*, Michael Kettle, p.49ff.

13. Telegram 3472 'Personal and Most Secret', 30 September 1918 (PRO FO/371/3319).

14. Letter from Lt-Col. C.N. French at the War Office to Ronald Campbell of the Foreign Office, 10 October 1918 (PRO FO 371/3319).

15. Letter from Mrs M Reilly to the Netherlands Legation (British Section), 17 October 1918, PRO FO 383/379, item 12, File 117953.

16. Letter from Margaret Reilly to the War Office, dated 16 November 1918 (*Reilly Papers* CX 2616).

17. Letter from Margaret Reilly to the Air Board, dated 4 January 1919 (*Reilly Papers* CX 2616).

18. The Last Will and Testament of Margaret Reilly, 15 May 1914, High Court of Justice, London, Principal Probate Registry, Ref. 1292, 2 February 1934.

19. *Go Spy the Land*, George Hill, p.262.

20. Ibid., p.263.

21. Letter from Sidney Reilly to Robert Bruce Lockhart, 25 November 1918, Lord Milner Papers, Great War, box 365c, Oxford University.

22. Letter from Reginald Hoare to Rex Leeper, 27 November 1918, PRO FO 371/4019.

23. Diary of Sidney Reilly, 10 December 1918; Passport No. 926 issued to S.G. Reilly, 12 December 1918, (*Reilly Papers* CX 2616).

24. *Go Spy the Land*, George Hill, p.264.

25. Ibid., p.266.

26. Diary of Sidney Reilly, 14 December 1918 (*Reilly Papers* CX 2616).

27. Dreaded Hour, George Hill (Cassell, 1936), p.63.

28. Diary of Sidney Reilly, 17 December 1918 (*Reilly Papers* CX 2616).

29. Diary of Sidney Reilly, 19 December 1918 (*Reilly Papers* CX 2616).

30. Diary of Sidney Reilly, 23 December 1918 (*Reilly Papers* CX 2616)

31. Ibid.

32. Diary of Sidney Reilly, 25 December 1918 (*Reilly Papers* CX 2616).

33. *Dreaded Hour*, George Hill, pp.61–62.

34. Ibid. p.62.

35. Ibid. p.70.

36. Diary of Sidney Reilly, 13 January 1919 (*Reilly Papers* CX 2616).

37. Reilly's Despatch No. 1, Sevastopol, 28 December 1918 (PRO FO 371/3962).

38. Reilly's Despatch No. 2, Ekaterinodar, 8 January 1919 (PRO FO 371/3962).

39. Diary of Sidney Reilly, 5 January 1919 (*Reilly Papers* CX 2616).

40. Reilly's Despatch No. 2.

41. Ibid.

42. Ibid.

43. Diary of Sidney Reilly, 8 January 1919 (*Reilly Papers* CX 2616).

44. Reilly's Despatch No. 4, Ekaterinodar, 11 January 1919 (PRO FO 371/3962).

45. Reilly's Despatch No. 5, Ekaterinodar, 17 January 1919 (PRO FO 371/3962).

46. Ibid.

47. Ibid.

48. Ibid.

49. Ibid.

50. Diary of Sidney Reilly, 14 January 1919 (*Reilly Papers* CX 2616).

51. Ibid.

52. The announcement that they had been awarded the Military Cross was published in the London Gazette, 12 February 1919; 'His Majesty the King has been graciously pleased to approve of the undermentioned rewards for distinguished services rendered in connection with military operations in the field: – Awarded the Military Cross, Lieut. George Alexander Hill, 4th Bn; Manch. R.; attd. RAF, 2nd Lt. Sidney George Reilly, RAF. On 5 January Denikin had also awarded Reilly the medal of St Anna.

53. Diary of Sidney Reilly, 22 January 1919 (*Reilly Papers* CX 2616).

54. Ibid., 26 January 1919.

55. *Ace of Spies*, Robin Bruce Lockhart, p.87. Lockhart refers to the street as Alexander III Boulevard. While indeed named after the former Tsar, city directories and street maps indicate that it was actually called Alexandrovsky Prospect. After Ukraine became a Soviet Republic the street was renamed Prospect Mira. When Ukraine became an independent nation following the collapse of the Soviet Union in 1991, the street once again became Alexandrovsky Prospect.

56. Novorossiyski address-calendar published by the Office of the Novorossiyski and Bessarabski Governor-General for 1871–74 and the address calendar of the Odessa City Governor's Office for 1877–80 and 1881–96.

57. Fond P-8085, Inventory 1, File 26, State Archives of Odessa Region.

58. Diary of Sidney Reilly, 4 February 1919 (*Reilly Papers* CX 2616).

59. Memorandum by G.E. Pennington, dated 20 March 1919 (Sidney Reilly's MI5 File PF 864103). The Brixton Hill address was that of John O'Sullivan, a friend of the Callaghan family.

60. Letter from Margaret Reilly to Capt. Spencer, dated 4 February 1919 (*Reilly Papers* CX 2616). Capt. Spencer was a correspondence name. As Sir Paul Dukes recalled 'I soon discovered that at least half a dozen persons either in the roof-labyrinth [Dukes' colloquialism for SIS headquarters at 2 Whitehall Place] and associated offices were all

called by that same name!' The
Story of ST25, Sir Paul Dukes,
p.35.

61. Telegram CX 066117, sent from
Odessa 1.20 p.m. 19 February
1919, received in London
1.30 p.m. 22 February 1919 (*Reilly
Papers* CX 2616).

62. Reilly's Despatch No. 13, Odessa,
18 February 1919 (PRP FO
371/3978).

63. Reilly's Despatch No. 15, Odessa,
21 February 1919 (PRO FO
371/3978).

64. Selby's comment made on 5 March
1919 is found on the Foreign
Office covering note to Reilly's
Despatches Nos 1–12 (PRO FO
371/3962).

65. *Dreaded Hour*, George Hill, p.95. The
'Council of Ambassadors' was
composed of Russian Ambassadors
accredited to European capitals
prior to the Bolshevik
Revolution. The committee had
been initiated by anti-Bolsheviks
in order to represent Russia's
national interests at the Peace
Conference.

66. Ibid.

67. Ibid., pp.99–100.

68. Ibid., p.102.

69. Ibid.

70. Reilly and Hill were not the only
ones to claim the honour of
passing this information to
Wickham Steed. Gordon
Auchinloss, the son-in-law of
American delegation member Col.
Edward House, was one of a
number to claim responsibility. *Iron
Maze*, Gordon Brook-Shepherd,
note 8, p.357.

71. *Daily Mail*, 26 March 1919, p.1.
William Bullitt's account of his
meeting with Lloyd George is to

be found in his statement to the
US Senate Foreign Relations
Committee (Official Report 1919,
p.1279).

ELEVEN – FINAL CURTAIN

1. Reilly sailed from Southampton on
15 April aboard the White Star
Line's SS *Olympic*, arriving in
Halifax on 19 April 1919. (US
Immigration, M1464 #365 Vol.
479).

2. US border crossing reference NYPL
Z1637, M1461 #326.

3. The St Regis was Reilly's favourite
New York Hotel. Vladimir
Krymov recalls meeting Reilly in
New York in 1917, by which time
'he was occupying an entire suite'
at the St Regis. Portraits of
Interesting People, Vladimir
Krymov, p.73.

4. Reilly had known Jaroszynsky in
pre-war St Petersburg. According
to the memorandum 'Character
Sketch of Karol Jaroszynsky' by
John Picton Bagge, the forty-year-
old Russian Pole was the son of a
landowner from Kiev who left
him 'a fortune of 3 or 4 million
roubles'. He used his wealth to
found the University of Lublin
and to buy up twenty-two sugar
factories and six major banks.
Bagge compared him to Cecil
Rhodes and paid tribute to 'his
genius for buying up banks and
enterprises' (CHAR 16/28/45,
Churchill Archives Centre,
Churchill College, Cambridge).

5. Telegram 10 May 1919, Sidney
Reilly to John Picton Bagge,
Foreign Office, CXC 416 (PRO
FO 371/4019).

6. SS *Baltic* 'inward' passenger list (PRO BT 26/653 & 654).

7. RAF Service Record of 2nd Lt Sidney Reilly (PRO Pi 21220).

8. Intelligence requirements were directed to the Production Section. It was then responsible for 'producing' the required intelligence by assigning appropriate personnel.

9. Memorandum dated 3 October 1919 from Maj. D.J.F Morton to Col. S. Menzies (*Reilly Papers* CX 2616).

10. Memorandum dated 16 October 1919 from Col. S. Menzies to Maj. D.J.F. Morton (*Reilly Papers* CX 2616).

11. *Secrets of Espionage: Tales of the Secret Service*, Winfried Ludecke, p.105.

12. *Britain's Master Spy – The Adventures of Sidney Reilly*, frontispiece.

13. *Velvet and Vinegar*, Norman G. Thwaites, p.181.

14. Memorandum from Sidney Reilly to John Picton Bagge, 10 October 1919 (CHAR 16/28/18 & 19, Churchill Archives Centre, Churchill College, Cambridge).

15. *The Russian Problem* (CHAR 16/28/170-189, Churchill Archives Centre, Churchill College, Cambridge).

16. Note from Sir Archibald Sinclair to Winston Churchill, 15 December 1919 (CHAR 16/28/150, Churchill Archives Centre, Churchill College, Cambridge).

17. Ibid.

18. G3/147 London to Capt. W. Field Robinson, 30 January 1920 (*Reilly Papers* CX 2616).

19. Ibid., attached report.

20. Letter from Sidney Reilly to C, 23 March 1920 (*Reilly Papers* CX 2616).

21. Ibid.

22. Memorandum from Section H to C, 5 March 1920 (*Reilly Papers* CX 2616).

23. Letter from Sidney Reilly to Robert Nathan, 13 March 1920 (*Reilly Papers* CX 2616).

24. Letter from Sidney Reilly to Robert Nathan, 14 March 1920 (*Reilly Papers* CX 2616).

25. Letter from Sir Archibald Sinclair to Winston Churchill, 24 June 1920 (CHAR 16/57/17, Churchill Archives Centre, Churchill College, Cambridge).

26. US Immigration, Port of New York, Volume 6489, 13 June 1920.

27. Entry No. 328, Register of Births in the Sub-district of Batheaston in the Registration District of Bath in the County of Somerset, Frances Caryll Houselander, 29 September 1901.

28. *Caryll Houselander: That Divine Eccentric*, Maisie Ward (Sheed and Ward, 1962), pp.72–73.

29. A Rocking Horse Catholic, Caryll Houselander (Sheed and Ward, 1955), pp.136–37.

30. Ibid.

31. Letter from Dermot Morrah to Frank Sheed, 7 October 1956 (Sheed and Ward Family Papers, Box 12, Folder 12, University of Notre Dame Archives, Indiana, USA).

32. Letter from Caryll Houselander to Wilfred Sheed, 12 October 1950 (Sheed and Ward Family Papers, Box 12, Folder 12, University of Notre Dame Archives, Indiana, USA).

33. Caryll Houselander: That Divine Eccentric, Maisie Ward, p.61.

34. *The Diaries of Robert Bruce Lockhart*, Kenneth Young (ed.), p.183.

35. Letter from Winston Churchill to Stewart Menzies, 29 October 1920, CHAR 16/49, Churchill Archives Centre, Churchill College, Cambridge.

36. Parmi les maitres rouges by Georgi Solomon (Paris, 1930), p248-250.

37. Memorandum from Naval Intelligence Division to SIS, 3 September 1920 (*Reilly Papers* CX 2616).

38. Memorandum from C to Naval Intelligence Division, 7 September 1920 (*Reilly Papers* CX 2616)

39. Memorandum from Naval Intelligence Division to SIS, 10 September 1920 (*Reilly Papers* CX 2616).

40. Ibid., handwritten note by C at foot of memorandum.

41. Memorandum dated 20 October 1920 (*Reilly Papers* CX 2616).

42. Telegram No. 983, dated 29 October 1920 (*Reilly Papers* CX 2616).

43. Memorandum from Section V to Production, 3 November 1920 (*Reilly Papers* CX 2616).

44. Telegram from Section G2 to Sidney Reilly, 8 November 1920 (*Reilly Papers* CX 2616).

45. 'Trust' File No. 302330, Vol. 37 (Archive of the Federal Security Service, Moscow).

46. *New York Times*, 1 May 1921, p.8.

47. Box 6, Robert Bruce Lockhart Collection (Hoover Institution Archives, Stanford, California).

48. Letter from H.F. Pougher to Air Board, received by SIS 12 October 1921 (*Reilly Papers* CX 2616).

49. Ibid. Note appended to foot of letter by Sidney Reilly.

50. Letter from Sidney Reilly to SIS, 19 September 1921 (*Reilly Papers* CX 2616).

51. Letter from Sir Eyre Crowe (permanent under-secretary, Foreign Office) to Lord Curzon (Foreign Secretary), 28 December 1921 (Curzon Papers), reproduced in Winston S. Churchill, Vol. IV, 1917–1922, Martin Gilbert, companion volume III, pp.1703–05).

52. Ibid.

53. Letter from Sidney Reilly to SIS, 23 January 1922 (*Reilly Papers* CX 2616).

54. From SIS (Vienna), 1 February 1922 (*Reilly Papers* CX 2616).

55. From G7 (London) to SIS New York, 24 July 1923 (*Reilly Papers* CX 2616).

Twelve – A Change of Bait

1. Letter from Edward Spears to Robin Bruce Lockhart, 2 January 1967, Robert Bruce Lockhart Collection, Box 6, Hoover Institution Archives, Stanford, California.

2. Diary of Edward Spears, 1 April 1921 (Spears MSS SPRS 2/4 Churchill Archives Centre, Churchill College, Cambridge).

3. *Diaries of Robert Bruce Lockhart*, Kenneth Young (ed.), p.17.

4. Diary of Edward Spears, 17 July 1921 (Spears MSS SPRS 2/4 Churchill Archives Centre, Churchill College, Cambridge).

5. Herbert Guedalla, a pre-war director of the Russo-English Bank. As a director of the Imperial and Foreign Company, along with Edward Spears, he was also involved in Reilly/Spears Czech Radium deal.

6. Lt-Col. Robert Guy (1878–1927), a war-time acquaintance of Spears (see *Who Was Who, 1916–1928*)

7. Reilly had recently moved from 11 Park Place, St James's, to Flat D3, the Albany, Piccadilly, an exclusive London address popular with peers, members of the government and upper-class society generally.

8. Reilly always liked to make out that he was a close confidant of Churchill's. While close to Sir Archibald Sinclair, it is most unlikely that Reilly was ever more than the briefest of acquaintances with Churchill. In Churchill's entire correspondence for the years 1919–25 there are but two letters written to Reilly, both in response to letters from Reilly. Both address him very formally as Mr Reilly. Anyone who was close or on personal terms with Churchill would have been addressed as 'My dear Sinclair' or 'Dear Spears', not as 'Dear Mr'.

9. Diary of Edward Spears, 17 August 1921 (Spears MSS SPRS 2/4 Churchill Archives Centre, Churchill College, Cambridge).

10. Ibid., 21–25 October 1921.

11. Ibid., 25 October 1921.

12. Ibid., 23 November 1921.

13. Diary of Edward Spears, 20 April 1922 (Spears MSS SPRS 2/5 Churchill Archives Centre, Churchill College, Cambridge).

14. Ibid., 30 June 1922.

15. *The Tatler*, No. 905, 30 October 1918, p.133.

16. Letter from Sidney Reilly to Boris Savinkov, dated 7 May 1923, State Archive of the Russian Federation, Moscow (Fond R-5831, Inventory 1, File 177).

17. Entry 462, Register of Births in the Registration District of Lancaster in the County of Lancaster, 4 May 1862. Isobel Burton died at the age of eighty-six (Entry 463, Register of Deaths in the Sub-district of Hythe in the Registration District of Folkestone in the County of Kent, 20 June 1948).

18. Letter to British Consulate, Hamburg, from Isabel Burton, 5 June 1888 (A6 Vol 33, Alphabetisches Register weiblicher Fremder 1868–1890).

19. Franz Kurt Burton, born 5 July 1888, Hamburg, Germany (Freie und Hansestadt Hamburg, Standesamt).

20. Nelly Louise Burton, born 20 January 1891, Hamburg, Germany (Freie und Hansestadt Hamburg, Standesamt).

21. 'Card File of inhabitants who left or died between 1892 and 1925' (K44320, Fotoarchiv, Hamburg).

22. No record of Alice Burton's birth has been found in Britain. She may have been born on the continent or registered in Britain under a name other than Burton. On her Marriage Certificate (Entry 124, Register of Marriages in the Registration District of St George Hanover Square in the County of London, 18 January 1918) column 7 – 'Father's name and Surname' has been left blank. Unusually, column 6 of her Death Certificate – 'Date and place of birth' (Entry 87, Register of Deaths in the Registration District of Westminster in the City of Westminster, 5 February 1972) simply states 'about 1894'

23. Programme of show 'Cache ton nu',

20 April 1914 (Ro 15743, Arsenal Library, Paris).

24. 'Pepa' is a shortened version of Josephina and 'ita' is a diminutive form, so Pepita literally means 'small Josephina'. Bobadilla is a town in the province of Jaen in the south of Spain and derives from the Arabic Boab'dil. Nelly first adopted the stage name Bobadilla in the summer of 1914. In 1916 her mother Isobel was interviewed by MI5, who were interested in her liaison with a Dutch merchant seaman. In a statement she explained that Pete Reyers was her intended second husband and that her first husband's name was Bobadilla. She never married Reyers and in fact never married anyone any time during her life. When she died in 1948 her death certificate claimed she was the widow of 'Frank Burton'.

25. *The Sketch*, 29 November 1916, p.6.

26. US Bureau of Investigation/ONI, memorandum to H. Hunnewell and A. Smith, 6 September 1918.

27. 1924 Electoral Register, City of Westminster, Knightsbridge St George's Ward.

28. Entry 96, Register of Marriages in the Regis-tration District of St George Hanover Square in the County of London, 29 October 1920.

29. This story is contained in a letter from Dame Rebecca West to Robin Bruce Lockhart, 29 February 1968 (Robert Bruce Lockhart Collection, Box 6, Hoover Institution Archive, Stanford, California).

30. The London Directory 1921.

31. Entry 95, Register of Deaths in the Sub-district of Mayfair and Knightsbridge in the Registration District of St George Hanover Square in the County of London, 28 March 1921; Charles Haddon Chambers died intestate. On 2 May 1921 the High Court of Justice (Principal Probate Registry) granted his full estate to Nelly (£9,195 gross, £8,240 net).

32. *Britain's Master Spy – The Adventures of Sidney Reilly*, Sidney and Pepita Reilly, p.105.

33. Ibid., pp.108–09.

34. *Caryll Houselander: That Divine Eccentric*, Maise Ward, p.75–76.

35. Nelly's claim to have been staying at the Hotel Adlon in December 1922/January 1923 is called into question by this letter. The Hotel Adlon was situated at Unter den Linden 77, Berlin (it was destroyed in the Battle of Berlin in 1945, but rebuilt on the same site in 1997). Reilly's letter of 9 January is addressed to her at Bamberger Strasse 38, IV Stock (4th floor), Berlin Wilmersdorf – not at the Adlon.

36. Cita is a reference to her sister Alice Menzies, who often referred to herself as Cita Bobadilla. She also aspired to a career on the stage, but was unsuccessful. During Nelly's marriage to Haddon Chambers she was apparently kept short of funds and was therefore dependent upon her sister Alice for support.

37. Letter from Sidney Reilly to Nelly Haddon Chambers, 9 January 1923 (Robert Bruce Lockhart Collection, Box 6, Hoover Institution Archive, Stanford, California).

38. Entry 29, Register of Marriages in the Registration District of St Martin in the County of London, 18 May 1923.

39. *Britain's Master Spy – The Adventures of Sidney Reilly,* p.111.

40. Ibid., p.115.

41. Ibid.

42. Margaret referred to their last meeting in her interview with HM Vice Consul Darrell Wilson in Brussels, Despatch No. 156, 29 May 1931 (PRO FO 372/2756) and in her untitled synopsis of November 1931.

43. In September 1921 Margaret journeyed to America (US Immigration Records, Port of New York, Vol. 6887, p.20, 16 September 1921). She was hardly in a position to fund her own passage, thus raising the question of who financed her trip and why. According to US Immigration Records, she stated that she was visiting the US in order to visit her friends 'Edward Moon and wife'. From the time Reilly initially filed a claim against the Baldwin Locomotive Company in 1920, their lawyers White and Case began assembling evidence on Reilly and his reputation. Private investigators were hired, including one Edward Moon.

44. Incorporation, Registration and Statement in Lieu of Prospectus documents in the file of the Modern Medicine Company Ltd, Registration No. 189767 (PRO BT 31/27894).

45. Ibid. Two further directors, Frederick Martin and Kenneth Fraser, joined the board in July and September 1923 respectively.

46. For documentation regarding Humagsolen, see PRO FD 1/953 and FD 1/3354.

47. Telegram from G7 London to SIS New York, 24 July 1923 (*Reilly Papers* CX 2616).

48. Letter from William Field Robinson to George Hill, 9 September 1935 (Robert Bruce Lockhart Collection, Box 6, Hoover Institution Archives, Stanford, California).

49. Ibid.

50. Letter from Edward Spears to Sidney Reilly, 19 July 1923 (SPRS 1/301 Churchill Archives Centre, Churchill College, Cambridge).

51. Ibid.

52. Reilly resigned as a director on 24 May 1924. A liquidator was appointed to wind up the company on 20 May 1925 (File of the Modern Medicine Company Ltd, PRO BT 31/27894).

53. *Britain's Master Spy – The Adventures of Sidney Reilly,* p.123ff.

54. Ibid.

55. Ibid.

56. Letter from Pepita Reilly to 'Cita' (Alice Menzies), 25 January 1924 (Papers of Mrs A.C. Menzies).

57. Letters from Sidney Reilly to Boris Savinkov, dated 19 February and 15 March 1924. (Fond R-5831, Inventory 1, State Archive of the Russian Federation, Moscow).

58. US Immigration, Port of New York, Volume 7978, p.50, 15 May 1924.

59. Letter from Sidney Reilly to Winston Churchill, 3 September 1924 (CHAR 2/134/110 & 111–114, Churchill Archives Centre, Churchill College, Cambridge).

60. *Morning Post,* 15 September 1924, p.11.

61. Letter from Winston Churchill to Sidney Reilly, 15 September 1924 (CHAR 1/134/130, Churchill Archives Centre, Churchill College, Cambridge).

62. Letter from Sir Archibald Sinclair to Winston Churchill, 23 September 1924 (CHAR 2/134/130, Churchill Archive Centre, Churchill College, Cambridge).

63. Because Reilly had destroyed his contract with Baldwins, his case was very much his word against Samuel Vauclain's. The best line for White and Case to take was therefore demonstrating to the court that Reilly was a dishonest and disreputable character whose word could not be trusted. This was not a difficult case to make and as the Bureau of Investigation had found during their probe, there was no shortage of people in New York willing to offer testimony. It is notable that Reilly did not permit Pepita to accompany him to court, which would clearly have exposed her to the many tales of his less than salubrious past.

64. Trading Ventures Inc., Certificate of Incorporation in the State of New York No. 1716116, 23 December 1924, p.4.

65. Letter from Sidney Reilly to Edward Spears, 22 January 1925 (Robert Bruce Lockhart Collection, Box 6, Hoover Institution Archives, Stanford, California).

66. Ibid.

67. See note 64, p.2.

THIRTEEN – PRISONER 73

1. Letter from Ernest Boyce to Sidney Reilly, 24 January 1925 (Robert Bruce Lockhart Collection, Box 6, Hoover Institution Archives, Stanford, California). Also reproduced in *Britain's Master Spy – The Adventures of Sidney* Reilly, pp.172–74.

2. Reilly's reply. Ibid., pp.175–77.

3. Letter from Sidney Reilly to Nikolai Bunakov, 27 March 1925 (Trust File No. 302330, Vol. 37, Central Archives of the Federal Security Service, Moscow).

4. Ibid.

5. Letter from Sidney Reilly to Ernest Boyce, 4 April 1925, *Britain's Master Spy – The Adventures of Sidney Reilly*, pp.182–83.

6. Ibid, p.185.

7. Ibid, p.187.

8. Letter from Sidney Reilly to Pepita Reilly, 22 September 1925, Papers of Nelly Haddon Chambers (Pepita Reilly). Also reproduced in *Britain's Master Spy – The Adventures of Sidney Reilly*, pp.188–89.

9. Ibid.

10. Undated report from Alexander Yakushev in 'Trust' File No 302330, Vol. 37, p.112 (Central Archives of the Federal Security Service, Moscow).

11. Ibid.

12. Letter from Sidney Reilly to Pepita Reilly, 25 September 1925, Papers of Nelly Haddon Chambers (Pepita Reilly). Also reproduced in *Britain's Master Spy – The Adventures of Sidney Reilly*, pp199–203.

13. Undated Report from Alexander Yakushev in 'Trust File No 302330, Vol. 37 (Central Archives of the Federal Security Service, Moscow).

14. Ibid. Margaret Reilly also quotes her husband as having said 'that he would believe Russia would be entering the convalescent stage when she would turn round and massacre at least one million Jews' (Letter from Margaret Reilly to SIS, 28 December 1931, *Reilly Papers* CX 2616)

15. See note 13.

16. Ibid.

17. SIS translation of letter written by Mikhail Trilisser of OGPU (INO), 1 October 1925 (*Reilly Papers* CX 2616). The 'valuables' more than likely belonged to Yaroslavsky, the former secretary to the Soviet Legation in Vienna. In June 1924 he absconded from his post with a considerable sum of legation funds and disappeared. The OGPU (INO) suspected that Yaroslavsky had asked Reilly to retrieve valuables of his located in Leningrad.

18. Telegram from Ernest Boyce to Pepita Reilly, 30 September 1925, Papers of Nelly Haddon Chambers (Pepita Reilly). Also reproduced in *Britain's Master Spy – The Adventures of Sidney Reilly*, p.193.

19. Letter from Ernest Boyce to Pepita Reilly, 1 October 1925, Papers of Nelly Haddon Chambers (Pepita Reilly). Also reproduced in *Britain's Master Spy – The Adventures of Sidney Reilly*, pp.193–94.

Fourteen – A Lonely Place to Die

1. Boris Gudz – interview with the author, 24 August 2002, Moscow.

2. Report by Vladimir Styrne, 7 October 1925, in 'Trust' File No. 302330, Vol. 37, p.241 (Central Archives of the Federal Security Service, Moscow). As we already know, Reilly attended neither Heidelburg nor the Royal Institute. Had he been an active Conservative, he would have been a member of the St George Hanover Square Conservative Association. Although the association's records still exist they contain no reference to him as a member (Records of the St George Hanover Square Conservative Association, 487/8–9, 487/13, City of Westminister Archives Centre). However, there is no reason to believe that his letter to friend Paul Dukes (see note 27), advocating the Conservative cause is anything less than sincere.

3. Ibid.

4. Ibid, 9 October 1925.

5. Mutt was Boyce's reference for Sidney – Pepita he referred to as Jeff.

6. Letter from Ernest Boyce to Pepita Reilly, 18 October 1925, Papers of Nelly Haddon Chambers (Pepita Reilly). Also reproduced in *Britain's Master Spy – The Adventures of Sidney Reilly*, pp.197–98.

7. *Britain's Master Spy – The Adventures of Sidney Reilly*, p.199.

8. Letter from Sidney Reilly to Vladimir Styrne, 13 October 1925 (Trust File No. 302330, Vol. 37, Central Archives of the Federal Security Service, Moscow).

9. Letter from Sidney Reilly to Vladimir Styrne, 17 October 1925 (Trust File No. 302330, Vol. 37, Central Archives of the Federal Security Service, Moscow).

10. The OGPU made photographic enhancements of the diary for the period 30 October–2 November 1925, which Reilly wrote in English, with occasional words or abbreviations in Russian. The entries for 3–4 November 1925 were not photographed but translated into Russian with the aid of magnification techniques. English translations of the Russian section of the diary have been published on several occasions during the past decade. The four most noteworthy are: 'How the Russians Broke the *Ace of Spies*', Philip Knightley (*The Observer*, 12 April 1992, pp.49–50); *Deadly Illusions*, John Costello and Oleg Tsarev, pp.38–40; 'Sidney Reilly's Lubyanka Diary', Richard Spence, *Revolutionary Russia*, Vol. 8, No. 2, pp.179–94; and *Iron Maze*, Gordon Brook-Shepherd, pp.300–04. Of the four, Spence is the most thorough, providing speculative additions where the original text is abbreviated by single or multiple letters. Due to the nature of English/Russian translation, there have inevitably arisen differences of interpretation in the above publications. The method used throughout this book to translate from Cyrillic Russian to English is based on a modified Library of Congress system and names have therefore been translated according to popular usage, i.e. Savinkov instead of Savinkoff, Gorky instead of Gor'kii, Zalessky instead of Zalesskii.

11. *Ace of Spies* (1992 edition), p.188.

12. Reilly's 'diary' is in 'Trust' File No. 302330, Vol. 37, p.366 (Central Archives of the Federal Security Service, Moscow).

13. Ibrahim Abisalov, an expert marksman with a pistol.

14. Pepita Reilly.

15. On the assumption that the diary was written for the consumption of Western eyes rather than the OGPU, this piece of bravado is perhaps not surprising. Although obviously not an 'Englishman', it is debatable whether he was, in fact, a Christian either. Caryll Houselander clearly regarded him as a fellow Catholic and from the testimony of Eleanor Toye and others we know that he certainly had a keen interest in the Christian religion and Jesus Christ. However, in the absence of any real evidence, his religious beliefs or lack of them must remain conjecture.

16. 'Trust' File No. 302330, Vol. 37, p.300 (Central Archives of the Federal Security Service, Moscow). The letter was first published in Moscow in the Literaturnaia gazeta, No. 51, 20 December 1967, p.2.

17. *Iron Maze*, Gordon Brook-Shepherd, p.301.

18. Secret Assignment. Edward P. Gazur (St Ermins Press, 2001), p.526.

19. Ibid.

20. Ibid.

21. 'Boris Savinkov pered voennoi kollegiei verkhovnogo suda SSSR, *Iron Maze*, Gordon Brook-Shepherd, p.276.

22. Mikhail Dmitriyevich Kushner was an OGPU doctor and mortician.

23. Veronal is a diethyl-barbituric acid or barbitone. As a white crystalline powder it would have been given to Reilly by Kushner to induce

sleep. As we already know, Reilly was possibly subject to severe headaches and mild epilepsy at times of acute stress. In New York he was apparently consulting Dr Anthony Bassler of 21 West 74th Street, who specialised in such conditions (US Bureau of Investigation/ONI, Memorandum of 9 October 1918, p.4).

24. A reference to the American Consulate's involvement in the 1918 'Lockhart Plot'.

25. A reference to the Soviet's claim that Reilly was involved in sabotaging food trains at Voronezh in 1918. See 'Sensational Plot discovered to overthrow Soviet Government' by Greorgi Chicherin (a handbill distributed to Allied troops in Archangel in August 1918). Reilly had always denied this.

26. Alexei Stark, a former naval Tsarist officer employed by the OGPU.

27. Ilya Kurtz had worked with Reilly in 1918 and Paul Dukes (ST25) in 1919. He is thought to have defected to the Bolsheviks in 1920 and become an OGPU agent.

28. Eduard Opperput, an OGPU agent involved in the 'Trust' operation. He defected to the West in Finland with Maria Shultz (Maria Zakharchenko) in April 1927 and disclosed that the Trust was an OGPU sham. He returned to Russia on behalf of anti-Bolshevik forces and was shot by the OGPU in Smolensk in June 1927. Richard Spence argues that his death was a sham and that he was re-recruited by the OGPU and sent to China (Revolutionary Russia, Vol. 8, No. 2, December 1995, p.189, note 38).

29. Alexander Yakushev, the OGPU agent who met Reilly on his arrival in Helsingfors on 22 September 1925.

30. Sir Robert Hodgson was a British diplomat assigned to Moscow in May 1921 by Lord Curzon as head of the British Commercial Mission. In March 1924 he was appointed Britain's chargé d'affaires by Ramsay MacDonald. The OGPU believed Hodgson's Commercial Mission was a cover for espionage.

31. Paul Dukes was a musician, civil servant and journalist who served as an SIS agent between 1918 and 1920. Knighted for services in the field, he was a friend of Reilly's during the 1920s. In 1922 Reilly endeavoured to persuade Dukes to stand in the 15 November General Election as a Conservative candidate (Letter from Sidney Reilly to Paul Dukes, 23 October 1922, Robert Bruce Lockhart Collection, Box 6, Hoover Institution Archives, Stanford, California).

32. Zinovy Peshkov was the adopted son of Maxim Peshkov (Maxim Gorky). He served with the White forces in 1918.

33. A Lycée was a secondary school organised along French lines. Both Christian and foreign, they were objects of suspicion. Jeanne Morans was the headmistress of the Moscow Lycée, a catholic girls' school, and had been arrested in connection with the Lockhart Plot in September 1918. She was tried but found not guilty.

34. Mikhail Gniloryboff was a member of Boris Savinkov's People's Union

for the Defence of the Motherland and Liberty.

35. OGPU official working with Dr Kushner.

36. OGPU agent Grigory Feduleev worked undercover on the 'Trust' operation and was in on the Reilly interrogation with Vladimir Syrne.

37. It would appear that what Reilly actually told Styrne about SIS was superficial, fabricated or already known to the OGPU, or a combination of all three. Following the breach of diplomatic relations between Britain and Russia in 1927, the OGPU arrested two of Ernest Boyce's agents and put them on trial for terrorism. The Leningrad Sunday Worker reported on 2 October that, 'evidence given by the notorious British spy, Capt. Sidney Reilly, in October 1925, was read out during the present trial of terrorists at Leningrad'. Reilly was quoted as declaring, 'The British secret service – called the Secret Intelligence Service – is an institution standing quite apart from any ministerial department… it is absolutely secret: neither the names of the chief nor staff are known to anyone except the principal cabinet ministers and military chiefs of the highest rank… since 1923 SIS has been headed by Rear-Admiral Gaygout' (this would appear to be a translation error for 'Guy Gaunt'). In reality, the chief was Rear-Admiral Sinclair, as Reilly well knew. (A copy of the Sunday Worker article is among the Reilly Papers CX 2616.)

38. Reilly could volunteer nothing here as he was completely unaware of SIS activities since his ties with the organisation were severed in 1921.

39. Norwegian military attaché in Moscow at the time of Reilly's interrogation.

40. SIS station chief in Prague, Czechoslovakia.

41. Reilly may sincerely have believed that SIS had placed no spies in Russia after Dukes. The OGPU, however, knew differently, thus their reluctance to take no for an answer.

42. Rear-Admiral Thomas Kemp had ordered Reilly's confinement on HMS Glory following his arrest in Murmansk, due to a passport irregularity, in April 1918.

43. This no doubt refers to the meeting with Lockhart following Reilly's visit to the Kremlin on 7 May 1918.

44. Artur Artuzov was head of the OGPU's counter-intelligence section (KRO), and therefore Vladimir Styrne's immediate superior.

45. The Zinoviev Letter was almost certainly a forgery and the Russians were keen to learn more about the anti-Bolshevik émigrés who were the prime suspects in the eyes of the OGPU.

46. Mikhail Frunze, Bolshevik Commissar for Military and Naval Affairs.

47. Wyndham Childs, Deputy Assistant Commissioner, New Scotland Yard.

48. John Carter, Deputy Assistant Commissioner, New Scotland Yard.

49. Sir Basil Thompson, superintendent, New Scotland Yard (Special Branch).

50. According to Winston Churchill, in a letter to Col. Stewart Menzies of

SIS, dated 29 October 1920, 'the other man whom I should be glad of any information which you can give me is one Boris Said [sic]. I am informed by certain persons that he was the principal Zionist agent in London before the revolution and having in his hands an exceedingly large sum of money he decided to appropriate it and throw in his lot with the Bolsheviks. I am told that he is now the principal Bolshevik agent and lives in style at the Ritz' (CHAR 16/49/64–66, Churchill Archives Centre, Churchill College, Cambridge).

51. Leonid Krasin was, from 1920, the head of Soviet Russia's Economic Mission to Britain. Reilly assisted Krasin in securing a trade agreement with Marconi, although it was suspected, but never proved, that both Krasin and Reilly pocketed money from this and other deals.

52. Amtorg was a joint Soviet-US trading company.

53. Arcos (Anglo-Russian Co-operative Society) was established by Leonid Krasin in 1921 to encourage joint enterprises with British companies. It was raided by Special Branch in 1927 who found evidence that it was being used as a front for Soviet espionage.

54. Edward Wise was a member of the British government's negotiating team that met with Krasin's Trade Delegation (Secret Service, Christopher Andrew, p.262ff).

55. Leslie Urquhart was one of a small number of British businessmen who endeavoured to negotiate trade deals with Arcos.

56. Reilly's approach to business.

57. During 1925, industrial unrest increased following Winston Churchill's first budget in April, which heralded Britain's return to the Gold Standard. This added greatly to the cost of exports and caused the mine-owners to announce wage cuts on 30 June. On 10 July the TUC General Council agreed to support the Miners Federation and declared a national embargo on the movement of coal. Prime Minister Baldwin judged that the time was not right for a national confrontation with the TUC and on 31 July – Red Friday – climbed down. The government offered the mining industry a subsidy of £23 million to stave off wage cuts.

58. Lieutenant Alexandr Alexeevich Abaza, a former Tsarist naval officer and White Russian.

59. Philip Faymonville had been in Russia during 1918/20 and was US Military Attaché in Tokyo in 1925.

60. See note 1.

61. Ibid.

62. This photograph appears on page 223 of this book. When the overcoat was later examined, a small Union Jack was found sewn into its lining. The Union Jack is now on display at the FSB Museum, Moscow, and was seen by the author on 26 August 2002, during a visit to FSB Headquarters.

63. This was more than likely necessary due to the fact that he had been officially dead since 28 September. Only the small circle of OGPU

officers involved in the Trust operation knew otherwise.

64. Secret Assignment, Edward Gazur, p.519.

65. Ibid.

66. OGPU File no. 249856. See also, Deadly Illusions, J. Costello and O. Tsarer, p.22.

67. By 1921 Hill, like Reilly and many others, found that due to budget constraints he had no future with SIS. Now unemployed he was reduced to living in a caravan in Sussex with his wife. He eventually found work in theatre management ('SOE's man in Moscow' by Martin Kitchen, Intelligence and National Security, Vol. 12, No. 3, July 1997, p.96.

68. Kim Philby was one of Hill's pupils at Brickendonbury Hall in Hertfordshire, a sabotage training school in 1940 ('SOE's man in Moscow' by Michael Kitchen, p.96).

69. Britain's Master Spy – The Adventures of Sidney Reilly, pp.285–88.

70. In a letter to Capt. William Isaacs, dated 17 November 1931, Margaret Reilly states, 'My firm belief is that Reilly is still alive in Russia working for England against Bolshevism' (Reilly Papers CX 2616).

71. Reilly: The First Man, Robin Bruce Lockhart, p.28ff.

72. Master Spy, Edward Van Der Rhoer, p.231ff.

73. 'Sidney Reilly's Lubyanka Diary' by Richard Spence.

74. Reilly: The First Man contains sixteen chapters. Chapters six–fifteen contain few references to Reilly, concentrating in the main on general East-West espionage issues.

75. Ace of Spies (1992 edition), p.188.

76. Letter to the author from Robin Bruce Lockhart, dated 9 January 2000.

77. CXM 159, 29 March 1918 (Reilly Papers CX 2616).

78. Report by Agent L.S. Perkins (US Bureau of Investigation), dated 3 April 1917 describes Reilly as of 'oriental appearance'.

79. Report by Kenneth Linge, BA, MSc, FBBIPP of DABS Forensic Ltd, 27 December 2001.

80. Ace of Spies, preface.

81. The Messenger of the Sacred Heart, Caryll Houselander, p.59.

APPENDICES

APPENDIX ONE – THE GADFLY

1. *Ace of Spies*, Robin Bruce Lockhart, p.27.
2. The American edition of *The Gadfly* was published by Henry Holt and Company, New York, in April 1897. The British edition was published in September 1897 by William Heinemann. They were identical apart from their respective covers. The British edition also contained an additional appendix of fourteen press reviews.
3. *The Gadfly* by E.L. Voynich (Heinemann 1897, p.341ff).
4. A collection of reviews and articles about *The Gadfly* are to be found in the Boole Family Collection, presented to Lincolnshire County Archives by Gabrielle Boole in July 1985.
5. 'The Gadfly and the Spy' by Tibor Szamuely, *The Spectator*, 17 May 1968, p.665.
6. BBC World Service, Russian Language Programme, broadcast 7.00 p.m. 9 June 1968
7. 'George Boole, His Life and Work' by Desmond MacHale, p.273.
8. Ibid., p.274.
9. E.L. Voynich, Evgenia Taratuta, Moscow, 1970.
10. 'Who Admired Pavka Korchagin?' by Boris Polevoi and Evgenia Taratuta (*Izvestia*, No. 11, 12 June 1968, p.3).
11. Giuseppe Mazzini (1805–72) founded the Young Italy movement in 1831, which was dedicated to achieving a united, republican Italian state.
12. From the Papers of Hugh Millar.
13. Letters from W. Field Robertson to George Hill, dated 6 and 9 September 1935 (Box 6, Robert Bruce Lockhart Collection at the Hoover Institution Archive, Stanford, California).
14. US Immigration Service, Passenger Arrival List Index Cards, Volumes 6332–14197 (1919–1941).
15. Letter from Edward Spears to Robin Bruce Lockhart, dated 2 January 1967 (Box 6, Robert Bruce Lockhart Collection, Hoover Institution Archive, Stanford, California).
16. *An Interrupted Friendship*, E.L. Voynich (Macmillan, 1910), p.139ff.

APPENDIX TWO – MISTAKEN IDENTITY

1. *Sidney Reilly – The True Story*, Michael Kettle, p.16.
2. Ibid., p.15.
3. Ibid., p.16.
4. Ibid., p.16.
5. Ibid., p.17.
6. *Ace of Spies*, Robin Bruce Lockhart, p.182.
7. *Mining the Challenge – 150 Years of the Royal School of Mines*, Anne Barrett, p.1, and *Imperial College* by Richard G. Williams and Anne Barrett, p.10.
8. City of Cambridge Directory 1906.
9. Minute Book of the Trinity College Boat Club, 14 October 1905 (Trinity College Library).

10. Entry 271, Register of Deaths in the Sub-district of Epsom and Ewell in the Registration District of Surrey Eastern in the County of Surrey, 13 June 1952.

11. Aline Reilly – interview with the author on 2 September 2000; Noel Reilly – interview with the author on 22 September 2000.

12. Indian Army List 1918/1920; Indian Army Reserve List (PRO); Thackers' India Office Biographical Index (India Office Records – British Library).

13. Baptismal Records for Dehra Dun, Volume 376, Folio 9 (India Office Records – British Library).

14. Entry 111, Register of Deaths in the Sub-district of Hornsey in the Registration District of Edmonton in the County of Middlesex, 18 September 1945.

Appendix Three – The Factory Fireman

1. *Spies*, Jay Robert Nash (M. Evans & Company, New York, 1997), p.412.

2. *Ace of Spies*, Robin Bruce Lockhart, p.36ff; *Reilly: The First Man*, Robin Bruce Lockhart, p.5. Curiously, when a revised edition of *Ace of Spies* was published in 1992, the reference to Krupps story was unaltered.

3. In Troy Kennedy-Martin's 1983 Thames Television adaption, *Reilly: Ace of Spies*, the Blohm & Voss shipyard in Hamburg is substituted for the Krupps plant in Essen, and Reilly's alias is changed from Hahn to Fricker.

4. *Master Spy*, Edward Van Der Rhoer, p.ix ff.

5. '100th Anniversary of Freidrich Krupp', 1912 (p.138/140), Historisches Archiv Krupp, Essen.

6. Ibid.

7. Ibid.

8. File WA 41/3–46, Historisches Archiv Krupp, Essen.

9. Ibid., File WA 41/6–64.

10. Ibid., File WA 41/6–255.

11. Ibid., File WA 41/6–274.

Appendix Four – The Battleship Blueprints

1. *Ace of Spies*, Robin Bruce Lockhart, p.54.

2. Ibid., p.51/54.

3. There are references on 2 March and 28 June 1910 to the recruitment and debriefing of Bywater in the diary of Sir Mansfield Cumming.

4. *Strange Intelligence*, Hector Bywater (Constable, 1931); *The Quest for C*, Alan Judd, pp.143 and 257.

Appendix Five – Rescuing the Tsar

1. The Plots to Rescue the Tsar, Shay McNeal (Century 2001), p137

2. Ibid, p120

3. Ibid, p121

4. PRO WO 33/962, Item 14, telegram 59154, Director of Military Intelligence to Brigadier-General Poole, 28 May 1918.

5. *The Plots to Rescue the Tsar*, Shay McNeal, p122

6. Reilly's report (Affairs in Russia, CX 038307, 22nd June 1918) is appended to a letter from the Director of Military Intelligence to the Under Secretary of State, Foreign Office, 9 July

1918, PRO FO 371/3315, paper 301.

7.   *The Plots to Rescue the Tsar*, Shay McNeal, p143.

8.   For example: Telegram CX 013592, 12th May 1918 (PRO WO 32/5669); Telegram 035402, 29th May 1918 (PRO WO 32/5669); Telegram CX 034907 (PRO WO/325669); Telegram CX 035176, 3rd June 1918 (PRO WO 32/5669); Telegram CX 038307, 22 June 1918 (PRO FO 371/3315).

9.   The orders concerning Reilly's mission to Russia are referred to in the letter from Lt-Col. C N French of the War Office to Ronald Campbell of the Foreign Office, 10th October 1918, PRO FO 371/3319.

10.   'Report of Work Done in Russia' by George Hill (PRO FO 371/3350/79980).

11.   *The Plots to Rescue the Tsar*, Shay McNeal, p58.

12.   Ibid.

13.   *Rescuing the Tsar* by James P Smythe (California Printing Company, 1920).

14.   *The Plots to Rescue the Tsar* by Shay McNeal, p131.

15.   Ibid, p234.

APPENDIX SIX – THE ZINOVIEV LETTER

1.   *Sidney Reilly – The True Story*, Michael Kettle, p.130.

2.   *A Most Extraordinary and Mysterious Business: The Zinoviev Letter of 1924*, Gill Bennett (Foreign & Commonwealth Office General Services Command), Annex A.

3.   *Sidney Reilly – The True Story,* Michael Kettle, p.121; 'Hand of British spy seen in Zinoviev Letter', by David Bonavia, *Sunday Times*, 15 February 1970, p.4. The handwritten copy of the Zinoviev Letter reproduced in Kettle's book was discovered by Harvard University Associate William Butler in the papers of former US Consul C.D. Westcott at the Harvard Law School (Harvard Library Bulletin, 1970).

4.   Ibid.

5.   *Britain's Master Spy – The Adventures of Sidney Reilly*, p.200.

6.   See note 3 above.

7.   Reilly's letter to Felix Dzerzhinsky of 30 October 1925 ('Trust' File No. 302330, Vol. 37, p.366, Central Archive of the Federal Security Service, Moscow) contains a number of words that occur in the Zinoviev Letter – president, presidium, Moscow, British and Russian for example. These are all markedly different in construction and appearance than those in the 'handwritten' Zinoviev Letter.

8.   'The Complete Diary of Donald Im Thurn' is reproduced in Appendix A of 'The Zinoviev Letter: A Political Intrigue' by Lewis Chester, Stephen Fay and Hugo Young. The diary was apparently found among the papers of Im Thurn's friend Guy Kindersley, the Conservative MP for Hitchin, who died in 1956.

9.   Ibid., and *Sidney Reilly – The True Story*, Michael Kettle, p.122/123.

10.   Ibid.

11.   Letters reproduced in Britain's *Master Spy – The Adventures of Sidney Reilly*, p.178/182.

12.   Sidney and Pepita sailed from Cherbourg aboard the White Star

Line's SS *Olympic* (*Titantic*'s sister ship) on 15th October 1924 bound for New York (US Immigration Records, Vol. 8155, p.5, 21 October 1924). Michael Kettle places their departure for New York after 25 October, the day the letter was exposed in the

Daily Mail (*Sidney Reilly – The True Story,* p.128).

13. *A Most Extraordinary and Mysterious Business: The Zinoviev Letter of 1924*, Gill Bennett, p.45.

14. Ibid.

15. *The Guardian*, 23 June 2000, p.5.

16. Ibid.

BIBLIOGRAPHY

Rupert Allason, *The Branch* (Secker and Warburg, 1983).

Christopher Andrew, *Secret Service* (Heinemann, 1985).

Christopher Andrew and Vasili Mitrokhin, *The Mitrokhin Archive* (Allen Lane, 1999).

Andreas Augustin, Igor Bogdanov and Andreas Williamson, *Grand Hotel Europe, St Petersburg* (London, 1996).

Geoffrey Bailey (George Vassiltchikov), *The Conspirators* (Harper, 1960).

Anne Barrett, *Mining the Challenge – 150 Years of the Royal School of Mines* (Imperial College, 2001).

Anne Barrett and Richard Williams, *Imperial College* (Imperial College, 1988).

Ralph Barker, *The RFC in France* (Constable, 1994).

Mikhail Beizer, *The Jews of St Petersburg* (Edward Elson, 1989).

Gill Bennett, *A Most Extraordinary and Mysterious Business: The Zinoviev Letter of 1924* (Historians LRD, No. 14, Foreign & Commonwealth Office, February 1999).

Sir Henry Brackenbury, *Some Memories of my Spare Time* (Blackwood and Sons, 1909).

Gordon Brook-Shepherd, *Iron Maze* (Macmillan, 1998).

Harold Brust, I *Guarded Kings – The Memoirs of a Political Police Officer* (Hillman Curl, 1936).

Hector Bywater, *Strange Intelligence* (Constable, 1932).

John Costello and Oleg Tsarev, *Deadly Illusions* (Century, 1993).

Derek Curtis Bennett and Roland Wilde, *Curtis – The Life of Sir Henry Curtis-Bennett KC* (Cassell, 1937).

Richard Deacon, *A History of the British Secret Service* (Frederick Muller, 1969).

Richard Deacon, *A History of the Japanese Secret Service* (Frederick Muller, 1982).

Richard Deacon, *A History of the Russian Secret Service* (Taplinger, 1972).

R.K. Debo, 'Lockhart Plot or Dzerzhinskii Plot?', *Journal of Modern History*, Volume 43 (1971).

George Dilnot, *Great Detectives and their Methods* (Houghton Mifflin, 1928).

Sir Paul Dukes, *Red Dusk and the Morrow – Adventures and Investigations in Red Russia* (Williams and Norgate, 1923).

Sir Paul Dukes, *The Story of ST25* (Cassell, 1938).

Herbert Finch, *Traitors Within – Adventures in the Special Branch, Scotland Yard* (Doubleday, 1933).

John D. Forbes, *J.P. Morgan Junior, 1867–1943* (University Press of Virginia, 1981).

W.B. Fowler, *British-American Relations, 1917–18, The Role of Sir William Wiseman* (Princeton University Press, 1969).

Charles Fraser-Smith with Gerald McKnight and Sandy Lesburg, *The Secret War of Charles Fraser-Smith* (Michael Joseph, 1981).

Edward P. Gazur, *Secret Assignment* (St Ermines Press, 2001).

Martin Gilbert, *Winston S. Churchill, Volume IV (1917–22)* and *Volume V (1922–39)* (Macmillan, 1971–83).

Teodor Gladkov, *Execution as a Reward for Loyalty* (Tsentrpoligraf, 2000).

Maj.-Gen. Lord Edward Gleichen, *A Guardsman's Memories* (Blackwood, 1932).

B. Green, *The Streets of London* (Pavillion, 1983).

Dame Elizabeth Hill (ed. Jean Stafford-Smith), *The Memoirs of Dame Elizabeth Hill* (Lewes, 1999).

George Hill, *Go Spy the Land* (Cassell, 1932).

George Hill, *Dreaded Hour* (Cassell, 1936).

Caryll Houselander, *A Rocking Horse Catholic* (Sheed and Ward, 1955).

Caryll Houselander, *The Messenger of the Sacred Heart* (The Society of Jesus, 1930).

H.A. Jones, *Over the Balkans and South Russia, 1917–1919* (Edward Arnold, 1923).

Alan Judd, *The Quest for C* (Harper Collins, 1999).

Michael Kettle, *Sidney Reilly – The True Story* (Corgi, 1983).

Michael Kettle, *The Allies and the Russian Collapse, Volume 1* (Andre Deutsch, 1981).

Grand Duke Kirill, *My Life at Russia's Service – Memoirs of Grand Duke Kirill* (reprint, St Petersburg, 1996).

Vladimir Krymov, *Portraits of Unusual People* (Paris, 1971).

David Lample, *The Last Ditch* (Putnam, 1968).

Henry Landau, *All's Fair* (Putnam, 1934).

Henry Landau, *Secrets of the White Lady* (Putnam, 1935).

Henry Landau, *The Enemy Within* (Putnam, 1937).

Henry Landau, *Spreading the Spy Net* (Jarrolds, 1938).

V.V. Lebedev, *Russko-Amerikanskie ekonomicheskie otnosheniia, 1900–1917* (Moscow, 1964).

Dr Richard Lewisohn, *The Mystery Man of Europe – Sir Basil Zaharoff* (Lippincott, 1929).

David Lloyd George, *War Memoirs Volumes 1 and 2* (Odhams, 1938s).

Robert Bruce Lockhart, *Memoirs of a British Agent* (Putnam, 1932).

Robin Bruce Lockhart, *Ace of Spies* (Hodder and Stoughton, 1967).

Robin Bruce Lockhart, *Reilly: Ace of Spies* (Futura, Macdonald & Co., 1983).

Robin Bruce Lockhart, *Reilly: The First Man* (New York, 1987).

Robin Bruce Lockhart, *Reilly: Ace of Spies* (Robin Clark, 1992).

E.V. Lucas, *The Highways and Byways of Sussex* (Macmillan, 1904).

Andrew Lycett, Ian Fleming, *The Man Behind James Bond* (Turner, 1995).

Donald McCormick, *Murder by Perfection* (John Long, 1970).

Donald McCormick, *Pedlar of Death* (Holt, Rinehart and Winston, 1965).

Compton McKenzie, *My Life and Times 1915–1923* (Chatto and Windus, 1963).

Shay McNeal, *The Plots to Rescue the Tsar* (Century, 2001)

Susan, Countess of Malmesbury, *Life of Major-General Sir John Ardagh* (John Murray, 1909).

Jay Robert Nash, *Spies* (M. Evans and Company, 1997).

Robert Neumann, *Zaharoff the Armaments King* (George Allen and Unwin, 1934).

E.K. Nozhin, *The Truth About Port Arthur* (St Petersburg, 1907).

John Pearson, *The Life of Ian Fleming, Creator of James Bond* (Jonathan Cape, 1966).

Henena and Dennis Pelrine, *Ian Fleming: Man with the Golden Pen* (Swan, 1966).

Bernard Porter, *The Origins of the Vigilant State* (Weidenfeld and Nicolson, 1987).

Dmitry Pozdneyev, *Trade in Port Arthur* (St Petersburg, 1902).

Eduard Radzinsky, *Rasputin – The Last Word* (Weidenfeld and Nicolson, 2000).

John Reed, *Ten Days that Shook the World* (Sutton, 1997 edition).

Pepita Reilly, *Britain's Master Spy – The Adventures of Sidney Reilly* (Harper and Brothers, 1932).

V.N. Sashonko, *A Documentary Story of Russian Aviator Nikolai Evgrafovich Popov* (St Petersburg, 1982).

Michael Sayers and Albert E. Kahn, *The Great Conspiracy* (New Boston, 1946).

Robert Service, *Lenin* (Macmillan, 2000).

Richard Shannon, *The Crisis of Imperialism 1865–1915* (Hart-Davis, MacGibbon, 1974).

Michael Smith, *New Cloak, Old Dagger* (Victor Gollancz, 1996).

Georgi Solomon, *Parmi les maitres rouges* (Paris, 1930).

E. Millicent Sowerby, *Rare People and Rare Books by E. Millicent* (Constable, 1967).

Richard B. Spence, *Boris Savinkov* (East European Monographs, Boulder, 1991).

Richard B Spence, 'The Terrorist and the Master Spy' (*Revolutionary Russia, Volume 4*, June 1991, No. 1).

Richard B. Spence, 'Sidney Reilly's Lubyanka Diary' (*Revolutionary Russia, Volume 8* December 1995, No. 2).

Richard B Spence, 'Sidney Reilly in America, 1914-1917' (*Intelligence and National Security*, Volume 10, No 1, January 1995).

Richard B. Spence, 'Trust No One' (Feral House, 2002).

Norman G. Thwaites, *Velvet and Vinegar* (Grayson, 1932).

Leon Trotsky, *The History of the Russian Revolution* (Victor Gollancz, 1934).

Edward Van Der Rhoer, *Master Spy* (Charles Scribners, 1981).

Samuel M. Vauclain with Earl Chapin May, *Steaming Up!* (Brewer and Warren, 1930).

Emanuel Victor Voska and Will Irwin, *Spy and Counter Spy* (Doubleday, 1940).

E.L. Voynich, *The Gadfly* (Heinemann, 1897).

E.L. Voynich, *An Interrupted Friendship* (Macmillan, 1910).

Maisie Ward, *Caryll Houselander: That Divine Eccentric* (Sheed and Ward, 1962).

Nigel West, *MI5: British Security Service Operations 1909–1945* (Grafton, 1981).

Nigel West, *MI6: British Secret Intelligence Operations 1909–1945* (Grafton, 1983).

Jules Whitcover, *Sabotage at Black Tom* (Algonquin Chapel Hill, 1989).

Kenneth Young (ed.), *The Diaries of Sir Robert Bruce Lockhart, volume 1: 1915–1938* (Macmillan, 1973).

The Security Service 1908–1945, The Official History (PRO, 1999).

LIST OF ILLUSTRATIONS

Illustrations courtesy of Andrew Cook unless otherwise stated:

Main Text:

p74   While staying at the luxury Hotel Bristol in Berlin in April 1909,
        Reilly wrote to Blohm and Voss, in an attempt to again undermine
        Josef Mendrochowitz. Hamburg State Archive..

p80   The Deed Poll application to the High Court in October 1908 finally
        made Rosenblum's adoption of the name Reilly legal. The National
        Archives.

p95   Advertisement in Vozdukhoplavatel announcing the opening of the
        Krylia Aerodrome in September 1910; another Reilly project
        financed by other people's money.

p103   On 25 April 1912 Reilly hypocritically complained to Obanowsky of
        insider dealing. Hamburg State Archive.

p112   Reilly's marriage on 16 February 1915 almost certainly saved him
        from arrest by the New York Police Department.

p143   Reilly's RAF service record (note next of kin 'Mrs A. Reilly').
        The National Archives.

p148   By March 1918, MI5's investigation into Reilly's background was
        making little headway. The National Archives.

p149   MI5 received a wealth of reports on Reilly's unsavoury past.
        The National Archives.

p150   When Reilly made an application to the War Office for intelligence
        work in January 1918, he was careful to submit glowing
        testimonials and references. The National Archives.

p151   MI5's surveillance of Reilly proved no easy task. The National Archives.

p159   Two of Reilly's 'top secret' reports from Moscow, commenting on
        Russia's intentions towards Germany. The National Archives.

p170   A Russian propaganda leaflet issued to Allied troops in Murmansk,
        naming Reilly as a conspirator in the plot to 'overthrow the
        Russian Revolution'.

p173   The key to the SIS dictionary code used by Reilly and Hill to com
        municate with each other while in hiding.

p223   The only true statement Reilly made about himself in the Marriage
        Register was his address; everything else from his name, age, former
        rank and the status of his father, was a complete fabrication.

p253   On 30 October 1925, Reilly wrote to Cheka boss Felix Dzerzhinsky,
        in a last ditch effort to buy himself more time. FSB.

p255   The last week of Reilly's life is recorded in the diary he wrote on
        cigarette papers in cell 73. FSB.

INDEX

If you are interested in purchasing
other books published by Tempus, or in case you have
difficulty finding any Tempus books in your local bookshop,
you can also place orders directly through our website

www.tempus-publishing.com

or from

BOOKPOST
Freepost, PO Box 29,
Douglas, Isle of Man
IM99 1BQ
Tel 01624 836000
email bookshop@enterprise.net